Running the World

Running the World

*My World Record Adventure to Run
a Marathon in Every Country on Earth*

Nick Butter

BANTAM PRESS

TRANSWORLD PUBLISHERS
Penguin Random House, One Embassy Gardens,
8 Viaduct Gardens, London SW11 7BW
www.penguin.co.uk

Transworld is part of the Penguin Random House group of companies
whose addresses can be found at global.penguinrandomhouse.com

Penguin
Random House
UK

First published in Great Britain in 2020 by Bantam Press
an imprint of Transworld Publishers

A CIP catalogue record for this book
is available from the British Library.

ISBN 9781787631724

Typeset in 11/14.75 pt Times NR MT by Jouve (UK), Milton Keynes
Printed and bound in Great Britain by Clays Ltd, Elcograf S.p.A.

Penguin Random House is committed to a sustainable
future for our business, our readers and our planet. This book
is made from Forest Stewardship Council® certified paper.

I am the sum of those around me.

To those with whom I shared footsteps,
To those who edged me closer to adventure and
away from the comfort zone,
To those who donated to help fight prostate cancer,
To those who believed,
To those who enabled,
To those who shared kind words,
To the schools who cheered me on,
To those who sheltered and fed me,
To those who humbled me,
To the selfless and the patient,

And to Kev; the man who sparked the dream
and changed my life for ever.

I am the sum of those around me.
To you all – I owe you the world.

Thank you.

Last, and by all means most – Mum, Dad. This was your journey as
much as it was mine. I really couldn't have done it without you.
Words will never be enough. I love you, and thank you.

Contents

Introduction: Tedious and Brief

I was coming to the end of a long run in Croatia when I happened across a motto on a sundial that has stuck in my head. Usually short and fatalistic, sundial mottos often refer to the passing of time; understandable, I guess. This particular sundial was old and scruffy, and the copper plate had oxidized over the years to a dirty green. After some cleaning, the words 'tedious and brief' were revealed. This, I assumed, was referring to our lifetimes. Brief? Yes, sadly. But tedious? 'Hell no, that's up to me,' I thought. And if it's up to me, I don't choose tedious. I choose full to bursting and downright chaotic.

This book is about that desire and drive to avoid the tedious and to squeeze every single second out of life. It is also about fostering a passion for adventure, and for the people and places that make up our wonderfully diverse planet.

Kev is tall, just over 6 foot, and well built. He doesn't possess a single strand of hair on his head and can usually be found wearing a warm ear-to-ear smile. And if the grin isn't visible on his lips, you can still see it in his eyes. A bromance, from my perspective at least, was blossoming. We met whilst running the Marathon des Sables ultra-event in the depths of the Sahara Desert back in April 2016; a seven-day, multi-stage race across nearly 300 kilometres of sand dunes – for fun. My brilliant rebel of a coach, Rory Coleman, had selected a bunch of us to join him. Rory is a 14-time veteran of the race and a legend in his own right. To be selected to accompany him was an honour. It was like being ushered into the VIP area at Glastonbury, except with no mud and certainly no rain; just a desert, sand and wind.

There's a lot more to say about the great bunch of people I met on that trip. Not only did we all bond so well that we are all still in touch to this day, but the conversations we had that week, under camel-hair bivouacs, in 51°C heat, were for me a tipping point. The desert is a harsh place. The dunes rise higher than you'd imagine, sometimes triple the height of double-decker buses, and with sand more golden than expected. With 700 or so people dropped in the middle of a vast nine million square miles of rolling sand dunes, it was here that my life was about to take a unexpected shift in direction.

As a kid I had always sought out adventure; as a 'grown-up' facing the prospect of 40 years of nine-to-five office grind and mortgage repayments . . . 'No thanks,' I thought. And yet . . . I had no other ideas. Ultimately the careers advice, along with my dad's, led me to exactly that kind of nice, sensible job and the comfortable normalities of office life: I went into banking. And whilst it paid the bills, it wasn't for me, as I was often reminded by work colleagues.

But throughout my ten years of office life, I was also mentally filing away all sorts of alternative advice: attending adventure lectures, listening to motivational speakers and inching further and further towards doing what I wanted. And then, after all those years of dreaming, of making plans and dipping my toes into a life I wished for but wasn't sure I could have, I met Kev. Kev gave me the push I needed.

On the face of it, Kev was a normal chap. Tall with a broad grin and infectious positivity, it was clear that he was a man on a mission and he seemed right at home during the desert race – much more than many of us, that's for sure. Kev wasn't like us other competitors. On day two of the Marathon des Sables, Kev and I were chatting, the usual stuff really, when out of the blue he told me that he had terminal prostate cancer and was dying, potentially very soon.

At the age of 49, in November of 2014, Kev and his family had their lives tipped upside down when a routine ultrasound picked up an abnormally high PSA (*prostate-specific antigen*) score. A normal score is about four; his was 342. He'd been given as little as two years to live. His three kids were aged just nine, 14 and 16.

As Kev told me his story, I was struck by his determination to live whatever life he had left to the absolute fullest, to make every day count. And here I was, complaining about the heat and my aching legs. The conversation was brief, but incredibly powerful. His words to me were: 'Don't wait for a diagnosis.' It's these words that resonated with me so profoundly. So, I'm not waiting. I am charging forward, filling my days.

I've realized that life isn't just short, it's that we can be so complacent with our time. After years of dreaming about something bigger, this Running the World trip was about acting on Kev's advice. I finally had the impetus I needed to give it a go.

I set out to 'live' Kev's counsel – to live life to the full, to dream big, and to use each and every one of those days with a smile on my face, appreciating how incredibly lucky I am to be alive. And the 'big dream' I reached for was that teenage 'what if': to run a marathon in every country on our planet. To do so in the name of a worthwhile cause, helping people with the same diagnosis as Kev, would be my motivation.

What happened over that 23-month journey was more than I could have ever dreamed of – and, better still, with the help of thousands of donations we raised over £200,000 for the charity Prostate Cancer UK.

What follows is an account of those months, of my travels around the world on a quest to run a marathon in every one of its 196 countries. Before I continue, you may be wondering how on earth I'll fit it all into a single book. Well, as I'm sure you understand, to assign a diary-style section of uniform length to each country would make for a pretty dispassionate account of an exciting expedition – and so while I'll include every country, this won't be an account of the 196 times I packed my bag, the 196 times I nearly missed the plane, the 196 times I really didn't want to get out of bed. Instead I'll share with you the life-changing memories, thoughts, struggles and emotional experiences, from wherever I happened to be at the time. It's a story from the heart, and I hope the reality of life on the road will shine through. Persistence and joy too – joy to live, and have the privilege to run free, and smile a smile of overwhelming appreciation for my short time on our planet.

This is for you, Kev.

1

One Step at a Time

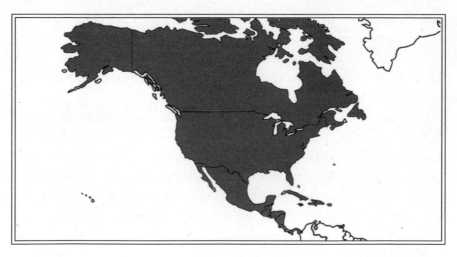

Canada	Grenada	Belize
United States	St Vincent	El Salvador
Bahamas	St Lucia	Guatemala
Haiti	St Kitts	Honduras
Dominican Republic	Antigua & Barbuda	Nicaragua
Cuba	Dominica	Costa Rica
Jamaica	Barbados	Panama
Trinidad & Tobago	Mexico	

Canada

At 7.14 a.m. on Sunday 7th January 2018 I took my first step of what I later calculated to be just over nine million. My toes already cold, my heart racing, I shivered with nerves; I was physically shaking. At the time I blamed it on the temperature, but, looking back, I was a mixed bag of excitement, tension and, if I'm honest, outright fear. It was surreal to finally begin something I'd been working on for so long. I had that strange feeling of looking down on the moment, rather than being in it.

I crumpled up two small hand-warmers, shook them a bit, and stuffed one in each glove – gloves that weren't mine; hand-warmers that I hadn't even considered bringing – and proceeded to throw on a jacket, hat and buff, all of which I'd had to borrow. The trip had taken about two years to plan, and on my first day, on my first marathon, in my first country, I still found myself utterly under-prepared. It was minus 25°C in Toronto, about 20 degrees colder than I was naively expecting, and I had to beg, borrow and steal 90 per cent of my running kit just to keep warm.

In the minutes between opening the door onto the frozen Canadian city and hitting 'start' on my watch, my mind jumped back to all that had led to that point: the heated discussions with my parents, the planning meetings and endless soliciting of potential sponsors. And yet . . . my mouth curled up at the edges. I was smiling, uncontrollably smiling, with both excitement and astonishment. Here I was, dumbfounded but overjoyed that I had got this far. It all suddenly became real. Crap, I've got to run 196 marathons now, and it's bloody freezing.

I was joined by a guy called Matt, a reporter called Virgil and another journalist whose name I can't now recall. Virgil seemed typically Canadian. Enthusiastic, with a gigantic smile and a voice I can still hear now – you know, that Canadian twang; relentlessly joyful (maybe too much so at 7 a.m. in mind-numbing temperatures). I hadn't met or had contact with Matt or Virgil at all before the morning, and I soon learned this would become a common occurrence as Carla (more about my long-suffering PA later) and the wonders of social media worked their magic. It was the beginning of an onslaught of new people everywhere I went.

We were all standing outside in the cold, doing the hoppy dance everyone does when it's too cold to stand still. I had the GoPro in my hand and was trying desperately hard to remember how to use it. Matt and I were both fiddling with our sleeves – our running watches were stuffed under several layers of clothing and we couldn't reach our 'start' buttons. I resorted to anxiously snatching off my heated gloves to rearrange mine. I was wearing two, one on each arm, in case one failed or the battery died because of the cold. This was a habit I later adopted for the entire trip – it seemed sensible to double my chances of not having to repeat an entire run because my watch had died within 200 metres of the finish. Guinness World Records needed every run to be tracked by GPS and recorded, amongst many, many other mandatory requirements. Each run had to be uploaded, logged and submitted. Getting the full distance, plus a little more for good measure, was my other big responsibility. Run and, whatever I did, don't forget to turn on the watch and track it – or else I'd have to run it again. Keeping my watches charged and ready to run was important, and later became a challenge in itself.

We looked at each other, took a deep breath, and set off into the city. It then dawned on me – just a few strides in – that I hadn't actually run a marathon for about four months, having broken my ankle in September after a rather stupid accident in Asia, thanks to a stag do and a rope-skipping competition on a Thai beach at one in the morning. Needless to say, it wasn't the best lead-in to a two-year running expedition.

I was starting this mission to run a marathon every couple of days without having really practised running marathons. I was pretty confused as to how I had ended up in this position. I guess I had just put it to the back of my mind – the planning and the preparation of finances, routes, flights, visas, security, kit . . . all that stuff had completely consumed me, and I had kind of forgotten the training. But I was hopeful that the 450+ marathons and various gruelling ultras I had under my belt from years prior would stand me in good stead. That said, I still felt beyond foolish – and proceeded timidly in blind hope my mind would conquer my body.

Fast forward to that cold wet morning of January 6th 2018. We left my family's home in East Dorset in the early hours, around 2 a.m. My parents were driving me to the airport and we were accompanied by my younger brother, who had the job of cameraman for the final goodbyes – it would have been great to have him, and indeed a crew with me at all times, but due to costs and logistics it was mostly down to me to take the photographic reins.

About halfway to Gatwick our phones all made their identical chimes – a BBC News notification. There had been a plane crash: a harsh reminder that plane crashes do happen and I was about to embark on a journey which would involve getting on, and hopefully getting off, about 300 planes over the next two years. We shared raised eyebrows as we looked at each other with unspoken concern. And this wasn't just any plane crash; this was a plane crash at Toronto Pearson International Airport, Canada. Out of all the countries and all the airports in the world, the one aviation accident that was taking place right then was at the one airport I was due to fly into in a matter of hours. As it turned out nobody, gladly, was injured and my flight departed and landed with no problems; but I think that was the moment that we collectively realized this trip had the potential to be far more fraught with difficulty than even we had first thought.

We cried, we hugged and I was gone, sitting on a plane wondering, 'What next?' No media circus, no banners and balloons, no good luck cards; just a cold sleepy airport with grumpy security staff and muffled Tannoy announcements.

After a reassuringly safe landing in snowy Toronto another wave of, 'Crap, it's happening,' washed over me. The weight of expectation was well and truly on my shoulders. That first night in the One King

West Hotel & Residence, just off Yonge Street, I had just a few tears slowly trickling down my cheek.

With my gear unpacked, my unworn trainers neatly placed by my folded clothes, and my alarm set for 6 a.m., I ordered some food to the room and planned for an early night. But, later, too excited to sleep, I dragged an armchair over to my 42nd floor window and sat for hours looking out over the frozen city below.

I'm not exactly sure what my expectations of day one were. I had, however, read enough adventure tales to know that things rarely turn out as you anticipate. This was true for me. No fanfare, no real sense of the epic challenge ahead. Most people were either asleep or entirely indifferent as I walked through the hotel. But a common theme of this journey is people. The famous phrase coined by explorer Christopher McCandless – 'happiness is only real when shared' – is so true. Forty-five minutes in, running with Virgil and Matt, my companions for the day, we were joined by Matt's running club. It was heartening to see the communal spirit of running alive and well, even at minus 25°C. Everything was frozen – the lake, the trees, the road, beards, eyebrows – it was an abnormally cold morning. There were about 15 of us by now and we spent the next hour or so chatting to one another as we ran. This is one of the many brilliant aspects to running – it's a social event. Or it would have been, if it wasn't for the temperature. The moisture from our mouths was freezing up our buffs and balaclavas around our faces. This made talking somewhat muffled, and with the wind increasing, especially along the waterfront, many of our conversations went unheard and needed repeating. It didn't bother us, though: we were all in great spirits. It's hard not to be when you're with Canadians.

Before I knew it, we were past halfway. As the hour of the office worker beckoned the city started to come to life, and our group dispersed. Just three of us were left when we made a short pit-stop in a café for a hot chocolate and a Canadian-style giant chocolate chip cookie. There was never any pressure on how quickly I should complete each marathon, but for pride I didn't want to be too slow, and for survival I didn't want to be too fast. A quick stop seemed reasonable.

The entire café, staff included, were wrapped up in big woolly clothes: hats, scarves and gloves, their hands wrapped around their hot drinks and their faces hovering as close to the mugs as possible to get the smallest benefit from the rising steam. Even for Canada, this was cold. And within about 90 seconds our bodies started to cool down. The sweat had oozed out through our clothes and was now freezing on the outside. Being so cold we hadn't noticed how sweaty we were. Someone pushed past me and placed a hand on the middle of my back. It sent violent shivers up and down my spine as my ice-lined top stuck to me. We took as many small sips as we could manage from our steaming paper mugs and ventured back into the icy world. We laughed at the situation, but really, we needed to warm up.

A few miles, slightly slower miles, later, the remainder of the gang peeled off to continue with their daily lives. I was, of course, just borrowing their precious time.

It became a common occurrence that various people from all over would drop in and out of the whirlwind ride of running around the world. The plan was to welcome the help and running companionship at every turn, but ultimately I'd be on my own in between. These self-less acts of kindness from strangers shone through more and more as countries ticked by.

We said our goodbyes in a rundown toilet block right on the south end of Yonge Street. 'Yonge's', otherwise referred to as 'Main' by the locals, connects the shores of Lake Ontario to Lake Simcoe in the north. It has been recognized by the Guinness World Records as the longest street in the world, covering 1,896 kilometres. After saying my goodbyes and warming up under the hand dryers I finished the last nine miles with an out-and-back along Yonge's. It would have been rude not to. My watches clocked 26.2 miles; I slowed down to a walk, and looked up into the sky. Big, thick snowflakes fell gently and covered my face. I was cold, wet through, my legs felt stiff and heavy from the clumps of snow stuck to my trainers. And I was grinning from ear to ear.

As with every project, big or small, there are always plenty of elements that are simply out of sight to the designer. I too was lured into this false sense of believing I'd thought of everything, or at least most of it. In reality there was rather a lot I hadn't considered. Meeting new people, bonding, and then leaving them, potentially to never see them again, was hard. It wasn't like meeting friends of friends in the pub where you moan about work, don't really know their name, talk about the latest Netflix series, have a pint and then leave. Most of the people I met over the 23 months on the road inevitably shared so many of the same values, attitudes and general excitement for life. I think it's a running thing.

The evening of my first marathon I went for a quick bite to eat in a nearby restaurant, and said goodbye to Matt over a pizza. That was that . . . bye. Two years on and we're still friends. Multiply that friendship rate by 196 countries and you get an idea of how friendship and people became such focal points of my day-to-day life.

I found some energy to gather my soggy clothes that lay strewn around my now smelly hotel room floor – I hadn't yet learnt not to just leave my kit in a wet mess post-run; thus guaranteeing that my next marathon would begin with the deeply unpleasant experience of pulling damp clothes over my tired and vastly unwilling body.

Shuffling around in my three-day-old pants, I folded my clothes, turned my crusty wet compression socks in the right way, grabbed my watch, various chargers, wash bag, and attempted to replicate the packing method I so diligently orchestrated back in the UK just a few days earlier. Naturally this was impossible, always is. I call it 'the luggage paradox'. A little sweaty after finally defeating the packing demons, I climbed into bed, untucking the duvet that needed a crowbar to loosen it, and let out a big exhale of relief at the feeling of being horizontal, warm and about to sleep. And within seconds, I was doing just that.

United States and Bahamas

From Toronto I flew the 2,000 kilometres south via Atlanta to Miami. It rained, I didn't sleep well (due to accidentally staying in a party hostel), and I ate nothing but bagels and Nutella pastry things for two days. From Miami I flew 900 kilometres further south to the Bahamas. It rained again. Despite the inches of water that drenched the island, there was somehow a shortage of bottled water in the small and rather odd B&B I was staying in. As a result, I ended up consuming seven litres of milk during my 48-hour stay. I like milk, but this was too much. I should probably have had some food too.

Both the run in Miami and the run in the Bahamas were not dissimilar – as in, WET. My view was one of blurry rain, through windscreen-wiper eyelids, as I splashed from one puddle to the next. I saw very little, thanks to constant squinting. The raindrops felt denser, larger and more wet than the wettest of wet rain. Still, I wasn't cold, and so made the most of empty roads. Avoiding any trips, falls or sudden knee-high water was the name of the game. Miami's beach and the metropolis of concrete-box skyscrapers is somewhat different to the quaint roads of Georgetown, but the feeling of being soaked through and heavier was the same. Likewise, as in any coastal town there was the same rust- and salt-covered buildings that made even new architecture look old. By sunlight I'm sure I wouldn't recognize either beach front. Miami or the Bahamas, they seemed the same. It was just a shame my feet were ruined from my sodden socks. I made a note to buy more back-up socks for future legs of the journey. I had to at least start the day with a dry pair.

Obviously, this was not how I envisaged the Bahamas, or Miami, or my nutritional plans, but hey, I was learning. As you'll come to read I did eventually rid my mind of any expectation, and instead just accepted the situations I found myself in. The world is too unpredictable for expectations.

Haiti

From the Bahamas I flew to Haiti, where it didn't rain, but I really wish it had. In fact, the sun decided to catch up after the last few days of absence with a rather unpleasant 43 degrees on the thermometer, cloudless skies and what felt like at least 1,000 per cent humidity. I exaggerate, but not by much.

The weather was my physical concern, but what I saw in Haiti will stay with me for ever. Haiti was my first experience of being around extreme poverty, and it's the small details I'll never forget. Only four countries in and I was witnessing small children bathing in mud. The human body I have seen – I have one – but these kids looked beyond hungry and desperate. Even the fortunate who had somehow found food and work were shoeless and appeared to be living lives of unimaginable struggle. The look of uncertainty in their eyes conveyed the harshness of their existences, making it all feel so real and alarming to me.

Turn the clock back 350 years and the island was thriving: a lush and tropical paradise. In fact, it was one of the richest islands on the planet. I couldn't help but spend a few hours doing some research that first night and, exhausted and battered by the sun, I learnt of the island's tragic demise.

A French colony, the Caribbean island of Hispaniola was known then as Saint-Domingue, and at the time of the French revolution it opened its ports to more than 1,500 ships per year. The French alone employed more than 750 vessels with as many as 24,000 sailors aboard. This, of course, was the effect of the western world's rapidly increasing demand for more and more luxuries, and led to slavery at its most extreme. Things like sugary tea, smooth cotton shirts and various other prestige items were in high demand – which led to over 12 million slaves being captured in Africa and transported to the Americas and the Caribbean during the 40-year abomination that was the Atlantic slave trade. Horrors seen on the island were a world away to the rich westerners. As they drank their tea and dined in fresh linen, conditions for slaves descended beyond inhumanity.

It was decades before the Haitian revolution brought about an end to slavery on Haiti, and it remains one of the only successful revolts against white enslavers in history. Sadly, once the whites had been defeated and moved on, the island was left in turmoil, and the remnants of this legacy remain today. Bleak, desperate and largely abandoned, Haiti is a shell of a tropical paradise. Aspirational desire for the luxuries we consume today (although now so readily available and affordable they no longer feel like luxuries) came from here, and now most of those who live here don't even have the cotton they were producing, let alone enough food or clean water.

Boarding the plane to Haiti, I was clearly the only tourist. I'm white – very white, actually. I was wearing shorts, and at this point I still had short hair and a shaved, unweathered face full of expectant energy. I stood out like an over-privileged sore thumb. I felt intimidated. This feeling grew as we landed, and then grew further as I travelled by car along dodgy roads that can only be described as bloody scary. The constant beeping of car horns, the higher pitched squeal of old battered motorbikes whizzing past just millimetres away, people and piles of smelly rubbish on all sides . . . it was chaos. I watched as motorbike madmen dipped their shoulders and squeezed their knees against their bikes to fit through virtually non-existent gaps in traffic. Needless to say, wing mirrors weren't a thing here. The sound of the horns, the dust-covered windscreen, the hot stuffy air and the fact I was tired ignited another wave of butterflies in my stomach. How was I going to run in this? I hadn't even reached Africa (the supposed tough bit) and I was already feeling out of my depth.

As my driver, Benjamin, weaved through the lawless traffic we passed scenes resembling dystopian action films: shirtless men wielding huge knives and looking menacing, piles of burning rubbish as large as buses, and buildings made from corrugated metal, mud and sticks rather than the more familiar building materials of the western world. This place was different, exciting even, but unnerving.

One sight in particular widened my eyes a little further: a burnt-out car with people crowding around it, all shouting at each other, in apparent disagreement – or perhaps just because that was the thing to do. It seemed as though there had been some form of accident moments earlier: the car was on its side with the driver's side sunk into a large drainage ditch full of human effluent and swarms of flies and bugs. Glass covered the immediate area, while smoke and flames licked up the underside of the bonnet. One chap, also shirtless, shoeless, sockless and rather angry-looking, sat on the upturned car, perched next to the petrol cap, swinging his scarred legs as if it were a playground swing. In his left hand he held a cigarette that was about to burn his fingers, and in the other hand, a semi-automatic weapon.

I quietly had a word with myself and came to the conclusion that I must be in a dodgy part of town, and my hotel would be in a safer area with less shouting, fewer guns, and no burning cars. As soon as I had reassured myself that the hotel would be different, safer and not near here, I felt the clutch engage, the clunk of the gearbox changing down a gear and then we stopped. We were at the hotel. Bollocks.

Two smartly dressed men in uniform with pistols on their hips and large guns over each shoulder pushed back an eight-foot-high solid metal gate and nodded to the driver. We drove in. Concrete walls with double-looped barbed wire acted as the perimeter to the compound, a space no bigger than a five-a-side football field. The hotel was simple but beautiful. Four or five small single-floor rooms all painted red and made from concrete blocks were dotted around a shallow ten-metre pool with some grass and sprinklers. In contrast to what was the other side of the wall, this felt like a tropical Narnia.

Check-in complete, bags unpacked, I put on my running kit, pulled my super-tight compression socks up and over my feet, heels and shins, and stepped out into the 39 °C heat. It was just before midday, just twenty hours after I'd finished my previous run in the Bahamas – my first back-to-back marathons of the trip. In hindsight, starting at midday was utterly stupid, but I was anxious to get it done.

I was already grateful to Benjamin, and he became what I thought of as my saviour. Sometimes you entrust your laptop or bag to the random stranger on the train, or in a café while you pop to the bathroom, but in the heart of volatile Haiti I blindly put my life in the hands of Benjamin, a man I'd spent just 20 minutes in the company of, doing so without any real consideration. (Often throughout this journey I've retrospectively been shocked at the lack of cautiousness I've shown. This didn't improve; if anything, I got more blasé, and yet things turned out OK.) I met Benjamin at the car near the gate of the compound. As I approached, he hastily hopped out, beaming a warm, inviting smile; a smile so broad that it appeared to require the use of all the muscles in his face. Infectious. He shuffled around to the passenger side to open the door for me. A tie lay in the back seat; he had obviously realized I was not a tie-worthy client. Benjamin is a short bald black man with a neatly trimmed 'tash and a jolly spring in his step. He is calm, patient and has an air of being entirely comfortable with whatever is going on around him. Which was fortunate, given he had no idea how miserable his day would be. This poor bloke was to spend the following six hours in a car without air-con, driving painfully slowly, whilst watching my spindly legs trundle along the dusty road at a snail's pace.

A short drive out of the main hubbub of Port-au-Prince and almost away from the obvious gang culture, we stopped and I got out. By this point I was fidgety to begin. I moved the plastic carrier bag from the rear seats into the passenger foot-well. Twelve one-litre bottles of water should do the trick. Little did I know what I was in for.

The first few miles felt stubborn and slow; it was only slightly uphill, but the anxiety I had built up for my surroundings was making every step slightly more tentative. The eyes of every single person on both sides of the road ahead, behind and to the side, were looking at me. Some wore frowns, there were some smiles, and some just stood in open-mouthed perplexity. The steps ticked on slowly and before long I had reached two miles. Yes, just two measly miles. The temperature was over 40°C and I could feel my skin really not enjoying the heat. You know when you lie on a beach and can feel you should probably cover up for a while? Needless to say, within only 15 minutes of starting to run in Haiti I had learnt my lesson: do not run in the midday sun.

The language barrier with Benjamin was real, but not impossible. I got the impression he spoke good English but was shy about trying harder in apprehension of getting anything wrong. He always spoke with a grin filling his face, and the joy was obvious in his tone, which made up for the fact he spoke so few words.

The plan for the run was simple. Run 13 miles in one direction up a transporter highway and then turn around and come back again. I ran about 100 metres ahead while Benjamin slowed traffic down behind, using the car as a big shoulder, pulling out if faster or bigger vehicles approached. For the entire marathon we reverted to hand signals. Upon needing water, which was often, I simply raised my hand above my head. He tapped the accelerator, pulled alongside, and handed me a bottle. This wasn't in the job description, but like so many times on this journey the support I had went above and beyond what was requested. Occasionally Benjamin would ask if I was OK. I clearly looked like I wasn't, and as the run progressed my legs became slower, my posture weakened and I was checking my watch at least every 0.2 of a mile.

I'd broken my ankle in the famous Marathon des Sables and still managed to finish the last 40 miles on crutches, so I'm no stranger to a hard run; but in Port-au-Prince my energy had been sapped by the sun, my legs were burning, and my mind was weak. Just when I thought it couldn't get much worse, we reached a bustling mini-village with street sellers lining the road. I had been warned not to carry valuables, and, for once, I had listened to the advice and had nothing on me worth nicking. The street hustlers didn't know that, of course, which made this advice seem a bit pointless. Nor did they know that the car a few metres behind had an eagle-eyed Benjamin at the wheel. Over the course of miles 11 to 13 I was approached by at least 20 individuals who were clearly not after a selfie or a nervous smile, and although I threw the smile in for free, they didn't smile back.

I lost count of the number of weapons I saw, ranging from semi-automatics to swords (actual swords, not just machetes). In a rather weird way I was sort of winning at this point – I was so tired, hot and sore that I had become desensitized to any terrifying behaviour but was still so distracted by it as to practically forget I was running. Besides, I was nearly halfway. This was my tired brain forgetting that, of course, I'd have to run past them again on the way back.

There were a few frantic moments when Benjamin jumped in to intervene. Some of these street fellas were clearly gang members but, in hindsight, most of the hostile experiences I had were probably just them showboating to their gang mates. In the moment, though, it felt very real, and very scary. A beep of the horn, and a sharp acceleration from Benjamin, followed by a quickening of pace from me was enough to deter most intimate attempts to mug me. Besides, I was smug in the knowledge that there wasn't much on me that they would want. My shoes? Surely not. My watches? Maybe. Nothing was safe.

At about 5.15 my feet carried me over the threshold of the Bel Fle Missions Hotel once again, clocking 26.2 miles plus a little extra for good measure. I'd survived and could now stop. My breathing was something that became very apparent to me once I got back. Due to the volume of speeding cars kicking up fine yellow and brown dust, I'd been running mostly with my mouth shut and finally breathing properly was like being born again. (Not that I remember being born but I imagine it was quite gaspy.) A cold blanket of air fell across my shoulders and further down my back as I stepped past the cool air curtain of the small conditioning unit above my room door. From baking hot to shivering in minutes, I sat on the edge of the bed with my feet swollen in my shoes and my hair dripping and let my heart slow down. With my eyes still semi shut and feeling weak, I gently uncurled my back and sat up to begin the next phase of the post-run ritual: the unpeeling of my socks from my shins and feet.

My Rehband compression socks are the only running socks I wore for the entire journey – hard to get on, even harder to get off, but totally worth it. Although only millimetres thick and designed for muscle support, mentally these socks gave my lower legs a layer of protection: a kind of psychological leg shield. My legs were safe, for now.

Jumping in the shower I let the steamy water run over my shoulders. With the sound of water splashing off my neck, down my back and pooling in a soapy pond around my tired feet, I closed my eyes and gathered my thoughts as I placed my hands flat to the wall and breathed in. The shower tap did that classic vintage metal-ware squeak as I turned it to the 'off' position. Peace . . . and then distant gunfire and shouting snapped me back to reality.

That evening I met a merry bunch of Canadians, the second group I'd met in as many weeks. Canadians really are scattered all over the world, and that's a good thing, they are lovely people. They were sitting around the small swimming pool in the courtyard as the sun went down. They'd been basking in the sun all day, actually enjoying it rather than being beaten up by it. After some brief tired words explaining why I was there, and why I looked like shit, they invited me to join them for dinner, saying, 'You need feeding up' – a phrase I've heard many times, mostly from people that don't realize I'm just naturally skinny and I actually eat like a horse. Their enthusiasm for my cause and mission was genuine and so a dinner chatting about my challenge took my mind off my fear for the remaining 192 countries and 22 months in front of me. I smiled as I explained my journey. 'Yes,' I said.

'Even North Korea.' An answer I would have to get used to giving very frequently over the next few months.

The discussion abated briefly and I took the opportunity to shovel pasta, chicken, bread and various other unspecified foods down my throat as fast as I could. All eight of these lovely people were in Port-au-Prince as part of a mission project with their church. The recent earthquakes, months earlier, had destroyed most of Haiti and killed thousands. These folks were here to celebrate an anniversary of building a school and an orphanage in memory of the disaster. Despite my eyes feeling heavier than my legs, and in the interest of not missing opportunities, I agreed to take a tour. It was Sunday tomorrow and thus church for the group and the entire country. Religion here was a must – I got the impression religion wasn't a maybe, rather the glue that holds everyone together; it's the only hope.

The following day, transport to the orphanage was a pickup truck, but not a US-style shiny beast with a five-litre engine – instead, a truck that was once white but now had more metallic silver scars than paint. We took it in turns to pick a spot and hang on. Once all aboard and holding on, off we went. Potholes, wind in our faces and even a singsong on the way. At high speed we were all virtually shouting at each other in an attempt to have a conversation over the sound of the wind and the orchestra of beeping horns. Once the traffic increased and the truck slowed, we could chat more freely. On the way we picked up four kids who needed a lift to church – two boys and two girls – all aged 14. These young teenagers had no parents or siblings, their families having all been killed in the earthquake. With the help of the group they now had a new family to call their own – an orphanage where hundreds of children robbed of their parents come together as a family unit. These kids sang, smiled and laughed their way to church. Happiness is all relative.

We eventually made it to the orphanage, which was also attached to the school and the church. After pulling into the complex, and with the big green metal gates and huge barbed wire-topped walls behind us, we parked up. I was struck by the sight of more than 400 people singing and praying in neat lines. A front man, otherwise known as a minister, was dressed in a bright pink dinner jacket that had seen better days. His sermon was one of gratitude for the alternative family and sense of togetherness that the orphanage offered. A young boy called Jeremy took me by my hand and led me to the classrooms to show off his home, school and life in this community. He was only ten, and whilst the look of desperation was still prominent in his eyes, his enthusiastic words were a pleasure to hear.

A collection of chairs, all identical and equally battered, with exam-style single-person tables was all that filled the five classrooms; these, and the one large green chalkboard at the front of the class. The walls and floor were a washed-out grey concrete – totally smooth, just like fresh plaster. There were no doors, no windowpanes, just the window holes, and a few small broken pieces of chalk dotted on the floor under the board. To my surprise there were outrageously advanced formulas on the board, which to me looked similar to those in the film *Rain Man*. I later found out a volunteer teacher was studying for her masters. I hadn't met her – but she clearly knew more about maths than I knew about anything.

I noticed more on the way back – it was just me and a driver, and more traffic, so my eyes wandered. I stuck my 200mm lens out of a crack in the window and grabbed a few shots before the driver told me it would probably be stolen if I carried on.

For every positive or hopeful sight – exchanging a smile or a wave with a smartly dressed local on their way to work with a bible under their arm – I witnessed many distressing scenes: children washing in filthy streams, poverty-stricken young adults with little or no hope of living a decent life. The brief moments of light-heartedness were made all the more poignant by the harrowing sights of Haiti's streets. Poverty is often just a word when spoken by us 'that have', but poverty has a whole different meaning when you're actually living it. People here had nothing and were living on far less than $1 a day. The closest I got to understanding the reality of that situation was seeing a dying child in the arms of its mother, who sat slumped in a foul-smelling gutter. And sights such as these weren't unusual, they were the norm, on every street we drove through.

It's encounters like this that make you question the way you live your life. During that 40-minute drive through the broken roads and broken lives of Haiti, my heart was heavy and my soul in a dilemma. Suddenly I felt obnoxious, spoilt and decadent by doing what I was doing. How could I do this amazing thing while millions of people around the world can't even afford food, water or medicine? Maybe I should stop right now and give everything I have to help these people? Then again, the purpose of my expedition was to raise awareness and funds for another deserving cause.

This was one of the first times I felt the extreme value of travel. Not travel to a comfortable resort with expensive restaurants, but travel to see the planet and its people in the rawest form. The mixed emotions and thoughts I experienced in Haiti were to recur in many other places over the next two years and continue to develop into more ideas of ways to use the benefit of privilege to make a difference for those who do not have it.

Dominican Republic

My tenth day on the road, heading to my fifth country. Goodbye Haiti, hello Dominican Republic. My legs were fine in the morning but horribly sore by the time I went to bed – and it wasn't even a run day. This was due to a long and unexpected bus journey. When planning this journey there had been many decisions that I had not really thought about making. Flying from place to place was the default assumption, but there were plenty of opportunities not to. I'd made the mistake of not checking my diary and had no idea I'd be bussing it rather than flying from Haiti. I looked at my iPhone calendar just five hours ahead of the journey time. My diary was my bible. It contained everything I needed to do: times, reference numbers, contact names, safety concerns.

My diary stated: 'Bus station in central Port-au-Prince – arrive by 2 a.m.' I did just this, and subsequently waited 3 hours in the dark being scared of angry dogs growling at me, along with observing dodgy-looking dealings out of car windows just metres away. I was still very white and rocking the classic traveller look. I may as well have had a sign above my head, saying: 'I have no idea where I am and

I have all my money, my passport and all my belongings on me.' At this point I also didn't have a ticket, and the bus terminal, which resembled an abandoned gas station like the ones in old western films, was closed till 4 a.m. I waited and made myself look as buff and as scary as I could. I don't think this really worked.

Once on the bus with my ticket, I had my passport taken away and was told I'd get it back when I got off. Apparently, this was standard. My bag was loaded, unloaded, loaded again, and I hoped not unloaded again without me realizing. My diary notes stated: 'bus journey approx. 6 hours – take water'. Six hours and no water later, I was quite keen to have a wee and get off. However, another four hours then passed before we reached the border, which was still two hours from my final destination in the city.

A man with a gun slung over his shoulder waved everyone off the bus and pointed towards the passport booth. 'Passport booth' sounds rather official but was in fact just a portacabin with a hole cut out at a comically abnormal height – seemingly made for toddlers at just below stomach level. Everyone had to more or less kneel to see through it. I would have found it all rather funny had I not been grabbed by the arm, spoken to in a language I didn't understand and dragged aggressively behind the portacabin and away from the rest of the group, past some bushes. My heart did a few wobbles and I protested in a classically British fashion. This naturally meant some quiet words of protest that did nothing. My heart rate was through the roof and my flight instinct had kicked in. I did however realize that it would be foolish to run away when all my gear, along with my passport, was in the hands of the armed officials and I was on an island thousands of miles from home.

I was put in a small empty room and the door shut behind me. My fear rocketed. Had I been locked up? It certainly had all the hallmarks. It was in fact just a 'waiting room' that looked, felt and smelt very much like an empty shipping container used to traffic people.

Thankfully, a cheery chap came in and ushered me to an 'office' moments later. A few questions, and then an aggressive thud as he slammed the stamp into my passport. After some groans and grumbles, he pointed vaguely towards the bus. I got back on, leaving my passport with him. I wasn't being trafficked, but I still didn't have my passport and wasn't sure if my bag was still on the bus. I'm pleased to report that all my worries were for nothing. My diary notes to myself read 'must learn to be less scared and pathetic – it's only going to get tougher'.

Judney was my companion during this ordeal of a journey. A Haitian girl studying to be an architect, she commutes from the bus station in Port-au-Prince over the border to Santo Domingo every week. She stays with a friend in the city centre, and then returns for the weekend. At 5 a.m. I caught the bus and shared the journey with her. At this point we were total strangers, but by the time we reached the city we knew enough about each other to regret having to say goodbye. Another key measure of the enjoyment of travel is sad goodbyes.

Judney was 19; her brothers and parents were back in Haiti. She was searching for a better life. I'm not sure how she was funding her studies, or how long it would take, but it became apparent she, like so many, was one of the good human beings. The media has a tendency to paint our planet with images of war, destruction and unrest, but so many times over 23 months I was reminded that people are innately good – in fact, not just good, but selfless, kind and warm-hearted. Judney was exactly this. She chatted to me about trying to find work as an artist in Santo Domingo so she could stay for longer periods to earn money and send it back to her family. She took it upon herself to teach me about the country's bank notes, and proudly instructed me on good places to eat, and where not to go at night. I got a sense she felt fortunate to be able to follow her dream when so many of her friends in Haiti weren't able to. I spoke briefly about why I was on the bus, the trip and 'the cause'. Upon saying goodbye, she handed me a fistful of cash and said, 'I don't have much, but your cause needs this more than I do.' I felt like she was working so hard to provide for her family and support herself that she shouldn't give me (the guy travelling to every country) anything – it felt wrong. With the charity in mind, however, I gratefully and humbly accepted the donation of £8. This level of selflessness could be seen as rare, but I've realized it often directly correlates with those who have less.

Not far from the bus station, along the coast, is the Marriott Renaissance Hotel, where I met the manager, Matt. I obviously looked rough because the receptionist jumped to the correct conclusion that I was the crazy guy running around the world. Possibly something to do with the bucket-like bags under my eyes and clothes that looked as if they could be harvested for penicillin. She promptly called Matt, who appeared in minutes. Smartly dressed, with little hair, he greeted me excitedly before introducing me to the majority of the staff on shift. Coming from Haiti, I felt uncomfortable accepting the refreshingly cold flannel and glass of (non-alcoholic) fizz. Having said that, I had just spent 12 hours on a coach without any food or water, so it was more than welcome. The tour of the hotel's facilities complete, I began the ritual once again. Shoes and running clothes out by the foot of the bed, and the rest of my bag open and accessible. Watches back on charge, a quick check-in with family and the team and then onto Wi-Fi to download an offline map ahead of tomorrow's run. I had no one to run with and no idea where I'd be running. I did, however, know that it was safe enough to venture out and explore on my own. And so I spent about two minutes examining route options before deciding I'd run with the ocean on my left, reach halfway then turn around. I set an alarm for 5 a.m. It was now 9 p.m. and I needed food.

At dinner with Matt I spoke briefly about Judney and her extraordinary kindness. I asked, hopeful, if there was any work available for her. We exchanged contact details and I thought little more about it. But eight weeks later I got a message from Judney. She was given work in the hotel and was able to earn money to help fund her education. Like many situations on this voyage of jogging around the world, it was a set of serendipitous connections and human kindness that led to opportunities, friendship and happiness. The spark for all this is always the willingness to be open to adventure and conversation. I didn't fly from Haiti, I took the bus; I didn't just sit on the bus silently and ignore my fellow humans; Judney was willing to chat, willing to share her stories, kind to donate to Prostate Cancer UK; and Matt was kind enough, not only to let me stay for free in his hotel, but even more kind to follow up on my request to reach out to Judney. This chain of events epitomizes everything that I love about people and adventure. As the sun set, I sat on the deep windowsill ledge of my top-floor bedroom window, reflected on life and recorded my daily video diary.

Running in Santo Domingo was pleasant and a far cry from the poverty in Haiti, but the Dominican Republic is by no means a tropical paradise. The early start helped avoid most of the searing 40 degree heat but I was a little disappointed, truth be told. Santo Domingo was just a bit of a mess compared to the brochure photos I'd so often peered at walking past the travel agent's. I resorted to running lengths of the coastline because the road was blocked by several layers of concrete and metal barriers after just four miles. No guns or violence here, just big bloody roads with cars driven by maniacs. The pavement, much like most (if not all) pavements in the Caribbean region, had been damaged by rain and poor maintenance, which meant that as I got closer to the end of the marathon I had to concentrate harder to avoid ankle-bending cracks and small bumps in the road that could lead to a face full of path. I was tired – the roads, dust and heat in Haiti had ruined my legs.

I listened to Chris Evans' latest book in audio form and generally tried not to think about what was ahead of me. This is a tactic I often adopt. Not Chris Evans every time, that would be odd, but audiobooks and stubbornly ignoring the pain. It wasn't a matter of having true grit, stamina or endurance; most of the time I was just trying to ignore the difficult bit around the corner. If you think no further than the next corner, you'll eventually be around them all and over the finish line. That was the mantra.

The highlight of my 72 hours in the Dominican Republic wasn't the running or even the luxurious hotel. Rather, in Santo Domingo, I got my first taste of visiting a school on this expedition. I was hopeful schools would be interested in the journey, so I could spread some of the messages I believe in. Value your time, live life with intent and direction, and always try to be grateful for each day. We get one shot.

St George's International School welcomed me, we played some silly running games, I spoke of my challenge, and the kids took it in turns to ask questions. Looking back to that point, I'd only been to five countries, so didn't have much to talk about, but it seemed to go down well, and we even managed to squeeze in a few bits and pieces for the documentary too. Drone shots and the like.

I so rarely had bonus days. By 'bonus day' I mean a day of no marathon-running or flying to a new country. Often these days meant exploring the country without running, so it wasn't quite 'rest'. I remember feeling an immense sense of calm after my post-run shower. Haiti had been so physically and emotionally draining that this, by contrast, was much easier, and close to luxury. On the odd day off, I'd grab some photography, and the bits in between the flying were often where I witnessed all the great sights, sounds and smells. Combine the lot and I was starting to see this becoming an incredible journey. I hadn't really thought of it that way up until this point; I saw it as a mission. A mission that I bet my life and all my money on – but I kind of forgot that it could be fun. That night in the safety of the Marriott I reminded myself it might also be something I could enjoy.

Cuba

The deep reds and oranges sprawled across the sky as the tinny airport PA system sounded in the classically muffled way an airport PA system must. Flight 0733 to Havana's international airport was due to take off at 04:00. The plane was delayed by two hours, and then another two hours. The reason – we never found out. Eventually arriving in Cuba, the airport seemed to be designed by someone that had never seen an airport or understood what they were for. The disorganized nature of the building, coupled with the fact they then lost my bags for a further few hours, wasn't helping my increasing frustration.

I was hoping to fly and run in the same day to give myself a little rest the following day. These delays were jeopardizing this and my exhaustion was getting the better of me. I was snappy, uncomfortable on the plane, grumpy, fidgety and generally showing all the signs of a tired workhorse. The final nail in the coffin of my plans to run that day came when I eventually found my bags. They weren't lost, after all – they were in quarantine. Cuban authorities didn't like me entering the country with a drone. I was half expecting this, but it would have been nice if they hadn't left me standing around for a further two hours. There was no hope of running, the sky was turning dark and the sun setting. Sitting on the floor by a door to the quarantine room, I waited. And waited. A headache brewing, dirt under my fingernails, tired feet; my mood was low, tending towards angry. The airport was one room: security, two luggage belts and a few empty, dilapidated information desks that stood unattended were the only recognizable features of an airport. The one member of staff I finally found informed me that the quarantine staff were on their break and I needed to wait. More waiting. With the place practically empty, I was eventually ushered along to another dingy area of the airport with a grunt from a large and stern-looking official. This patch of airport open space came with two little plastic tables and a box of rubber gloves and a collection of papers. The official had various badges and brooches fixed to her breast pocket and epaulettes. Her hat was comically large for her head. The blue plastic latex gloves finished off her ridiculous authoritative presence rather nicely.

After some long vacuous form-filling and various scans of my passport, they still wouldn't let me leave the airport. After several deep breaths and much biting of my tongue, I couldn't help myself any longer. I thrust my phone in the face of Miss Trunchbull. I was showing her my calendar and the dinner appointment with the British embassy that evening. Cuba is one of those places where embassy relations matter, and I was just desperate to get out of the airport. I'd try anything – even name-dropping. I offered to call the embassy in an attempt to hurry things along. The drone was the cause of the problem, but my frustrations were starting to show to the point where I was in danger of getting into worse bother. They didn't want me to call and instead insisted I return to my patch of floor in the corner and wait for a further unspecified time. I did, although not willingly, and then called the embassy anyway. Twenty minutes later Lesley, the embassy liaison, strolled straight into the luggage hall, flashed some documents and collected me. I'm relieved to say the drone was finally handed back to me upon leaving.

It was a weird combination of feeling: on the one hand as if I were being collected from detention by my mother, but also with the sense of 'I told you so' to Miss Trunchbull. Poor Lesley; she took me under her wing and apologized, reassuring me that it wasn't just me that this had happened to. I tried to not let my annoyance show, but failed, and within seconds I was ranting. Apparently I couldn't outrun the sleep demons. I made a mental note: more sleep needed from now on.

I racked up another 26.2 miles the following day running in the rain. This was another solitary run with no support but even in the rain the magic of running transformed my mood. I was even singing while trotting along in my own bubble. A Cuban classics playlist, of course, including Buena Vista Social Club and 'La Bruja'.

Havana showed me many of the classic sights of Cuban guide books. The growl of old engines trundling by, shiny classic cars lining each side of the streets, and the Spanish colonial-style buildings standing tall and stubborn, combined with various Caribbean smells, all added up to cultural overload – all in the best possible way. I hadn't yet been through the rest of the Caribbean, but I was aware of the unique cultural heritages of these places. Mile four and only a few steps after being covered in muddy water from a passing lorry, I bumped into another runner. 'Bumped into' in the literal sense – a guy whose name I couldn't recall, but, to my amazement, lived just four doors down from where I'd lived in Bristol. Although we'd never met, we chatted briefly and ascertained he was a member of Southville running club. My running club. In the excitement of encountering a British accent so far from home, it slipped my mind to explain why I was covered head-to-toe in muddy brown sludge. He must have thought I was quite peculiar. After a few more words of surprise at bumping into a neighbour and various 'nice to meet you' pleasantries, he ran his way and I ran mine. 'See you soon.' I hadn't yet learnt to encourage passers-by to join me.

Havana was more of a flying visit than I had hoped, thanks to the airport hassle. The only full evening I had in Cuba wasn't wasted, though. I enjoyed a few hours with the embassy staff at their residence, wading into a huge spread of British and traditional Cuban dishes while a quartet played Cuban music. Over dinner-party chatter a number of the group kindly pointed out how tired I looked, which I took as a welcome invite to have an early night as soon as I'd eaten. Sitting around a large circular garden table, I hunched over my plate of barbecued food and didn't come up for air until the plate was devoured. Not a word left my mouth, and I didn't even raise my head. I must have appeared rude, but I remember reassuring myself that they'd understand as I shovelled large spoonfuls of potato dauphinois into my mouth. Letting out a replete sigh, I sat back, held in a few burps and immediately stood up and weaved my way through the small gathering of guests all gently swaying from side to side to the music, a few granddad dancers amongst them. It was time for round two. It was a free buffet – don't judge me. Lesson number one of long solo expeditions: eat all the free food you can get. What with all the delays and faff in the past 48 hours, plus foodless plane and bus journeys, I was ravenous. I was only at the get-together for an hour, but in that time I managed to scoff down at least four sittings of food, and then felt sleepy. Looking back, I was definitely rude, but at the time was focused on refuelling and sleep. This took priority over any pleasantries.

Lesson number two of solo travel: hotel buffet breakfasts are for the most part crap. I principally stayed in mediocre and budget accommodation of varying standards and Havana was no exception. Stale pastries and some tap water, along with a cuppa, was all I could hope for. I'd also miss most breakfasts due to the early morning starts to beat the heat. Food was becoming a bigger focus than I'd originally planned. Cuba done, I was off to the land of jerk chicken and reggae, reggae sauce.

I'd run 157 miles now and was getting in the swing of things. I was slowly making the dream come true. Hopping from one new country to the next, three a week so far, and loving it. Despite the problems, rain, frustrations and lack of sleep, my body was holding up. The adventure had really begun and so, after a few phone calls back home from the airport, I was feeling pretty sprightly. Carla, my assistant, had informed me that the Jamaican leg was being supported by the British embassy once again.

Let me tell you a little about Carla. She was my 'go to' for every problem, and more or less every question or concern. She was employed as my 'assistant' but, in reality, did far more and never complained once. Although she wasn't with me from the very beginning she took to the mission like a duck to water. In the early planning stages my team wasn't a team in the slightest. It was just me, with help from any friends and family that could spare the time. Nine months or so into trying to juggle all the planning, management and logistics myself, I realized I needed to bite the bullet and hire some help. Then, for the entire planning phase, it was a brilliant person called Ali. I found her through a Gumtree ad asking for help with a world record attempt. She organized everything from the launch event to various sponsor meetings, and management of nearly every aspect of my life. All meetings, all planning, everything was done between us. We lived not far apart and so spent many hours ordering copious coffees and teas in various Bristol coffee shops making plans.

In late October 2017, around two months before I was set to begin the journey, Ali informed me she had to leave. I simply wasn't paying her enough to match her needs. I knew that, and wished I could have paid her more – it was a friendly exit from her post, but a massive loss to the team. She wanted some job security and some decent wages – I could provide neither. We were already running on empty, even with some small backing. I posted the same ad again on Gumtree and within 24 hours had received 48 responses. I spoke to a few but Carla stood out. She'd worked as a remote assistant many times for various corporate executives and, while I couldn't pay her well, she was keen to be involved and within four days she and Ali were chatting and beginning a handover. Ali remained on the sidelines of the mission, managing the newsletters and various needed but lesser roles on a volunteer basis. The amazing thing about the relationship I had with Carla was that we never met. She and her family lived up in Scotland, and with only six weeks till I was due to begin the mission we had very little time. The reality of the mission was I'd never have any team members with me, and so it was pretty perfect to work entirely remotely. She put up with enormous amounts of impatience and over-tiredness from me, and worked tirelessly answering the phone every time I rang, no matter what time of day it was. Carla was a star for taking the reins so late on and steering me through the mission. Her position only came to an end when, once again, we ran out of money. She, along with Veton (who took up the reins – more about him later) and the rest of the team, held everything together.

The Caribbean

Back on board the plane and ready to fly the 500 miles south from Havana to Kingston, Mrs Moulton was sitting in seat 5C, an aisle seat, and I was 5B, the middle seat, on an old 737-800. This lovely lady never gave me her first name, but Mrs Moulton had a smile nearly the size of her head, with deep red lipstick framing her mouth. She was Jamaican, about 50, and for the first time in her life had left Jamaica, to visit Cuba, a three-week trip. The Caribbean Airlines slogan is 'the warmth of the Caribbean', and with Mrs Moulton sitting next to me that's exactly what I felt. She was a bag of excitement, chatting about her recent visit, and was also nervous and on edge about flying. This was the second flight of her life, the first being the initial journey to Havana. She showed off her knowledge of how to fasten her seatbelt, and of course I thanked her and clipped in as she instructed. I noticed her hands shaking as she fastened her own. She was brave and proud, despite the nerves. I, in my privileged bubble, had never been on a plane with someone who had hardly ever flown. Needless to say, hundreds of flights later, I have now. A small lady with a dark denim jacket, high cheek bones and a hefty smudge of blusher, she exuded happiness and contentment. Just her presence was enough to make me feel more thankful for the enormous opportunity that lay ahead of me and the experiences I'd already had. I felt guilty for the frustration I'd felt in the airport a couple of days ago, and ashamed to have been so short tempered over a delay caused by my bloody drone.

We touched down only 40 minutes later and hugged goodbye. Her parting words were: 'God bless you, go strong in all you dream.' I had been so caught up in my mission, this lovely lady felt like an angel providing the gentle nudge I needed to reset my compass. A bearing of appreciation and gratitude, steering away from ill-temper and impatience. Mrs Moulton was another significant person that reminded me of the saying: 'Who you surround yourself with, you become; what you think of yourself, you are; who you speak to, reflects.' I was keen to keep meeting people like her – it felt good for the soul.

With my reinvigorated positivity from the flight, Jamaica was to be a great 48 hours. I had support from the British embassy and, as a runner, I was in the home of the world's fastest man: Usain Bolt. His statue had been ceremoniously erected less than 24 hours before I arrived. Nick, the deputy high commissioner, was tall and oozed ambassadorial charm. His years in this position shone through, his experience apparent in his body language: a straight back, careful with his words, humorous, but with a gravity befitting his rank. I liked him. We got on instantly.

Just hearing the word 'Jamaica' is very evocative, and for me it conjured all the usual images of chilled reggae music, tasty barbecued food, a laid-back-to-the-point-of-horizontal approach to life, Bob Marley, beaches and rum. I no longer drink, and substituting the rum for a coconut just seemed to make the stereotype even worse, so I decided to forget about preconceptions and find out for myself what this place was like.

Shortly after arriving, I was treated to a tour of Usain's home stadium and where it all began. Setting foot on the lane in which he ran his last professional home race was another special moment. I pondered in admiration of the effort and sheer volume of hours and sacrifice required to reach the top of the sport. I try hard to bottle such feelings and use them like collected tokens won on computer games when I need them the most. I did a lap of the aptly named Usain Bolt Stadium with Nick, just so we could say we ran together on the track. A few photos and off we went. The air was hot – too hot, actually; I was now a little closer to the equator, and so the temperature was uncomfortable, like a hairdryer coming at you from all angles. Burning down, the sun had turned the once-green grass to a pale yellow, and turned me from white to red. I burnt badly on my nose, ears and shoulders during just the first few hours in the country.

I was staying in what seemed like a rather plush hotel; still basic and rundown in a classically Caribbean way, but pretty, all things considered. Large oil paintings on the wall, thick rugs on the floor by the entrance, and comfortable armchairs hooded with oversized lamps in the corners. The place was cheapened a little though by the painted Jamaican slogans on any available wall space, daubed in incongruous colours and makeshift fonts. I was welcomed with a friendly smile and a strong handshake by the enthusiastic reception-ist. I'd always previously thought this meant they were probably getting paid too much or had something wrong with them. Why were these people so happy? They were working behind the reception of a tiny hotel! Having learned so much more about the world, I now real-ize that, generally speaking, anyone who has a job is one of the lucky ones, relatively speaking, and probably has a great deal to be happy about, compared with so much of the world's population.

The Jamaican marathon was my first but not last encounter with balancing safety and running depressingly dull laps. Nick, informed by some recently updated FCO advice, had suggested it was best to stay indoors and avoid a handful of areas. Gang violence is big in the capital of Kingston, and there had been 67 murders in the 24 hours preceding my arrival. I had no idea that the land of rum and reggae also has the highest murder rate anywhere in the world. Organized crime, gang culture and poor or corrupt policing was apparently mostly to blame.

I got the sense that the embassy would rather Jamaica didn't become known as the country that killed me. And so, it was agreed I'd run around their compound. I consulted my diary for notes on the agreed set-up; things like run location, if I had any runners – I hadn't – and the rough distance. The distance read: 'compound 3,000-metre loops'. Loops. OK, I can do that – if I have to.

The high commissioner was on leave and his beautiful home was being renovated. Like with most small embassy units, staff all lived in shared accommodation or in close-knit communities within a compound – one of the perks, or in some cases necessities of embassy life, I guess. Of course, some countries' compounds are more extrava-gant than others. This compound consisted of four buildings. There was an office where the official visitors' book stood proudly on an antique colonial table, a large photo of the Queen looking down from above. Off to the left, in the rear courtyard, was a small gardener's shed, surrounded by beautiful floral colours and shrubs. Nick's small but beautiful home was on the right, no more than a hundred metres away, set back among some tropical palms and foliage. The occasional hummingbird could be seen hovering near nectar-laden plants. The high commissioner's home was in the middle, on a slight hill, and the centrepiece of the compound. Scaffolding smothered much of the frontage and some local staff were working to restore damage following a recent storm. Out of sight from the main entrance, behind a trellis and past Nick's house, was an outdoor pool. Pristine, neat and inviting, considering the beads of sweat that were now falling down my back.

After a quick visual recce, I calculated that the loops couldn't be 3,000 metres – this place was tiny. Nick chimed in, as if my thoughts were made vocal: 'So the loop you'll be running is around past the trees up there, in front of the commissioner's house, back past the entrance gate and . . . do that a few times and you'll reach your distance.' He laughed with the understanding that this would not be fun. The loops were in fact 300 metres not 3,000; 140 laps, not the 14 laps I had in mind.

Lap 1, lap 2, lap 3 . . . 'This is all right,' I thought, as I trotted around with various staff looking on as if I was already a little mad . . . lap 54, lap 55, lap 56 – 'This is NOT all right!' Always turning in the same direction – this must be how it feels to be a racehorse. The slight incline, anticlockwise up past the swimming pool to the house, was now a mountain, and my feet dragged and dawdled under my flagging body. That bloody swimming pool could speak, I'm sure of it. Her gentle whispers of: 'Go on, just jump in, cool yourself down' beckoned to me like a siren on every lap. The whispers became a loud shouting cry after another 80 laps. The heat was too much and I experienced my hottest temperatures yet: 46°C. The shade I had in the early morning was now gone, and each lap, although horribly repetitive, somehow still seemed longer. I had set up a GoPro at opposite ends to capture the monotony – they warped in the heat and the memory cards corrupted.

To make matters worse, the stomach upset I'd been trying to ignore for about three days was now in full flow – literally. I'd spent much of the night frequenting the toilet. Although it was unfortunate that gang violence had confined me to the compound, the upside meant I now had a clean, flushing and, more importantly, readily available toilet never more than 150 metres away. My dashing to and fro, however, was increasingly laboured as the sun further sapped my energy. By lap 90 I had got through all 11 bottles of water laid on for me. I resorted to asking a gardener to spray me with the hose. He seemed to enjoy it as much as I did. Nick hurried around to top up my water and later returned for the final lap. I was totally pooped – in both senses of the word. My bottom had been experiencing its own marathon, and when I thought it was all over, lying on the melting tarmac, exhausted, as Nick took some snaps on his camera, my rear end rumbled again. It was time for yet another toilet visit. Coincidentally, I visited the little outdoor toilet booth exactly 19 times during that marathon, and got through 19 bottles of water. Correlation, maybe? Probably not.

I never did take a dip in the pool, despite 'her' siren calls. Although I did have a little time, I wanted to avoid any misjudged bottom burps while in the water. There were plenty more opportunities for ambassadorial *faux pas* to come on this trip. Instead, I was driven back to the hotel, where I fell asleep instantly – still in my sweaty clothes.

After waking up briefly for another episode of toilet time, still fully clothed in my running gear, including my shoes, I decided to get undressed and get into bed properly. I was too tired to pack for the morning. I eventually won the battle of removing my compression socks and sweaty clothes and threw back the cover to get into bed. The bed was full of cockroaches. For the past few hours I'd been the insulating blanket lying on top of the cover, attracting the little buggers without realizing. At least 40 scurried off to find darkness. Now, standing in my pants and startlingly awake, I wasn't sure what to do. I picked up a shoe and with one heavy blow splattered one on the architrave near the door. I immediately felt bad and decided to brush them off the bed and let them find somewhere else to hide. Besides, there were too many to splat – the bed would have looked like a bloodbath. I was also too tired to object to them using my body as a home if they wanted – I just needed to sleep.

As I tentatively crawled into bed, creeped out by the ugly creepy crawlies, I smiled and laughed at the situation. I'd been so focused on the mission that I'd forgotten, or not even initially realized, that all these frustrating interruptions: the heat, the shits, the insects, the laps were in fact the journey! It's not the destination but the path you take. I was likely delirious, but content in the fact. I slept happy.

Barring a few further dashes to the toilet, I slept well. No cockroaches up my nose or in my ears. My flight wasn't until the afternoon, so I had time to attempt some laundry in the sink of the communal hotel bathroom. I was confronted with two problems: no soap and no water. So that idea was abandoned, and I ventured out to the infamous Devon House Bakery. This place is well known for their great patties of which I scoffed down two of the curried goat and chicken variety, washed down with a huge cone of vanilla ice cream. An added perk of all the running is that I can eat and eat and eat – rarely healthily.

You may question why on earth was I eating such stomach-harsh foods that are likely to only prolong my unpleasant illness. My rationale, I suppose, was, 'I'm in Jamaica, I'm already as rough as hell, and let's face it, there's a chance it could flush something out.' Either way, having been so ill, a piece of dry toast and some water after another marathon wouldn't have left me with much, if any, energy to get the next one done. It was a gamble. Besides – those who know me well know I don't like to make things easy for myself.

The sleep I was getting wasn't enough. I couldn't afford to keep getting ill like this. Less than three weeks in, and I'd struggled with diarrhoea for the past eight days, and I'd averaged 4 hours 20 minutes of sleep per night.

The free time I did have was spent mostly on backing up photos, liaising with the team via Skype and WhatsApp, but, where possible, I did prioritise seeing as much of each country as I could. Thankfully I saw quite a lot on the run days: 26.2 miles on foot is a bigger distance than it would be in a vehicle in terms of being able to absorb the sights, sounds and smells of a place. I'd arrive a stranger, but by the time I'd finished running (if I wasn't running around in circles, that was), I would know my way around enough to be able to give directions to people in shops and eateries in the area. In fact, I did this a number of times. I felt worldly.

The ocean my friend. The hills my foes. Marathons eight to 15 took me through Trinidad and Tobago, Grenada, St Vincent, St Lucia, St Kitts, Antigua, Dominica and Barbados. (Puerto Rico, British & US Virgin Islands, Turk & Caicos Islands, Anguilla, Montserrat, Martinique and Guadeloupe are still colonial outposts of the British or Dutch and/or French overseas territories, so technically not independent countries recognized by the UN; the list I was following for 'the 196'.) The air miles now totalled 10,723, and my feet mileage 393.

In Barbados I had an early morning interview with BBC Radio 2 on the breakfast show with Chris Evans. It was breakfast time at home but most definitely pre-breakfast for me: 2 a.m. I was sitting in a beautiful suite of the Cobblers Cove four-star hotel, right on the beach. I could hear the waves through the window. Not British seaside waves crashing on concrete, rather, calm waves lapping at the shore. The dull hum of the swimming pool's electronic underwater filter system was the only other noise.

In my week-old boxers I sat on the edge of the living-room sofa on hold: 'Chris will be with you in a moment – just hold on the line – and remember you're live on the radio so please don't swear.' While waiting I scrolled through the memories of the last few countries I'd completed. Trinidad had been another looped course with a lovely chap called John. Fewer laps, and less punishing than Jamaica, thanks to a 2 a.m. start with head torches. The temperature was similar to that of a summer's morning in Dorset: crisp but promising. John's knowledge of the city centre Queen's Park Savannah kept my mind busy while his car, parked on the corner of every lap, acted as a fuel station. Loaded with bucketfuls of fresh coconut water from his garden, it was a welcome stop on each of the eight laps.

In Grenada I was hosted by the incredibly luxurious hotel Maca Bana. They had just eight private villas, all with staff. For this marathon I was accompanied by ten of the country's finest British expats. We shared running stories, talked about pets, jobs, travel and all the surprising connections we had. They took it in turns to run one of the four legs of the out and back route, which meant I was repeating answers to the same questions over and over again. We ran from the hotel to the downtown harbour and back. A road route, boring, but I didn't care. It was enjoyable to have company and finish before 11 a.m. The run done, I sat on the terrace of the beach-front restaurant and leisurely gorged on fresh fish and pasta – all with the view of crystal-clear water and bright white sands.

St Lucia, St Vincent and St Kitts were also beautiful hotels, but the hills of the Caribbean coast roads ruined my legs. The quick succession of these 3,000-feet climbs, coupled with cramped and foodless flights, caused me to have less sleep and subsequently I moved deeper into exhaustion. Happy in mind, my body was shouting at me to rest, my legs tighter than ever, and my hips, feet and knees aching and sore.

Antigua was next; a benchmark I'd been waiting for: my first package from DHL. As part of the two years' planning, we had come up with an ingenious way to tackle the issue of travelling so light. How would I get new trainers, more supplements and nutritional goodies, fresh clothes and new documents? DHL turned out to be less helpful than we had hoped, but they did give us a tiny discount and solved a problem. The long-winded process of naming each package item and its value, and filling out countless forms, turned into a hassle we later abandoned. At the time, though, 4 February marked 'special delivery day'. A few messages from home, some chocolate, my next new pair of running shoes, and various important flight documents that saved me the job of printing and sorting were all that was in the box. I even had fresh underwear provided by Runderwear, seamless pants to help stop chaffing in the undercarriage area.

From Antigua to Dominica, where the hills punished me and the rains came harder than before. The tropical paradise that was the Caribbean was reminding me that tropical doesn't always mean sunshine. My fresh shoes were soaked within minutes of stepping out of the door, as I plodded my way up the first of many hills. Running past broken bridges, land-slipped roads, and houses crushed to piles of rubble, I was reminded how weather is king in this part of the world (increasingly throughout most of the world). Hurricane Maria had decimated this island in 2017. The recovery efforts are estimated to last 50 years. Although the run was wet, windy, humid and frankly horrible, everything paled into insignificance next to the state of the country. The taxi driver who drove me from the airport to the hotel told me stories from the day the storm came. He still hadn't returned to his home he'd abandoned 12 months earlier. He couldn't face it. His family simply started again, with support from strangers, aid and anyone who'd help.

Once my mind was back on the present, and having chatted with Chris and Vassos on the radio, recalling the various trials and tribulations of the first few weeks on the road, before I knew it, it was nearly dawn in Barbados. I couldn't sleep. I was ready to run. Will, the manager of the beautiful Cobblers Cove hotel, along with my team doing their bit to publicize my being there, had landed an impressive haul of 11 friendly faces who greeted me in reception. Everything was still quiet and so my initial hellos to the gang in multicoloured running gear, complete with head torches, was in hushed tones. It was predawn and the birds were only just coming to life. The route for me and the gang armed with backpacks to carry bottles, snacks and some coconut water was a run through fields, along narrow coast roads, through Georgetown and past massive rich, classically Barbadian homes.

At the risk of understating things, it was hot. We survived off water from a number of standpipes around the island. I was cautious at first, with a desperate wish not to become sick, but I got involved. The water was cold and fresh and the little taps appeared out of nowhere far more often than I'd seen anywhere before, even in local parks back home. It was a great system and one the island is proud of.

By the time we completed the meandering loop around Georgetown and were back at the hotel there were just four of us. The rest had work and real responsibilities and so had peeled off at various points. It was my first really peaceful run of the journey. Everything was in slow motion. I loved it. It felt like I had more time.

Before checking out and moving on, I was invited by Will and a few other staff to join them for afternoon tea of scones with all the trimmings. To my delight but extreme surprise he presented me with an envelope. They had donated some cash to the charity already, but wanted to give me a gift as a thank you for staying and spreading awareness to fight prostate cancer. They gave me a complimentary one-week stay, for when the journey was complete. This was one of the nicest places I'd ever stayed and now I get to go back! I got the distinct impression that it wasn't just a publicity stunt and that they really cared and were grateful. They certainly weren't short of guests, and so I was thankful and moved by it.

I left the hotel later that day, but before I reached the airport I was diverted by the driver to visit the British ambassador and a cancer rehabilitation centre. I was in for another tear-jerking surprise. I was becoming aware that cancer sadly touches many, many lives, families and communities. A small group of embassy staff, the cancer centre nurses and some patients gathered for a photo to thank me. A touching speech was then read by the ambassador and another by the cancer centre chairwomen. I was honoured and moved to tears. I felt totally unworthy of such thanks. I was just running, they were doing the hard work. I came away with a bag of goodies, snacks for the plane and a small enamel pin. It meant the world. That day's events lingered on my mind for some time afterwards.

The Caribbean is an expensive place, and it may appear that I was living pretty luxuriously through these first few weeks. Hotel-wise, I certainly was, and while that wasn't the initial plan, it was a bonus, and I wasn't about to turn it down. For this initial handful of countries we had the benefit of time in the lead up to the start line, and the team had worked wonders finding some willing hotels to put me up free of charge. Remarkably, in these first 15 countries, I'd only paid for accommodation twice. I'd hoped that having heard why I was doing this, hotels, hostels, guesthouses and families would offer to take me in and want to help the cause, and I was incredibly fortunate that plenty did. In return I would thank these hotels on social media, share some photos and be available to speak to management about the journey. I had imagined that it would be the smaller hotels that would welcome this publicity, but it tended to be the more wealthy establishments, with bigger budgets and more rooms lying empty, who were keener to help.

Of course, with people working so hard for me, I had to pay the team . . .

About a year into the planning, around January 2017, I was still managing everything myself. I'd taken time out from working and competing in various races to solely focus on piecing the trip together. I believed I could put all the various pieces in motion and manage the rest on the road. Naïve, really, but I couldn't afford to pay anyone. Financially, I was all in. I used all my assets: home, car, any cash, the lot. I wanted to be all in – this was a cleansing exercise and the trip of a lifetime. But it turned out that my cash wasn't enough, not by a long way. It was the world, or bust – and bust happened long before the trip was over.

Funding soon worked its way to the top of the list of priorities. My carefully calculated budget totalled all the basics, like accommodation, flights, visas, supplies, and a small amount of contingency. The upshot was that I needed to find £97,000 more than I had. I made a list of all the things the trip was not to be, what it was not to include, and what I didn't want. This was designed to translate the many small cost-cutting measures I had in my mind into numbers on paper: 200+ flights with a snack could mean £1,000 spent on things like Twix bars. No-brainer.

Then, as the planning months went by, I consulted various experts, bloggers and other explorers. I wanted to learn of the pitfalls before going any further. The overriding consensus was one of madness. Some simply thought I couldn't even access every country, others believed the timescale was impossible, and some thought my body wouldn't cope. There were also those that were jealous and damn right rude when approached for help. A shame, really. From my perspective, I welcome, in fact urge, anyone thinking of attempting an expedition like this to come to me for advice and contacts. I'm by no means an expert, but I do have a long list of what not to do, and an even bigger address book of totally brilliant friends all over the world who would be willing to help.

Mr Mark Beaumont, a man I hugely admire for his various ridiculous feats of endurance, physical and logistical, was a huge help, and has since become my unofficial mentor in all things adventure. He is a rare breed and so totally selfless, gentlemanly and generous with support in any way he can be – even if it means going out of his way. I can't speak more fondly of him. If you don't know about him, he's cycled around the world in 80 days – that says enough.

On the funding side, I'd spent about eight months sending 10,000+ emails to potential sponsors, media outlets, running brands, embassy contacts; you name it – I tried everything to find avenues into funding. We even got very close to Mr Branson – his people were kind to connect us, but I have a feeling bad timing played a part in the breakdown in communication. Necker Island was hit by a storm and his focus naturally wasn't on helping an unknown bloke halfway around the world. I still admire you, Richard, and if you're reading this, it's not too late to chuck me a few grand. I jest. Let's make it 50 grand?

In the quest to find funding and to reduce my workload I eventually adopted the position of 'speculate to accumulate'. Enter Jeff Smith, as key a figure as Kev from the Marathon des Sables in contributing strongly to my belief that I could give this mission a crack. Jeff Smith is one of the most modest men I know: a mountaineer, an Everest summiteer, a brilliant father, and a guy who dedicates his life to helping others. He happened to be sitting next to me on the bus for the six-hour drive into the sandy depths of the Sahara Desert.

Jeff spoke to me about the precious nature of life and how his life was transformed following the death of his friend, known as 'Moose'. (I'm not entirely sure why 'Moose' was called 'Moose', but they played professional ice hockey together.) He subsequently set up my all-time favourite foundation in memory of his friend, a non-profit foundation which goes by the name 'Big Moose'. Their mission statement reads, 'Leaving the world better than we found it.' They do just that. He and his family are the embodiment of everything I now stand for. I got to know and admire Jeff, aka the 'adventure whisperer', and (later his family) after our week together in the desert, and he became something of a guiding light. He edged me closer to embarking on this trip, encouraged me to move into the world of adventure, and told me stories about how having people to support my expedition would, in the long run, benefit me.

Still not really knowing where the money would come from, I posted my first advert on Gumtree the next day. It read: 'Help organize a world first expedition. Virtually no pay and lots of long hours – with me as a boss. I'm often snappy, and determined to the point of selfish in trying to raise awareness to fight prostate cancer.' Perhaps surprisingly, a number of people responded, including the aforementioned Ali. Skip forward several months, and Ali was managing my life.

By the time January 2018 came around, my team now consisted of many pivotal individuals and companies. Mostly volunteers or on minimal pay, they all got stuck in and got me to the start line with a rough idea of what we were doing. It was far from ideal, but a world away from what I could have achieved on my own.

In terms of finances the plan initially was to find full funding from sponsors or ideally one sponsor. We got close many times. On two occasions specifically we had months of discussions with finance firms willing to sponsor – only for them both to pull out at the last minute. Both for the same reason: the fear that their sponsorship could result in something horrendous happening to me and they would be at fault. This was something I understood but was eternally frustrated by.

The advice from several quarters was to make a start and that once I got going, and the media kicked in, the sponsors would follow. In truth, however, the funding never really came in the quantities we were hoping for. We relied on lots of smaller donations through varying businesses and individual donors. The vast majority of money that was spent ended up coming from either my savings and investments, which I hadn't intended to use, or out of the pockets of my parents, extended family and very selfless brilliant close friends. It was clear early on that if a big sponsor didn't turn up I would have to borrow most of the money to make the dream come true. Frankly, I was amazed that we didn't land at least one substantial sponsor. In hindsight, many realisations about money hit home, including the fact that my calculations of our expected spend were embarrassingly and wildly wrong. That put further strain on the process.

Another puzzling aspect of the planning was that, initially, we did approach travel agents – but they just didn't want to know. Well, they did, but for huge fees. Not a single agency offered any kind of discount if we agreed to book all 200-plus flights through their business. This I still find baffling. We went back to the drawing board.

The drawing board revealed that individual flights booked directly through various independent sites would save us around £20,000. This was a surprisingly huge saving, so my parents Mike and Sally reluctantly took on the task of overseeing logistics. They were in charge of all flight bookings. Their number-one job – aside from worrying, and arranging my insurance cover (when I was in the dodgy countries in particular), and managing the funding – was to link country to country logically and sensibly. This role inevitably snowballed, and their time stuck behind the computer scratching their heads increased tenfold and then tenfold again as we got deeper and deeper into the expedition. I know for a fact this is a regret. If you ever meet this brilliant duo, it's probably best not to bring it up. Every day further into the trip, they did more and more to rectify various problems and miscalculations. It's no understatement to say that without them this dream would have failed.

It would have failed without Maz and Faisal too. I'd budgeted £5,000 for visas. After approaching eight companies, the cheapest quote I had back was £15,000 – only three times my initial budget. Mum WhatsApp'ed me one day with the message: 'Try these guys.' Universal Visas was their company name. I later found out that they operated out of a small office in London with only half a dozen staff, all working till the sun set, eight days a week. They agreed to help and waive all their fees. They'd only charge us what the embassies charged them. (At one point I was accidentally sent a file from another visa company that included their costs and mark-ups. This was rather telling: a Canadian e-visa costs about £5. This company was charging an eye-watering £250.) Having UV on board took £11,000 off the initial cost and brought it back down below what I'd estimated. The best part was that UV helped not for exposure and didn't put any contract in place. They helped because they wanted to be a part of the mission.

And this dream team didn't let me down at any point from start to finish. The nature of such a long journey meant that people's lives moved on and developed. While I was still on the same mission, other people naturally moved on with their lives, changed jobs, got married, had babies ... but Maz and Faisal were always there, truly dedicated to helping me and the cause. I owe them a lot.

The final piece of the jigsaw to slot into place involved promotion. Before this life of running, I had hated social media. I thought it was a waste of time and anybody who used it was either out to make money or was wasting their lives sharing pointless updates with photos of food or of them getting pissed every Saturday. But the truth is without the likes of Facebook, Instagram and Twitter I would never have attempted this mission. For one, I wouldn't have found runners all over the world to run with, or to host me. Without social media there would have been no way to shout about Prostate Cancer UK at all. Emily would regularly receive WhatsApp messages from me asking for more posts, ideas to engage more people and generally reach a wider audience. The point was simply to bring in more donations for the charity. Dawn also volunteered to help edit my blogs and social content ahead of publication, a task I hadn't even thought of, but obviously one that needed doing. Years later she is still reviewing and publishing my blog on my behalf, without any reward. Another individual crucial to spreading the word was Mr Scott Barnett from Spark Media – along with the crew behind the documentary. Scott approached me at the end of a networking event in Birmingham where I was talking about my plans to run the world. He was impressed, and luckily co-owned Spark Media, which in turn happily enabled me to capture the entire trip in a finished article worthy of the big screen.

So those are the headliners. It feels harsh not to include many of the other brilliant people. If you're not in that list, but supported, please don't take offence. There are simply too many people. For example, Rebecca, who approached me at the end of a talk in Bristol to ask if she could help with logistics. She had a full-time job but wanted to do what she could. She was initially given the mind-numbing task of insurance. Twenty-five insurance policies later she had painstakingly picked apart the small print of countless companies and ensured (and insured) all eventualities were covered – even the likes of war zones. She worked tirelessly behind the scenes and then popped her head above the surface to say, 'It's done.' No doubt you get the picture – these are just a few of the influential contacts that have made all the difference to the success of a long and complicated expedition. I can't thank them enough.

Mexico, Belize

Mexico could have been a very different story. We (the team and I) had opted to fly me to Cancún and not Mexico City. This was mainly because the flight path worked out, but also because the crime rate around Mexico City is somewhat (massively) higher than Cancún. I did feel a little that it was a cop out. Instead of culture, cuisine, history and architecture I landed in what felt effectively like Benidorm, Spring Break and Magaluf rolled into one. Not that I'm dissing those things (I am), but it wasn't my cup of tea. Without meaning to be rude I was in Cancún to get the Mexico leg done and to move on. I could do Mexico properly another time. It did make sense to avoid any unnecessary dangers and so I was happy enough to sit at the 'all you can eat' human trough and watch the trumpet-wielding imported mariachi bands prancing along with slightly overweight, slightly over middle-aged hen parties in tow.

Despite my slight snobbishness regarding the overall vibe in Cancún, the run was surprisingly beautiful. The coast and the vast expanse of beaches pre-dawn were an amazing sight – especially because they weren't littered with people. Instead, perfect barrel waves crashed to the shore, birds picked through the tide-line wash, and the massive sun rose over the ocean. I had the place to myself for most of the morning. It was so impressive that I even taxied there post-run with my drone and camera gear to get some shots. The bright white beach, with the black seaweed tide-line and the deep blue ocean, was even better from the sky. The drone was over 500 metres above

when I took the best shot. Thanks to the views my anti-Cancún attitude made a u-turn.

Belize was a funny one too. Amongst the many Lonely Planet
guidebooks that littered my book shelves at home, the Belize book
had sat at the top, more visible than the rest. I'd often pick it up and
flick through, occasionally turning corners over to mark wonderful
photos I liked. (Let's face it, the photos are the best bits, aren't they?)
Ninety-nine per cent of those lovely photos referenced the various
islands and atolls off the east coast of the mainland – and not Belize
City, where I was staying. I had seen thousands of backpackers at the
airport, all arriving in vests and thongs (as the Yanks call them), but
me, I was to run around the dusty unfinished and pretty busy roads of
the city. It was a shame to miss out on the islands, and so I hatched a
last-minute plan to run immediately upon check-in and then find a
boat to take me to an island.

The largely un-scenic and very dry, dusty run along long, wide
unmade roads was complete. As far as venturing to a nearby island, I
chose Caye Caulker. Remarkably, I made it, mooched around the tiny
beach-style town centre and outdoor barbecues, where fishermen and
palm trees surrounded little huts, had lunch, made some friends, went
for a swim, bought a few souvenir bracelets and got back before dark.
The whole thing cost me less than $35 although, annoyingly, I did
manage to lose a few camera and drone accessories, mounts and gim-
bal clamps, which I needed for the rest of the journey.

I had let my beard regrow, and my hair began to get to the annoying in-between length. I had made a pact with myself that I wouldn't
cut my hair for the entire trip, the plan being to donate it to a children's cancer charity to make wigs. This was, at the time, a great idea.
As the temperature reached nearly 50°C, not so great. My teeth were
also not brushed as often as they should have been, and my bag was
now becoming a friend rather than an object. I was slowly morphing
into a different person. The Caribbean had changed me – for the better. At the time, I felt very scruffy and unkempt, but that's just me
now. Before heading to the airport, after a restful morning ticking off
a few interviews in Belize, I packed my bags. With some music from

the Spotify playlist 'let's get shit done', and looking much like a robot on an assembly line, I twisted, spun and reached around the room picking up items and packing them in the specific order I'd become accustomed to. I was saying the names of each thing out loud as I packed. Packing was a challenge initially, but now I had it down to just four minutes and 20 seconds. Neat, exactly the same as the time before, and I knew where everything was. I felt smug in my efforts. Life on the road on your own – you make your own fun.

El Salvador

On the plane to El Salvador I peered out of the window and let my mind wander off, enjoying the sun falling below the horizon and casting deep, vibrant colours across the sky. I had seen so many mesmerizing sunsets over the last month. I thought of the uniqueness of this kind of trip: the ever-increasing collection of weird and wonderful bank notes; the various critters and creepy crawlies, such as the gecko that had stowed away on a plane; and, of course, all the strangers that were now 'contacts' in my phone book. I wrote my diary in an upbeat, excited tone before falling asleep, only to be woken what felt like seconds later by the thud of the wheels touching down into yet another country.

Bernhard, the British ambassador, was my liaison in El Salvador, and very much archetypal as such. He got things done with a best-of-British attitude. Other hosts would have to go some to match what he pulled off. He only had two weeks from our initial contact with him. It wasn't always possible to track down the right contacts in time and it was also often unfair to give contacts specific dates further in advance in case things changed. And things did change – a lot. I say this with absolutely no knowledge of what went on. El Salvador was a good example of how Carla and Bernhard had sorted everything between them to make what happened next happen.

Flying in, on the evening of 14 February, I had one full day in El Salvador, which involved a run with over 1,000 people ranging from school kids to elite athletes and elder retirees. I was interviewed on radio for two hours and had an additional five interviews with other

TV news channels. Medals were produced for all who took part –
these had my face on the back. Roads were closed, I was gifted a large
glass trophy of a motmot. It meant nothing to me but it's apparently
their national bird. The trophy was made by a world famous Salvado-
rian sculptor. And if that wasn't enough I was whisked off to watch
the premier of the film *Churchill* – of all films. Red carpet, the works.

The lengthy radio interview took place very early in the morning
and was in Spanish. My Spanish was limited to 'si' and 'no', which
meant a translator. I'd never experienced parallel translation live in
such a mind-jumbling way. As the words left the Spanish-speaking
host's mouth, a Spanish English-speaking woman would translate. I
had the gentleman looking at her but speaking to me, and she was
listening to him but looking at me. I was listening to both but had no
idea where to look. Do I look at the person I understand? Or at the
man who's not looking at me? All in all, this was as exhausting as the
marathon running. What made the morning especially memorable
for me was the coffee moment. That particular episode of the radio
show was sponsored by a coffee company. I eat more or less everything and drink most things too. I don't drink booze, hate cabbage,
and, above all, cannot stand coffee. An entire section of the show was
set aside to review coffee. As their guest for the morning, I was the
one to taste all the various coffees. In that polite British way I couldn't
let the side down and pass on every coffee thrust in front of me, so I
went for it. I figured running around the world or drinking coffee –
what could be harder?

After the first few delicate sips of round one, it was all I could do
not to vomit – I really do not like coffee. Opting for a more devious
tactic, the following rounds were less of a struggle. I put the large
bucket-like mugs to my lips, and ensured no liquid entered my mouth.
Instead some would spill down the back of the cup, and the rest just
stuck to the edge of my lips. No taste, winning! Just the 'perfectly
roasted world famous' coffee-bean smell scorching my nose. I must
fess up to Pencho y Aida radio station and apologize for my terrible
reviews of coffee.

Mid-run I was treated to a special surprise. An international school
had been told of my arrival and were patiently waiting for me. They

were eight or so miles down the road from the starting point, next to the beach. I rounded the corner, up a slow grind of a hill, with the beautiful coast and waves on my left and the mainland to my right. I heard them before I saw them: 400-plus kids all screaming, waving flags and generally excited to welcome me. I was topless, due to the crazy humidity, sweating out of every pore, running with as much enthusiasm as I could muster. I remember my smile hurting my face. It was such a great feeling, to feel so impactful to these young minds. Hundreds of kids lined either side of the road waiting for 'high fives' and shoving notepads in my face while shouting for autographs. I was convinced they had the wrong guy. Little did I know, my trip was causing quite a wave down the Caribbean and into Central America. This may have been due to the popularity of running but more probably was because of the high incidence of prostate cancer, which kills more men throughout Central America than any other cancer.

After pouring a few more bottles of water over my head I pushed on. Four TV stations filmed the entire run. I was surrounded by news crews. The group that lasted the distance were a mix of club runners, a few national elites and some very good amateur racers. All of these people were better runners than me, but still somehow looked to me for advice. I didn't know what I was doing, really. Just run until I'm done – that was the only plan.

I left El Salvador exhausted and bedraggled. The onslaught of everything other than the running had mentally worn me out. I slept like a baby on the plane to Guatemala the next day. Bernhard had had the awareness to offer to take the enormous glass trophy back to the UK on an upcoming trip. It was a more than common courtesy that most wouldn't have thought of. He, like many, I wanted to thank more fully.

Guatemala

By Guatemala I was well and truly in Central America. Ahead of the expedition, Guatemala had been spoken about more than other countries in the region because there was a slim but possible chance of visiting one of four charities helping to offset my carbon emissions. Carbon, the climate and excessive burning of fossil fuels was a sensitive subject when it came to this trip. In all honestly, my first thought about carbon emissions was that the trip could attract bad press because of all the flying. Facing potential questions and scrutiny from the press I thought it would be wise to maybe plant some trees, or something. I now know that's very naive and not really how it works.

I researched a little more and, as Google tends to do, it made me worry even more. I was more concerned than ever. Concerned about all the emissions from not only flying but my diet, and all the bits of my life that I hadn't really considered would be harmful, I found a few companies that offered professional accredited offsetting. To my surprise a company called Natural Capital Partners (NCP) got back to me. It turned out NCP were the first to provide a set of clear guidelines for businesses to achieve carbon neutrality. As of 2019 they had won best 'offset retailer' for a record ninth consecutive year. These guys were the bee's knees of offsetting and, unbelievably, wanted to talk to me about supporting the trip.

After a couple of phone calls I sent over all the projected estimates for various bits and pieces, ranging from flights, distances, transport types, diet and where in the world I'd be going, and let them work their magic. Three months later they got back to me with a full offsetting proposal.

A great chap call Tom sorted everything and I learnt that there were better, more complete ways to offset and support the environment. There were other ways that helped the environment more than just planting trees. You could start by reducing the amount of trees being cut down in the first place. This is obviously a crude example, and only one angle, but the general message is clear: it's not just about carbon emissions, it's the bigger picture. NCP's model operates by forming and then harnessing a huge network of projects around the world. At the time of writing they have over 350 projects across 40 countries supporting the environment in countless ways. They look at the environment as a whole, the planet and the people as one.

As part of my offsetting package they selected four key initiatives already in operation around the world that I could support and,

better still, they could sponsor. I naturally bit their hand off. One specific gold-standard project was a 'non-profit' in Antigua (not the
country but a village of the same name) in Guatemala. Primarily
focusing on water filtration, they also delivered health benefits to
more than 230,000 Guatemalan families – this directly through the
use of fuel-efficient stoves and ecofiltration pots. With over 40 per
cent of the world population still relying on solid-fuel stoves, many
use open fires and burn tons of wood for warmth and cooking, which
is largely ineffective. Efficiency is paramount and on a large scale the
impact is of course massive. This project also has a positive knock-on
effect with improved health due to the reduction in smoke inhalation
in small spaces. Burn wood more efficiently, burn less wood, create
less harmful smoke = less harm to the planet and its people. Very
quickly I understood that carbon offsetting can and does have a far-
reaching impact if tackled correctly. We totalled 45 tons of carbon
equivalent offset. This not only made the entire journey neutral but
delivered exponential good alongside.

As with most behind-the-scenes logistics I was the last to know I'd
be meeting the owner of this brilliant offsetting initiative. I was probably told but had forgotten. My memory was really struggling to
recall various names, places, and even at times which flight I'd just
come from. It's rather embarrassing to be asked by an immigration
officer where I've flown from and not be able to remember. Everything was merging into one big blur. In the early days I'd just stare
blankly and stutter with my face shocked and confused. I'd since
learnt to disguise my face with some small talk allowing me enough
time to look at my diary. I'm really not joking. This happened regularly. It certainly pulled things into focus. My body was just about
coping, but my mind was lagging a little further behind.

Once landed and tucked up under fresh hotel linen once again I
thought I should probably check the calendar ahead of the run tomorrow. 23:50, with the light already off, and having no energy to move, I
lifted the phone with a heavy outstretched arm. My eyes still virtually
closed, and letting out a groan, I read 'EARLY START – 03:30 meeting with Philip Wilson from "EcoFiltro" – factory tour.' I hadn't
thought about this for months and was really not in the right frame of

mind. Reluctantly, I scrolled back the alarm time on my phone and fell asleep with it still in my hand on my chest. The early start was simply because there weren't enough hours in the day. If I visited at 8 a.m. I'd be running in the midday sun, any later and I'd be too tired for the following day. This was a regular problem, and because the EcoFiltro factory was just opening up it had made sense to fit it in at what felt like the middle of the night. Despite the exhaustion, early mornings did elongate the day and slowed everything down. It was a blessing, really. I woke up what felt like minutes later. Like with an early training session, or a cold windy morning run, I knew I'd feel grateful for getting up. So I did. Phil was waiting in the lobby at 3.15 – a firm handshake from him, and a weak wrist from me. I simultaneously used my other arm to snatch at a few peculiar-looking pastries on the side by the hotel reception. 'How are you, Nick? A pleasure to meet you.' His voice was very awake and full of excitement. I have no idea what my response was – but if you're reading this, Philip, I'm sorry for being totally overtired.

I'll never forget the sunrise over the ancient city as we drove east to the factory – the beautiful buildings, with Mount Fuego as backdrop. In the central highlands of Guatemala, known for its impeccably preserved Spanish Baroque-influenced architecture and colonial churches, the city has the look of a painting and the feel of a welcoming home. This was the splash on the face I needed to wake up and smell the roses – or at least the street stoves cooking fish and corn.

The tour of the factory, a non-profit manufacturing water filters mainly for the rural poor in Guatemala, was comprehensive and impressive. I've vowed to go back and volunteer, and I will. The work, while scientific and incredibly impactful, meant a great deal to Philip personally – I could tell he loved it. This was his baby. The factory wasn't an obvious assembly line, but with a tour of each element it was incredible how the components for the filters came together to form such a brilliant invention: from ceramic pots, to the special furnace and drying areas, plus the various different moulds and the complicated science bit with the special layers that make up the filtration system.

A set of brilliant connections were about to unfurl as he dropped me back to the hotel a little after 5.30. Philip turned out to be one hell of a guy. He dropped me back about 40 minutes later than planned, and to my surprise, because I hadn't checked the calendar again, there were a group of random people in the hotel lobby in running gear. I looked them up and down a little, but began to walk past, not wanting to assume they were there to run with me. Philip cleared it up in an instant, announcing in his commanding and eternally charming tone, 'You must all come back to my house after the run and I'll cook dinner. This man is on a mission of a lifetime, and you, fellow pilgrims, you deserve a banquet.' (Or words to that effect.)

There were four groups of runners – two couples – and two groups of running buddies who knew each other. By the time we finished the run, half of them had bailed to go to work, but were brilliant company nonetheless, and the remaining half have now become lifelong friends, one of which, Nick, I've run with on four other continents. My tired mood had been extinguished by the energy of others and I'd made some brilliant friends. I felt on top of the world.

With me bringing up the rear, stopping to take photos of various colourful market stalls, and old peoples' faces, the group was strung out in front of me in peloton-esque fashion.

The unexpected gathering was in fact a result of social media. It transpired that our Facebook posting approach was beginning to work. The plan with Facebook was to approach all the running clubs in every city I was due to run in, but it turned out the most success we had was by good old fashioned word of mouth – with the help of Facebook's worldwide network and the added boost of the six degrees of separation concept. More often than not, someone I was running with knew someone I'd already run with. It happened more and more as the journey went on. Is the world small or are we just really good at chatting to the right people? The word of mouth nature and the wonders of social media meant the journey was creating a wider and wider network. Even so, early on, the connections were much further reaching and more helpful than I could have imagined.

To cap it all, Mount Fuego, the massive volcano, decided to erupt more or less as soon as we set off. Just before mile two we heard a boom, and then watched as bellows of grey smoke soared into the cloudless blue sky. All of us reached for our phones. I couldn't believe my eyes. Should I panic? Was this a Pompeii moment? The locals amongst us said, 'You're lucky, that happens, but rarely – that's the second time in the last month though – it's happening a little more often these days.' The entire marathon was to the backdrop of this pristinely conical mountain belching ash with flashes of red lava into the sky. We were about 11 miles away, but were in fact on the outer edges of Fuego itself. I ran open mouthed for a while, initially a little worried, and then just in awe.

Only four weeks later Fuego blew in a more deadly way, killing over 140 people. The eruption I experienced was certainly not small and perhaps again I'd come close to things going wrong. This part of the world is ruled by much more than governments and politics. Mother nature holds many of the cards.

The runners with me that day included Nick Kershaw, James Campbell, Abi Jones, Rocio Aldekoa, Ana Maria Gonzealez de Ruano, José Fernando Toje Maldonado and Silvana de Rash. Nick not only has one of the more easy names to pronounce but owns a charitable marathon company called 'Impact'. They 'run', quite liter-ally, marathon events all over the world. All of these races are designed to support the local community and, as the name suggests, make an impact to help towards various initiatives in the country. I've learnt more and more about his efforts and his attitude to help as I've got to know him. He's a man of complete dedication and authenticity. A brilliant bloke. The kind that will go above and beyond to help in any situation. He did just that orchestrating the whole day for the group.

Remember the meal offer from Philip? Well, that was where our temporary running family bonded even further. The run done, showers completed, we reconvened once again in the lobby of my hotel. I only later found out that some of the group travelled for over an hour to get back to the hotel. A brilliant effort, especially post-run. We ventured, on foot, only a few streets down to Philip's family home in a gated community of large well ordered houses in a sweep-ing crescent before the backdrop of looming mountains in the shade of the sun.

None of us left until the early hours of the morning. With pizzas and beer flowing all night, sitting in the rear courtyard, we chatted for hours. Philip had a beautiful grand piano in the living room – and I'm not sure how it came up, but I was ordered to play the piano. I don't play officially, but I can, and enjoyed a few minutes of musical release – nothing but some classical improvisation.

Later, I realized I'd somehow lost a microphone from one of my cameras, and in testament to the group's kindness, the reclined, beer-sipping atmosphere abated for a good half an hour when, one after another, these lovely people joined me in the search for my missing microphone on the streets. It was pitch black outside, we could hardly see a hand in front of our face. Armed with phone torches we collectively squinted at the grey cobbles looking for a similarly grey microphone. I was grateful for the help, but couldn't put them all through it any longer so called off the search without success. To this day I don't know where that mic went.

My ethos was this: 'always try to go to bed having squeezed every last drop out of the day'; I was after as many sounds, smells and sights as possible. I went to sleep wanting more days like this, while also acknowledging I wouldn't last very long if I did. I needed to hit pause and sleep for a week or ideally longer.

Honduras, Nicaragua, Costa Rica, Panama

In my tired state, the next few countries flew by. After Saturday night in Guatemala, I flew to Honduras on the Sunday, ran on the Monday, flew to Nicaragua on the Tuesday, ran on the Wednesday, and had finished marathon 22 in Costa Rica by Friday afternoon. The first of many spells of extreme blur.

In Honduras, and the un-pronounceable capital of Tegucigalpa, I was hosted by George and his wife Dilcia. They opened up their home to me, fed me and organized literally everything from touchdown to take-off. Dilcia spoke no English – or so I was told. I later found out her English was rather good. My poor attempts in Spanish often ended in a lesson around a particular phrase or pronunciation. Language was fast becoming something I noticeably didn't have.

That first night in their home I played table tennis with their two young children. Aged 11 and 14 they were inquisitive of me and shy but keen to play. I remember clearly the feeling of being so unbelievably tired – in contrast to their bounding youthful energy even lifting the table-tennis bat was an effort. We played in the night air on their roof-top terrace. Their puppy spaniel was also keen to play but ended the match quite abruptly by eating the last table-tennis ball.

We then tucked into delicious mountains of home-cooked chicken pasta while sitting around their kitchen diner set-up. Midnight bedtime once again; up at 5 a.m. The mountains of marathon 20 beckoned. With the sky still black we drove an hour north under a scattering of stars and light cloud. George was a keen runner but sadly was unable to join us due to work – Dilcia, it turned out, was a brilliant ultra runner and made it look easy and me feel even more tired. From mile one running down the twisty switchbacks in the dark, to mile 26 in the blazing sunlight, I was educated on everything from farming, to language, race and culture. I even learnt an impressive vocabulary of ten phrases. Things like *¿Dónde está el baño? Por favor espera. ¿Puedo tomar un poco de agua?* (Where is the bathroom? Please wait. May I have some water?) All of which were much needed phrases.

We ran along the CA-6 highway out of the capital for 24 of the 26 miles. Lined with endless flat fields that eventually rose to faraway mountains, the road was dusty, with the only traffic consisting of huge double-length sugar-cane trucks that were bigger than traditional lorries, made up of two conjoined trailers with countless sprigs of sugar cane sprouting into the sky like punk-rock hair. The old and laden diesel engines could be heard slogging through the long straight roads miles before they reached us. We'd hop into the fields to let them past and gawp at the mind-boggling number of watermelons littering the land as far as the eye could see. The green cylindrical dots against harsh muddy flats were like a polka-dot patchwork; the distinctive smell of sugar cane and diesel filling the air as plumes of smoke wafted past us. The air was so sweet, had it not been for the fumes that followed I would have opened my mouth to try to chew it. Freshly cut sugar cane is one of my favourite smells in the world. Post-run, I even had my first taste of sweet pizza. After eating a large normal savoury pizza in a beautiful Italian themed kitchen I was presented with another pizza the same size to the tune of happy birthday. It wasn't my birthday, but without wanting to be rude to my guests I accepted this second pizza and tucked in. It was sweet, covered in honey and syrup – apparently a Honduran thing – not quite a delicacy but I needed sugar nonetheless. It was a weird occasion, but I ate the lot and later slept like a baby in a sweet sugary mess.

With another aggressive thud of the stamp in my increasingly mosaic passport I moved deeper and deeper south. I never have understood why immigration officers deem it necessary to slowly lift the stamping machine off the table to then smash it into the page with such force. Perhaps that's the only perk of the job.

In Nicaragua I visited one of the few places you can see freshwater sharks in the world, sat dangling my legs over the lip of an active volcano, and was met, hosted and pampered by another couple, this time a father–daughter combo. Carlos and Maria had the widest smiles, with crisp white teeth, and their energy was infectious. They were successful in business and keen runners so had the means and inclination to not only pay for my hotel and treat me to a steak dinner, but also put on a brilliant early morning race around the capital's central lagoon. Twelve of us mingled around a small plastic trestle table at 5 a.m., TV crews shot some footage, a couple of cars provided support in busy traffic, and a big red cool-box, which held all the goodies we needed to keep us going for the hot 16 laps around the lake, sat on the table.

On our first lap we passed what I coined 'the screech bird tree'. I have no idea what these birds were called, or what the type of tree was, but every available branch held tiny little birds, all of which were making a racket. Wow, did they sing at dawn: the volume from these birds was so much that all conversations were halted as we passed. They were so loud that they could be heard for over a mile away after the tree receded. As the fatigue from the run set in, the birds, although still mesmerizing, were starting to get my goat, and so we all covered our ears as we plodded past lap after lap.

Another key moment reminded me how far from home I was. A large platoon of military – all with weapons, camo clothing and shiny high-laced boots – marched past. Chanting their military phrase of determination and solidarity, my mind briefly turned to all the discipline and hard training miles over the years. From slogging it out on my Thursday morning hill sessions on the inclines of the Bristol streets, to the often windy and rainy 5 a.m. starts with training partners. The dark, wet mornings, with low-hanging fog and eerie quiet of British towns were, however, something different to the recent miles of this journey.

Only one of the 12 runners in Managua intended to do the whole distance – and he happened to be the eldest. Everyone called him Don – as a sign of respect for his age and being the senior athlete amongst us. He came with extra kudos due to his previous professional running career. Aged 60 he chatted and smiled his way to the end, his feet never leaving the floor by more than a few millimetres. The art of efficiency in his running was quite something; his mouth was the only thing that seemed to move.

Four hours and 40 minutes after clicking 'start' on our watches the marathon was done, celebratory photos were taken and we all went our separate ways. By this point, I was pleased to be in the habit of writing names and making notes in a little black book (along with countless entries on the notes app on my phone). In the back of this book there's the name of almost every single person that has had anything to do with the expedition. The focal point of every day on the journey was starting to become much less about the running and far more the community, people and humanity. The list of names was my very simple attempt at highlighting the importance of togetherness and the 'one world' view I'd taken to.

Later, on the journey to the airport, I was shocked and honoured when Maria and Carlos presented me with an envelope. Inside a letter read, 'In your name we are opening a prostate cancer drop-in centre. You have inspired us to do more. With your help we will launch the drop-in centre next year.'

Not to take away from the generosity and donations so far, but this was the first time on the journey where the reason for the expedition was not only being heard but acted upon, and in a big way. With help and kindness from so many like Carlos and Maria, prostate cancer is ever closer to being extinguished. It was a good day. I went to the plane knackered but with a spring in my tired step. On the plane to Costa Rica I wore my official Running the World t-shirt with sponsors smothering the front and back. Although it was becoming yellow with sweat and grime I felt like this was now my travel top and I would wear it, regardless, with pride.

Sponsors, as I've mentioned, are hard to find, but once found, they are the lifeblood of any expedition. Contrary to the belief of many, wearing sponsors' logos on my clothing wasn't actually a contractual obligation. Not least because nearly all my dealings with sponsors weren't formalized in contracts – they were arranged in good faith and so I felt like it mattered even more to support them and give them the exposure they deserved. In the odd few interviews to this point I was pleased to stand in front of the camera with brands that literally made the trip happen. Admittedly, of the 48 sponsors I'd secured in the lead up, only five of them were offering up any cash. I'd often speak with fellow passengers about how the brands had supported the trip – the top was a great way to spread awareness for the journey when I wasn't in running gear. I was a walking advert.

On this flight in particular, from Managua to Costa Rica, I spoke with a man named Peter, who was half-American and, as Americans often are, very enthusiastic, intrigued and keen. We spoke for a while about raising money and the dangers of prostate cancer, and then some more after a mid-flight nap. I encouraged him to get himself checked for prostate cancer. He said he would, but, if I'm honest, I thought he was just being polite. We parted without exchanging any details. Weeks later I received an email from him – more of an essay – that stated he had hunted me down to thank me because he had followed up with the prostate cancer screening. He thanked me profusely for my encouragement. He then went on to tell me that sadly his check came back with a higher than expected PSA score, which had since been confirmed as prostate cancer. The overwhelmingly sad but lovely email concluded with the more positive news that he had caught the cancer early and he would live, although without his prostate. My chat about running around the world had led to a man getting checked. Immediately, I got on WhatsApp and messaged Kev about the news and told him he was saving lives without even realizing it.

In truth I had been feeling more and more fatigued with telling the same stories over and over again, and had become rather lax in shouting about the whys of the journey. Not because I didn't care any more – quite the opposite. I had simply said the same thing so often that I either didn't connect with my words any longer or perhaps I was just overtired and fed up of talking. This was the kick up the backside I needed to refocus and reconfirm with myself what this trip was all about.

The 'why' behind this journey can be broken down into three parts. First of all, rather obviously, who wouldn't want to travel the world for two years? And, as a runner, who wouldn't want to run? I was always quite up front with the fact that I was running a marathon in every country in the world plainly and simply because *I wanted to.* The whole idea, however, had come to be because I met Kev. He was dying, and, following only some brief conversation, he opened my eyes, shook up my entire outlook on life, the time we have, and the opportunities and indeed responsibilities we have to ourselves to follow our dreams. To chat with a man who knows he may only live for two more years and yet see a happy content face staring back at you – that is life-changing. Kev showed me that I had control of what I did in my life; by contrast things were being taken out of his hands. I needed to make the most of life while I could.

The second reason behind this mad mission was to do something big enough that would raise a large sum of money for the principal prostate cancer charity in the UK – Prostate Cancer UK. And, more than that, raise awareness of what prostate cancer is. To get people talking about it was coupled with the funding goal. Prostate cancer has a stigma – men are embarrassed talking about their prostate. Men in general are particularly crap at going to the doctor or showing much or any suffering. A cancer that sometimes has no symptoms, combined with an embarrassment or even fear of having a 'finger up the bum' test, has literally been killing men for years. Over 12,000 every year – and that's just in the UK. That's more than the number of women dying from breast cancer. If I could somehow shout about it enough, maybe I could stop other men like Kev dying. The trip was inspired by Kev, but really the journey and the challenge was for the men in the future who could potentially have their lives saved by us all knowing how to talk about prostate cancer more. An early test saves thousands of lives every year.

The third 'why' was, of course, the world record(s). I'd been running in various competitions for a long time. It was my life – but, as yet, I hadn't taken on a huge world record, and never attempted a world first. To become the first person to run a marathon in every country in the world ticks off many brilliant bucket-list items. Being the first person to do something is always pretty cool. I also had an opportunity to make new friends all over the world, to inspire others to other crazy challenges, to take photos, to learn, to grow. The world was literally at my feet – and I had the chance to turn my passion, my hobby and my deep want to stop men from dying from this cancer into my legacy. This journey had it all. Do good, do something for the first time, inspire people all over the world, and, ultimately, follow your dreams. In my mind, when you put it like that, who wouldn't do this?

I continued south, away from the rich north. Honduras and Nicaragua were very much Central not North America. Men with only one tooth, vultures circling, mud brick-making by the side of the road, farm workers with various utensils over their shoulders; the atmosphere of the north was gone and I was edging closer and closer to continent number two, South America. Although North America is often seen as just Canada, the US and Mexico, it actually totals 23 countries, including all of Central America. South America was my next benchmark.

Airline lounge, airport trolley, long queue, laptops out of bags at security, liquids in stupid separate plastic bags, more queuing, some more standing-up sleeping, then boom: airport time complete. I was getting rather good at, but also fed up of, airports.

Costa Rica came and went without me realizing. I had reached total fatigue. Like my body dwindling, my sun cream and anti-inflammatory gel supplies were reduced to nearly nothing too. My trainers were worn and crusty with dried sweat; ditto my socks and hat. My bag was worn and grubby, my hair even longer, and my body weight dropping. Due to my mind and body being so pathetic I found myself sitting on the central reservation of a busy four-lane motorway on the outskirts of San José. I'd eaten a hefty breakfast that morning and headed out for my 22nd marathon. I then proceeded to get a little lost in the back streets before getting even more lost, ending up in the middle of this highway. In order to find a way out of this weird situation, I attempted to cross the road four or five times before I gave up and started to walk between the two barriers separating the southbound and the northbound traffic. I was stuck in the middle and my mind was too tired to judge distance safely. I'm glad I was aware of this drunk-like feeling so I didn't step out at the wrong time, but my eyes were heavy and I was yawning every few seconds. Whichever way I walked, I was stuck. Traffic was fast and heavy. I couldn't go back, I couldn't go forwards. I sat on the barrier for a few moments and closed my eyes. It was only when a few horns woke me up that I had a word with myself. I was falling asleep five miles into a marathon in a country I'd never been to before. I remember thinking how peculiar my life was at that moment. On my own and so tired that I couldn't cross a road. I did eventually cross but, as my Strava data shows, I was stuck for only five minutes, but five minutes seems like a lifetime when you're in the middle of a central reservation mid-marathon. I did eventually finish the marathon with the help of four energy drinks, a McFlurry and some chips.

With a bonus day off before flying out I had a decision to make: sleep all day and catch up so my body doesn't crumble underneath me and produce an injury? Or throw caution to the wind and get up nice and early to explore the Costa Rican mountains, and maybe photograph some exotic animals? From the shots of snakes, leopards, frogs, waterfalls and, of course, the iconic toucan birds, I think we know which option I took.

Arriving in Panama I was determined to gain back those extra hours of sleep. I scribbled down a few sleep calculations on an airline napkin before landing. I needed three extra hours a day for the next three days to give myself enough to rejuvenate. Of course the calculations were totally made up and I had no idea if it was possible or would help . . . but it focused my mind a little. Three days later? I'd had even less sleep than before and I was now ill, but in love with Panama.

Still in shorts and flip-flops (and with new white-rimmed glasses and a cap) I rocked off the plane in Panama City feeling well in my groove, very much in the 'goldilocks' zone of running: the moment in a marathon a few miles in when you're well on the pace and can visualize yourself cruising to the finish line significantly under personal best pace. This is before the wheels come off.

An eclectic gang of supporters made up the Cutarra Runners. Some were in their fifties, some in their late teens, all of them were buzzing to meet me thanks to the spread of media attention over the past month or so – I was being interviewed by at least one major national news station in every country I visited; word was getting out. I met the Cutarra Runners at 4 a.m. in a car park not far from the famous Panama Canal. Everyone was a little sleepy. As we gathered for pre-run group photos I answered the usual questions and chatted to a few of the group. Some of them had taken the day off work, and even flown in especially to be there. I did make the joke that they could have waited to run with me in their own country – but apparently they were attending a wedding on the scheduled day and so flew to Panama instead.

In the early few miles I was told by various members of the group where we'd be running and what we'd be doing. They were aware that I had no inclination to run particularly fast and so took me on a tour all over Panama City at a slow and steady pace. The group were all the same ability and ran strong without a hint of tiredness until 20 or so miles in. There were some hills towards the middle and end. It may have helped that we stopped for a few minutes for ice cream, and then again at the Instituto Oncologico Nacional. This time, no ice cream – but dying people. The mood changed. This was a hospital that was keen to meet me. The oncology ward wanted to say hello as I ran past, by way of support and acknowledgement of the journey. A sort of tipping of the hat.

We kept our watches going, of course, but spent just a few minutes meeting various cancer patients. The two large swing doors squeaked as they were pushed back to reveal a large room with damp yellow stains on the square ceiling tiles. The place was clean, but rundown and classically Central American in decor and condition. Twenty-eight patients filled a crowded whitewashed room. Each of them sat in faded leather green armchairs full of scuffs, scratches and holes. Alongside each chair there was a drip connected to a patient; all of them sat slumped with dour faces in old blue hospital gowns. Slippers and a few cups of tea or the odd patient reading a book were the only real signs of normality. These people were all dying of cancer. While their life was being prolonged thanks to science and support from the hospice, it was gut-wrenchingly sad and hard hitting. I had a lump in my throat immediately. The youngest person was 11, the eldest 71. My eyes welled up, and my thoughts spiralled to thinking about the countless lives that had been lost – and of course to Kev or members of my own family being sat in those chairs. It was a sight I'll never forget.

I met the owner of the clinic briefly. She had come in especially to see me. This was her first day back at work after her father had died following a long battle with cancer. With one eye on the run, and the fact I was now shivering due to the air-con making the room about 30 degrees colder than it was in the blazing midday heat outside, I left with a few smudged tears on my face and reflected in a daze on what I'd just witnessed. I'd only spent a little time with them, but it was enough to see hope, fear, loss, sadness, anger, defeat and gratitude. I spoke to two women who had become friends there, and who were being treated together. In just a short conversation we covered the whole spectrum of emotions. We spoke, had a cry, laughed, exchanged glances of encouragement and then I left. I was touched by their bravery more than anything. Jokes were made, laughter heard, and the enormous sense of 'I will win this battle' shone through and hit me hard. It was sad to think I'd likely never see any of them again after leaving that room.

I cried for a few miles, just to myself, and towards the back of the group so few people would see me, but I cried for them, and for everyone in that position. Although sad and tragic, my morale was lifted and I was given yet another lease of life and motivation to make this trip a success, and in turn shout more loudly about cancer. The miles ticked over and before I knew it I was nearly done. I had a lesson about the Panama Canal, ran past the boat previously owned by Pablo Escobar, and witnessed a perfectly round and pristinely red sun. As a surprise, and I guess to balance the scales of sadness in my heart, I rounded the corner into my final few hundred metres and was greeted by 400 young kids from King's College International School. All waving flags, just like in El Salvador, they were buzzing and all screaming for autographs. It was still very funny to hear requests for autographs but I obliged in a sea of kids. I crossed the finish tape with the rest of the group following behind me.

Once I was dragged from the horde of kids surrounding me who were shoving notepads and pens in my face, I was offered tea. I politely declined because it was over 40 degrees and I was dripping with sweat. A hot tea was not what I had in mind, but I suppose was typically British. Instead I opted for the dregs of my water bottle and shared with the kids tales from the day, promoted the work of the hospice and put in my two pence worth of life advice.

Another marathon down. To the tune of traffic, beeping horns, and some tropical rain hitting the windows I tucked myself up in my nice white sheets of the top-floor hotel suite and fell asleep quite sad. It had been a brilliant day, but I was conscious of so many people suffering. I woke up overtired and emotional. Sad for the previous day, full of cold and snot, I snapped at the airport staff, which made me feel worse, but South America beckoned, and Colombia wasn't going to run itself. I had to sort my mood out before I let it ruin me and the trip.

As lovely as it was to run with so many people, I think I was ready for a few runs on my own. Running had always been a mental release and a way to escape. I believe that everyone suffers mental health issues in one form or another. Everyone deals with ups and downs differently. For me lacing up and getting out the house meant I could be free and mentally tidy myself up. Because of the sleep deficit, along with the sore throat and the now ever-worsening flu symptoms, I was letting my mental state become messy and irrational. I needed to fix my weakening state of mind and push aside the weight and scale of the future that lay on my shoulders. At this stage, 54 days in, and with 172 countries still in front of me, I think I was getting scared and doubtful. I'd been shovelling most negative thoughts of fear and doubt out of my mind and out of sight – but rather obviously they were still there – and had to be dealt with. I'd never really allowed myself to think of the scale of the journey from a personal perspective. It had always just been a plan on paper. But I was now nearly two months in. It was all starting to feel very real.

2

Yes, Even North Korea

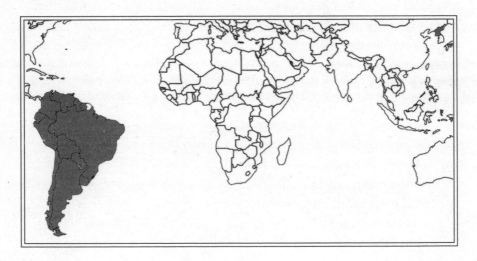

Colombia	Argentina	Peru
Venezuela	Uruguay	North Korea
Guyana	Paraguay	Ecuador
Suriname	Chile	
Brazil	Bolivia	

The month of March looked like this: Colombia, Venezuela, Guyana, Suriname, Brazil, Argentina, Uruguay, Paraguay, Chile, Bolivia, Peru, North Korea and Ecuador. It was a brilliant but relentless month. My route was a sort of clockwise circle working from Colombia in the north around to Brazil and then Uruguay on the east coast, down to Argentina, across to Chile and then back up to Colombia's neighbour Ecuador. Twelve countries in 28 days – and, yes, not a typo, but North Korea too.

North Korea, officially the People's Republic of Korea (although I can tell you it's certainly not the 'people's' anything), was and still is hard to access, for obvious reasons. In fact it's always North Korea that comes up when being interviewed. The general consensus is that North Korea must be hard to access, and, yes, it is – except for one key opportunity each year. Fortunately, the capital Pyongyang hosts an annual marathon. This race is one of the very few ways to enter the country without huge difficulty. Don't get me wrong, there's certainly scrutiny by the bucket load. Their race, however, takes place in late March/early April, meaning I'd have to whip around South America quick enough to tag this on. I left the UK in January with three months of flights booked, and another five months lined up ready to book. Although we had every flight planned out it was a game of chance with airlines. Airlines, as my dad puts it, are 'all bastards'. I tend to agree. Cancellations, overpriced baggage, and generally never answering the customer service desk phones. Anyway, that's a rant for another day.

So, we'd booked all the flights, including North Korea. North Korea was our benchmark. I must finish South America ahead of 5 April 2018. This would mean 27 days to run a marathon in every country in South America then fly halfway across the world to tick off this potentially problematic country before starting my next continent – Africa.

Some of the smart ones amongst you may question why we didn't just schedule Korea for the following year. But the political landscape was uneasy at the time, with the Trump administration stirring the pot and with missile-test rumours being bounced around, so we took the decision to get it done and ticked off the list before anything changed. North Korea was in 47 days' time – let's worry about that then.

Colombia, Venezuela

Bogotá, Colombia. South America kicked off in style with a classic airport delay and then eventual cancellation. In the marble-floored check-in hall of the Tucumán International airport in Panama, the departures board read: 'AV 8383 flight to Bogotá, gate D6, expected departure 10:35.' I was almost exactly two hours early. Perfect! At this point the flight was on time, and even when I reached the gate the flight was still showing the original boarding time. Boarding was in less than 15 minutes. Those 15 minutes came and went, as did the next 30 minutes. A crowd started to form around the gate counter. Me and my trusty bag were slumped against the glass wall separating the departures lounge from the runway and airfield. I even propped my phone against the glass and started a time-lapse film. Our plane was there but nothing was happening. I later ascertained that it wasn't our plane, after all. Many planes came and went. The jetway arm on its little wheels docked and undocked. The hold door opened and luggage emptied and refilled, and the passengers streamed on and off like lemmings. The whole beautiful sequence unfolded over and over again with the warm sun on the glass gently fading to darkness. In my delirious state I was rather enjoying being still and thoughtless. To cut a long story very short, it was an additional five long hours until our bags were returned to us having passed back through from airside to the original check-in counter. The flight was cancelled; the race to find another flight was on. I had to stay on schedule to avoid compromising the rest of the onward flights. I remember the day well because it was also my dad's birthday. But in my delirious haze I had totally forgotten. I called him with a snappy, overtired demand for flight options. I was panicking. In hindsight there was nothing to worry about (and had I known there were far worse scenarios to come, I wouldn't have stressed at all). I hung up and frantically darted around to the various airline desks for support. This wasn't an ideal start to a hectic month with a hard deadline looming before North Korea. My bag weighing me down and my tired feet ready for a sit down, my phone rang again. Dad had worked his magic. I would arrive at night and have very little time to sleep before running, but at least I'd get there. It was only when I got through security again and the madness had subsided that I remembered it was Dad's birthday.

South America is home to many household names. The Amazon River, the beautiful Aconcagua mountain, alpacas, condors, Lake Titicaca, Rio, São Paulo, the Atacama desert, and the world's highest capital, La Paz in Bolivia, to name but a few. These were amongst my imaginings as I stared out of the plane wondering what adventures were in store as I approached the runway into Colombia.

Colombia didn't go exactly as planned. My legs were starting to give me some jip. Nothing serious but enough to make me worry. Five miles in, running around Simón Bolívar Park in the centre of Bogotá, my knee was more sore than usual. The thing with running so much is you make do with various aches and pains and just push on until you've forgotten about them. This time my brain wasn't able to forget. By halfway my right knee wasn't happy and it was becoming a concern; not just for the marathon I was trying to finish, but the bigger picture – the 172 ahead. It didn't help that Bogotá is located at 9,000 feet above sea level. It's so high that I was noticeably out of breath. I felt very unfit and my mind started to tangle in worry. I ran uncomfortably but finished with a limp. Not good. My diary read, 'My knee isn't OK, have iced it this evening for an hour, and doubled up on anti-inflammatory tabs – I'm worried about the run tomorrow.' I was worried for more than one reason.

In this region Simón Bolívar was a name that popped up many times. After the short flight from Colombia, and with my dodgy knee still feeling delicate, I landed in Venezuela. The airport had the same name as the park I had run around the day before. But I was now in Caracas – and while it's 8,000 feet lower in altitude it's rather scarily known as the kidnap capital of the world. The Foreign Office advice for Caracas was to avoid all travel. And the words of advice I'd had from security consultants mentioned that I was far more likely to be kidnapped than not in some areas of Caracas. On my own, and with the knowledge that I must spend four hot hours running around a city known for kidnapping white tourists, I was anxious.

Remember February 28? The day of the cancelled flight to Colombia – my dad's birthday – just three days prior? Well, in my many hours at the airport I decided to conduct a little experiment to test my security protocols. Back over 12 months prior to starting the expedition I began what turned out to be four months of discussions with a security firm, chewing over the potential dangers of worldwide travel. The idea was to put various procedures in place to ensure my family were updated and reassured as I hopped from one place to the next. Mostly this boiled down to keeping tabs on my location, ena-bling easy lines of communication and ensuring my team and the security company had heard from me at regular pre-determined intervals. It was also important that we weren't jeopardizing the expedition by simply not having enough awareness of the actual pol-itical landscape. Upwards of ten meetings took place in London in the months leading up to the challenge and, among other things, we even-tually categorized each country and city by its relative safety concerns, a gauge that took in accessibility along with any political or religious elements I needed to be aware of. Things like learning I'd be ques-tioned more in Israel, for example, and what I should expect; or where to be more patient, or perhaps where I should not have my legs on display. Also, where not to spit on the floor. And, just to clarify, I don't go around spitting on the floor all the time – but for a runner spitting is slightly more of an accepted thing. We marked each coun-try with a traffic-light system. Green – no problems at all; amber was difficult but safe; red – be on high alert. There were 95 green, 86 amber and 15 red countries. Venezuela was the first of the red.

Some countries we assumed would be difficult were actually green when I had imagined them to be red, and vice versa. North Korea was a classic example. Yes, not the most normal of places, but to be a tourist, once you're granted access, you're looked after relatively well.

The idea was to make all amber and red countries as green as we could through various means. Each of the three categories had a communication plan and a protocol to follow. For green countries I didn't need to check-in or make contact at all; for amber countries I should make communication at least once every 24 hours by phone or text. And for red countries I must ensure my satellite phone was on me at all times, my GPS tracker turned on and recording at all times, and I must check-in every waking hour. The plan was also to communicate when I was about to sleep and then when I woke up. The extra agreement was to have a video call prior to entering any of the red countries. This was designed to run through any last-minute security updates, protests or visa problems.

Three days prior to landing in Caracas I decided to put this protocol to the test. I simply wanted the assurance someone was watching over me and actually checking my updates, which should have been daily given I was in Colombia, on our amber list. I didn't check in at all for each of the three days, closed the communication app entirely and waited to see if the protocol we put in place worked. If they hadn't heard from me, they should call me, or email me or call the hotel, try somehow to get hold of me. Three days later I'd had no responses and was now in Caracas having not had any phone or video call as agreed. I was hours from my run the following morning feeling like all the months of effort we'd put in to ensure my safety were out the window and wasted. To make matters worse my sat phone wasn't working at all. I'd carried this useless piece of kit around for months.

It was no surprise that Venezuela made it to the red column. As with many nations in the red list it's more often than not down to politics, money and corruption. For many years Venezuela has been crowned the most dangerous country in the world with its capital, Caracas, also taking the title for highest number of murders relating to petty crime. More or less every nation has blacklisted Venezuela as a 'no go' country, and Caracas is particularly high risk because of the vast number of kidnappings in recent years. This was aside from the bloody violence, murder and rape. The kidnap rate had alarmingly multiplied over the previous decade (potentially in correlation to the financial crisis). 2007 saw as many as 380 people kidnapped for ransom; by 2018 that had risen substantially to over 3,400. That's over three a day. By 10 p.m., from the safety of my hotel near the coast, I called the security company to rant about my fury at being left out on a limb. I was hoping they'd answer the phone, confirm my location and reassure me. The phone rang and rang and rang – no answer. I tried all the numbers I had. I even rang the emergency line. Nothing. I was fuming as I paced around the room in my pants getting more worked up with every passing minute.

By the time I got to sleep there were only a few hours before I was due to be awake again and ready to run. I procrastinated a little in the morning. I was overtired but scared more than anything. The run had to be done. I just went for it. I stepped out tentatively after making phone calls to the team. I told them of the failure of the security company, my proposed route, and the time I was expected back. That's all I could do.

Although I got back safely the run wasn't without its issues. I was on high alert for every mile. That feeling of being followed or having someone walking in my shadow wouldn't leave my mind. It was exhausting. The only few scary moments came when the occasional car drove past with hooded men wielding guns and shouting in slurred Spanish. I think they were Caracas' equivalent of yobs and nothing more – but scary nonetheless.

There was however just one more thorn in my side – water. Thanks to the dwindling financial situation in the country cash was hard to get hold off. My attempts to find cash in the airport, at the hotel and numerous ATMs around the city were all in vain. Cash simply wasn't available. I paid for my taxi and hotel with the last remaining British sterling and was left with only three dollars to pay for water. With over ten miles remaining and far from the hotel I resorted to begging for water. And to my surprise on the three occasions I asked for a free bottle of water – in my horrendous broken Spanish – all three warm-hearted shopkeepers said yes and gave me a bottle happily. Oh, how my pre-conceived ideas changed.

My running route didn't cover the entire city – I wanted to keep away from downtown Caracas as much as possible, and so stuck mainly to the coastline of outer-suburbs. I was stunned at how gorgeous it was. If I could have stopped worrying about potential kidnaps and death it would have been rather enjoyable. The city's coast was the highlight in terms of views. The waves were big, the white water crashed on the rocky beaches and the sun glazed the various bays of water with warm light. Despite the buildings being littered with bullet holes, over-occupied with a dozen family members in each, plus the extreme smell of rubbish – with a bit of a cleanup I could see Caracas turning into a bustling tourist spot. Crime, of course, was the only real sticking point, but fortunately I managed to get the miles in without incident.

Guyana

From Venezuela I plodded through South American beauty until I reached Bolivia. Guyana was marathon 26, Suriname number 27, Brazil 28, Argentina 29, Uruguay 30, Paraguay 31 and Chile the 32nd. All of which were ticked off with support from new friendships, bucket loads of selflessness and many hot and sticky long miles in the sun. The days flew by as I clocked up the mileage day after day. I was doing all I could to keep further flu symptoms at bay, and it seemed to be working. Although so much went on in those 20 days there were two significant memories of note. In Guyana I learnt of the unbeliev-able gambling habits of the locals and their finches, and in Rio I was joined by my good friend Mr Andy Swain, who ran with me not only in Brazil but in Argentina and beyond.

The Guyana gambling phenomenon encapsulates the wonders of the world perfectly. Magic and madness at every corner. While there are stereotypes for more or less every nation, I certainly hadn't come across this one. I was mid-run, about mile 8, running with a few locals through Georgetown, a small quiet capital with large pigs that roamed the verges. A couple, Silas and her husband Vada, their friend Cyrleen and the driver Jason were my running crew that morning. They'd all been in touch with my team after seeing a news article online. We were running on the roadside of the 13-mile out and back route – no hassle, just very humid. Every few miles there were stalls selling bird-cages, bird feed and the birds themselves. I thought nothing of it until we passed the fifth roadside stall. This stall was more like an outdoor market with hundreds of birdcages in varying colours, from brand new sparkling silver ones to old rusty orange and green ones. Some were big and some small – but always rounded at the top with a circular base and metal bars spaced less than five millimetres apart. The birds were noisy and singing in an orgy of clashing tones. I also noticed that most of the houses either side of the road, of which there weren't many, all had birdcages out front; very similar to the style of an American mailbox at the end of the drive – except full of finches instead of post. I looked at Cyrleen with an expression of confusion and bewilderment. He smiled and said, 'I wondered when you were going to notice the birdcages.' He told me that finches were a very important part of the Guyanese culture. Many people own these birds to earn money, he explained. Thousands of people buy a cage, find or trade a bird, and then train it to sing loudly and quickly. Why, you ask? Well, the concept involves a faceoff with one or multiple con-tenders. If I had a bird I could challenge you, or you and others, to a match: either one against one, or one against many. Everyone gathers in a circle with the cages on the floor or on tables. The birds are sitting on their individual perches in their respective cages. The owners wait for silence and then the battle begins. The bird owners simply watch as they wait for noise.

The winner is the bird that sings first. Any noise wins. Bizarre, and something of an anti-climax when onlookers have waited for so long to hear just the faintest of noises. Upon a little internet research later that evening there were also various accounts of competitions where bird owners would count the number of songs in an hour, or measure the length of song for each bird. Despite that all sounding totally nuts, that's not actually the crazy part. Even more mad is the amount of money that exchanges hands in this game of what looks like luck. For about $4 you can eat a decent evening meal in a restaurant in George-town. In these competitions, though, it's not uncommon for over $2,000 to change hands. This is the equivalent to five months' wages for most families. A few wins can change a life; a few losses can ruin a family.

As we ran and eventually crossed our finish line back in the car park of the small town centre, I kept quizzing Cyrleen and the others about the birds. They'd all had birds at one point, but spoke of the stress it can cause. 'Stress', in a place that's safe, quiet and relatively well off compared to most cities in the region. Gambling, once again, not a friend to man.

Suriname

Not an easy place to get to or to get out of. I had to fly back to Trinidad, then endure a ten-hour wait before a connecting flight to Paramaribo, the capital. I had one day (actually only a total of 28 hours) so it was up early the next morning and onto the wide sidewalks next to the main highway. The people were so friendly, with many motorists and bikers stopping to find out what this mad guy was doing running in the heat of the day. Their confused faces were only made worse when I explained why. I was tired and slow despite the refreshing coconut milk straight from the coconuts on the side of the street. I had no momentum whatsoever for sightseeing once the run was done. Food, then straight to bed before an exhausting series of flights – four in all – taking me, eventually, 20 hours later, to Rio.

Brazil, Argentina

By now I was getting used to the three-day cycles of meeting new people and running in strange and wonderful lands – and my mood improved even more so when I heard the last-minute news that Andy would be coming to see me in Rio. Andy was a good friend from home and we'd both worked together in the finance world for many years. Andy is a top bloke but also happens to be a superb runner. He was the perfect chum to spend a few days with. It was only when he arrived and I started reeling off stories that I realized how much there was to say. I was talking fast like a hyperactive child on Christmas morning. It was so nice to see a familiar face. We chatted over dinner for hours in

a nearby outdoor restaurant. He asked me if it was what I had expected
so far. I was so focused on getting each marathon done I hadn't really
considered anything other than that. Andy laughed at how much at
home I was in hotels, and how my laidback attitude was now even
more horizontal. I greeted him barefoot in the lobby of the Marriott
hotel overlooking the Copacabana. He smiled and commented on my
attire being similar to that of the old office days. Back then I was forever being asked to put my shoes back on or wear something smarter.
While I enjoyed dressing smartly every now and then, I hated wearing
a suit and tie at work. I was often seen hovering by the water machine
early in the morning post-run with bare feet, a shirt half open, running
shorts still yet to be changed and a tie chucked over my shoulder in a
mess of sweat. Andy could see I was in my element.

Seeing Andy was a total pleasure. We had three days in Rio and
then three days in Buenos Aries. Great sunsets, great food, loads of
new faces, and of course having someone I knew with me meant I
realized how unkempt I had become. Although Andy is in his forties
(though has always looked annoyingly young) and I was only 28 at the
time, I looked old and haggard in comparison: the travel-bracelet
souvenirs had accumulated on my wrist, my hair was longer and dirt-
ier and my face had gone unwashed for quite some days. Andy was the
surprise messenger that although I was on a mission that would eventually end, my life, looks and personality were changing for ever.
Seeing every country and running 26 miles in each was eye-opening,
wonderful at times, sad at others. But what I was just starting to grasp
was that by seeing more, I was beginning to understand more. A lesson in race, religion, cultures, class, road safety, weather patterns – the
list is close to endless. Chatting with Andy was my first realization
that things would be different once I finished. I would be different.

No day in Brazil or Argentina passed with a dull moment. My bag
was lost in Rio's Galeão–A. C. Jobim International airport. I ran
through motorway tunnels in Argentina. I paddle-boarded in the
Atlantic Ocean. I even bought a small green stone necklace from an
eight-year-old girl by the beach in Rio. Her name was Jamai – her
parents were hippies dressed in floating brightly coloured drapes
who sat crossed-legged smoking on the patterned mosaic tiles of the

famous Copacabana beach. The atmosphere was one of bustle and sandy shoeless locals with surfboards tucked under their arms. The young girl gave me her best sales pitch and I bought the necklace not really expecting to wear it. She put it around my neck as I kneeled on the hot stone floor. I grew to love it. It subsequently stayed hanging around my neck for every single remaining country.

Andy and I gorged ourselves on huge steaks in roadside eateries in Argentina, wandered markets, surfed, joined the gaggle of tourists, like we had on Sugarloaf Mountain and by the Christ the Redeemer statue in Rio. We'd also been fortunate enough to meet and run with a couple of groups of runners and supporters. I had relaxed: having another person to check flight times and help with routes eased the pressure. It may seem trivial but even that little let-up in responsibility was the mental rest I needed. More importantly for Andy he got to experience what life on the road was really like. The quick succession of marathons was certainly a shock and his legs were ready for a rest. After Argentina Andy flew home and back to work. I missed him afterwards – I was back to making decisions on my own.

Uruguay

Leaving Argentina, Andy and I also waved goodbye to our daily breakfast view. The famous Recoleta cemetery had been the view from the hotel window every morning. We were incredibly lucky to have a brilliant (and free) hotel overlooking the entire plot. Imagine gothic horror at sunrise: large grey stone sculptures casting dark and beauti- ful shadows across the maze of graves. I could almost feel the texture of the stone from the balcony. This was the resting place for Eva Peron, Nobel Prize winners, heavyweight literary figures and the grand- daughter of Napoleon; needless to say, I felt small and in awe. We watched the sunrise over the mesmerizing space as the shade withdrew and unwrapped the graves to reveal their full beauty. It was calm, still and silent. What a way to spend our last breakfast in the city.

If I could sum up my Uruguay experience in one word it would be 'wind'. It was to be my first properly windy run of the journey, and when I say windy I mean very bloody, powerfully, unrelentingly windy. Montevideo being a coastal capital, it was unavoidable from start to finish. Perhaps I could have coped with the wind if it wasn't for the sandblasting on the backs of my legs, or without the need to chase my hat along the ground repeatedly for a few hundred metres, much to the amusement of passers-by.

The advantage of wind on an out-and-back route, however, is that it'll be in your favour in one direction. On the way out for my first 13 miles I was trotting along with the wind lengthening every other stride as it pushed me along effortlessly. I was basically floating, with the occasional sidewind taking my legs from underneath me like the instant wave of a magic wand had somehow shunted me sideways. On the way back I was bent over leaning heavily into the gale. She wasn't giving up. I gave myself a bit of a pep talk and battled on with sand pebbles dashing my grimacing face. Every so often I found cover for a brief break – as much from the sound of the wind in my ears as from its strength. For the last mile the sky cleared and the wind dropped. The rest of the afternoon turned into a lovely and virtually breezeless day. Typical.

By the end I was covered head to toe in sand and sea salt, my ears were sore and every crease of my skin held as much sand as it could handle. My clothes weren't entirely dry either owing to the occasional big wave that would breach the wall along the corniche. It caught me out every time as I squinted away the sea water ready for a fresh pelting of wind. It was a battle to the end, but I enjoyed it. I couldn't defeat Mother Nature, I just had to endure.

Paraguay

The one with the sombrero. Being a landlocked country, Paraguay's route was far from coastal, a struggle, or windy – and I had friends along: four brilliant runners supporting every step of the way. The set-up for the day was simple: a support car to provide water, snacks and coconut water that would stop ahead every 3 kilometres, leapfrogging us to make sure we had everything we needed. We started at

6 a.m. while the sun wasn't quite awake yet. You could say the same for me.

Despite not being able to see the big ball of raging hot gas, I could certainly feel it – 27 degrees pre-dawn; at mile two we were literally dripping. The humidity was so intense that I could ring my top out and collect a decent half pint. It was a sticky first few miles. When the locals tell you it's 'especially hot at the moment' I start to worry. They were right. At mile 25 it had reached 45 degrees. Like rats hunting for cover, we darted from one small patch of shade to another, avoiding the sun at all costs.

Having been given strict instructions from the team my four amigos were keen to do a good job of supporting. The run was split into three stages. The first was the responsibility of a chap call Juan, with help from a fab lady called Rico. This was all at dawn, so he and I saw in a spectacular sunrise over the city of Asunción as we ran through the sleeping streets.

The middle section was with Rico and Eugenia. Eugenia was a speedy runner and a seriously competitive athlete. She ran on her toes the whole time and set a good pace. I was struggling to keep up. I may add that she had only just given birth to her second child four months prior and so was showing me who's boss. Rico was another one of the most instantly lovable people. So warm-hearted it just oozed from her.

The last eight miles or so were spent with Hugo and Eugenia, running around a lovely flat park. Considering the heat we were actually all pacing along nicely. We had the comfort of ice blocks, oranges, Powerade and water, all cooled in a chill box every few kilometres, supplied by Juan and his wife, who had retired to provide support from the car. This was support of the highest order; a total cluster of lovely people – then Hugo decided to raise the bar. Post-run he drove me to his house via a general store to collect some ice. He had a plan. Together we bought 100 kilograms of ice so we could soak our legs. Once at his house, Hugo converted his empty hot tub into an outdoor ice bath. Bloody brilliant. We took it in turns from the car to tip huge bags into the tub. I lasted no more than 15 minutes. The ice lasted about 60 seconds. It must have been over 50 degrees in the sun. This, however, wasn't the highlight of the day. Hugo had been wearing a massive straw sombrero for our run together and now we'd iced off together he told me of its significance. He had worn the now battered and well loved hat for every single training run and every single race for as long as he could remember. He spoke about it with such love and pride. As I was hugging him and saying goodbye he said, 'I have one last surprise – I want you to have the hat. Take it on your travels.' It made me well up a little, and him too, I think. I thanked him and as I left we mutually agreed to meet again and run with the hat once more. The level of this man's selflessness was getting a bit much. I didn't deserve it. I'm just a runner. What an honour.

Chile

The story of Chile is one of mountains, smog, the special mountain city in the basin of the Andes, Santiago and, you guessed it, even more overly kind people. This time I owe my thanks to a chap called Bernar.

I wasn't expecting it to be chilly in Chile, but there you have it. From 50°C+ I was now experiencing my first long-sleeve day since Toronto. Despite the cold, it turned into one of the most stunningly peaceful runs, with views to match.

I hopped in an Uber at about 5 a.m. to go to the home of Bernar, who was keen to run with me. This was all thanks to Juan from Asunción. If it wasn't enough that Juan had orchestrated the whole relay support system, he had also roped in his mate Bernar, who jumped at the chance to help. The rest is history.

Bernar is a fellow ultra runner and so we had a lot to chat about. We drove north from his home towards the Andes in the early morning haze which clung to Santiago's skyscrapers. It was dark, but the large shapes on the horizon were peeping through and it got me a little excited as we drove higher to our start point a little way out of the city. The crisp ridges of the mountains were looming over us as we parked up, about 45 minutes out of the city. Bernar had sorted the route so we were over the other side of the valley in time for sunrise and with enough distance to run back to total 26.2 miles. Fab.

The sunrise was like a pastel painting of deep reds, oranges and yellows. It was so good I had to keep stopping every few minutes. As we climbed higher the view got better and better, outdoing each last photo. It wasn't long before we started to descend from the north and head south, with the sleeping volcano the other side of the city acting as our marker. Run towards it and stop when we hit my hotel – that, Bernar said, would be a marathon. He was spot on. What a day. We could have finished a couple of hours sooner if it hadn't been for me insisting we stop for countless photo opportunities. Santiago was another city I would need to revisit.

For a long while I was thinking about something Bernar had told me. Just 40 days prior to our meeting, and while I was in the Caribbean running another marathon, Bernar had had a terrible accident. He'd hit a pothole while cycling in the mountains we'd just run down. He lay unconscious for over half an hour and was only saved by a random post-sunset passer-by. He had broken ribs, a broken collar bone plus a bunch of bad head injuries I can't remember or pronounce. He only told me once we'd run an entire marathon that our run together was the first form of any exercise since his accident. My admiration for the man shot up even higher than it already was.

Bolivia

High in the Bolivian mountains – which put the Chilean Andes in the shade – the terraces of tin shacks act as mirrors for sunlight as the beams bounce from roof to roof and glare brightly until nightfall. The beams of light are gradually replaced with the soft orange glows of small street fires, surrounded by the shadows of large families. The smoke lingers in the valley as the locals tuck into various chargrilled foods. The sound of horns dying down in the evenings ushers in a brief period of sleep for the city, before everything ignites again to a chorus of dogs barking and birds slowly joining in. No matter where I was in South America I always felt I was more outdoors than in.

La Paz sits at just shy of 12,000 feet. From landing, to beginning my 33rd marathon of the expedition, I had just five hours to sleep, eat and attempt to acclimatize to the altitude. And then another 24 hours to run and leave the country. In the tiny downtown district of the city I was given a free night in a small attic room of Hotel Casa Fusión. After a bowl of strangely thick soup I took myself to bed immediately and slept like a baby, but the acclimatization was impossible and I woke up what felt like minutes later.

I'd fallen asleep in darkness, cockily confident the altitude wasn't going to bother me. I'd skied all my life, climbed, ran and hiked in mountains much higher. I was actually quite excited to see the city. Upon waking, my banging headache had given me a clue that my day would be tougher than anticipated. I hadn't even moved and my body wasn't happy with the lack of oxygen in my blood. Under the sloping Velux windows in my room, I stood for a while in my pants and messy hair and downed a litre of water before getting changed. I was still half asleep and felt so rough. The view from the window looked out onto the city below. Hills, hills and nothing but bloody great steep inclines as far as the eye could see.

Having been driven from the airport I'd got an idea of the general elevation but the fact it was night time had disguised the extent of the potential problem. By day the reality was obvious. For every one of my 26 miles there was not a single flat enjoyable moment. I climbed steps over and over again at every corner, was chased by huge stray dogs, and, gasping for air, ran past countless outdoor cooking hobs belching wood smoke. My plan for the route was up, up, up and then a long slow descent completing a big loop around the surrounding rim of the city. Although the miles were tough and my body incredibly tired, the route accidently and rather fortuitously took me through every district in the city, so I experienced most of what La Paz had to offer. The city was busy, full – full of colour, full of smells; the lights bouncing further. The small side streets weren't just quirky for quirky sake, like trendy cities elsewhere in the world – this place was genuine and held new gems of meat markets, hat sellers, kids making skate-boards, and lines of women squatting over their stalls preparing food at every turn. Every corner of every street was bloody brilliant and teeming with life: the wrinkled faces of the women in bowler hats and conical skirts, the street vendors, the profusion of coloured fabrics lining the markets – what a delight. Although out of puff and feeling very unfit, my few moments of rest were spent to the backdrop of a wonderful view. It made stopping and sitting all that more appealing.

Run complete, and with a sense of great accomplishment from a very tough day, I arranged to meet with some new friends, a great couple of a similar age to me. We initially got chatting on the plane, having played musical chairs with the seating arrangements. They were spending six months travelling, and welcomed company besides each other. The dinner we shared that evening was one of the best on the continent. Thanks to the ridiculously cheap prices we ordered more than we should have, agreeing that it was a special occasion to honour the audacity of our different adventures around the world. Sitting on the floor of a quirky loft-space restaurant we had streetlamp views of the city as we tucked into platters of fish, linguine, falafel, dips, pitas and strange sausage things that tasted of bananas, but weren't.

The following day, leaving the 'city of headaches', as I called it, was bitter sweet. I was pretty keen to get low and release the throbbing in my head, but on the other hand there were so many great little streets full of new smells, colours and curious little places to explore – and everywhere more smiling people.

Peru

By 24 March I had reached Peru having circled my way around the continent and was now back in the north-west, just below the Equator. Peru offers a truly magical aura with unrivalled colours at every turn. There's something unique about the smell of wood smoke on roadside fires coupled with big top hats on old sagging tanned faces and heavy woollen ponchos. Similar to Bolivia, the open-toe sandals, street food and markets look like they've come from the imagination of an artist or film director. Machu Picchu, condors and shepherds herding alpacas – Peru is a photographer's paradise and a truly idyllic place to run and explore. For me, a runner who loves to take photos, I had the best of both worlds. I got the run done as soon as I arrived:

a quick meandering route around the capital Lima. Not very pretty, but coastal. Because Peru was a 'must visit' in all the guide books I pre-planned a handful of extra days to take some photos and do the tourist things. Peru is one of the continent's richest countries and feels free and easy: shopping centres that look like shopping centres, and transport links that actually transport people were giveaways to the prosperity of the land. This was my first country since the United States that resembled the 'western world' I was used to. I could even buy Marmite and protein bars from the supermarket.

North Korea

My journey from Peru should have been directly to Ecuador, completing the continent and then flying out on the 5th to Pyongyang for the 8 April marathon. But because of a few more cancellations and redirections, as well as my determination to enjoy South America and have an extra day here and there to take it all in, it meant I'd still be going to Ecuador – but after North Korea. North Korea was nearly 10,000 miles away across ten time zones via five connecting flights. In hindsight I shouldn't have had that extra day here or there. My mind was knackered more than anything.

As you can imagine, direct flights from Peru to North Korea simply don't exist. The flight path was beyond long winded. From Lima I flew north to Atlanta in the US, and then to Canada before flying to Beijing, with a technical stop in Doha. Beijing is home to Adrian and his wife Hannah, who had contacted me to show their interest in helping me on behalf of Koryo Tours. Without us even making initial contact, they had heard of my plans and had got in touch to offer their expertise. On top of this they volunteered a free place in the race, flights and even a specific package to allow other supporters to sign up to the event as part of my party. This gave subscribers a hefty discount and extra 'in country' perks too. Koryo Tours are a big deal and the only tour company taking foreigners into North Korea. They paid for the lot and simply asked for some exposure in return – no contracts, just good old fashioned good faith. The first phone call I had with Adrian (on the platform of Earl's Court tube station in London in July 2017) was the turning point for much of the planning phase – after that I received more interest from sponsors, more support and additional interview requests.

Once in Beijing I was met by a friendly driver from Koryo's team, whose name I forget sadly, who drove me to their office to meet everyone for the pre-race 'foreigners' briefing'. I was unfortunately three days late to that briefing and so my version was done over dinner with Adrian and his wife, who had kindly offered to put me up for the night. The Koryo office is small and somewhat squished in amongst other high rises. It's nothing to look at from the outside. On the inside, though, Beijing was no more: North Korean art, posters and literature littered the walls and shelves. I whipped the camera out and recorded some interviews with their staff. It was fascinating and I was buzzing to see a country so few people get to see. I left most of my luggage, including the drone, in Beijing as I'd have to return in a few days. I couldn't simply fly out of North Korea to Ecuador: I must fly with the group back to Beijing. Those were the rules. The rules, it turned out, were a focus for every day in Korea.

Early on the day of the collective journey to Korea I met with my group. These were the folks that had paid their £2,000 for their four days to see the hidden, restricted world of North Korea. We bundled on buses and started to make introductions. The group were complaining of long flights from London or Australia. I'd been on five since I left Peru after having spent nearly 100 days on the road. While I felt a little smug that I was about to run another marathon after already running 34, and they were all worried they hadn't trained enough for one, I realized the joke was well and truly on me. I was pooped. It was 5 in the morning but I was ready for bed and still half asleep while everyone else was excitedly chatting. My brain was shutting down as my attempts to be social diminished by the second. My voice was hoarse and involuntarily broken. Another of my rundown colds was well and truly on the way. I'd tried so hard to keep these at bay and, with the help of my concoction of 11 supplements a day, I was doing well considering I was practically living in planes, which are, of course, known for being unavoidable bubbles of germs. Even under

normal circumstances my ability to sleep in cars, on planes, on horse-
back and many more moving objects is one of my most mastered skills.
In my tired man-flu state I fell into a deep slumber on the bus to the
airport. Then once again on the Koryo airlines jet to Korea, and then
annoyingly again from the airport to the hotel once landed. I needed
the rest but was frustrated I missed the initial experience of the city.

Finally awake, the view from my 16th-storey room of the 'tourists'
hotel' in Pyongyang was remarkable. While it looked bleak, the city
had a definite beauty about it. Grand and neat, yet demeaning and
hollow, the streets held no sign of litter, no advertising, no brand
names, no communities, just oversized buildings, majestic in scale but
without life or enjoyment. Somehow, everywhere I looked the underlying politics of the country seemed to seep through. Looking down
on the city the fog of the early morning added a haze of gloom. Some
of the buildings were brightly coloured, painted in various pinks and
greens, with the Taedong River carving through the middle. But the
city is grey: it's as if the colours of the buildings are there to disguise
the bleak nature of the place. A city with the infrastructure and people
that could one day become a great home to many, might one day
be liberated and burst into life, but for now it stands in the mist, sad
and without heart or soul. With a different leader, in a different time,
perhaps playgrounds will come to life, bars and shops will surely
appear with smiling faces, and love, friendship and compassion will
be visible. For now, though, Pyongyang appears a city of buildings, of
concrete and neat roads with nobody smiling amongst them. Our
hotel was known as the tourists' hotel because it's rumoured to be the
only place where foreigners are allowed to stay. This was a very bla-
tant example of how the state controls everything, and is happy to
make it known. The state police are ever present at major events, the
city lacks any hustle and bustle, there's no internet access and the flow
of information is heavily censored, and the all-seeing eye of the government constantly monitors every move. There's a great deal to say
about the city, and I think most people that visit will come away with
a similar opinion – it's a fascinating place, but if I put myself in the
shoes of the citizens of North Korea, I feel sad and squashed.

The day of the marathon was unique, just like most experiences in those 36 hours. Arriving early by coach to the Rungrado May Day stadium we parked up to join the other Koryo tour group who had opted for the ten-day package. They were all a little more worn down, and had travelled into the city by train rather than by air. We gathered, were briefed on the strict four-hour cut-off time and began to gather our things. It was cold, the coldest I'd experienced since Toronto. I had been living in the unbearably hot and humid climates of South and Central America for three months. I felt I'd been taken from an oven and rammed into a freezer with nothing but my birthday suit. In Pyongyang, no matter how many layers I put on, I was still cold and blue-lipped.

I was also adjusting to being around people, people that were excited, far more awake, and who were looking to me as 'the runner' – I felt pathetic, cold, exhausted and fed up with the 'What's your favourite country?' or 'You must be quite tired?' questions. The saying goes, it takes more energy to be sad or moody than it does to be happy. For me it didn't feel like that at the time. I felt like an old Windows PC trying to attempt more than one task at once.

Once in the confines of the stadium, with the start line ahead and two pairs of leggings hugging my now scrawny and worn-out thighs, plus a dirty pair of socks over my mittens, we all huddled together in the tunnel under the grandstand waiting to enter the stadium. We could hear loud and intense clapping from above. The mood of the group, and even myself, lifted. We were getting excited and I think we were also a little warmer too having been shoulder to shoulder for a while. We laughed and collectively stuck our phones in the air, above the trail of troops heading into the stadium ahead, to take pictures and capture the moment.

I have a superb video of the bizarrely orchestrated clapping of the North Korean fans. We all discussed whether the grandstands were full because the crowd had all voluntarily turned up, or were otherwise summoned out of fear. We settled most definitely on the latter. It was bloody cold, and everyone looked miserable as sin. The controlled nature of the state came through in their clapping too. While it was great to have the applause for a good hour by over 50,000 people, in the lead up to the starting gun it was strange to witness just how the clapping was achieved. As with most stadiums the stairs leading to the upper and lower levels act as a corridor for each section of the grandstand. Standing in each of these areas situated on the lower tier on all four sides were chaps dressed entirely in white with a flag in one hand and waving a conductor's stick with the other. The 'fans' meanwhile sat with their painted-on smiles in uniform grey heavy jackets with what looked like fox tails wrapped around their hats. The clapping wasn't achieved the conventional way either. Rather than one hand hitting another hand, which I imagine would cause an uneven sound, all of the crowd were given silver 'clap boards', as we collectively named them. We stood in our shivering huddle for longer than we would have liked and stared open mouthed at the sheer oddness of what we were seeing. The conductor's white stick would fall to his side (always his, not her), and the clap boards would mute in an instant. Totally crazy, but so effective – it made a Sunday lower-league football game look like a riot. North Koreans would all be appalled at our lack of coordination, or indeed the lack of conductors.

The run circled the stadium, and out through the main highway into the city. After eight miles or so we were out the other side with nothing but industrial mining and construction flanking a new, as yet unfinished, motorway. Bleak and cold, we circled a tiny orange cone and made the return journey to the stadium. With only 500 or so participants the field was rather spread out, and so it was a solitary run for Eddie and I. I shared a hotel room with Eddie, who had joined my Koryo tour group, and we made up two of the 300 or so foreign participants. He was a smiley chap who always looked to the positive. His energy was what I needed to brighten a cold dreary run. We bonded as we both observed the various quirks of the country. Mostly, though, we were keen to get it done and get warm. Then it snowed in the final few miles, which made for a nice dusting of white across the city – from black and dreary to bright and fresh in just a few minutes. Bloody cold still, though.

The run wasn't all plain sailing for me. My exhausted mood, coupled with my old foot injury playing up, meant I was reduced to a hobble by the end. In hindsight the pain was nearly all psychosomatic. My mood was just getting the better of my running brain. Everyone else was experiencing a few gripes in their legs too. It wasn't the best run in the world, but it was Pyongyang, and I'd say 99 per cent of us were just ticking it off so we could say we'd done it, more than anything.

The rest of the stay in Pyongyang was spent seeing as much as possible. Early mornings and late evenings. My camera was in my hand every second of the day. Despite all the repression and the overarching cloud above the city and country, Pyongyang was totally mesmerizing. Neat, orderly queues in the spotlessly clean underground metro stations, vast high rises, school students learning English, multicoloured architecture, and not a single advert or billboard of any kind. What's so intriguing about Pyongyang is that it feels so empty. Be it buildings, shop frontages, buses – it's like a computer animator had designed a city but not yet coloured in the elements to make it feel real. All the small details like litter on the streets, scrapes or scratches on cars, potholes or graffiti were all missing. The buildings were also slightly out of proportion, as were the roads. Bigger than most cities, and wider, and with basic shapes and designs. The whole city felt like a simulation. Perhaps it was. Maybe we were only shown the clean, empty bits.

While the country offered much to gawp at, I won't miss the food. Their speciality of cold-glass noodles with various unidentifiable objects floating in the silver dish was frankly revolting. I even opted to heat mine up in an attempt to add something resembling taste. Apparently flavour isn't allowed either, and that attempt failed. Maybe I didn't try enough food, but the odd fatty barbecue thing on the final night was moved around on everyone else's plates too. When anyone asks me about North Korea all that comes to mind is grey, control, the cold, and wanting to have a Mars bar or to be able to pop into a McD's – even though I hate that that's the reality.

North Korea done, it was a quick hop back to Beijing for a night then back to Ecuador to finally finish South America, via another five flights.

Ecuador

Ecuador felt more like a layover than a marathon. The marathon wasn't easy. My body clock, combined with the altitude and change in temperature, contributed to a nice headache, dehydration and general deliriousness. I got changed ready for the run, only to then step out of the hotel lobby in Quito in slippers rather than my running shoes. It was early and I was still half-asleep. I soon woke up abruptly, though, with a hard thud to my head. An elderly drunk, possibly a homeless man, shoved me square in the chest as I ran past. I was running at a gentle pace up a hill, about four miles in. He simply stepped out, and as I went to manoeuvre around him he double-handedly pushed me with full force in the chest. It knocked the wind out of me and I fell backwards, slipped on the recently rain-coated concrete and smacked my head on the floor. If I didn't have a headache before, I certainly did now. I opened my mouth and held my hands in the air, as if to say, 'What was that for?' But I stopped myself. 'Let's not get into a fight in my last American country.' Besides, I have never been much for confrontation – at least not physically – I'd rather just crack on and get the run done. A great deal of me wanted to have a very British stern word – but I couldn't have even if I tried: he was already quite a way down the street.

It was such a strange thing to have happen that the rest of the run flew by. My adrenaline was up and my body wide awake. I thought about it so much that I can't remember a single thing about the run. Looking back through my Strava feed it looked like a lovely route, though. I even popped into the Equator visitors' centre and ran along the Equator for a while. I don't know what the elderly man didn't like about me.

I had such a happy celebratory phone call with my family that evening in Ecuador. I called to say I'd finished South America – we were elated to have the second continent done. Off the phone and back in my own head, the path that lay ahead was uneven, potentially emotional, dark at times, and hard to navigate in every sense. Time to head to the continent where running began – Africa.

3

Stepping into Africa

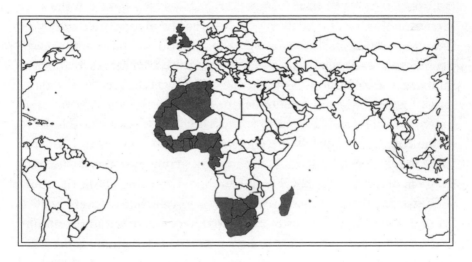

United Kingdom	Sierra Leone	São Tomé & Principe
Morocco	Liberia	Namibia
Mauritania	Ghana	Lesotho
Algeria	Burkina Faso	South Africa
Tunisia	Togo	Botswana
Senegal	Benin	Zimbabwe
Gambia	Nigeria	Eswatini
Guinea-Bissau	Cameroon	Mauritius
Ivory Coast	Equatorial Guinea	Madagascar
Guinea	Gabon	Seychelles

For the past three months while I picked my way through the Americas, the brilliant Universal Visas had been working hard to secure the next batch of visas in my second passport, ahead of the upcoming Africa stage. Holding two passports meant that while I was using passport 1 to travel from country to country, passport 2 was in the hands of Maz and Faisal at the visa office. The plan was to hand back passport 1 and collect passport 2 at the right time on a London stopover, so that the next batch of visas could be obtained, seamlessly allowing me to progress without delay. That was the theory. The passport juggling act was about to begin.

Everything was made more complicated in this respect thanks to some countries not allowing entry if I'd had stamps from countries they weren't friendly with, Israel being a prime example, or perhaps Yemen, or Syria – the list is long. On top of it all the passports would fill up unexpectedly thanks to an entry visa taking four pages instead of one. Plus many airlines require 'advanced passenger information' (APIs) at the time of booking. This required booking the right flight with the corresponding passport or forfeiting a fee – or, worse, risking refusal to board the plane.

On some occasions I ended up travelling with both passports in unison. My tired brain had to work hard to avoid presenting the wrong passport at the wrong time when passing through immigration. I can't tell you how many times I simply forgot which country I was standing in, let alone which passport to post through the immigration-booth window. On a number of occasions I had to talk my way out of it, not always successfully. (Without Universal Visas' 24/7 approach to getting me around the world, or my dad's ability to map out every eventuality, I simply wouldn't have made it. I wouldn't have come close. The phone calls at 2 a.m. asking them which passports I should use were always answered, and mostly politely.)

So at 10.20 a.m. on 18 April 2018 I landed in London with just a few days to clean my clothes, repack my bags, back up photos from multiple devices, swap hard drives with the production company, attend embassy appointments for visas, and then pick up my fresh passport. I'd also totally forgotten that I was supposed to be running my official United Kingdom marathon, aka the official London marathon. I was so caught up with everything else it had passed me by. I only remembered when I had a few text messages from friends asking if I was being interviewed on the famous London Bridge celebration BBC spot. Amazingly, I was, even though I didn't really have time for it. The icing on the cake of the entire few days back home was seeing Kev. He was on one of the Prostate Cancer UK support stands cheering as I ran through the streets of London along with tens of thousands of others. I knew he'd be there but was unsure if we'd have time to chat let alone hug at the side of the race. It was perfect. They even caught it on camera too. Then my brother, for the FIRST TIME IN MY LIFE, had come to watch me run. I was so shocked to see him that I had to backtrack against the flow of runners to say hello and chat for a while with him, my parents and other friends. We also managed a few extra donations for the charity on the Just Giving page, and for the first time in a long time, it wasn't hot. I think it was one of the hottest on record for everyone else, but for me, coming back from the Equator, I was the only person avoiding the sprinklers. It was a magical day. But, the following afternoon, lugging my bag around London, my feet ached and I cursed the lack of time I had to recuperate. I thought finishing a continent meant rest. I was wrong again. I was experiencing a bodged Formula 1 pit stop, not a weekend getaway with a warm bath and a lie-in. I stopped off at Universal Visas by Angel tube station to exchange my tatty and very full passport for a fresh-smelling new one. Time to get back on a plane again.

I was so rushed that day that I actually boarded the plane without any idea of what was next. I knew it was Morocco but after that – not a clue. I hadn't had time to look at the plan and it certainly hadn't registered that I was now heading to Africa for two solitary months. I wasn't even sure what I'd packed or even where Casablanca was. This was also the first of many occasions the airline resorted to calling for me by name – I was late.

Twenty-nine countries over 127 days, mostly in north-west Africa, taking me up to a total of nine months on the road. That was the plan anyway. After a 2 a.m. start, my little brother Chris and my dad dropped me at the airport, before promptly breaking down on the ramp out of Heathrow. Sorry, guys. While I was on the plane they were waiting for the AA in the rain. I flew from London to Madrid for a short layover, and when I say short, I mean running to my gate to make a 25-minute connection. Running I can do, but I didn't really want to have to run through airports as well, given what lay ahead. From Madrid, I flew onward to the less glitzy but more evocatively named city of Casablanca, Morocco. This was my first stop on the continent of Africa. Coming up was the glorious diversity of land-scapes, cultures and languages in a part of the world which is often sweepingly referred to as 'poor'. Steeped in history, and in terms of human evolution, the birthplace of running is where I'd spend the next four months. If successful, by summer I'd have 53 per cent of the continent complete. I would, however, have to hop back to the UK sooner than planned. Things were about to get bumpy. And not just the potholes – although they were terrible. The route, safety, food, hydration – more or less everything was far less straightforward.

The cultural peculiarities from place to place had so far been a learning curve, steep at times (to match the gradients), but on the whole it was manageable, if exhausting. I had also spent most of the trip so far within the relative comfort of the Spanish language. While I can't speak it well, it was at least familiar, and I was able to hold my own to an extent. Now, though, I was about to be dropped into a whole new world. In addition to the language barriers, I was trying to open my mind to the huge cultural differences I knew I'd be living with for the next few months. With the commonly perceived views of corruption, war, suffering, instability and poverty in the back of my mind, 'Let's see what Africa is really like, first hand,' I thought as I sleepily and slowly passed through the immigration queue once again.

I knew Africa would be different and difficult but, despite my attempts at mental preparation, this phase was to be a pebbledash assault on my senses. I was trying to second guess and plan for every eventuality, when in reality I didn't know anything – it was all new, and I'd just have to roll with it.

Africa has 54 countries; the most of any continent by some margin, and with that came enhanced focus on passport juggling, so much so that we had to tackle it in bite-size chunks. We realized quickly that in order to 'complete' Africa, we'd have to split it into four phases in order to accommodate the logistics of obtaining the relevant visas and access. With certain countries requiring scans of my retinas and fingerprints this, on more occasions than I'd have liked, meant sometimes flying halfway around the world just to attend a visa appointment in person, given that I was unwilling to part with my eyes and fingers.

Before flying to Casablanca, in addition to the brief pleasures of a home-cooked meal from my mum and a bed I knew, I had taken the opportunity to update my kit and make adjustments based on what wasn't working and what could be improved. Time to shed some unnecessary items from my beast of a bag. My kit consisted largely of the usual items you'd take on holiday, but a stripped-down version to allow space for items that wouldn't normally form part of holiday luggage, like large tripods, drones, microphones, spare cameras and several kilos of batteries. And this was just the gadgets. Nutrition took up another chunk of space in my bag. My bewildering array of colourful tablets, 11 per day, had been diligently sorted into neat piles on the dining table and individually packaged into a pill bag for each day, by my mum, like a sort of WI drug dealer. All four months' worth were then squeezed into a large and very old wash-bag. Among the contents of each bag were a probiotic tablet for gut health, to give my body a fighting chance of avoiding unpleasant stomach upsets, a cod liver oil capsule for my knees and joints, a green-tea tablet to help with recovery, and two Juice Plus tablets – one fruit and one veg, for a bit of variety.

There was also a very small corner of my bag reserved for three items of great sentimental value. From the beginning, I'd carried a photo, a cap and a water card. These items were precious to me and not to be removed from the bag for any reason, and being back in Morocco stirred memories of the Marathon des Sables and meeting Kev for the first time. In this race, every competitor is given a water card, which is strapped to you by various clips and tie-wraps, and is essential to have on hand at all times. Every morning and at each checkpoint during the seven days of battling over skyscraper sand dunes, we were presented with varying amounts of water. Our water cards were marked using a hole punch, to show we had had the correct amount of water. It's very easy to under- and over-hydrate and, in extreme conditions, incorrect water intake can result in death, so the water cards become part of your lifeline. Before leaving for this expedition Kev and I met for dinner and, as we were saying goodbye, he presented me with his water card. He said, 'Do me a favour and look after this for me – take it to every country.' He was gifting me a precious item to treasure. To most, it's just a card, but I knew how much it meant to both of us, and him giving it to me was another shove in the direction of success.

The cap was just a cap I had bought in a race in Australia a few years earlier, nothing special. I collect caps, but this was the only one to go to every country, and I wanted a personal memento to pass on to my future kids. Silly, I know, but there is comfort to be found in sentimental items like these. The photo was of three dear friends, all of whom I've mentioned before: Jeff, Rory and, of course, Kev. They were the collective force that, unbeknownst to them, had led me down this path.

Morocco, Mauritania, Algeria, Tunisia

While my brother and dad were still stuck with a broken-down car at Heathrow, I had made it to Morocco. However, my bag hadn't. Great start. The shoddy luggage belt in Casablanca airport ground to a halt, the shutters leading from the belt to the luggage handling area crashed shut, and I was left staring at an empty carousel, with just a few members of staff hanging around, busy smoking some pretty foul-smelling cigars. After pacing around in the luggage hall to check all the other luggage belts, there was still no sign of my bag. Day one in Africa, and no bag. It was fairly obvious where it was – with such a short connection in Spain, my bag hadn't made it through Madrid airport as quickly as I had. Meanwhile here, in a dusty luggage hall on the west coast of Morocco, I was struggling to find anyone who cared about my predicament. One particularly unhelpful member of staff gestured to me without raising his head from his Gameboy. Although I don't speak Arabic, his meaning seemed to transcend language: 'I don't care, tourist.' His fingers were frantically tapping away, head bowed, eyes fixed on the tiny screen; he was clearly at a critical stage of Super Mario. Such was his fixation on the game, I almost became distracted, wondering which level he was on, before reminding myself that this deeply uncooperative man might be my only hope of finding my bag.

To cut a long story short, I left the airport empty handed. With help from my team, we confirmed that my bag was indeed still in Spain, and I was reunited with it the following day, using my only day off to shuttle backwards and forwards from the airport by train, queuing in the enormous and disorganized crush of people to push my way into the terminal building. Once that mission was complete, I had at least five entirely contradictory conversations about how to get to the lost luggage area. I resorted to chuckling to myself as I was pin-balled from one information point to the next. I eventually reached the correct grotty corner of the airport, staffed by some people who appeared to have attended the same customer-service training course as Gameboy man. Having retrieved my bag, it then took me an hour to get back out of the airport, thanks to some enthusiastic 'patter downers'. Very friendly, but perhaps going above and beyond what was required for a basic body search. Then another hour on the train, by which time I was more than ready for sleep before the following day's marathon.

Annoyingly, when packing my bag I hadn't checked the shoe size of my new pair of trainers. This was my third pair of the challenge, provided by my brilliant sponsors Pro Direct. Unfortunately, on this occasion, they seemed to think my feet had shrunk from a size 11 to a size 9.5. Running a marathon in shoes a size and a half too small is uncomfortable, particularly in a place where your feet swell due to the heat. I had also developed horrendous toothache – my tooth was now attempting to outbid my sore feet to become my primary source of pain.

However, the run complete, and nursing my aching tooth through the night, I headed in the very early morning to my second African country. I was warned it would be even hotter and unsafe in the city, and arriving into Nouakchott, Mauritania's capital, the Moroccan airport experience was soon trumped.

Mauritania is in the far west of Africa, with the Atlantic lapping at its shore. With 90 per cent of the country's landmass within the Sahara desert, it's a dry and dusty place. After the Marathon des Sables I had a little clue of the dry heat to come. Nouakchott airport hinted at the state of the city I was about to step into. At 2 a.m. I arrived at the airport (which looked like it hadn't yet finished being built) about an hour later than planned, and lined up in immigration for about 40 minutes. Reaching the front of the queue, I was told I needed a visa, which required joining another queue for a further 40 minutes, all the time my tooth was kicking me in the face from the inside. I made it to the front of the second line and attempted to pay for the visa. They only accepted cash. Cash I had, but not in the correct currency. An official then dragged me off to the other end of the airport to find the right cash. The machine didn't accept my card, so it was over to the exchange centre. This was to become a common occurrence in Africa – no matter what currency I had, they always seemed to want something else. Anyway, after finding cash and yet another 40-minute queue, I had my visa and some more funny looks as I was passed from one security guard to the next, my bag was inspected and my drone removed. Here we go again.

This is where my patience ran out. The guy who removed the drone didn't appear to speak English, French or Arabic. On top of the language barrier, he was seemingly caught up in a separate argument with a colleague, which was much further up his list of priorities than dealing with me. It was now 4.30 a.m. and my tooth pain was close to unbearable.

After much hassle and arguing, I left the airport with a handwritten scrap of paper bearing some Arabic scribbles which apparently instructed me to call him when I came back to fly out in order to collect my confiscated drone. In normal circumstances this would have made me livid, but, with all my pain and tiredness, they could eat it for all I cared. I have a brilliant photo, now framed. It shows me looking up at the camera as they photographed me for my visa sticker. I look like a kidnap victim. Shaggy beard, huge bags under my eyes and the side of my face swollen with the infection. I still felt worse than I looked, though. With my awful photo, visa and official scrap of paper, I bundled into a dodgy taxi and went to the hotel. It was only when I reached the hotel that I noticed the phone number I'd been given to collect the drone was only five digits long. Can a phone number be only five digits? It felt like the equivalent of being given a false mobile number by a girl who doesn't want a second date. I fell asleep with the piece of paper in my hand on my chest then five hours later, my energy levels still desperately low, dragged myself out of bed for 26 hot exhausting miles.

I was reminded that my trainers were still over a size too small when trying to step into them with my eyes half shut. It wasn't like there was an Adidas shop on the corner either. I was in the strange position of feeling grateful that my tooth was so painful because it took my mind off my feet. Due mainly to tooth pain, I was awake early enough to catch morning prayer at the main mosque, which was 30 minutes away. I had just enough time to jog down and witness the goings-on. With the sun rising, I watched hordes of people praying in silhouette. The sounds, smells and sights took my mind off everything. The mosque resembled a sort of church-like car port – open but sheltered at the same time; a totally beautiful and peaceful reminder of the wonders of the world.

The run can be summed up very simply: one straight road, a few donkeys, and a massive burning ball of hydrogen in the sky scorching everything it touched, including me. Roumald was my driver, crawling along behind me in his very old 4x4. He had no idea he'd be driving for hours at a snail's pace, but he wasn't going to turn down the cash. In my battered mental and physical state I couldn't help but compare myself to the thin, sluggish and seemingly dying donkeys we passed.

If anything, the donkeys seemed perkier. I'd read about the influences of the French on Mauritania's cuisine and music. My soundtrack, however, was the occasional donkey eeeorr and the cuisine was mostly dust and grit from the road.

Less than 12 hours after running my 39th marathon, I was up and out on a 4 a.m. flight to Algeria having spent a good hour retrieving my drone from the custody of the airport officials. No rest for the wicked, as my nan would say. I gobbled down a double dose of painkillers to numb my horribly throbbing tooth and got on with it. Despite the sore tooth and lack of sleep, I was due to be joined by my mate Andy, who'd been with me in Brazil and Argentina. Just for a few days, but running together would be a welcome distraction and an opportunity to see some non-touristy parts of Africa. Although I felt bad for Andy – he was about to play nurse.

I arrived in Algeria in the early evening. I met Andy and spent a few hours moaning about my tooth while attempting to prod and poke it in front of the bathroom mirror. My gum was definitely infected. We were staying at Hôtel Lamaraz Arts in complimentary rooms generously given to us by way of supporting the challenge. I wasn't in the mood for company, though, and I felt bad to have to decline the offer of dinner with the staff, knowing my mouth couldn't handle food.

One of the most noticeable elements of the trip so far had been the prevalence and visibility of religion in so many of the countries I'd visited, in the Caribbean especially. Coming from a relatively secular country, I've always been aware of the fact that religion features far more prominently in the lives of many people around the world, but visiting cities like Algiers really brings home how much a part of daily life it is. Part of the stunning view from the top of our hotel was the remarkable and brand new Djamaa el Djazaïr mosque, a vast edifice with the world's tallest minaret, standing at over 250 metres. With such a conspicuously magnificent reminder of the fact that we were in a Muslim country visible from our room, Andy and I found ourselves talking religion. While it has been the root of much conflict around the world, it remains at the heart of so many communities, bringing people together in vast numbers, no more so than at the Djamaa el Djazaïr, which can hold over 120,000 people. Now that's community. Through a little reading and some conversation with locals we learnt of the sheer scale of worship in Algeria – 99.7 per cent of the population are not only religious, but actively practise Islam. It's this strong gathering that gives Algeria most of its culture and societal identity. It is fascinating to view the changing ways of the world based on the pockets of faith globally.

That night was one of the most painful nights of my life. Maybe I was being pathetic and overtired, but all I wanted to do was pass out. My toothache had reached a new level of pain, to the point where I was ready to jump on a flight and get it fixed. Yes, there are plenty of dentists in Algiers, but with a strong fear of dentists back home, the thought of braving a dentist elsewhere was a no-go. It seemed a molar was the main culprit and the heart of the infection, which had spread throughout my bottom gum and surrounded other teeth that felt delicate and beyond sore. A painful strain to open my mouth and look in the mirror revealed the extent of the mess. If you've ever seen the film *Into the Wild*, I looked like Alexander Supertramp in his dying moments.

I sent a text to Andy in the early hours of the morning instructing him to knock on my door as soon as he was awake. We decided the hunt for antibiotics was a must. Andy kindly went on a search and returned quickly with an array of drugs. No breakfast, no food, no sleep, and after attempting to eat a banana, which felt like chewing glass, I dosed up on painkillers and antibiotics, and we headed out to run. I was in the country, and could physically run – so we did. Those were the rules of the game, really. The copious amounts of codeine and the antibiotics started to take effect, my tooth started to throb less. My face still felt the size of a beach ball and my mouth was red and swollen, even from the outside.

Chats with locals, coastal paths, interesting buildings and a nice breeze – the run, all things considered, was decidedly pleasant. For Andy it was a little different, but I'd become accustomed to the ever-changing landscape from one day to the next. Despite that, I tried my best to not take it for granted. It was a pleasure to have Andy along to chat with about anything and everything. We took our time, and attempted to snack as we ran. I was starving, but couldn't manage much above a few more bites of a banana.

After an entertaining four-hour delay before our flight to Tunisia the following day, we eventually reached the sunny coast of Tunis and made our way to our host's house. Natalie works for the British embassy and was incredibly kind to let us crash at hers. She lived in the centre of Tunis, in an airy open-plan two-bed flat complete with a cute breakfast balcony. She'd made it home with various personal touches of art and memorabilia from other postings, and it did indeed feel homely. A pleasant, slowly chewed evening meal spoilt by my bloody tooth, a brief tour of the seafront, some more drugs then off to bed. I was still in a fair bit of pain, and with an early start the following day I attempted to get my head down around 7.30 p.m.

Another marathon on little sleep and with an aching face. Some days during this challenge I felt the world was just throwing everything it had at me. Around mile 22 of my 41st marathon, Andy and I were feeling surprisingly fresh for a change. We were meandering past some houses on a quiet section of beach when we realized that we were running towards some aggressive-looking feral dogs and, in such a quiet spot, we were very much on their turf. (Well, sand actually, but still not good.) We slowed, turned around and did what you're supposed to do. We ignored them and walked slowly away, but almost immediately we had five very angry street dogs snarling at our heels. This had happened to me in a few South American countries, and I just assumed they'd get bored and go away. However, without fair warning (aside from the barking and snarling), the leader of the pack launched itself at my scrawny left thigh and had a good chomp. 'Ouch, you bastard!' I yelped, as Andy and I ran into each other in an attempt to get away. Andy thought on his feet much quicker than I did and used the dregs in his water bottle, along with the actual water bottle, to eventually deter them. With some extra adrenaline soaring through the both of us, we put some distance between us and the dogs. They galloped off to their sand dune. Four puncture wounds at the end of some tooth marks started to bleed immediately, and my Do Running shorts were missing a mouth-shaped segment. Although deep enough to bleed a fair bit, it was just a small bite, really, but nonetheless a trip to the doc for a rabies jab was now a must.

We rinsed the bite with our remaining water and set off back the way we'd come, gradually hobbling back into a run. With adrenaline pumping, we were now running our fastest miles of the entire marathon. I hoped that running wouldn't cause any possible infection to spread through my body more quickly, but getting to a hospital was urgent, and with only two miles to go, we just went for it. Still in shock, the realization suddenly dawned that the expedition was close to an abrupt end here. Had that dog bitten my ankle rather than opting for my succulent thigh, it could have been game over. There's not a lot I could have done with a damaged Achilles tendon. I felt fortunate to be able to run, but frustrated we hadn't thought to just kick sand at them. We were on a beach, after all. Hindsight, as so often on this journey, is a wonderful thing.

Having run the middle section of the marathon with us, Natalie was surprised to see that I'd managed to become bloodied in the short time since we'd parted. With her great knowledge of all things Tunisian, she agreed that a rabies vaccination was essential and urgent. I'd had my full complement of pre-trip vaccines and spent several thousands of pounds returning weekly to top up the whole catalogue, including hepatitis A and B, typhoid and paratyphoid fever, meningitis, yellow fever, Japanese encephalitis and, of course, rabies. While some of these would protect me for ten years without worry, even with my pre-trip rabies vaccine I'd still need another jab. The chances were that I was totally fine and it wasn't a rabid dog, but a quick Google search revealed that there were only 14 recorded instances of people having survived rabies after the onset of symptoms. Not great odds.

It was all very dramatic for a little bite, but the jeopardy was real. Still in my running kit, including the ragged semicircle of fabric now hanging from my shorts, I lay face down on Natalie's balcony, partly so Andy was able to daub iodine from an embassy-issue first aid kit on the back of my leg, and partly to avoid getting blood all over the soft furnishings. Meanwhile Natalie had contacted a doctor, and obtained the details of a vaccination clinic. She was clearly concerned for my wellbeing, but also keen not to have a British citizen die of rabies on her watch.

First aid complete, we bundled into a taxi and headed for second aid at the clinic. The shock had now worn off, but so had my second lot of painkillers – the ones I had taken mid-run for my tooth and sore feet, rather than the bite. Crammed in the back of the car with my leg on a towel and clutching my aching face, we arrived at what looked like a small house and were met at the reception desk by a chap in jeans and a pullover with some holes in. He asked what was wrong, took my name and then asked me to take a seat in the empty waiting area, before disappearing through a door. Barely had my sore nether regions touched the plastic patio chair when the same man appeared through another door, now wearing a white doctor's coat with a stethoscope around his neck – the classic fancy-dress doctor – and asked me to follow him into a small surgery. Andy followed, camera in hand, to capture the moment, as I sat down gingerly and we exchanged some confused/concerned looks, and then without warning the needle was in and out of my arm, no words exchanged.

I was in the building for a total of about three minutes. No forms, no fee, barely any communication. Just a jab in the arm and a piece of paper informing me I'd need two more injections; one and two weeks later. Job done, no messing around. We were more shocked by the efficiency of the service than we were by the dogs. Having phoned for the taxi that had taken us to the clinic, the final surprise of the day came when trying, very unsuccessfully, to hail one to take us back. Tunis taxis are a lot newer and smarter than a lot of other African taxis but, bizarrely, as we later learned, they display a red light when they are available and a green light when they have a passenger already on board. It took us a while to get back.

Waking the following morning, I now had four attractive yellow circles of bruising around the teeth marks. The dog wasn't huge, but it had certainly left its mark. With my flight to Angola not until the evening, I had time to think things through, and so over a breakfast of pastries and painkillers I called home to update them on the situation. After many conversations with my team, embassy staff and

Andy, it became apparent that I couldn't just carry on to the next country. The piece of paper the doctor had given me showed the dates I would need my follow-up vaccinations, which would put me in Niger and then Mali, both unknown quantities in terms of healthcare. I couldn't take that risk.

This meant taking a £1,500 hit on flights and heading back to the UK for just one top-up jab. The tooth also played a part in the decision-making – if it wasn't improving, I'd rather be in a country with good and easily accessible dental care. So the plan was set to get back to the UK, get a proper inspection of my tooth and gum, top up my rabies vaccination and get a new pair of shoes that actually fitted my feet. Tunisia was actually pretty close to home, relatively speaking.

My dad's study is a large, cube-shaped room in our family home in Dorset. One wall is covered, floor to ceiling, with shelves of maps all filed by their Ordnance Survey-assigned numbers, pink for Landranger, orange for Explorer, with various atlases and larger books acting as bookends. This is as a result of his life as 'the map man', drawing maps for most of his career with the OS. Printers, computers, scanners and various other gadgets are all arranged on the opposite side of the room. With a desk in between looking out onto the garden and fields, this room became known as the Yellow War Room, the room in which all the careful planning and flight logistics were orchestrated. The 'yellow' came from the hundreds of post-it notes bearing document numbers and flight iterations which littered the room. During every phone call home, I imagined my dad surrounded by his 'organized chaos', as he sat waiting for the crappy internet connection to load another check-in screen.

It was in this room that we discussed the first big re-jig of the trip, necessitating the use of orange post-its among the sea of yellow. I can make light of it now, but at the time we were all starting to become stressed. We couldn't afford to keep spending money on things going wrong, but we had no choice but to put my health first on this occasion. We knew I'd already missed Niger and Mali but it was possible I'd miss two more with the logistics of flights and connections in Africa.

Within just 72 hours I was all fixed up and the various appointments ticked off. I even managed to see a dentist and have another jab
at very short notice on a Bank Holiday. As I flew to Senegal to restart
the journey after rearranging 12 flights, I stumbled upon a website
called Worldometers.info which highlights key stats from around the
world, many of which made me think about how fortunate I am. At
the time of writing, there were at least 826,916,525 undernourished
people in the world and at least 298,895 people had died due to poor
water sanitation. In 2018 2.9 million people died from cancer. As I
mentioned before, problems are always relative.

Senegal

I flew via Lisbon into a beautiful sunrise in Senegal. It's amazing
what a difference a few days can make. An airport lounge, free food,
three seats to myself on the plane, I even slept all the way. Everything
was starting to look more optimistic for this second crack at the first
phase of Africa. Approaching Dakar I peered out of the porthole
windows and muttered under my breath, 'Please be kind, Dakar.'
Aside from what felt like slightly more than the usual amount of staring at the pasty white boy, it seemed I was back to normality. Life on
the road. Just six miles into the marathon, I passed a couple of runners, possibly runners by profession. They were speeding along,
cadence in sync and chatting away as if it was a warm-up, and gave
acknowledging nods as they whizzed past me in the opposite direction. With my spirits slightly higher and feeling as if I should try to
re-engage fully with the world, I turned around, raced after them
and said, 'Bonjour.' Being in a French-speaking country, I felt that
was a safe bet. The run began to fly by as we trotted along somewhat
quicker than I'd hoped, but with fresh and correctly fitting shoes and
my mind in the right place, it was a pleasure. Thirteen miles later one
of the chaps was still running with me. He showed me around a fish
market, bought me water, which he then carried for me, and offered
me the use of his home any time I revisited the country. I learned that
this guy, who looked about 35, was, in fact, ex-army, and 55. Retired

for two years, he just ran because he loved it. Now that's a man after my own heart.

The power of 'hi' is remarkable. As a kid I was super shy, hardly said hi to anyone without hiding behind my mum's legs. But things change, and I have discovered how great it is to meet new people. I am that weirdo on a train, plane or bus who will say, 'Hi.' And I don't apologize for it. Saying hi on this journey was a no-brainer. It opened so many doors, corrected any preconceptions I had based on first impressions and, above all, it was the first step to new friendships and connections. On so many occasions I have politely initiated conversation with a stranger only to learn that we both had something in common, or made a connection which led to an opportunity. Meeting new people made me feel like I was really back in the swing of things. And as yet nothing had gone wrong. Yet.

Gambia

Day 129 was another one to file under 'not going to plan'. At 2 a.m. I found myself sitting in a taxi surrounded by armed guards peering into the vehicle and having a heated conversation in what sounded like a mix of French and an African language. It was pitch black outside, and all I could hear was the sound of dogs – big dogs – and deep angry voices.

Roll back a few hours, and I was at the Brussels Airlines desk ready to leave Senegal and fly to Gambia. A smiley chap with dazzling white teeth informed me in the most cheery manner, 'No flights today. Cancelled,' and continued to smile at me as if it was a joke. It really did seem like a joke. It wasn't. In fact, there was no flight to Gambia until Friday, in four days' time. This situation was made worse by the fact that I had no form of communication in order to make alternative plans. No Wi-Fi. With my so-called 'worldwide' internet box not working, my sat phone wasn't receiving a signal, and both my phones had no service. I resorted to hunting for a phone box. There were none. The excessively jolly Brussels Airlines chap could see my concern and offered me the use of his tether. High-five to technology and to kindness.

Once again, an early morning call to base camp to assess options.
I couldn't wait four days, I knew that much. I would miss another two
or three countries. We came up with a new plan: get back to the hotel
and arrange for a driver to take me overland to the hotel in Gambia.
Easy, right? It should be about five hours to the border and a little
more to the hotel. After some discussion, we agreed a price, I scoffed
some food down and my driver collected me. I sat up, lay down, curled
up and basically attempted to get comfortable in every conceivable
position while he drove me for what turned out to be nine hours to the
border. The roads felt like they'd been ploughed.

At the border, plastered with military logos and surrounded by
battered old army trucks, the aggressive and heavily armed guards
were staffing what turned out to be the first of four checkpoints set up
for little else than relieving travellers of their money. This was referred
to as a 'toll'. For 'toll', see 'bribe'. These checkpoints often consisted
of a full car search (presumably to find a reason to extort further),
having fingerprints taken (in ink, of course, not digitally) and entries
into one of the mountains of dusty and scuffed leather-bound ledgers,
presumably full of decades' worth of passport details.

Once at the *actual* border, I was gently hauled out of the car and
put in a 'holding cell'. The driver gestured to me with a nod and a
downward-facing palm, implying that I shouldn't panic, it's just what
they do sometimes. All well and good, but I was the one behind bars
in a foreign country in the middle of the night. You can imagine the
fear creeping into the back of my mind, and then quickly making its
way to the front. The driver and the guards disappeared, and I
instantly made the natural assumption that, of course, the driver was
in on it and they were currently round the back sharing out my
belongings – or, worse still, in the process of kidnapping me. Out of a
sense of necessity, more than anything, I forced myself to be calm, sat
down and waited, quietly cursing Brussels Airlines.

I was in the cell for at least 100 years. That's what it felt like anyway. It transpired that we didn't have enough cash left to pay the
border people off, and the border didn't officially open for another
five hours. To make matters worse, my driver had neglected to tell me
that a ferry crossing was also required to get into Gambia, which

didn't become evident until the sun came up and I could see the issue for myself.

I'm not entirely sure how my release was negotiated. I think they just got bored of me. We played the hand of having no money, because we had no money – and so when they realized we were telling the truth they just gave up and let me go. Either that or the driver conducted a dodgy deal I was unaware of. I think the former is more likely. I was too tired to care and, frankly, was just pleased to be making progress again.

The driver and I decided to sleep in the car until the ferry started running at 8 a.m. I woke up in a dirty, sweaty, thirsty mess, huddled under a blanket on the back seat. Looking outside, to my huge surprise, the empty landscape from the night before was now filled with hordes of people, completely surrounding the car. They'd turned up early to get their place on the first boat. I later learned that this was due to Ramadan and people were travelling to be with families to begin their fasting and celebration. Our car was now part of the crush to get on the ferry, and was rocking from side to side as people jostled for position.

So despite being there all night, we had both slept through our first opportunity for a spot on the ferry. We would need to queue for the next slot, and managed to inch forward in the car until, by 10 a.m., we were in the middle of a ramp laden with people carrying all manner of belongings and large household items. It felt like sitting on a supermarket checkout conveyor belt while people passed their shopping around and over you. Slightly scary at first, then ridiculous, and eventually just amusing. Three hours later we finally negotiated our way to the front spot on the boat, with more money changing hands. Africa was clearly going to require saintly patience and a relaxed attitude to health and safety. As the ferry ploughed its way across the river, waves splashed over the car, and I mean the entire car, with foot passengers crammed in like sardines – hundreds of people on a boat about the size of four large buses, many using buckets and various rugs and clothing items in an attempt to shield themselves from the soaking. Of course every passenger disembarked wet through. I couldn't have got out of the car if I'd wanted to. Finally, at 1 p.m., a mere 20 hours later than planned, I made it to my hotel in Gambia, Kololi Beach Club. My incredibly patient driver, facing the same return journey to get home, still carried my bags to my room with a genuine smile of accomplishment.

It was now too late to start running, so everything was pushed back a day. I slept all afternoon, ready for a 5 a.m. run with my hotel hosts and avid runners, Katie, Tina and Martin. The trip to Gambia hadn't been pleasant, but the running made up for it: a gorgeous sweeping beach at sunrise, gentle waves, local fishermen going out for an early catch, and a few other local joggers who, without fail, said hello – as did everyone else I passed. With so many friendly people this was a marathon of smiles as well as miles. Katie supported in the car when we rejoined the road. Warm, but not hot, windy, but not blowing a gale, and the road was busy, but not deadly. Perfect. Out and back by 11 a.m. Katie then waited on me hand and foot – making me an omelette, baked beans, French bread with Marmite and butter and bacon – all in her lovely, open-plan coastal-view kitchen. For someone who had missed this kind of food, I was in heaven, especially after a great run with great people. Africa's rollercoaster of ups and downs continued.

Guinea-Bissau

With the delays getting to Gambia, I was already up against it to find transport and get to Guinea-Bissau for marathon 44. Guinea-Bissau was one of the very few countries that we hadn't found a way to get into in advance. We knew there were no flights, but had heard tales of a potential bus service. This was apparently a long, slow journey, stopping at many villages not necessarily en route. The internet seemed to confirm that the bus existed, but didn't allow us to book in advance. Unfortunately this, like my financial forecasts for the trip, was simply wrong. There was no bus. It hadn't operated for over five years. So the objective was now to find a safe, reliable driver who could speak the necessary languages to get me through potential danger, take me from my hotel here in Gambia, back into Senegal, and then into Guinea-Bissau at a reasonable price. Gambia is a small narrow inlet within the country of Senegal, and so driving practically in any direction you must pass through Senegal to get anywhere (unless, of course, you drive west and then have the ocean to contend with). On a map it looks a little like a carpenter's tongue and groove joint. The entirety of Gambia is engulfed by Senegal – hence the double border crossing (once to get out of Gambia into Senegal, and then from Senegal into Bissau).

I would then tackle the problem of finding somewhere to stay. I felt very much on my own at this point. My team would usually have done this for me, but now with no communication options, it was back to good old fashioned 'asking around'. To cut a long story short, Omar would be my driver for a fee of £300 and drive me door to door. As it turned out, he was accompanied by his Portuguese-speaking friend, who had come along to help with the border crossings, and was named Smiler – presumably because of his one and only tooth, which was gold.

The journey felt like being immersed in an over-the-top 4D cinema experience, but without the comfy reclining seat or air-con. I was sitting in a noisy, bumpy torture chamber with what felt like a thousand hairdryers blowing in my face, with no popcorn, no food and no water. Aside from the endless potholes, hairpin bends and relentless 'checkpoints' (extortion stations), we had some seatbelt-wrenching emergency stops for everything from children to pigs. The roads were unkind, to say the least, but we were making progress. With every bump and bruise I was getting closer to my next country, and that was fine by me. After a few hours of politely staying awake, I even managed to doze off for a bit whilst rattling around in the back. I was soon awake again, dripping with sweat, my mouth dry, and filthy from the dust and grit blasting in through the open windows. There was still about half a day of driving ahead of us.

After several more bribe payments and pointless bag checks by dodgy guards, our next problem came in the form of a breakdown, as the jeep shuddered and stopped. I literally put my head in my hands. We were miles from anywhere. Just swathes of arid nothingness as far as the eye could see, in every direction. The only option was to go for help which, to my horror, meant both my driver and his Portuguese-speaking friend flagging down transport to hitch a ride to the nearest town, leaving me alone, with all my gear, on a dusty single-track road in the middle of West Africa, with no means of communication. In addition to feeling tired, dirty and frustrated, I now felt vulnerable and scared. Would they come back?

An hour later they returned with a tow truck, having found a garage in a town ten miles away, and my growing sense of panic subsided, a feeling which always tends to be accompanied by a mild sense of foolishness at having panicked in the first place. I hadn't really doubted them, but in situations like that it's difficult not to assume the worst, especially in a state of exhaustion. After hooking up and bumping our way to the next town, we pulled up alongside various other battered vehicles. Had we arrived at the garage? Or were these roadworthy cars? As I was pondering, a few grubby-looking men came out of a nearby shack and gathered to poke around under the bonnet. I came to the conclusion that 'garage' was a fairly loose term around here.

Being Ramadan everyone downed tools mid-repair and went to pray – Omar and Smiler too. Although I was anxious to get going, I loved witnessing these displays of faith taking priority, and I took the opportunity to sit on the side of the road and watch the world go by. Whole villages were commuting from miles around to the mosque, looking at me with inquisitive eyes. I wasn't really blending in, with my sunburn and skinny white legs. Some people were kicking a football, others riding bikes, skipping or generally just being joyous. A while later they passed me again on their way back. They seemed to have taken on a spiritual glow from their short time praying.

It turned out the jeep wasn't being fixed any time soon, and my hopes of getting to Bissau were reducing by the second. However, I was back in another part of Senegal, so why not explore? I had no idea if it was safe, but it was better than sitting in a pool of my own sweat, feeling grumpy. I had a little wander around and chatted to a few locals. Fortunately, I speak a little French, and it was enough to meet and understand Denny, a tailor who was just 18 and made shirts and local garments. Denny's little set-up was a table and a chair under a makeshift lean-to outside a small shack that stored fabric and materials. Made of offcut pieces of wood, it was a classically African affair. It was all he needed, the embodiment of no-frills working. I admired it. He had what he needed and nothing more. He was incredibly welcoming, and we ended up spending over an hour together, during which time he expertly taught me his trade and we made an outfit together. It was a traditional combo, a *boubou*: a tunic-style top together with long pleated trousers; heavy material, brightly coloured with eye-watering patterns from head to toe. For me, in the heat, there was no way I would last more than five minutes wearing it – the material was so thick my body temperature wouldn't stand a chance. That said, it was a work of art and Denny was proud of it. I offered to buy it from him as a thank you and a show of friendship, but he insisted it was already mine.

I had no idea what was wrong with the jeep – but it eventually started and the small crowd that had now assembled to take part in the repair whooped and cheered in celebration. We ventured on, surviving many more stops, and at long last completed the 300-kilometre journey in just over 15 hours. We reached Bissau at 1 a.m. on the day of the marathon.

During that trip we paid off a total of 12 officials at 'checkpoints', survived a breakdown, Denny had taught me how to sew, and I had another four stamps in my passport, despite only travelling through two countries. We'd even driven through a forest fire. I was knackered, and whilst it had been a difficult day, it had been utterly fascinating, and in retrospect was one of my favourite days in Africa. Denny and I are still in touch now. As I fell asleep, with four hours before I needed to run, my thoughts were with Omar and Smiler as they turned around, switched seats in the car and began the journey back home – and all during Ramadan. Legends. The Guinea-Bissau marathon was thankfully uneventful, and I spent the rest of the day in bed after eating two bin-lid-sized tuna pizzas. Might not sound noteworthy to you, but I loved those pizzas. Food, glorious crap food.

Ivory Coast

The next fortnight was hot and dry. From Guinea-Bissau to the Ivory Coast, to the pungent-smelling streets of Guinea, to new friends in Sierra Leone, then the green, green grass of Liberia and the dusty suburbs of Ghana's capital, Accra.

The Ivory Coast was a fairly uninteresting marathon (out and back along a single dusty, straight road), hard and hot but noteworthy for another interesting African airport experience and an embarrassing blunder. Despite already having my entry visa, which we'd spent months obtaining, I was still required to queue, deli-counter style, for the officials to rigorously and pointlessly check it, along with all those that didn't have a visa at all. I was handed an actual deli-counter ticket bearing the number 106. The big red number in the corner of the box room was displaying 56. With no sign of anyone entering or leaving the tatty back office, my heart dropped. I spent an agonizing five hours curled up on cold metal seating, trying to sleep while I waited my turn. Patience, by necessity, has a whole different meaning in Africa – I was beginning to realize that nothing happens fast here. By the time I left to face the argy-bargy of the taxi hustle, it was 7 a.m., 12 hours after I'd landed.

As with most countries it was my first time visiting and, wherever possible, I had arranged transport in advance to avoid having to jump into an unknown taxi. Here, I was looking for my driver and didn't need a taxi but was mobbed by at least 15 drivers, some of whom were physically pulling me towards their vehicles. I shouted at the last one, wrestled myself free of his grip and retreated back into the terminal building, slightly overwhelmed, and tried to make contact with the hotel that had kindly offered a free night's accommodation and the much-needed shuttle from the airport. With my phone giving me the now familiar 'no connection' tone, I unleashed the satellite phone, eagerly pulled up the aerial and made a call. It was the first time I'd relied on it during the trip. I wanted to understand if there were any safety issues with the taxis, if my driver actually existed, and, if so, where he was. And thank goodness I did. The hotel, once I finally got through, confirmed that taxis shouldn't be trusted by tourists and to wait for their driver. In an embarrassing turn of events, it turned out that my driver was already there, and was none other than the guy I had yelled at to stop pulling me. He just spoke no English, and, in my alarmed and tired state, I hadn't made the connection. I made a couple of mental notes: 1) try to get more sleep; 2) remember that normal rules don't apply in Africa.

The port of Abidjan is the largest city in Côte d'Ivoire, with office blocks, the odd skyscaper and a bustling, congested market area selling everything conceivable. The standout memory was the kindness of my host Isabella at Villa Oasis, who not only let me stay for free but actually washed my smelly sweaty clothes too.

Guinea

From one run to the next. The runs were ticking by slightly faster than usual thanks to a rare (and short) spell of single-flight access. The lack of direct flights in Africa, I learned, was often down to disputes with neighbouring nations. Now, though, despite my body being largely unwilling, I was motoring along from one to the next, covering four countries in a week. My body was knackered and sluggish, but that was more generally from early starts, lack of calorific food and needing sleep more than anything. My legs, and the running side of everything, seemed to be working OK. I wasn't really sore, because I'd made sure all my runs were completed slowly and without too much struggle on the legs. My hips and my back were a little buggered due to lugging my gear in and out of planes and up and down stairs. Other than that, I was holding up – at least enough to avoid too much running pain. Guinea was marathon 46, day 138, and with it came a new challenge, in the form of powerful smells.

In terms of infrastructure, Conakry feels like a city that has tried to run before it can walk. Narrow, dusty roads with no road markings, separating concrete structures, built mostly through Chinese investment, lie unfinished and abandoned. Deep, dug-out drains overflowing with effluent line each roadside – meaning there's no escape from the stench of raw sewage. Single lanes of assorted traffic squeeze past each other, while motorbikes precariously duck and weave between lorries, all vehicles honking their horns for no apparent reason. The roads are lined with street traders selling everything and anything from moonshine to wooden beds to barbecued corn on the cob. Everything is dirty, and everyone is hustling for business. There are car-sized piles of burning rubbish at almost every turn, in addition to actual burned-out cars. Goats, sheep, dogs and cows roam the streets searching for food, all of them desperately skeletal, many having already given up and lying dead and decaying where they had fallen. The continuous cacophony of car horns and motorbike engines blended with deep-voiced shouting and barking dogs to form the soundtrack to my run. The midday sun bounced off the road and onto my face and body. It was like a filthy oven – and I was in it.

The unpleasant sensory overload and the heat was all too much for me and, unable to control my gag reflex any longer, I was physically sick three times in the space of a few miles, leaving me feeling even weaker than before. I finished the run feeling horrible, with two small burn marks on the backs of my left calf where motorbike exhausts had rubbed past me and burnt through my compression socks – as if I wasn't hot or uncomfortable enough already. Thankfully, I managed to avoid all the wing mirrors that seemed to be targeting the back of my head as lorries rumbled by, the wind rushing past signalling another near miss. Africa wasn't letting up, and the thing about travelling on my own was that there was nobody to bounce ideas off, so I'd begun to talk to myself as a form of therapy more than anything. I'd ask myself questions like: 'Was that too dangerous?' 'Should I have abandoned that one and started again elsewhere?' And sometimes I'd just give myself vocal encouragement to reassure myself that I wasn't going to get hit by a car, or be sick again. I was starting to become a little isolated and alone in my head. Thankfully, the next four days, although emotional at many points, I spent with a new friend and a great group of people.

Sierra Leone

Marathon and country number 47. I was about to be immersed into a country that was needy beyond belief. I think I cried every day. All in all, the short time I spent in Sierra Leone was an unbelievably positive experience, but I learned a great deal about how 'those without' really live, and I reflected a lot on myself and how I still took pretty much everything for granted. Children roamed the streets with nothing but an empty plastic bottle. Some were without any clothes, family or any sign of hope for the future. The streets were littered with groups of young kids trying to make trades. Most buildings were rundown, made of wood cladding and seemingly without power or water. The concrete buildings with amenities were often foreign aid projects or shops. Stalls and traders were the hub of every street, whilst aid agencies provided a vital lifeline to those who couldn't afford even the most basic items, including food. Even for those fortunate enough to have money, tar roads, fourth-hand cars and the occasional small-shack stores were as rich as it got.

We'd rescheduled a few countries to free up more time so I could run the official Sierra Leone marathon – held in Makeni, and organized by Street Child, a charity that supports the wellbeing of children living on the streets – and explore the capital, Freetown.

The race was fab, and it was a total delight to run as part of an organized event in a country where the supporters, particularly the kids, are so smiley and happy. Some of them ran with me for miles, cheering and chanting in support. Running mostly in trail conditions with rocks and mud made for an interesting change. The route also skirted many small communities as the ascents and descents edged us closer to the finish. Mud huts, makeshift thatched roofs, and hordes of small children mostly under ten who ran alongside, smiles covering every face that spoke of genuine hospitality in their hearts . . . getting hold of an empty water bottle and having photos taken made their day. I didn't want to stop running. I was back in the wonderful, familiar-yet-unfamiliar situation of being in the company of other runners. Chatting with other competitors, I learned more about how locals lived and I was reminded of my privilege and counted my blessings. The official street child marathon was organized exceptionally well and worked wonders to reinvigorate my soul after all the toughness of recent weeks.

In the planning phase of this mad mission, during discussions with the security firm and the insurance company, we covered everything from how kidnaps happen to the things that go wrong, and how ransoms should be paid. I was completely surprised to learn that a) kidnaps happen all the time, and b) ransoms are often paid, despite what you hear on TV. My contact who made the insurance cover possible was a guy called Nick. He was initially a contact of a contact of a contact. As was so often the case on this journey, I had reached the perfect person for the job via three or four degrees of separation. Nick also has a brilliant daughter called Gen, a volunteer doctor in the children's hospital in Freetown. I was shocked to learn that she was one of only 150 doctors in the entire country, compared with 290,000 doctors in the UK. That means there are roughly 50,000 patients per doctor in Sierra Leone. It's simply not workable, safe or humane to have so few doctors. Gen works heroically to support an absurdly overstretched healthcare system. The civil war between 1991 and 2002, plus the Ebola outbreak which killed seven per cent of the medical workforce in the country, goes someway to show just what the country is up against. Free healthcare for under-fives was finally introduced in 2010, but, with most of the population still having to pay for treatment privately, the healthcare problems continue. Healthcare in the simplest of forms – like malaria meds – are just not available for all who need it, free or otherwise. The country is embroiled in a constant battle to do more – there's just not enough help, resources or education. It's tough to witness.

During my remaining time in Sierra Leone, I travelled from Makeni back to Freetown and stayed with Gen and her housemates. All are doctors – they live in a small home provided by the institute organizing Gen's voluntary position. Over dinner on the first night, I heard many of their stories and was horrified by the country's shocking child mortality rate. In 2018 that stood at a horrific 11 per cent. That's 110 deaths for every thousand birth – five times higher than the UK.

The following morning I witnessed first hand the harrowing nature of Gen's job and the plight of her community when we visited her hospital for the day. We arrived equipped with consent forms to allow us to film and to discuss some of the patients' situations. I wanted to capture the reality of this place for the documentary. Even though the conflict ceased in 2002, the human development index still ranks the country in the bottom five per cent of the world, with close to 80 per cent of its seven million inhabitants living below the poverty line. This place needs help and I wanted to at least try to capture something of its struggles, in an effort to show the world that we have a duty to help.

It was an emotional battering. The state of the hospital and the lack of medication, equipment and beds were gut-wrenchingly appalling. In one small room, with holes for windows, there were 12 beds. Everything except the patients was old. There was no equipment and, with the handful of staff not being able to offer much in the way of help due to a lack of medication and means of diagnosing and testing patients, it felt like Gen and her colleagues were fighting a losing battle. I was introduced to partially sighted orphans who lived in the hospital and came running up to Gen as she arrived. The hospital staff cared for and supported them as best they could. They relied on nothing but the compassion of strangers. While I sat and observed their afternoon, two more children were effectively dumped at the hospital, disabled, abandoned and with very little hope for the future.

I then met a woman called Adanna, in hospital with her two children. Gen translated for me, speaking mostly Creole. I learned that Adanna couldn't afford to pay for their treatment, which was largely academic, as the hospital lacked the means to work out what was wrong with her. Gen was sure it was likely to be something curable, if they had the necessary tests and medicines. Despite this, Adanna remained hopeful, but although initially happy to talk to us, recounting her situation was incredibly emotional for her. At the end of our chat, almost as a passing remark, Adanna mentioned that she was actually a mother of nine, and that seven of her children had already died of unknown illnesses. Their father had abandoned them and, with no time to work, there was no food to eat for her remaining sick children. A few weeks later, Gen told me the heartbreaking news that these children, as well as many others I saw that day, deprived of proper healthcare, had died.

My experiences that day changed my outlook on everything in my world for ever. If nothing changes, eight out of ten children under five that come through those hospital doors will die. Talking more with Gen, I ascertained that about £90 could clothe, feed and educate each child for a year, and when I posted this story on social media there was an influx of people offering help. I did what I could, passing on donations to the hospital and individuals, but I came away knowing more was needed at an infrastructure and political level.

The politics in Sierra Leone and in Africa as a whole are as fragile as they are damaging. Many African nations are outrageously corrupt, and are often run by governments made of a handful of senior officials who are self-elected. Problems like unbalanced wealth, government-approved violence, lack of access to credit facilities, poor health facilities, and horrendous civil unrest are linked to lack of well-rounded governance and exploitation. Corruption is king, and it rules and ruins the continent. Manipulation of electoral processes (if there are any), the weakness of political parties and constrained societies, collectively has hugely disrupting consequences. Many individual men hold the power, wealth and freedom of others, which is a complex legacy of the colonial rule so many of these nations have lived under, and are still very much influenced by.

I've since set up the 196 Foundation to support communities around the world. By accumulating small donations from many people the aim is to support pockets of need around the world. £1.96 or $1.96 donated per month from eventually thousands of kind donors – we have the opportunity to make a big impact on those who need it the most. One project every year – all delivered without any of the donated money being spent on staff. At the time of writing, we are gearing up to gain support and funding for our first project. What's so remarkable and special about countries like Sierra Leone is the correlation between those without, and their want to give. Leaving Freetown was hard. It was back to the grind without my new friends and, still struggling to come to terms with what I'd witnessed, I was again feeling conflicted. On the one hand, putting what I was doing in the context of what I'd seen in Sierra Leone made everything all the more relevant; the run was for a specific charity, but also to be used as a springboard for community projects around the world. On the other hand, while I was travelling around the world virtually every person I set eyes on in those four days was more or less certain never to leave their own country.

Liberia, Ghana

I landed at Roberts International, which serves the capital of Monrovia, and, rather than taxi into the city, I stayed on the outskirts. I had just 24 hours here, so my dad and the team had made the good call of keeping me close to the airport, which I was pleasantly surprised to find was surrounded by sweeping hills and greenery – the perfect location for a run, with the sounds of heavy traffic replaced by the gentler accompaniment of birds and trees. The roads were quiet and I had my very own escort, thanks to the hotel manager Richard and his colleague Mark, who joined me as my drivers. Peace, and time to process everything that I'd experienced in Freetown, my footsteps underneath me, kids shouting hello, and water whenever I needed it – in these pleasant conditions, and with two extra rest days under my belt, Liberia did not feel like a marathon. I then took my happy and contemplative mood to Accra, Ghana, the last country in the second phase of Africa, after which I would need to pop back to the UK to pick up passports with my visas for the next 20 or so African countries. This was all about timing. There had been no point getting all these visas months ago, because now they'd be invalid. Maz and the gang at Universal Visas had had their work cut out, but had once again worked their magic to satisfy all the paperwork requirements for each of these countries. Ghana also gifted me an unexpected treat in the form of meeting a man called Alem, which was yet another humbling experience.

As mentioned, I always relied heavily on my calendar to tell me pretty much everything that was going on in my life while I was on the road. My assistant Carla, and later Veton, would add everything from accommodation, travel, visas, payments and news of any dangers to the calendar. It was my bible and my source of all the information I needed to plod on. Also inserted, of course, were the entries detailing where, when and whom I was running with. The calendar entry for marathon 49 in Ghana read: 'Alem to meet you in lobby at 07:30 a.m. Police motorbike support, water on bike, route unknown.'

So the following morning, still half asleep, I trotted down the stairs of the hotel to the lobby, a little late, but not by much. Nobody in sight. I did a quick circuit of the car park and then a lap of the building to try to spot anyone looking like they were looking for me. Nothing. A one-legged man in a vest, with crutches, approached me, and asked if I was Nick. Alem had been in the lobby the whole time. I'm ashamed to say I'd just looked straight past him because he lacked something that I generally associate with running: two working legs.

Once we had introduced ourselves, Alem, wearing a beaming smile, told me a little about his life while we waited for our support vehicle. Having survived polio, he spent the first ten years of his life crawling. He eventually learnt to walk with an aid, and then to cycle with modifications. He battled, suffered, trained and struggled, and eventually became world champion in the C2 class cycling event before competing in the 2012 and 2016 Olympic Games and was, back then, still scheduled to take to his wheels in Tokyo 2020. 'Ah, so he'll be cycling in support,' I thought. I was wrong again.

Although he could have hopped on a bike and cycled the whole thing, this would've been too easy for Alem, who opted instead to run ten kilometres with me. He crutched his way through the heat of the day, and I am not exaggerating when I say he was travelling so fast that I was struggling to keep up towards the end, as he powered through, gaining speed. His arms have more muscle than my legs, and he was sweating and hurting hard.

Alem is not only one of the nicest guys I've ever met, but he has an attitude I wish everyone had, including me. No challenge was beyond him, no obstacle too hard to overcome.

Along with Alem, Richard, who lost one of his arms in a road traffic accident ten years ago, cycled the entire route. A quiet and also very smiley guy, Richard stuck with me and held off traffic along with Nat, a police officer and fellow cycling club member who also joined our merry band. He helped immensely by holding off traffic at round-abouts and stopping cars from whizzing past me too close. Last, but certainly not least, was Victor, also a national cyclist and friend of the gang. He cycled in front of me, warning me of potholes and handing me water when I needed it. It was hot and humid, but it was a day I'll never forget.

My next flight took me back once more to the UK for an unavoidable embassy visit for a visa. After the disjointed and troublesome nature of the first African leg, the decision to divide the 54 countries of Africa into three smaller and more manageable chunks was feeling like the right one, and phase three of the trip (leg two of Africa) would take me from the still unpronounceable capital of Burkina Faso, Ouaga-dougou, around the west coast, all the way down to South Africa and then up the eastern side of the continent to Zimbabwe, covering off island countries like Madagascar and the Seychelles on the way. My route would take me through nearly all the coastal countries, leaving the central countries for the third leg of Africa much later in the journey – for the usual reasons: my health, sanity and visas. This phase was to be more pleasant, I hoped. The dangerous countries we'd put in the red column as part of the security breakdown were far fewer in this phase (only two of 17). I was looking forward to the pros-pect of more time off my feet and getting to see each country while I was awake.

That said, I spent most of my brief return to London in the Nige-rian embassy, handing over six months' worth of bank statements, fingerprints and full documentation outlining the journey, all of which had to be provided in person. The bank statements revealed lots of money going out all over the world. Not suspicious at all. Other more pointlessly bureaucratic stipulations like having every page of each statement signed by the bank manager amounted to little more than time-wasting security theatre, something I really didn't have the time or energy for mid-expedition.

With only a few hours left to sit around the kitchen table with my parents, and a few members on the team on speakerphone, we rattled through my current position. I had already missed Mali and Niger following the canine intervention, and these would have to be wedged into the calendar at some point. We put a pin in that for the moment – it would be expensive but not the end of the world. Chad and Angola we still didn't have visas for as they had now expired, due to the earlier delays. It was looking like they'd take too long to be issued to be attached to the correct passport, or at worst be refused. This was where pre-booking flights that required passport numbers became a real bugger. We were also still waiting on my Nigeria visa to be approved, having spent hours in the embassy submitting reams of documents. And on top of this, my visa application for Equatorial Guinea seemed to have gone AWOL, and we couldn't get a response from the embassy. I always knew it wasn't going to be easy to run a marathon in every country in the world in under two years. That Frantic Friday, as it became known, came to an end at 11.15 p.m. when I finished packing and got into bed for three measly hours of sleep. I now had the right passport but it was missing four visas. I hadn't achieved as much as I'd have liked. At 3 a.m. on 9th June we left the house for the airport. Day 155 – straight back to Africa.

Burkina Faso

Exactly 24 hours after leaving my own bed in little old Dorset, I landed in Ouagadougou, Burkina Faso. Country 50. It began to dawn on me that I really did enjoy living outside the much-referenced comfort zone. While I was still under no illusions about just how huge this challenge was, in some ways I had become more comfortable away from home than at home. I was in another crappy hotel, in a city I didn't know, but I had all my kit with me and, with a sort of exhausted elation, I smiled to myself as I fell asleep. I remember thinking, 'This is bonkers. And I have such a long way to go!'

I saw some pretty funny things on that run, most of them involving unusual things carried on motorbikes. Top of the list was a man riding side-saddle on a tiny moped with two sides of beef on his lap.

Travelling at less than walking pace, he was seated right at the back of the bike, reaching over most of a whole cow to grip the handlebars. Wearing flip-flops, his feet were scraping along the dusty road, rendering the moped almost incidental to his trip. Another chap was in the unusual position of travelling by motorbike whilst carrying another one as luggage, with a small motorcycle strapped to his back, the front tyre dangling to the left and the rear tyre sticking out into the passing traffic on the right. To top it all off, there was a family of five who had unwittingly formed a sort of motorized Von Trapp circus act. The mother was sitting right at the back of the moped, with three of her children sitting in front in height and age order, eldest at the front, driving. At the rear, Mum was pulling a pushbike along by the handlebars, upon which was balanced her youngest, a girl of around eight, completely oblivious to the danger, her tiny feet nowhere near the pedals. Forcing her peril from my mind, I smiled and wished myself a happy 50th marathon.

The fierce African weather had relented for a while, luring me into a false sense of security, with refreshing rain for the first 14 miles, but then normal service was resumed as the sun blazed down on me for the remainder of the run, in a deeply uncomfortable 46°C. I was sore and heavy footed for the last five miles, but it was another one down and another few steps closer to the finish line. Just another 519 days to go.

Togo

The following day I made my way to Togo on Air Burkina. The airline wasn't up to much, really – old seats, missing life jackets, and no food or water, plus the plane was clouded with mosquitos. I didn't care. My eyes were glued to the spectacular view below, my nose pressed against the tiny plastic window for most of the flight, as the breeze from the air-con chilled my neck. Like a shoelace draped across a quilt, a huge dry riverbed snaked through the patchwork of the planet below. Brown, orange, yellow and occasionally green, dotted with small fluffy clouds. Beautiful.

I was only occasionally reminded that we were travelling at great speed when the larger clouds buffeted the plane. I smiled to myself smugly as the shudder made some of the first-time and infrequent fly-ers sit up and grip the arms of their seats, while I went back to appreciating the view. By now I was hardened to flight turbulence, and even felt a bit short-changed after a smooth flight. Togo from the air was how I pictured Africa in my mind, pre-trip. Vast, empty, bleak, yet beautiful. The horizon was hazy; light blues seeped into darker blues as the huge sky reached for the stars. What a wonderful planet we have. And how wonderfully privileged I was to explore it.

My hosts in Togo were the lovely Karen and Jerome, who were ori-ginally from Belgium but had moved to Togo four years earlier before setting up their cute guesthouse, Ahomé –Maison d'Hotes de Lomé, just a brief walk from the beach. I was spoilt once again as they waited on me as if I was royalty, asking for nothing in return. My diary notes for that day read: 'No car, no driver, and no support . . . but also no need. I felt safe and able to explore. I jogged the first few miles to the Ghanaian border and then along the coast with the breeze in my face. I was planning to run from the Ghanaian border all the way along Togo's coast to the Benin border. I thought it would be interesting to run the length of the coastline, but I didn't quite make it because I'd underestimated the distance somewhat. I reached the 13-mile mark and wasn't close, so I turned back. It was hot, and that's something that I will never be comfortable with, although I'd rather be running in it than sitting in it. At least running you sweat more and create a little breeze that makes it slightly more bearable. The run felt a little longer than usual. I stopped many times to buy water and some sugar to keep me going. No music, no audiobook, no car behind me. Just me and the open road. It's quieter here than in other African countries to date, as well as cleaner and more orderly. The coastline reminds me of the Dominican Republic. I like it here. Love it, in fact.'

Benin

Sometimes it felt like I was just landing to get a connecting flight somewhere else, despite having to run 26 miles before doing so. I had one night in Cotonou, but with the marathon taking up a sweaty five hours, and factoring in time to eat, change, shower and pack, Benin was one of the countries where I felt like I didn't see much at all. When I was running well, and without pain, but was also tired and generally rundown, everything was a bit of a blur and stopovers and marathons would fly by. But the run was not without its moments, including a new mental note for future countries: confirm that the people running with me actually know what a marathon is.

My companions were a merry bunch of staff from the Posso Hotel, who had laid on a car for support. The car, full of bottled water, trundled behind, while Marie, a receptionist, ran with me. At mile four she asked when we'd stop. I laughed and assumed she was joking. She wasn't. The driver of the support car didn't understand the concept that I needed to run 42 kilometres either. Every now and then he'd ask me, 'Finished? Do you want to get in now and go to the hotel?' 'No, we still have 22 miles left.' And so it continued, with my replies gradually counting down the marathon distance. At mile eight Marie revealed that she had never run further than five miles in her life, but was very optimistically planning to stick with me to the end. After my lengthy lecture about the history of the marathon in ancient Greece, she became familiar with the concept, but was still grossly underestimating the distance. She didn't call it a day until 14 miles, though – an incredible effort, all things considered. I never saw her again.

The locals also got stuck in with frequent friendly heckles and the occasional jogger changing direction to join in for a few miles, or at least until the song finished – the support car was blaring out loud African music on speakers that sounded like they were full of broken crockery, and that was a beacon of interest in itself. We trotted to the finish along a gorgeous beach with crashing waves and clean white sand. One young child, around eight years old, with tightly curled brown hair, his huge smile full of gappy white teeth, waved enthusiastically as I ran past. I had to stop and say hi. We had very little to talk about, but his smile seemed to fill me with energy. It was this kind of small gesture, in such a beautiful spot, that made a difference to my days.

By now the heat had branded me with horrendous tan lines. After the Benin run, I took my running vest off to hang it over a chair to dry on the balcony. I caught a brief look at myself in the mirror. I was still wearing a white vest. Along with my sunglasses, my running kit had caused me to look like an unfinished painting-by-numbers picture. My tired scrawny body, now virtually devoid of muscle, looked ridiculous, with dark brown shoulders and a moon-white skeletal chest. I couldn't help but chuckle to myself. A country and a marathon without any hiccups. Was this a turning point? Nope.

Nigeria

Nigeria, specifically the city of Lagos, was a place I was more than a little apprehensive of. Having heard tales of extortion and violence, my preconception of Nigeria was one of corruption and lack of security. That said, I arrived feeling mildly positive, knowing I would have some support here, and not being a war zone, it could be worse.

It was day 163 and Father's Day back home, which meant time for a phone call. My dad was the person I could rely on to look at the bigger picture with an analytical eye, calculating various worst-case scenarios. On a superficial level, I found this eternally frustrating, not just on this trip, but in life generally. I'd always seen things more positively and tended to sweep potential problems under the nearest carpet. Dad would bring them into focus, by explaining how something so small like an extra day here or there or just one missed flight at the wrong time could cause havoc and make all the difference to the eventual success of the mission. He is a man of detail, precision and perfection, and it was exactly his approach that was needed. After all, growing up, I'd never make a decision without his opinion. Infuriating at times, but exceptionally valuable and absolutely essential on a journey like this. We spoke briefly and I did my best to thank him, but he was in re-plan mode and also on the landline phone to an airline, waiting on flight-amendment details. The work he did on the expedition never stopped, was unpaid, stressful and absolutely vital to completing the trip.

Phone call to Dad complete, it was time to run. In Nigeria, Dayo was our principal contact. A very well-decorated runner, this lovely Nigerian lady was keen to help and made her home and resources available to me. She owned a house a stone's throw from the city centre and, despite the fact she wasn't in the country at the time, allowed me to stay for two nights in her home. Her friends Suen and Queen were to look after me.

I set off running in the early morning, around an area just outside the main hub of Lagos, which was quieter and likely to be less dangerous. The marathon route was boring and dusty, but it was hassle-free and I had the company of some fantastic people. One in particular was a short 16-year-old lad called Peter Pan. I've seen his passport and his name really is Peter Pan. I ran with him, his running coach and a few of his friends. It was a lovely experience, and completely the opposite of my expectations of gang violence and robbery. I felt guilty for that.

Until my worst fears were realized.

Post-marathon, a few of the runners offered to take me on a sight-seeing tour and, despite my nervousness, I was by now in the habit of saying yes. We walked arm in arm through the main market, arm in arm apparently being the best way to avoid kidnappings, as it's not uncommon for locals to take tourists for ransom. With company for safety, I decided to take my camera. I hadn't considered getting mugged, I just didn't want to get kidnapped, mainly because it would mean missing countries and having to reorganize them. Such was my focus on the trip that I'd forgotten about the additional considerations of eternal imprisonment or death.

Lagos market is one of the biggest open-air markets in the world, not your average car-boot sale. The streets, sellers and everything in between were all permanent fixtures, with most walkways ankle-deep in mud. Sinister-looking back alleys were the only paths through the elaborate maze of knock-off watches, not-so-freshly butchered meat and livestock auctions, with any space in between blanketed with people, standing, sitting or lying. The whole place was a claustrophobic riot of chaos, noise and menace. You'd have more space right in front of the main stage at Glastonbury during the headline act. And you'd be a lot safer.

We were right in the heart of the market when, without warning, five men appeared from all sides with knives and guns. They were after my camera, plus anything else I had on me, which amounted to a few banknotes from Benin. One guy shoved me to the floor and wielded a knife in my face, shouting while two of the others pulled semi-automatic weapons from their jogging bottoms. I was kicked and shouted at aggressively. My heart rate shot up and I did all I could to hang onto my camera, curled in a ball on the floor, while the locals attempted to protect me. They did an incredible job of calming the situation and eventually appeased the gang momentarily with what little money they had on them, along with a few watches. By now, three more members of the gang had become involved and, as the circle of eight muggers around us broke up for a few moments to take the loot, I was instructed by one of my helpers, in a very immediate tone, to run.

Now run I can do. And I did.

My senses were on high alert and my body was shaking with fear and adrenaline as I fled. Sprinting is not really my thing and made me feel very unfit but, nonetheless, within seconds I was totally on my own in the middle of Lagos with an expensive camera and no sight of anyone I knew. I was conspicuously white, sweating from head to toe and gasping for breath. I have never before or since felt so vulnerable. It dawned on me that I was now probably even more exposed to danger than I had been a few seconds before. Shit. I had no phone, no map, no money, nothing except my mugger-magnet camera. I had been told to leave everything else in the car.

After the longest two minutes of my life, a familiar friendly face appeared and one of my new running friends grabbed my arm and pulled me through the crowds heading back to the car. However, instinct told me that we were going the wrong way and I started to panic again. My brain was working overtime, and I started to convince myself that this guy was part of the set-up and I was being kidnapped. It turns out he was just trying to help, but couldn't work out which way to go. Meandering through the streets as he held my wrist with a tight fist and a nervous look on his face, it felt like it took an age to reach the car. Rubble on the streets, the eyes of every single local piercing my skin, we eventually made it. We drove with the windows up and my head down, back through the noisy, busy and stressful streets to Dayo's place.

With very bruised ribs, which were later confirmed as fractured, I had a long sit on the bed to calm myself and process what had happened. The brutal kicking made me wonder, 'If this happens here, what about Mogadishu or Kabul?' What made the incident more alarming was the presence of two fully uniformed police officers, who stood idly by and watched the entire event take place. I was later told that the police mainly just enforce the good old 'no murder' rule, and not a lot else. I packed my bag, keen to get out of there. I still had 24 hours before my flight but I was ready to go. Needless to say, I wouldn't be venturing out again before heading to the airport, but at least it was over. Or so I thought.

Dayo's offer of a place to stay for a couple of nights was kind and genuine. Suen and Queen, the people trusted to look after me in her absence, were not. In their car, ready to leave for the airport, they presented me with a half-baked invoice demanding 1,100 US dollars for their 'hospitality'. When I say invoice, they had typed a few words into the notes App on their phones, informing me that somehow their time, mileage, plus a few bottles of water had put me in their debt by $1,100 (I guessed they'd added an extra hundred so it didn't look like they'd just pulled a round figure out of the air). Was this a joke? It wasn't. And so began a conversation which quickly progressed from awkward to heated to hostile on both sides.

Sat in the passenger seat with Suen driving and Queen in the back with her eyes fixed on me through the rearview mirror I was feeling intimidated to say the least. I was desperate to reach the airport and escape. The conversation came to a head when Suen slowed down. At this point I was already going to miss my flight and was livid. I said, with a snapped voice, 'We can't slow down, I'll miss my flight.' Suen had been driving fast and erratically to get me there on time (with a little aggression thrown in) but as he started to slow his driving and linger at traffic lights my heart sank. From their perspective they had spent time conning me for the past couple of days and were about to get paid. From mine, I just wanted to leave. I made the excuse that I couldn't use the cash I had because I needed it for visas (this happened to be true, but at the time it felt like a lie). Thinking on my feet, I made a deal and calmed the situation down by thanking them for the hospitality – totally insincere, of course; I was in a headstrong state of anger and desperation. I agreed to pay them – but it came with a deal. They had to get me to the airport on time. Once there and checked in, I would then call my team to make a bank transfer. No part of me thought that this obvious lie would work – but it was all I had. The other option was asking them to stop the car and get in an actual taxi to the airport – this I wasn't keen on either, mostly for safety reasons. A part of me knew that they knew I wasn't going to pay them – but I said, repeatedly, 'You must get me to the airport first. I must catch my flight.' The car fell silent as we started, once again, to speed through Lagos.

To cut a long story short, I didn't pay, and it all made for a pretty nervy and heated hour's trip to the airport. There was no way I could miss that flight.

I felt for a long while like I was the one ripping them off. I wasn't. Once out of the car, I grabbed my bag from the boot and ran to the airport door. I was the last to check-in – but I made it. Did I call my team to make a payment – yes, I did. But only for the amount that I actually owed them and nowhere near the $1,100 they'd tried to get their hands on. It was scary to be ripped off by the people I trusted, with the only way out to lie and be deceitful. I felt terrible – but I was safe at least.

Cameroon

After the ordeal in Nigeria, Cameroon's economic capital Doula was my sanctuary and home to my 54th marathon. Again, I was only there for less than 24 hours, but I made time to settle and reset, and running in the warm, windless rain I let my mind ponder everything that had happened. Running was my therapy. I was so relieved to be out of Nigeria and back to what I knew: the comfortingly familiar territory of dusty roads, constant car horns and smiling roadside vendors.

That night, post-run, and with my sweaty clothes drying and festering in the evening sun, I wrote my diary, went for a dip in the pool and had an early night, falling asleep in my nice safe hotel. My mood was high, all things considered. It had never occurred to me before to feel grateful for not having been mugged on a given day. What a difference a day makes. The routine of running an uneventful marathon in a strange new country was now given a rosy tint – positivity through relativity.

Flying out of Doula, I was heading for Equatorial Guinea. On the plane I jotted down some observations based on what I'd seen so far whilst running the streets of this incredible, vibrant, infuriating, wonderful, scary and surprising continent. Surprised by the positive reaction this got on social media, I turned these notes into a set of rules for getting by in Africa:

Rule One: You must own and drive a motor bike, regardless of age. It cannot be new, and it must have an annoying horn and several terminal defects.

Rule Two: Always sound your horn, especially when there is no reason to do so. A minimum of 500 times a day is suggested.

Rule Three: Never stop at traffic lights or wear a helmet. If you do wear a helmet it must be broken or unstrapped.

Rule Four: Regardless of your job, you are a taxi driver. If you have a car, the outside, including the bonnet, roof, boot and doors, is all available space for passengers.

Rule Five: No matter how many passengers you have, you will always have room for three more, especially when driving a motorbike.

Rule Six: When travelling on foot it is essential to wear open-toed sandals that are either a size too big or a size too small.

Rule Seven: If you are trying to attract someone's attention you are not permitted to use any words. A mouse squeak through pursed lips is the suggested method.

Rule Eight: You must never read the *Highway Code* and never give way to any human, animal, or other vehicle, especially at speed or at junctions.

Equatorial Guinea

Arriving in Equatorial Guinea I disembarked from my 82nd flight of the journey, and with another new country came another absurd scenario, culminating in five armed police officers in my hotel room, looking to arrest me. In my underpants. More on that shortly.

Initially, my experience of Malabo was one of pleasant surprise. In Africa, I'd got used to relentless swarms of mopeds and motorbikes whizzing past me, bumping into me, honking their horns incessantly; as well as the roads being busy with hustle and bustle, the smell of sewage and rubbish, potholes, kids washing in streams, and having 'white boy' chanted at me by passers-by. However, everything in Malabo was just different and I loved it.

On my 26.2 miles around the capital I ran down the middle of miles of deserted motorways and along overgrown forest paths. I saw fewer than 15 cars during the run, and felt the overwhelming sense that nature had won. Imagine a film set where they close roads to shoot post-apocalyptic scenes. It was like that, but real, bigger and nicer. I later found out that most of the peace in Equatorial Guinea derives from the discovery of oil and therefore a hike in GDP in the early 1960s which caused the country to shift from being one of the poorest to one of the wealthiest in West Africa. Malabo is quiet and peaceful and my mind was relaxed and at ease. I saw a grand total of zero motorbikes, at least 1,000 frogs, over 500 brightly coloured lizards, and thousands of birds. The trees were full of life. Running can be peaceful even when it's busy and hectic, but to be in the middle of a tropical wilderness, with wildlife engulfing everything from lampposts and bins to abandoned cars, was special. The noise of nothing was the best treat I'd had in months. It was another fantastic day.

A fantastic day, that is, until I rather Britishly refused to pay for meals I hadn't eaten. I was staying in a really crap hotel with staff that were either new or inexperienced or beyond incompetent. Arriving the previous night, I had frantically ordered a meal before a very late bedtime. Twice they tried to serve a meal that was not what I'd ordered. Twice I sent it back, and as time ticked on I finally gave up on trying to eat. As I tried to leave and go to my room for a shower and bed, I was accosted with a bill that I refused to pay. Anyone who knows me knows I'm not the type to shy away from things like this. Money was tight at the best of times, and this was a large chain hotel trying to charge me for something they knew I hadn't ordered or eaten. Mid-shower there was a knock on my door. I jumped out of the shower, put some underwear on and opened the door in a towel.

Five tall and grumpy-looking military men pushed their way into the room and questioned me, accusing me of stealing from the hotel. I hadn't stolen anything, I had simply refused to pay for something I hadn't had. The conversation continued and eventually I was threatened with jail if I didn't pay. I then started to suspect that this was likely to be another organized group set up to extort solo tourists. They knew that I knew this wasn't legit and, as the conversation continued, I began to question them, which wasn't a smart move and was likely to end in incarceration or a beating. As time dragged on, with the talking going round in circles, they gradually appeared to acknowledge what I was saying and, seeing that I was not going to give them any money, they simply gave up and went away. Victory was mine and I felt elated, until I remembered that I'd still had nothing to eat. Then any elation was completely squashed when, on attempting to check out of the hotel, the receptionist demanded I pay. I had used up all the fight I had in me, plus it was now dangerously close to the time of my flight, with less than an hour before takeoff. I had no choice. I gave in, paid and angrily left, with the words of Alan Partridge in my head: 'I'm going to absolutely rinse them on TripAdvisor.'

Funnily enough, several months later, chatting to a man (whose name I can't remember) at an airport (I can't remember), he told me he'd experienced a similar scenario at exactly the same hotel, confirming my suspicions. He was charged for a missing pillow. And so the peaceful, almost spiritual feelings I'd felt for this place had been tainted by greed and dishonesty.

Gabon, São Tomé & Príncipe

Before you continue reading, please be sure your window blinds are open, your seat backs are upright, and your tray tables are stowed. A hundred and seventy-four days in, and having clocked over 100 flights, I was now able to successfully recall the entire airline safety briefing off by heart, and in one go. From Equatorial Guinea, it was on to Gabon, and then São Tomé & Príncipe.

Libreville, Gabon, started badly after waking up to run and realizing my watch was out of battery and I'd have to wait at least an hour for an 80 per cent charge. It did mean I had a rather long sitting at breakfast, but with the downside that breakfast was just a platter of stale pastries. Once I finally did get going, it was a seaside coastal run typical of West Africa with the midday sun burning down on me. The run wasn't terrible but I was kicking myself for the watch mistake. I put a line through my tired brain and slept early after the exhaustion of the day. That was that. Gabon was ticked off, but I was in a grump with myself.

My journey from Gabon to São Tomé was a classic example of African air travel and something which I imagine most people don't realize: flights are very rarely direct in Africa. This journey took me from Gabon back to Togo, covering 978 miles over five hours' travel time. From Togo, there was a hot and frustrating wait on the tarmac before flying 135 miles to Ghana, by which time another four hours had passed, followed by the final leg from Ghana to São Tomé, 749 miles and five hours. That's 14 hours in total, with three check-ins, two bag collections, two aisle seats, one window seat, two different passports, two visas, zero meals, two naps, three stupid immigration form thingies and one mad rush.

That last connection was a close call and, even at this stage, would have resulted in serious impact on my overall schedule, had I missed it. Connecting to my final flight, on little to no sleep, I had just 42 minutes to get off the plane, stand in line at immigration, smile politely at passport control, show my vaccination card for the health check, fill in the stupid immigration form thingy, wait for my bag, go for an emergency wee, push my way through customs, exit the airport, run from arrivals to departures, find the check-in desk, check my bag back in (in a very sweaty state), push through security, fill out another stupid immigration form, find my gate, make it to the shuttle, shuttle to the plane, and endure the evil eyes of other passengers waiting for me to board, before finally taking off, exhausted, and not particularly looking forward to getting my running gear back on upon landing.

Once I finally arrived in São Tomé, I decided it was well worth the wait. I'd recommend this gorgeous island to anyone that wants to witness what life could be like without technology. Naturally, there were still pockets of the twenty-first century dotted about, but on the whole its simple living was bloody brilliant. The sun was out, the breeze in my face, the waves crashing. Everyone said hello, kids ran with me for a while, and the occasional group of fishermen even invited me in to watch them fillet fish or repair fishing nets. For a while I chatted to a bunch of boys with their handmade skateboards. The country speaks Portuguese and, as such, the conversation wasn't really working, but their smiles and gestures made it clear they wanted to proudly show off their skills.

One of my main logistical challenges was, of course, water. A human can't survive much more than three days without water. Running a marathon in this heat, I couldn't really last much more than six miles before my tongue was completely white and my mouth was dry and gasping. Once that happens, the body starts to crave water, the muscles are using all the wrong fluids and any post-run soreness gets worse. Despite my usual attempts at drinking more than I thought was necessary, my pee was nearly always more colourful than I'd have liked at the end of a run. Sometimes I drank eight litres, and still my body craved more. That day in the beautiful hills of São Tomé I spent the first 15 miles trying to find money in order to pay for water en route. The two banks didn't accept any of my cards, so no cash meant no water. The alternative was to repeatedly return to the hotel every few miles to drink from their supplies, and I didn't want to miss out on the beautiful scenery. On one of the very few countries in Africa that's actually an island, it seemed a shame not to explore the coast.

The hotel managed to reluctantly exchange some dollars and I skipped off to buy water. These dollars had lasted me for months as emergency cash for paying for things like bribes and unexpected transit visa costs. Problem solved, I spent the last 11 miles in bliss, on the coast. Legs fine, water on board, and the ocean by my side: a day without too many problems and I was in high spirits. The rollercoaster of emotions continued, but for the moment I was on the up, looking forward to a well-earned day off in Namibia. No running – and no flights.

Namibia

I arrived in Namibia via another series of convoluted flight connections, and marathon 58 was to be an early morning loop around the outskirts of the capital, Windhoek. It came with a sudden and serious temperature drop. On most of mainland Africa, I experienced an average temperature in excess of 40°C. Landing into Windhoek, up at 5,500 feet, it was four degrees below freezing, and I was underprepared. In our planning we had missed this one – we'd simply overlooked the altitude, which obviously causes a drop in temperature. Even so, they'd had a particularly hot front in the months prior which somehow had been balanced out by an extra cold spell. Being July, the height of the southern winter, we weren't expecting anything less than 5°C but it was below that in the early morning.

I reached for the bedside light at 5.30 a.m. I had been blissfully cocooned in my fluffy duvet, forgetting that when I woke up I would be able to see my breath, it was so cold. With half-closed eyes, I reached for my gear as usual. As my eyes began to adjust I could see frost on the ground outside, and it was clear I couldn't wear my usual kit. I emptied my bag and found a jacket and leggings. No hat or gloves, though, so I'd have to improvise with socks as mittens and a hotel flannel in my pocket to wear under my cap as an insulating layer.

I waited a while for the bunch of runners who were supposed to be running with me. For the first time on the trip, I was let down by all of them. Nobody turned up and nobody contacted me to say they wouldn't be there. A bit disappointed, I set off on my own in the dark. The morning was crisp, quiet and beautiful, with the sun slowly peeping over the mountains. I devised a route around the entire city following a mountain pass and a ring road. The haze of the morning reminded me of early mornings spent skiing, with the heat of the sun and the cold of the wind chill. I loved that run. I spent most of it daydreaming about skiing and being in the mountains. Despite my yearning for snow, the views were stunning. What a morning. I was back in time to catch the end of breakfast service.

Due to the pre-dawn start, and the fact that I didn't have a flight to catch the next day, I wasn't sure what to do with myself. After a quick chat to some locals and a few experienced travellers, I ventured out up into the mountains.

Dressed in close to nothing, and living in straw huts, the San people, otherwise known as Bushmen, are members of various Khoisan-speaking indigenous hunter-gatherer groups who live off the land across southern Africa. I spent several hours learning how they live, hunt and make fire. They were welcoming, didn't ask for anything, and were happy to have an interpreter relay everything to me. Their mother tongue sounded, to my untrained ear, like a series of clicking noises made at the back of the throat. I learned that there is a significant linguistic difference between the San of Namibia and, say, those in Botswana or South Africa. In the middle of the Namibian bush the San showed me their complex hunter-gathering techniques, including a demonstration of how they track animals and people. I was invited to hide in the bushes and to be silent and still. I did just that – although I was within a few hundred metres of their camp they had no idea in which direction I'd headed but found me within minutes. They offered the same exercise again but with my guide hiding and me observing. Much like many of the tracking segments of TV shows, I witnessed first-hand how their use of smell and extraordinary eyesight can find small breaks in branches and imprints in the dry soil. It took a while longer to find my guide and without the interpreter I was left following things through hand signals rather than words. Once found and back at camp, they demonstrated a fire being lit from twigs and flints. This was something they managed in min-utes using their young children as wind shields around the pile of sticks. When I attempted to start a fire nothing but frustration, dust and cramp in my hand resulted.

The colours of brown, orange and cream of the surrounding straw-like crops were a delight. Wearing nothing but a small selection of foliage around their waistline, the San live without most things I take for granted – and yet are as happy and content as anyone I know – and in many things, more skilled. I was left in awe at their way of life and conscious of how the twenty-first century, my relative wealth and west-ern culture had molded mine.

The following day started with a long drive north into the bush. I had 24 hours to kill before I'd leave for Lesotho, and I decided to go in search of animals. First stop at 8 a.m., just an hour out of the city, was a small private game reserve, where black and white rhino were being rehabilitated from recent poaching attempts. It was off season and close to empty. A small private tour took me through the enclosed wilderness, past giraffes, warthogs, zebra and rhinos. A large female white rhino walked towards us and stopped just two feet away, so close that I could smell her and hear her slow, steady breathing – three and a half tons of powerful, prehistoric-looking beauty. As I admired her placid majesty, I realized I had a big silly grin on my face to greet the unicorn of the savanna.

I felt like I was on a roll, and asked my very patient hotel driver to take me somewhere we could see cheetahs. In an attempt to keep me sweet and earn some extra money, he called around to friends, and friends of friends, to find a guide and the best spot to take me. The western world survives on the use of the internet. I was learning that elsewhere human networks were far more useful. We travelled along a long and bumpy dirt road, during which time I fell asleep with my head rattling on the side of the car for a couple of hours. By 2 p.m. we had pulled up alongside a white jeep and I was introduced to a chap in his late thirties or early forties, quietly spoken, who came across as both nonchalant and professional in his camouflage gear, with a rifle slung over his left shoulder as if it were a handbag. We walked for about 20 minutes and, as we approached the brow of a hill, he said to

me, 'I'm going this way, you go that way. We may not see any cheetahs, but if you do, just shout. I have a gun. Oh, and watch for snakes.
You don't want a snake bite.' I didn't particularly want a cheetah bite
either but I was now more concerned about huge man-eating snakes.
I needed my legs intact for this little run around the world I was in the
middle of.

I was really not expecting to see any big cats at all, I was just hopeful that maybe I was in with a chance, and it was worth spending the
rest of the day trying. About 40 minutes into a blissfully quiet wander
through the knee-high grass and dry bushes, I heard a rustle off to my
right. Not loud, but not far away. Something was definitely there. I
stopped, listened for a while, looked around, and waited – nothing.
Nothing but the sound of birds in the distance. Just as I was about to
continue walking, I did one last visual sweep of my immediate surroundings, mainly to check for snakes.

And there she was.

Not a snake, but a cheetah. Totally still and her eyes fixed on me. A
massive surge of adrenaline shot up through my body until my fingertips
tingled. My guide's advice – 'If you see a cheetah, just shout' – suddenly
seemed utterly absurd. There was not a big cat in hell's chance I was
making a noise. I had practically stopped breathing.

For a brief moment I made peace with myself – this was it. I was
going to die at the hands, or paws, of a cat. I was terrified. Thinking
of my options, I reached slowly for my phone. If I was going be eaten,
I at least wanted to capture it on video. It would make great footage
for the documentary, generate a big donation spike if it went viral. I
nervously pointed the camera at her and waited. Within ten seconds
it was all over. She just walked right past me, and I mean so close that
her fur brushed my jeans. Presumably I had by now become too
scrawny to make it worthwhile biting into.

I later found out that although cheetahs aren't picky when hungry,
they're not keen on the taste of people and generally don't see us as
prey. To make the whole encounter feel even more like a dream, when
I found my guide (once shouting became an option again) and told
him about it, he didn't believe me. It was only when I showed him the
video that he laughed in shock. 'You are so lucky, so lucky, so, so

lucky. To be that close is very special. You should have called me over,' he said.

My adrenaline was still through the roof and I talked incessantly at my driver for the entire journey back to the hotel. It was late, and once it wore off, I fell asleep in my clothes.

Lesotho

Due to some passport logistics it was to be a brief stop-and-go in the mountains of Lesotho. The smooth flight in from Namibia via Jo'burg mirrored my calm, peaceful state of mind. I woke up from a few hours' sleep mid-air, wiped the sleepy dust from my eyes, yawned, and squinted out of the window into the morning sun. A white sea of perfectly flat, light and fluffy clouds was my highway for the next 600 kilometres. With a clear day and clear air, the plane glided peacefully and effortlessly over the smooth mattress of clouds. The words 'cruising at 37,000 feet' were a perfect description of what we were doing.

Upon landing and exiting the airport with my grubby bags over my shoulder, I was met by two different people, both holding signs with my name on. This was new. We had somehow ballsed up and found two hotels willing to give me free accommodation, but failed to cancel one of them. There was a brief discussion, and Griffin, the owner of a guesthouse, explained, with heartwarming honesty, that the other hotel was far nicer and I should probably stay there. As if this wasn't enough he then, despite me passing on the offer to stay in his guesthouse, offered his entire day to be my support driver for the run. Deeply touched, I accepted. The hotel I ended up staying in was a small collection of yurt lodges in the mountains. They were basic, but it was a beautiful place. I quickly changed and got my trainers on. I had energy and was keen to get the run done, to give myself an extra day off. The cheetah and hanging with the San people in Namibia had made me want to take any opportunity to squeeze in a bonus day.

Griffin was English-speaking, from South Africa, and so we chatted for a while and I explained it would be nice to have some photos of me running. He jumped at the chance to help and subsequently took over 2,000 photos and videos during the marathon that day, as I ran along dramatic sweeping roads in the hills, around the northern town of Maseru. It was all by chance that everything happened the way it did, but once again, I was benefiting from the selflessness of strangers. One of the photos he took is now the front cover of this book, and we're still in touch today. Griffin, you are a brilliant human being.

Lesotho is a country not on the tip of everyone's tongue. As you look at the country of South Africa on a map, Lesotho is one of two nations nestled within it. It's hard to see without zooming in, but what it lacks in size it makes up for in beauty. The mountains are vast, the hills long, and the silence deafening. All I could hear were the occasional sounds of cows, birds, goats and the distant clang of the bells hung around the necks of livestock as they sauntered through their day. The palette of this land is full of dark oranges and glowing browns, delineated by the black of the new Chinese tarmac road that runs the length of the barren landscape. The rocks and cliffs that break up the flat were mesmerizing. There was no town out here, just tiny farms consisting of a few small but homely-looking huts made of mud, concrete and sticks, with half a dozen cattle and clothes hanging on washing lines. Kids played with old tyres and sticks. I could see shepherds and cattle herders strolling through the fields so slowly they barely seemed to be moving. A cloak of heavy, coloured wool and a large staff was all they carried. It was cold, only about two or three degrees. I ran with a permanent smile on my face. Empty space, and peace. I loved Lesotho. The evening was crisp and still as the sun set around the hills, long light reaching every corner of the valley. I could see my breath as I ran and heard only my feet underneath me. Occasionally I would stop and stand in the middle of the road just to hear the sound of nothing. This is why I run! I was on an extreme high made possible by the kindness of others and the beauty of our planet.

South Africa

Day 185 was a Tuesday, not that days of the week meant anything to me any more; the world was my office now, but it was a Tuesday nonetheless. It was the second day of week 27 on the road, and the first of a wonderful ten-day break of discovering the wilderness and wildlife of South Africa. I flew into Johannesburg but connected immediately for a flight to Cape Town where I hired a car. Me being me, I wasn't going to rest too much in this rest time. Instead, I decided to spend a few days driving the famous Garden Route, a 300-kilometre stretch of the southern coast of South Africa, extending from Witsand in the Western Cape to the border of Tsitsikamma Storms River in the Eastern Cape.

After a brief stop at a penguin-covered beach near the Cape of Good Hope, I set off on my mini-adventure, stopping in any cheap motel or B&B I could find. I did as I was told and rested my running legs, but nobody said I couldn't drive, kayak, swim or hike, so everything else was a go in my eyes. I wanted to make the most of the diversity of land-scapes, wildlife and cultures. In those six days of hopping from one place to the next, I was fortunate enough to visit four game reserves and lay eyes on the big five multiple times, along with dozens of other equally worthy animals, stayed a night at the most southerly point of the entire continent and spent an entire day kayaking on a quiet reed-fringed river. Camp fires, new travelling friends, great food, and no bloody airports. South Africa fast became a firm favourite.

The day I visited Robben Island would have been Nelson Mande-la's 100th birthday. While I drove I listened to his autobiography, and learned further of his sacrifice and will. While Apartheid may have officially ended in the 1990s, racism and a strong racial divide were more evident here than anywhere I'd ever been. Anyone who has ever made light of racism should visit the island. I was shown around by a guy who, like many others, was locked up for five years for no other reason than the colour of his skin.

After a few days of no running, I decided that, rather than travel-ling all the way to Durban to run my South Africa marathon on the famous Comrades Route, I couldn't miss the opportunity of a glori-ous run around the islands of Knysna, 34 degrees south of the Equator and 55 kilometres east of the city of George on the N2 highway, a highway I was now very familiar with.

Marathon done, I joined a whale-watching tour, and after a couple of hours of waiting around eight miles off the coast, our reward was a stunning encounter with a family group of four humpbacks. Even if you've never watched whales surface to breathe before, the sound of their exhalations feels so familiar from the endless wildlife documentaries we've all seen. But something I hadn't considered before was a whale's 'footprint' – apparently, this is how the mark left on the surface of the sea by a submerging whale is often described. The glassy, smooth patch of ocean where a large whale recently surfaced, caused by the vortex generated by their tail flukes, can remain visible for three or four minutes after the whale has disappeared, and can be used to track them. We watched these mesmerizing animals until they disappeared and the boat's gadgetry tracked them deep into the ocean, heading on a course that would eventually take them towards Antarctica. As soon as the four-hour whale-watching tour ended, I immediately joined the next one.

I drove a further 200 kilometres east, heading for Port Elizabeth. Vast orange farms lined either side of the empty highway, polka-dotting the blankets of rolling green hills with splatters of orange. I must have passed literally billions of citrus fruits. Power lines stretched high above the road and disappeared into the distance, drawing me towards the horizon. Music on, windows down, wind in my hair – my now very knotty and long hair.

Reaching the airport, I dropped off the little car and flew back to Jo'burg. From there I picked up another car and, tired but still exhilarated, drove for five hours to the legendary Kruger National Park. Crocodile Bridge Safari Lodge was to be home for my last three nights in the country. The lodge was a luxury tent with a hefty communal barbecue, or *braai* as the South Africans call it. The compound backed onto the park, and each morning I awoke to the sounds of lions, rhino and cheetahs patrolling close to the bridge that connected the park with the big wide world. It was a great mix of the familiar picture-book animals and the less photographed characters: lions, baboons, hippos, vervet monkeys, white rhino, giraffes, warthogs, elephants, kudu, buffalos, wildebeest, duikers, impala, striped skinks, brown snake eagles, hornbills, crested barbets, zebra, mongooses and crocs. The list was endless. I also witnessed a nail-biting standoff between a lion, a crocodile and an antelope. For the antelope it was clearly going to hurt.

Botswana

Goodbye luxury Africa. Back to real Africa. Back to business. Back to tiny, shoddy-looking planes, filling in immigration forms, standing in slow-moving queues and waiting for luggage. In reality, Botswana was surprisingly pleasant. The feeling of Botswana in the most part is laidback and calm, far less hectic than the Africa I'd began to know well. Mostly, this calm feeling was due to the nature and the scale of the place. With a population of only two million, and most of that sum residing around the capital and a handful of cities, the outskirts were full of nature, greens and space – which so many of the cities in Africa lack. In terms of health, my legs were rested, my mind at peace – I had found my balance. The running was becoming easier, and I was well versed in, and dare I say, more tolerant of the frustrations of African customs, in both senses of the word 'customs'. I felt slightly unwell and sluggish, but this was just down to my excessive meat intake at the Kruger *braai*, and nothing to complain about. Running alone, through empty city streets and out into deserted scrubland and dirt roads, with the straight tracks of the railway line disappearing into the dawn, was unexceptional but that suited me just fine.

Zimbabwe and Eswatini (Swaziland)

On the morning of 1 August I ventured out along the banks of the Zambezi river with a friend and client who I coached for a while. Her name is Wen, and she came out especially to run with me. We stopped off at a local shop, with our driver, Emmanuel, and filled the car with bottles of water and snacks and headed out into the heat of the day. We spent 99 per cent of the marathon running through the national park, alongside Victoria Falls, with Emmanuel patiently following behind. With the sound of the water roaring over the falls, throwing up a fine mist overhead, we ran just feet away from elephants, monkeys, impala, kudu and warthogs. It was all very distracting, and just when I thought I had this running thing down I fell flat on my face, the first time while running at speed. Fortunately, my Jedi-like reflexes meant I escaped with grazed hands, knees and chin. I was sore, but relieved to be in one piece. I was on a perfectly flat road. I blame the view.

No small part of which was the Zambezi river, a sinuous lifeline serving African communities for thousands of miles. At Victoria Falls the river acts as the border between Zambia and Zimbabwe, with a rickety wooden bridge separating the two – the bridge that crazy people choose to jump off and plummet head first towards the river below. Three months earlier a bungee jump had infamously failed when a woman dived off the bridge to what was, miraculously, not her death. The bungee cord snapped at the end of its extension, and she simply plopped into the crocodile-infested water, where she was pulled to safety by locals. Anywhere else in the world this would have resulted in the closure of the business while a full investigation took place and preparations were made for litigation. But this was Africa, the snapped cord was hastily hidden in the nearest bin and bungee-jumping was back up and running by the time I got there. I'm terrified of heights, but I calculated that my odds were good, given that the new elastic band was less than three months old, and in the spirit of saying yes to as much as I dared, I decided to give it a go. I wanted to feel what it was like to fall for that distance – in my head, a metaphor for taking the plunge into this whole adventure. They wrapped my legs in towels, fastened me in, told me to stand up and jump. In that instant, I was surprised to find that all my fear and nerves had gone, replaced by a sort of blind resignation. Despite my life being in the hands of some blokes on a bridge, I jumped.

I wasn't overly wowed by the experience, due to it lasting only about five seconds while the long queue to jump felt like weeks, but the sense of having survived gave me a high that was still with me as I headed for Eswatini, one of the two countries that changed names during the trip, as if things weren't complicated enough already.

Eswatini, formerly Swaziland, came and went pretty quickly. My memory, prompted by the photos I have to hand, reminds me that Eswatini, marathon 63, mirrored most of this part of Africa: pale green to burnt-yellow palms edging dusty orange earth roads, sweet-corn cooking over open fires and a distinctly African sign that read 'DANGER! Animals Crossing, No Fences 60 kilometres'. My chosen route through the Hlane Royal National Park could be interesting, as the image that accompanied the sign wasn't the horse or cow that I am used to from back home, but instead a lion.

Mauritius

A country I had been looking forward to, and I wasn't disappointed.

An African nation, Mauritius is situated about 2,000 kilometres off the south-east coast of the African continent in the Indian Ocean. Still closer to Africa than Asia, it feels, smells, sounds and looks like India.

The Be Cosy Hotel in the north-west of the island hosted my stay. Fronted by a palm-fronded white sand beach, it is everyone's idea of the perfect location and tempted me into running 80 per cent of the marathon along the surf line. The only downside was the packs of dogs sleeping in the sun as I ran past. I love dogs, but Tunisia had made me wary. These dogs, lulled by the heat, stayed asleep thankfully. I had an ice cream mid-run, which was becoming a recurrent theme whenever possible, then finished the 26.2 miles by running straight into the bathwater-temperature sea. I had a couple of rest days built in, in case of rescheduling or other calamities, and I used them wisely – surfing, swimming, kite surfing and making the most of this spectacular island. I left with regret, feeling that this treat was part of the balance for those other 'not so good' experiences on the road.

Madagascar

Perhaps thanks to DreamWorks, Madagascar, the world's fourth-largest island, was not what I was expecting, and in sharp contrast to Mauritius it provided the kick up the backside any pampered west-erner needs. Whilst further afield the island has idyllic, picture-postcard spots teeming with animals, with only two nights here I would be in the heart of the capital, Antananarivo, a poor but hard-working city, with brick-making one of the main industries. It was a familiar blend of poverty, chaos, dust, smiles and busy roads. It was impossible to run fast – the potholes, traffic, cobbles and fumes put a stop to that – but I also wanted to take it slowly to get some good photos. I took over 500, mostly of families and kids grinning dazzlingly white ear-to-ear grins, smiles that still make *me* smile to this day. I previously hadn't made the connection between poverty and white teeth, but it struck me here: how was it that people living in such poverty had such sparkling white teeth? The answer is obvious: because they can't afford to eat anything that degrades teeth – no sugar, no sweets, no chocolate. Around 70 per cent of people in Madagascar live on less than $1 a day. It's one of the poorest places in the world and, just like in Sierra Leone, I had been made to feel so welcome and safe and witnessed only kindness from everyone. Having spent a few hours dodging lorries, cars, motorbikes, chickens and piles of rubbish, I finished marathon 65 with brick dust in my eyes, covered from head to toe in dirt, my lungs full of exhaust fumes and smog from the wood fires that line the streets.

Before leaving the country I made time to go all tourist and visit a part of the island where all 115 different species of Madagascar's lemurs can be found, although I only saw six up close. While the ring-tailed lemurs are your classic Hollywood lemur, the others were actually more fun. I particularly liked the dancing sifaka lemurs, who were very energetic, despite looking like wizened old men. I walked through forests of enormous bamboo shoots, many species of which were endemic to Madagascar, feeling like a miniaturized human walking across a lawn. Emerging from the forest and trekking along a riverbank, I saw some of the island's iconic baobab trees and also traveller palms, named for their usefulness to travellers, with their ability to store huge amounts of clean water in their trunks. High in the canopy, I saw the huge nests of the hamerkop – dome structures made of intricate layers of intertwining twigs and leaves to hide them from predators. On the way back we passed a radiated tortoise. I think tortoises are my spirit animal. That's it, guys, keep going. Slow and steady wins the day.

My flight was approaching, I was eventually forced to down my camera and, after a long traffic jam on a nervy journey to the airport, I made it with just ten minutes to spare. By now planes were like buses to me – I just turned up and jumped on them. I was well and truly done with pointless queuing to board, and I'm ashamed to admit that, depending on my mood, I'd often wait to be called by name to the plane. If you were ever sitting on a full plane waiting for the doors to close and you saw me in flight-diva mode, last to board – sorry.

Seychelles

The Seychelles is a much-dreamt-about destination and is made up of 115 islands. I flew into the capital Victoria, so named I supposed because it was part of the British empire and only gained its independence in 1976. Any anticipation was dampened by the dodgy feeling in my gut which meant the first day in paradise was spent close to the bathroom. The following day, the run day, I felt much better, which was fortunate because the British embassy staff and minister for sport had amassed a group of ten to run with me and had organized the route and water stations. Paradise indeed.

Caron became the first British diplomat to run with me and she stayed alongside for ten miles. Ana and Geno, both seasoned runners, kept me company for the rest of the way as others gradually dropped out. We chatted as we ran past beautiful beaches and crashing waves. Run complete, I did a couple of interviews before heading over to the high commissioner's residence where I met the Seychelles swim team over lunch and was dropped back to my hotel by Dean, Theresa and their coach who were all part of that team. I had a couple of rest days built into the schedule, mainly due to flight timings, so the next day, with Theresa as my guide, we hiked over the Mahe mountains, alive with the island sounds of birds and running water.

The expedition was now attracting a fair bit of attention, with a lot of interest from media and fellow runners, and countless messages from people sharing their sad but so often inspiring stories of living with cancer. I felt like the limelight was on me personally, while my

Above: My first running group, sheltering from the minus 25°C temperatures in Toronto, Canada.

Right: Visiting an orphanage in Haiti.

Below: The finish line in El Salvador, where my hosts had organized a fantastic run complete with specially made medals.

Left: In Guatemala, with Mt Fuego erupting as we ran around it.

Below: Watching the sunrise over the tin shacks in La Paz, Bolivia.

Bottom: A young girl sells fabric with her mum in the mountains of Peru.

Above: The North Korean skyline. Simultaneously colourful and bleak.

Below: I join in with the annual celebrations in Pyongyang.

Above: A warm welcome to Africa. Local fisherman pose for a photo in Gambia.

Left: Learning to be patient, at a typical overland immigration booth in Gambia.

Below left: Passengers on the very busy and very dangerous ferry crossing into Gambia.

Below right: Alem, a paralympian C2 cyclist, crutched 10km with me at an impressive pace in Ghana.

Left: In Lesotho a young boy rushes to school as I run past (**below**).

Bottom: Surveying the world from the top of Table Mountain in Cape Town.

Above: Back in colder climes, with Duncan, Mike and Jay in Iceland.

Below: Switzerland – catching up on sleep on the way to start the run around Lake Zurich.

Above left: Pakistan. A wet busy run through the streets of Islamabad.

Above right: The magnificent Sultan Qaboos Grand Mosque in Muscat.

Right: Taking on the Bosnian wind, rain and snow with great company.

Below: Running along the beach in Oman.

Above: A little boat trip in Ḥa Long Bay, Vietnam.

Below left: In the Philippines a group of kids want a photo mid run.

Below right: Talking with fellow running fans in a local stadium in Laos.

Preparing to run the mountains of Kazakhstan.

team beavered away in the background, invisibly and anonymously. I sat on white sand at sunset on my last night of the phase and it crossed my mind that maybe I'd been having too much fun, taking too much time out of my otherwise relentless schedule. Would this cause problems down the line? Longer stays in countries like South Africa had always been factored in, not just out of necessity for rest and recovery, but to allow time for travel arrangements and lengthy access requests to be processed for places like Libya, Iran and Bhutan. And, as it turned out, some small but significant problems were cropping up back at the ranch – a couple of airlines had gone bust, planned flight routes had been scrapped and a couple of visas had been refused. But sitting on the beautiful beach in the Seychelles, I was blissfully unaware of these issues, and I soaked up the last few moments of paradise before rinsing off the sand, stuffing my dirty clothes and kit into my bag, minus the now empty sun cream bottles, and heading for London.

4

Making Tracks

Spain	Iceland	Finland
Andorra	Ireland	Russia
France	Malta	Estonia
Monaco	Croatia	Latvia
Italy	Belgium	Lithuania
Vatican City	Netherlands	Belarus
San Marino	Switzerland	Ukraine
Germany	Liechtenstein	Moldova
Czech Republic	Luxembourg	Romania
Austria	Denmark	Poland
Slovakia	Norway	
Hungary	Sweden	

23 August 2018. Halfway through Africa. I was in good spirits as I landed at Heathrow, but I was soon to be brought down to earth with a bit of a bump. The two days I was expecting to be at home had turned into four, thanks to my parents arranging for me to be home on my birthday, as a surprise present. The other surprise they'd kept from me, to avoid causing me anxiety, was the growing list of things that had started to go wrong, not least the fact that we were running out of money. Fast.

To top it off, when I wasn't working on the remainder of the route in the Yellow (increasingly Orange) War Room with Dad, sitting in long queues at embassies, sorting kit or doing interviews (I had 19 over four days), I was battling one of those heavy colds that inevitably pop up when you have a few days off and your brain says to your immune system, 'Hey, you've been putting in the hours lately, have a break!' More red tape and bureaucratic bullshit. I'm aware that the overarching principle behind this kind of officialdom is security, but it was occasionally difficult not to answer questions like 'Why do you want to go to Iran?' with 'Because it's a country.' Travelling on the tube, I was also reminded of my old life in finance, the life from which I'd escaped. Looking around at the obsessively coiffured hair, patent leather, bamboo-framed glasses, tie-pins and laptops, it all felt very sterile and superficial. Office workers travelling on London Underground have, in their attempts at dressing to impress, unwittingly crossed the line between noticeable and ridiculous. One man seemed to be trying to tick every aspirational box: laptop, waistcoat, brightly coloured socks, pin-striped shirt, *those* glasses and a bluetooth earpiece. He was having a loudly self-important phone conversation about his upcoming purchase of a Mercedes, occasionally glancing around to see who was impressed. We were on the DLR (Docklands Light Railway), and I prayed for a tunnel. The poverty I'd witnessed among the disadvantaged communities I'd visited was still fresh in my mind, and I tried not to judge my fellow tube passengers for not appreciating how lucky they were and, instead, smiled inwardly as I reflected on how lucky *I* was.

I had 34 marathons in 34 countries during the next leg, taking me all the way through autumn to Christmas. All were European, most would be warm, but a few very cold; from the relative ease and familiarity of Italy and France, to less-visited places such as Ukraine and Belarus. It was my chance to reach a massive milestone: 100 marathons in 100 countries in less than a year. On the day I left for Spain, country number one of the phase of 67 overall, the team and I still had no idea if it was possible, but if we were to stay on track to finish in Athens on 10 November the following year, we had to try.

My bag was packed: three power packs, two GoPros, my Spot Gen GPS tracker, laptop, headphones, Garmin and Suunto watches, the SkyRoam Wi-Fi box, drone, many batteries, toothbrush, iPad, wallet, back-up wallet, my phone, emergency phone, notepad and pen, both passports, SD cards, spare bags and emergency pair of boxers just in case I ended up with the shits again and was more than a short sprint from the nearest convenience. Oh, and my Dictaphone, to help me make notes for this book. Although that list seems long, and doesn't include all the things I needed for running – like clothes, socks, hats, sunglasses, sun cream etc., etc. – I was actually travelling very light for the next phase, with just a few lightweight winter items curled up at the bottom of my backpack ready for the cold ones. I was now managing with two small backpacks, one for electronics and one for clothes and essentials, like my trainers, the sixth pair of the trip.

By now, you'll be aware that this wasn't an all-expenses-paid package tour managed by an operator who took care of everything. Via the wonders of WhatsApp, my assistant Carla, Maz and Faisal from Universal Visas, security consultants, my UN contacts, friends, family and I all sat down around a virtual table, with a world map and all manner of paperwork to hand. My mum made notes, and chaired the call. Item 1 on the agenda was a biggy: funding. One of the little concerns my parents had decided not to burden me with in Africa was that the money had run out. The £100,000 we had budgeted for the expedition, including every penny of my savings, the small sponsorship pot and the £20,000 my parents had kindly loaned me, had been swallowed up. I was already over budget, a third of the way through the expedition.

Digging through card statements, it was clear that there wasn't a single cause for the overspend; everything was just costing more than expected. I'd hoped to be offered more free accommodation as a result of hundreds of begging emails; we hadn't factored in paying for taxis and drivers; and certain visa fees were much higher than anticipated. We'd also budgeted far too conservatively for food, partly because it simply cost more than we thought, and also because of the number of calories I was having to put away to be able to run. I was already 12 kilos lighter than when I started, and for a 6-foot man (who likes to mix imperial and metric), 55 kilograms was already unhealthily underweight, especially with 130 marathons ahead of me.

As I left the UK, the possibility that this trip wouldn't be sustainable, felt, for the first time, very real.

Spain, Andorra

The plan was to travel by rail around western Europe, meaning no flights for a month. I landed in Barcelona with Dani, a good friend of mine, who had ditched work for four weeks to join me on the road and act as cameraman. Dani hadn't seen much of Europe, so was looking forward to some country-hopping. I was a little tentative, as Dani is a very laidback character, and I wasn't sure if he had any idea what he was letting himself in for.

Europe felt familiar, local and neighbourly. Arriving in Barcelona at 6 p.m., we were met by a lovely lady called Rowena. There was something very warm-hearted about Rowena, and we bonded instantly. She drove us the 30 minutes from the airport to her stunning home in the mountains, from which the view was jaw-dropping. Back in Barbados, several months earlier, when I had my 2 a.m. radio interview with Chris Evans on his BBC breakfast show, little did I know then, but Rowena was listening and got in touch with the team. In fact, with Europe's

large running community, the team were now being contacted frequently with requests for interviews and offers of accommodation,
which would certainly help with the financial situation.

After a quick change, we went out to dinner, where we met Mauri,
the maître d', who not only served us some of the tastiest risotto I've
ever eaten, but would also be accompanying me for 26.2 miles around
the hills on the outskirts of Barcelona.

Woken early by the weather, we sleepily counted the gap between
lightning and thunder as the storm moved overhead, until eventually
lightning struck Rowena's house, and we collectively jumped back from
the large floor-to-ceiling window. It was 6 a.m. and still dark and gloomy
outside. Dani, Rowena (Ro) and I looked down the valley towards the
city, listening to the rain batter the glass. The sky was apocalyptically
black. Dani gave me a look as if to say, 'Are you really running in this?'
To which my look replied, 'Yep! You see, while on paper this trip may
seem glamorous, in reality it can be an absolute shithouse, and you've
just got to get on with it.' A lot to convey with a mere facial expression,
but Dani and I have known each other for a long time.

Ro drove us down the winding hills to meet Mauri and his son Pau.
Pau, at 16, had been assigned to cycle the entire distance with us to
supply food and, despite the rain, water. I'm not sure if I would have
done that at 16. Champion. Our route took us over long, winding hills
with a few kilometres around the city, ending at Gaudi's staggering
masterpiece, the Sagrada Familia, all in unrelenting rain.

But Rowena's hospitality more than made up for the weather. Her
kindness and selflessness were unsurpassed, and we were treated to
every meal during our stay. As if this wasn't enough, she announced
over dinner that she had been in touch with Carla, and between them
they had hatched a plan to save Dani and I some tricky train journeys: Rowena offered to drive us the 200 or so kilometres to Andorra,
and then a further 600 kilometres into France, where she would drop
us in Nice! (Ro, if you're reading this, we can't thank you enough.)

In the comfort and luxury of the kitchen, we made fluffy scrambled
eggs on seeded toast with a good strong cuppa. The rain had passed
and we breakfasted overlooking the warm early morning haze of Barcelona. Bags packed, a quick shower, we said goodbye to Rowena's

palace in the sky and meandered down the mountain to begin the drive to country number 68, Andorra, where we were to be met by a fellow runner and fan of the expedition. His name, rather aptly as it turned out, was Angel.

Angel had been following the trip on Instagram and online since the journey began. He was a great runner and, sadly, his father was suffering from cancer, so felt a strong connection to what I was doing. He was kind enough to organize everything for us, including food, accommodation, a running route and a press conference. The four of us checked into our rooms at the Centric Hotel in Andorra, which we discovered had been both booked and paid for by Angel. As discussed, I was strictly teetotal for the duration of the expedition (and still am), a fact which Dani used to his advantage, immediately getting stuck in to our complimentary bottle of champagne in the bath, nonetheless. So this was how it was going to be! I've known Dani for a very long time, and although he spells his name the girl's way and always copies my hairstyles, we've shared many happy memories together, and I'm very fortunate to call him a friend. With that in mind, only a carefully handpicked selection of Dani's drunken escapades will be described in detail. Post-champagne bath, we went down for a press conference, followed by dinner at Angel's home overlooking the Pyrenees. Maria-José, Angel's wife, fuelled us up with delicious pasta and incredible chocolate brownies.

Up at 5 a.m., I dragged myself out of bed and wrestled my new compression socks over my sore feet and calves – a chore at the best of times, but trying to do it while half asleep and with the extra challenge of a large and deeply unattractive bunion on my left foot . . . all this before an 18-kilometre uphill stretch led by Angel along cobbled lanes, forest trails and dirt tracks, still in darkness. Dani had kindly donated one of a great many pairs of socks he'd brought with him, for me to use as gloves, but, even so, my hands were numb, and my sweat-soaked clothes were making me very cold. We reached the top of the climb, and after several cups of hot chocolate and snacks provided by Dani and Ro in the support car, which had leapfrogged us on the road, we turned around and headed back down into the valley with the city ahead of us, the tree-covered mountains on either side now visible in the morning light.

My foot had been pretty sore on the way up, with some bruising and a possible strained muscle. So, to avoid any further damage and pain, we opted to run back down the road, which made for a much more enjoyable second half. The sun came out, the roads were empty and our spirits were high as we flew down the mountain. We even passed a group of supporters waving hand-decorated banners bearing enthusiastic mottos such as 'Running the World 196' and 'Woooo Wa' (the latter I assume was a message of encouragement, but in truth it could have been anything – I took it positively, regardless). Glitter and every colour of Sharpie had been put to heart-warmingly good use. We ended our run in the stadium, where there was some more press, and then it was back to pack and rest before an early start and the eight-hour journey north-east to Nice. French service stations will forever remind me of long journeys to the mountains for skiing holidays as a boy, and we stopped several times, just because we could. Ice creams for me and several large, strong coffees to feed Dani's addiction. Rowena had offered to drive the first leg, so I could rest after the previous day's run. I tried to do my bit by joining in the conversation, but with my total running mileage hovering around the 1,700 mark, I dozed in between breaks.

The Pyrenees are stunning in all seasons, and we stopped for a few shots of the road winding down through the valley, and then, in stark contrast, we passed the scene of a serious road accident which had clearly only recently happened, with the injured still being attended to. Witnessing things like that is always gut-wrenching, because, consciously or subconsciously, it makes you think of mortality. It put me in mind of Kev and others facing similar situations, and triggered a similarly themed conversation in the car. For me it was another reminder of how every moment of every day is valuable, and we should all try harder to appreciate what we have.

France, Monaco

We made it to Nice, and the time had come to reluctantly say goodbye to Rowena. I was so grateful for everything she'd done for us, not just because it was so helpful, but because it allowed us to spend more time with her. For the last five days, we'd laughed, sung in the car, chatted about life, love and everything in between – even the Brexit disaster and the embarrassment of British politics had seemed like light-hearted conversation topics. We hugged and, as we waved her off, I'm not ashamed to say I had a tear in my eye. Dani, hardened by years of kung-fu and strong coffee, is not a crier, so I hid my eyes from him.

We had been dropped off on the corner of a road where a couple called Phillipe and Jean-Michel live. A guy named Jean-Christophe (JC), who lives in Luxembourg, had been in touch with the team, and not only offered to host me in Luxembourg in a few months' time but had arranged for us to stay at Phillipe and Jean-Michel's B&B at his expense. What I didn't know at the time was that JC had been donating to the cause every week without fail since the beginning of the trip. He wasn't a runner, but loved the idea of what I was doing and wanted to help.

Although I love Paris, I'd opted for Nice as the obvious choice, due to its proximity to Spain, Italy, Andorra and Monaco. Plus I hadn't been there before, so it would be yet another new experience. Being in France, breakfast – in fact, every meal – was quite an occasion, featuring a fresh warm baguette with all the usual toppings, fresh juice and, of course, pastries. All to the backdrop of the early morning sun lining the tops of the buildings as the city awoke, the sound of the odd moped or dog in the distance. I had forgotten how beautiful old French buildings are, with their shutters, elegant wrought-iron-railed balconies and overflowing window boxes and hanging baskets.

Some marathons can feel like a lifetime, some are dull, some are painful, but this one flew by, with no after-effects from the uneven surfaces of Andorra – 13 flat miles one way, and then another 13 miles back, plus the little extra. Perfect. The Nice coastline is made for training, and I must have seen around a thousand runners and cyclists on the route.

Post-run, I used the 'Find My Friends' app to locate Dani, who was enjoying a morning beer in a small café on the seafront. A quick debrief and a dip in the sea rounded off a great morning for both of us: 26 miles for me, two pints for Dani. Had it been the other way round, we'd have both felt a lot worse. We spent the afternoon listening to some live music from a great jazz/swing band next to the beach. It was hot, but not Africa hot, so while Dani was lapping up the sun, I still needed a hoody – 33°C was still ten degrees cooler than what I had become accustomed to. We went back to the B&B to change and eat and then went back out for my first proper night on the town for eight months. I hit the H2O hard, while Dani took it easy with beer and shots. It was a late one, and we eventually crawled into bed around 4 a.m. I certainly looked more spritely than Dani the following day.

Monaco is a one-of-a-kind place, and even if, as with me, it's not really your cup of tea, it's still a remarkable and intriguing place to see. Cars that cost more than houses and super-yachts that cost more than the value of several of the countries I'd be visiting. Hard to believe it was on the same planet as some African nations, let alone only a stone's throw away. Whatever your view on Monaco, it's a beautiful place, but one that certainly makes me think about horrendous rich–poor divides.

A man named Lorenzo, who owned a lovely Airbnb property in the city, had contacted me to offer us yet more free accommodation. Yet another person to whom I'm indebted. We got the train from Nice, dumped our bags, Dani went to find coffee and I spent a few afternoon hours weaving around the tiny country. I'd had romantic visions of running around the Formula 1 circuit, making high-pitched engine noises as I tore down the straights, but in reality it was a twisty run, and I not only covered several repetitive F1 circuit laps but ran on almost every street in the city. Although the border with France was further away than my map suggested, I was checking my position constantly, to avoid accidentally running out of the city and therefore the country, which would have invalidated the marathon and resulted in my having to start it all over again. This generated a very messy-looking route map full of boat jetties and u-turns that looked like something a two-year-old would draw on the kitchen wall. I ran, Dani drank, we both slept, and before we knew it, it was time to board an early train to Rome. Monaco was ticked off.

Italy, Vatican City, San Marino

Although still infinitely better and cheaper than air travel, the 30-day InterRail passes we had both purchased were starting to feel like a bit of a con. We had to pay additional booking fees, reserve seats (if there were seats available), and we discovered early on that our tickets were often only valid on certain trains. To quote one of the grammatically dubious labels of our time, we'd been 'mis-sold'. Our fight for justice took the form of skipping the reservation process, boarding the first train to wherever we wanted to go and seeing what happened. We dodged conductors, argued with ticket collectors, were frequently asked to leave and board the correct train, and occasionally just slept to avoid interaction with staff. I'm usually a law abiding citizen but it really felt like we had the moral high ground here. Maybe in reality I'd spent too long in countries where anything goes, and I just wasn't used to European levels of red tape.

After three connecting trains, we made it to Rome, feeling sluggish due to lack of sleep and the life-changing amount of pastry we'd put away in Nice and Monaco. Vespas, pizza and pasta eateries; loud, emotional conversations with excessive gesticulation – Italy welcomed us with a flurry of clichés. The sun was shining and there was a breeze. Dani had now seen more countries in the last week than he had in the last few years, and although he was loving the adventure I could tell he was finding the quick-fire travel tiring, especially when combined with late nights. He had become a part of the journey. I'd be sad to see him go when this month of roaming the European cities was over. We could jest, joke and jibe at one another as much as we wanted. Dani's laidback nature is something nobody can miss. His walk is one that amuses me to this day – it's the saunter of a contented, quiet and at-peace man. In all the years I'd known him, I hadn't realized his calming affect. In terms of travel companions – they don't get much better. But this was to be a two-marathon stop without leaving Rome – a country within a city, a marathon within a marathon. I'd be running in Rome, plus the smallest country in the world: Vatican City.

It's hard to go anywhere in Rome without feeling the weight of history in the very fabric of the city, and I used the Tiber cycle path to connect the classic sight-seeing locations, including a lap of the Colosseum, as I ran through the centuries, taking care not to stray into the Vatican. After a tour of the centre, I still had the majority of a marathon to run, so I rejoined the river and ran north out of the city. Trees provided welcome shade and my route became more peaceful as the pace of life around me slowed, symbolized by a tortoise I passed. My spirit animal seemed to be a minor tourist attraction, and was being heavily photographed as it slowly chomped its way through lunch. For the last ten kilometres, I popped my earphones in, occasionally singing out loud (nothing particularly Italian, instead a horrendous mix of Beyoncé and other running classics like Kate Bush. My taste in music isn't exactly taste, but it is eclectic). I was in my element, and flying along. My body was now so accustomed to the distance that I was often feeling more energetic in the latter stages of a marathon than at the start. I should add the caveat that I'm not boasting or showing off when I say it gets easier. I am in fact not really a natural or great runner in any way – I've just put the miles in. As my father's incessant advice as a child stipulated, 'practice makes perfect'. And while I wasn't perfect and more practice was needed, by this point I'd had many miles under my feet, and, as importantly, in my mind. If my mind allowed me, I could put one foot in front of another now, and enjoy it if – and it's a big IF – the stars were aligned. If the weather was pleasant, if I had enough water, if I felt safe, if I didn't have the stresses of running quickly to get to a plane, and, above all, if I was in the mood. I think most runners will relate to the really enjoyable runs that have been born from such a mindset.

A couple of days later I was facing the obvious question: not the one about the pope but, how do you find 26.2 miles in a country with an area of one fifth of a square mile? Assuming his role as cameraman, Dani walked to the tiny country with me. He had never seen me run a whole marathon before, and was only doing so now by virtue of the fact that I couldn't run more than 200 metres away from him at any point. I'd have to run laps of the perimeter of the only easily accessible part of the tiny city-state, the oval of St Peter's Square, which, at around 500 metres, would mean about 80 laps.

It was early, and the square was more or less empty when we arrived, so we recorded a piece to camera as the sun was rising. Dani took photos as I ran, and we exchanged a few words each time I passed. After several laps, he made the astute observation: 'It takes a while, doesn't it?' before sloping off to find coffee. I plodded on, my left leg rapidly becoming shorter than my right. After eight miles and 28 laps I was ushered over by a uniformed man, an Italian police officer who worked for the Vatican. By this point there were several hundred people in the square, and he told me that I couldn't continue in case I injured someone. He spoke no English and I spoke no Italian, so it was impossible to get across what I was trying to do, but he called his colleague over to interpret, and while I attempted to explain why I was there, Dani sauntered over with his latest coffee and began unsurreptitiously filming the exchange. This didn't go down well with the officials, and Dani was soon brusquely reprimanded, before making a show of pretending to turn the camera off whilst still secretly filming. The police position seemed to be that if I wanted to move any faster than walking pace in St Peter's Square, I would first need permission from the relevant authority, whatever that meant. His holiness? His holiness's boss? After ten minutes of pleading and arguing, I had resorted to jogging on the spot, although this was a waste of time, as I wasn't covering any distance, but the police had their orders and didn't seem to be budging. They told me about an office where I could enquire about obtaining permission to run, but it was outside the perimeter of the city, and leaving would mean having to start the run again. I was only eight miles in, but eight miles is eight miles, and there was no guarantee that the office would even a) be open or b) exist. Luckily, I was able to dispatch Dani to investigate, and he returned shortly, confirming my suspicions that the office was closed.

Another 15 minutes passed, during which time they had various phone calls and walkie-talkie chats, suggesting that all wasn't yet lost, so we gently persisted. I kept moving in tiny circles, hopefully small enough to avoid further pissing them off, but large enough to keep the distance increasing a little. Dani and I had noticed that the English-speaking guy, the 'good cop', seemed a little more sympathetic to my cause than the 'bad cop'. Through chatting to him we discovered that he was sporty, and when we showed him the website, plus some photos and videos from the trip, he was clearly interested. It turned out that he was also a keen martial arts fan, particularly kung-fu, giving him common ground with Dani, who has been doing kung-fu since he was a boy. Suddenly, we were making headway, this was our way in!

Just when it seemed we were getting somewhere, we overheard a radio message from their superiors, in English, confirming that I must not only stop running but also *leave*. Shit. I'd basically been excommunicated. Fortunately, though, I now had a supporter in the form of the 'good cop' with whom we'd developed a rapport and, amazingly, he said that despite what they'd been told I could carry on – but if anyone else asked us to leave, we must go immediately. Phew! I didn't really want to become the man who'd run almost every country in the world.

Skip ahead another 30 laps and the police were waving and cheering me on, and, as I dipped and weaved around tourists, people had started to grasp what I was doing. By lap 50 groups of foreign exchange students were running with me trying to capture an action-selfie, and the place suddenly felt like a stadium. Sitting in the shade of the vast colonnade, couples, families and groups watched me chase my tail, and started to cheer as I passed; a Mexican wave of noise began following me around the square. It was bizarre and brilliant. By the time lap 80 came around the watch showing the shorter distance told me I had just two more to run. Relieved, I jogged the last two circuits to clock 26.4 miles (the extra 0.2 to ensure I'd definitely covered the distance). Perhaps by divine intervention I'd run a marathon in the Vatican City, and despite the problems and repetitive laps I'd loved it. As I slowed to a walk and downed the last of my water, the police officers gave us a wave and a thumbs-up. Common sense had prevailed. Praise be.

It was off to the hills for number 73 – San Marino – to complete the trio of Italian marathons. We caught the train to Rimini before paying for an expensive day-return coach into the mountains, leaving our bags in a small seaside resort hotel to collect later that day. Once the run was done, we'd have the rest of the day off and I could sit by the beach and recuperate.

Approaching San Marino from the east coast of Italy, the place looked like the set from *Game of Thrones*, with mist shrouding the lower ground and dramatic towers topping the citadel. I was lacking sugar and energy, and, as the bus laboured its way around tight hair-pin bends bordering vertical drops, my legs felt achy at the prospect of some serious ascent. It was to be another run where I'd have to check the map constantly to ensure I didn't cross the border back into Italy.

A mile after starting the climb, my heart was pounding and up to around 190 bpm, but my legs felt surprisingly fresh and, to my amazement, the next few hours of running flew by as I made my way three times up and down Monte Titano. I was even feeling cheery enough to befriend the bus drivers, who waved to me out the window, ferrying people to and from the city. At the end of the run, I went to remove Dani from a coffee shop before he took root, and we still had time to film some footage for the documentary before catching the bus back to Rimini. I was sweaty, tired and in need of water, but it was another one done. My legs generally felt light, and the run, for the most part, had been comfortable in ideal temperatures and straightforward. Although the regular sniffles and headaches were my body's way of telling me I still needed more rest, I found that the more frequently I ran, the more I was ready for it.

Germany

Rimini to Berlin via Bologna, Bolzano and Munich was a long day's travel, made longer by us twice sleeping through our train stops and having to backtrack. We arrived in Berlin late, still tired, to run the city's official marathon the following day.

I'd run in Berlin before this trip, and having run a great many organized events, I've kind of grown out of all the peripheral marathon ceremony and paraphernalia. The big races are always great occasions, and I used to love the atmosphere at expos – browsing

more running kit I didn't need, sampling new gels and energy drinks –
but now I'd rather just spend that time chatting with locals or exploring
a city. Maybe organized marathons like this had come to feel just a bit
tame and predictable. Without having to concentrate on planning a
route or finding places to buy water, the Berlin marathon passed
largely without me noticing. The psychological boost of getting from
country to country without flying, and running in places that lacked
the dangers of Caracas or Lagos, made me feel like I was powering
through these marathons.

Czech Republic, Austria, Slovakia, Hungary

Prague, to me, conjured up images of stag dos and Brits abroad giving us a bad name, but the stunning architecture and the hustle and
bustle of the riverside endeared the city to me, and I was looking forward to pounding its streets. Could do with fewer cobbles though . . .

I enjoyed a lie-in followed by a breakfast that was very much about
quantity rather than quality, followed by a relatively late start to the
run. I'd be running with a guy called Nik (full name Dominik), who
was 16 and had never run a marathon before. Nik's dad had driven
the 200 kilometres to the city so his son could run with me. They'd
even paid to stay overnight to be ready for a morning start. It was
bizarre but an honour to have someone drive so far just to run with
me. This wasn't a friend or someone I had spoken to – this was a guy
who was inspired by me. I was so chuffed to have had an impact, but
felt a responsibility to do him proud. Nik seemed very nervous to
meet me, but once we got going I was impressed by how well he
spoke and ran. For someone who had never covered the distance
before, I was amazed at how he coped, especially with the heat and
cobbles.

I, on the other hand, had been experiencing some pain in my right
heel within a few minutes. By around mile 17 I'd gone from running
with a sore heel to being barely able to walk. A quick pit-stop in a
pharmacy for painkillers and anti-inflammatory gel took the edge off
it, and I limped on, telling myself it was just another twinge that I

would run off after a few miles. Tens of thousands of miles over the years had conditioned me to just keep going, think away the pain, and hope that I wasn't doing any lasting damage. Runners know the drill: let the mind control the body; not the other way around. By 20 miles Nik was also feeling the strain and, with visible salt lines all over him, started to cramp badly, but he soldiered on without a murmur or any intention of stopping. I was so inspired by the grit and mental strength of this 16-year-old. We limped on for the last few miles and finished with smiles on our faces. Before we parted ways, Nik gave me a hand-made bracelet as a memento of the city and our marathon together, which I still wear today.

It turned out that the pain in my heel was caused by fibres in my right Achilles tendon starting to fray and tear. This was the first proper running injury I'd experienced since my ankle break the previous year, and was a big worry. Were the wheels about to come off? Just when I was in my stride, running well, enjoying the trip, and even the weather was treating me kindly?

Vienna. Another hotel breakfast buffet of old pastries, machine hot chocolates, small European-style 'toast', tiny rock hard packets of 'butter' and UHT milk did the job, but I just couldn't help but crave pork and apple sausages, fried eggs with runny yolks, crispy streaky bacon, proper baked beans and some homemade hash browns, mopped up with a fresh, thick-cut white loaf and soft Devon butter. Mmmm, heart-attack food.

I'd spent the previous evening icing and elevating my heel, and with this injury justifying (in my mind) a short lie-in, I left the hotel late in the morning, pushed the start buttons on my watches and set off gingerly, anxious not to do any more damage, promising myself that if I was struggling to run or walk before the ten-mile mark then I'd call it a day and revisit Austria later on in the trip. It would be inconvenient, but I couldn't afford a snapped tendon. Fortunately, the TLC, anti-inflammatories and painkillers seemed to be doing the job, and my heel felt OK. As the run went on and I became immersed in the relaxed ambience of Vienna, I too relaxed and, before I knew it, I was cruising again, heart and breathing steady, legs floating over the ground, the heat on my face and the wind in my hair. Any runners reading this will know this feeling – the runner's high. After my injury concerns in Prague, I hadn't expected to be feeling it in Vienna, but it was a beautiful place to run, and easy to see why it's been voted the world's most liveable city on more than one occasion. Marathon complete, I felt good and so did my heel. Post-run, I tucked into a super-tasty chicken, mushroom and broccoli risotto. It was a huge portion but I still had some room for chocolate cake. I was thoroughly enjoying the process of trying to regain the 12 kilos I'd lost in Africa.

In Slovakia Dani and I met up with mutual friend Andy. This was the same Andy that had already joined me a couple of times on the trip and, in fact, later spent time editing and fact-checking this book. (I've somehow landed myself a bunch of brilliant mates, willing to give up their time and holidays to help in so many ways.) While I tended to stick to pastry and orange juice before a marathon, with no concerns about unwanted mid-run stops, Andy preferred to ensure such matters were taken care of before the start. It had to be carefully scheduled though – a badly timed morning coffee could potentially land him in the shit. Literally. As it was, we had zero bathroom stops during our run in Bratislava, but we did stop for a few minutes for some shelter from the rain, to FaceTime Andy's Auntie Vida. It was her 100th birthday and worth at least a quick stop. Talking to someone who has spent a full century on our planet, living through the enormity of change that has taken place in that time, is thought provoking, and Andy and I marvelled at this landmark as we ran. The day had started with sunshine, and in our enthusiasm we had lost our bearings and come dangerously close to running back into Austria. Easily done when following the Danube. Soon the weather took a turn for the worse, and after a more or less unbroken month of European sun we were running in wet and very windy conditions. For miles we ran single file, taking turns to act as a windbreak for each other, peloton-style. We reached the 26.2 miles suspiciously close to the door of a McDonald's. It was mid-afternoon, and as we sat, soaking and cold, gorging on chips and ice cream, we glanced out of the window. There, outside a café across the street, sat Dani, beer in hand. He'd earned it, though.

His month on the road with me was coming to an end, and he'd spent a lot of it filming, taking photos, carrying my bags and listening to my whinging, but most of all just being there with me – the unspoken support. We all had one last city together, though: Budapest.

Hungary welcomed us with more drizzle. Having learned our lesson in Bratislava, we donned an extra layer and set off, taking in the sights of the city. We ran up to and around the Buda Castle complex, passing Hungarian horse guards past and present (both a historical re-enactment and actual military) before snaking back down to run by the Danube once again, passing the spectacular parliament building. Towards halfway, approaching our turning point, we were on the outskirts of the main city and the neighbourhood was starting to look a little derelict, even Soviet. And that, as with so many similar places, meant stray dogs. As the barking that foreign runners seem to trigger in dogs worldwide increased we looked at each other with the unspoken resolution that dogs were not going to get us this time. Andy had been with me in Tunisia, and didn't want to develop a reputation as some sort of arse-about-face dog whisperer, so he darted to the side of the road to select some ammunition in the form of a few rocks. We both love animals but he wasn't going to let either of us get bitten again. We carried on for a while, and eventually made our way back into a more populated area before rejoining the river to head back into the city, thankfully with no shots fired, and Andy disarmed himself to save weight. The morning after the run before, it was time to wave goodbye to my two great friends. I would be seeing Dani and Andy again, but this mini central European phase was complete and the fun of InterRailing was over.

Iceland

A flight, a hire car sorted, some local money extracted from the greedy jaws of an expensive airport cash machine, and within 24 hours of saying goodbye to Dani and Andy in Budapest, I was having dinner overlooking the wonders of the Icelandic skyline with three new friends.

Duncan owns a hydraulics company called Hydraquip, and, pre-trip, got in touch to suggest doing some fundraising with his customers and staff. His son Jay, a triathlete who was also involved in the business, was keen to get on board too. At this point Duncan was a stranger but, even talking to him on the phone, I could tell he was an endlessly kind soul. In Reykjavik Duncan, Jay and I were also joined by Mike, a mate of mine. Mike's one of those guys you can rely on in any situation – a hard-working, decent and brilliant bloke. He and Jay shared stories of those silly events where running isn't the only discipline. Mike's into triathlons too.

We had three glorious days of rain and bitterly cold wind in and around Reykjavik. With all the rain in the last couple of countries, and without the heat of Africa to dry things, I'd been putting on damp, if not wet, running kit for the last couple of runs. For the majority of marathons, I'd don a white vest covered in sponsors' logos: shorts from my main clothing sponsor, Do Sport Live; Adidas Ultraboost trainers provided by Pro Direct Sport; Rehband socks; Runderwear pants, plus an Arch Max runner's belt. All this gear was very kindly provided by each of those brands, and I was grateful. I just wished I had fresh stuff every day. When packing, I'd carefully isolate this kit in a small shoe bag in a bid to protect the rest of my luggage from its bouquet, but to no avail. The 'infuser' would always manage to make the rest of my bag smelly and damp. Despite the occasional special delivery from DHL with new items, even my non-running clothes were getting worn and grubby. I was quickly chaffing my way through pants, and I'd try to wear my socks in such a way that the holes wouldn't get bigger, but I was fighting a losing battle.

The dramatically barren science-fiction landscapes of Iceland, dotted with waterfalls, mountains and volcanoes, were a welcome change from the cityscapes of central Europe. Due to the wet weather and two bonus days in Iceland, I didn't run on the first day and, with a car at my disposal, opted to explore this awe-inspiring landscape. The wet and wild weather actually lent itself to the drama of the place, but we eventually had a few hours of sun to explore on foot, trekking among towering waterfalls and simmering geysers, until we came across the long-abandoned wreckage of a plane crash on a volcanic beach. I was getting through SD cards at a rate.

For marathon 79, around Reykjavik, the sun disappeared again and we were treated to snow, sleet and highs of 4°C under a grey sky. Despite Duncan being a runner and Jay's triathlon credentials, neither of them had run a full marathon before, but they both looked spritely as we set off and didn't complain at any point during the distance. However, I still hadn't adjusted to the lower temperatures, and we were running slower than my body needed to go in order to keep my central heating on. Being wet and cold is my least favourite state of being. The four of us weaved our way around the dramatically bleak coast, Duncan and Jay working hard with tired legs towards the end, until we reached a slow and shivering finish. Mike was the unsung hero of the day, providing motivation and enthusiasm throughout this wet, chilly marathon.

Ireland, Malta, Croatia

Another day of saying goodbye, and I travelled a stupidly long distance from Iceland to Ireland, via a quick stop in Chicago. Although my US marathon had already been ticked off way back with marathon two in Miami, I couldn't pass up the opportunity to run in the famous Chicago Marathon. For the non-runners among you, there are six marathons in the world that make up the 'majors'. These marathons – London, Berlin, Tokyo, New York, Boston and Chicago – are on the professional circuit and some of the best and largest running events in the world. So I sacrificed a day and hopped over the pond to the Windy (and, as it turned out, rainy) City. I was hosted by the spectacular Viceroy Hotel for a night, ran the Chicago Marathon and then flew straight to Dublin, pleased that I'd ticked off another major, but instantly regretting the additional tiredness and jetlag I'd chosen to pile onto my body.

Despite dashing between continents, the journey back across the Atlantic was oddly peaceful. I'd forgotten how the duration and relative luxury of transatlantic air travel is conducive to both sleep and reflection. Although being among friends for a spell had been uplifting and therapeutic, the prospect of travelling alone again was no longer daunting, just slightly dispiriting. It was a different mindset. As the clouds rolled gently by, tiny interlacing ice crystals spread across the scratched plastic of the plane windows and the wings occasionally twitched, reminders of the inhospitable conditions outside this snug, seemingly stationary cylinder full of people. The drone of the engines, murmur of conversation and occasional cabin announcement blended to form that comfortingly monotonous white noise, an audible silence that allowed my mind to leave my surroundings. By the time I landed in Dublin, my tiredness and acceptance of being a lone traveller once again had translated into a downbeat and anti-social mood. It was raining here as well and the weather was really dampening my spirits. After the highs of the last few weeks and a long-haul flight to reflect on things, I suddenly felt unready to face the next 20 European countries. I just wanted a home-cooked meal, slippers, a log fire and my own bed. While I was generally very receptive to the inevitable questions and conversations about the journey, at times like this I just found them draining. But I was in an English-speaking country, close to home, and it was inevitable that I'd try my best not to appear rude, keep the smile turned on and answer questions as enthusiastically as I could. I was getting used to these rapid changes in mood, and with the physical and mental strain I was under, I was never more than a reality check away from feeling down, or a chance encounter away from feeling cheery. Despite the rain, Ireland provided just such an encounter and plenty of laughter in the form of four exuberant Irish women who ran with me whilst sharing eye-popping stories of mischief from their long friendship together – a welcome distraction that lifted my mood. I'd love to tell you the anecdotes that they shared with me, but I have been sworn to secrecy. In a mental battle to stay positive, I then plodded the streets in Malta and Croatia on my own and in my own head. The marathons were straightforward, with no dramas, and, in my mindset of one foot after the other, I left with little memory of the few days I spent in these countries. This was the first point at which it fully dawned on me how much further I had to go. Looking back, I was probably at the worst stage in the trip for psychological disheartenment. At the start, I had it all to do, but it was new and exciting, and I felt fresh. Over halfway, and I would be ticking them off, counting down to the finish. But approaching halfway, I'd already done so much, yet I was still going uphill.

Belgium

I was in need of company, or at least a distraction, and fortunately Brussels was another place notable for the kindness of friends. A friend named Andre and his family had been following my journey since the beginning, their bright eight-year-old, Thomas, tracking my progress on a light-up globe from his bedroom headquarters back in the UK. Andre and his family were in Belgium where their friends, Fred and Kathleen, offered to put me up for my brief stay.

I heaved my bag off the luggage carousel, met them all in the arrivals lounge, and was driven to their home in Laken, just a few kilometres from the centre of Brussels. A quick change and we went out for a delicious meal, for which they insisted on paying. With the benefit of cheerful company, I suddenly felt silly for feeling so down in the dumps over recent days. But it wasn't without good reason – there were still problems to be solved, and they were weighing on my mind. As well as the financial situation, a few team members had moved on and others had less time to offer because of work commitments. All perfectly understandable, but feeling down about it was of no help to the remaining team whatsoever.

Having started early we finished the marathon around noon, after which I had until around 6 p.m. to try and make some headway. I changed, grabbed my laptop and found a busy café in the centre of Brussels. Amidst the hubbub and barista noise, hugged by a small, salmon-coloured armchair, I frantically emailed people and researched potential solutions to some of the issues. The travel arrangement to Amsterdam, and accommodation when I got there, had fallen apart – funding, always an issue, was extremely tight and loans were being explored. We still had arrangements to get in place for some of the remaining European countries, plus I'd misplaced some really important travel notes I'd made. To top it all the visa I needed for Russia was in my other passport that was still in being processed by Universal Visas in the UK. Instead of just being the guy in the running shoes, I'd now have to be more actively involved in all aspects of the trip. Having made this mental shift, I'd also lost track of time, and dashed back to my hosts' house to pack, shower and grab some pizza before heading to the train station. Big hugs all round and it was onwards to Amsterdam.

The three-hour train journey from Brussels to Amsterdam took just under six hours. A minor train crash, then a broken-down train, followed by hundreds of passengers being asked to get off the train, then being told to get back on, then another breakdown. I was impressed – in terms of rail service, these were almost British levels of unreliability and incompetence. Another reminder that however tightly I planned things, shit could always happen.

Netherlands

It was raining in Amsterdam. Longfellow once wrote, 'Into each life some rain must fall.' While I agree with his words, at this point I really did feel like I'd exceeded my quota, literally and metaphorically. Early the following morning, dry and warm in my hotel bed, I tentatively stretched out to pull the curtain to one side. The sky was grey and dark. Raindrops were cascading down the glass. I was going to have to hit snooze on my alarm. Eventually, around 8 a.m., I braved the day. Still full of sleep, I sat up and hauled my legs out over the side of the bed until my feet touched the cold wooden floor. Miserably, I looked down at my eight remaining toenails, soon to be seven.

I was met at the hotel by three enthusiastic runners, Miriam, Sara and Sofie, and tried to muster the energy for both running and conversation as we donned our layers and rain jackets and began to pound the flat but cobbled streets of Amsterdam. Admittedly, once we got going, I was glad of the company, and shared 11 miles with them before they peeled off to resume their lives. I trotted the rest of the way with my soggy poncho flapping in the wind, stopping briefly in a small corner shop to buy some overpriced gloves. My hands were so numb I couldn't handle the money in my pocket, and had to ask the shopkeeper to assist. He seemed more than happy to relieve me of my cash.

Amsterdam complete – marathon 84 of 196 – I opted for an early night in a bid to catch up with some sleep, both to improve my mental state and prepare for another, perhaps foolhardy, transatlantic addition to my marathon tally. Like Chicago, it wasn't necessary for this challenge, but I wanted to tick off all the majors, and New York was one of them. Plus I had a few days' break to look forward to.

From Amsterdam to what was once New Amsterdam. The day of the New York marathon was significant, as it was my 300th day on the road. A hard and brilliant year, a year of emotional turbulence and incredible experiences and, above all, a year of my life which I was enormously privileged to have lived. I'd run over four million steps, more than 2,000 miles, flown on hundreds of flights, and met so many brilliant people. And it was far from over; soon enough it was time to return to Europe. Switzerland beckoned.

Switzerland

For my two-day stay in Zurich, I was hosted by friends and runners Jon and Julia. It was such a pleasure to be with friends again, and we were joined for dinner on the first night by their friend, Pascal, who at one point used the words 'only a marathon' in a sentence. He seemed to be a like-minded guy. Jon and Julia made an outrageously tasty raclette supper with all the trimmings, and we soon slipped into soft-cheese comas.

Marathon day brought a crisp autumnal morning of reds, oranges and yellows. I ran with the previous night's gang, along with my friends Marieke and Jack. Beyond the tree-covered hills lay the Swiss mountains, and as we weaved our way for 11 miles through the trees to reach the summit, we were rewarded with spectacular views. Fluffy clouds hung just below the top of the tree line, with the jagged horizon of snow-capped peaks in the distance. Looking back the way we'd come, the morning mist of Lake Zurich was lifting, slowly revealing the city as it came to life.

With a spare day to enjoy in Zurich, I went for a wander and discovered a marvel of a shop named Transa. This was a shop made for me; an outdoor enthusiast's paradise selling everything you might need for any adventure, including, of course, Swiss army knives. Massive ones. With no space in my bag and no money, I shopped with my eyes only. It was then off to meet up with Jon so we could make our way to Vaduz, Liechtenstein.

Liechtenstein

Having collected my bag from Jon's, it was just a short walk to the local station, a brief connection at Zurich central station then on to Sargans, on the Swiss border. Jon's good friend Marcel met us off the train and drove us into Liechtenstein. It was, of course, raining again.

Another day, another marathon and another new running buddy. Marcel and I shared our running tales. Marcel told me about his 15-year-old son who had recently completed his first marathon. It was always inspiring to hear about young runners getting into endurance distances. We snacked as we ran. After what felt like a quick jog along the river with a slight detour into the city of Vaduz, the capital, we were done. It really did feel that easy. We changed into our warm puffer jackets by the car, had a few swigs of water and the hot chocolate we'd brought with us in our flasks, and headed back to Zurich. A country ticked off within eight hours. The sun came out to mock us on the journey back.

My documentation for Russia had now been approved and returned, but with no obvious opportunity to complete a return trip home to collect my new passport, my endlessly obliging and selfless parents flew from the UK to Zurich to drop it off. We had a very brief early lunch, discussed the next few weeks' admin, and swapped passports. This would be the only time I'd see them on the road mid-trip, and I saw them for less than 20 minutes.

Luxembourg

The following day in Luxembourg my busy schedule started at 10 a.m., speaking for an hour at an international school in the city. My attempts to inspire the next generation of adventurers must have struck a chord, as at least two of the young adults I spoke to are now accomplished world travellers. I am, of course, taking full credit. From 11 a.m. I ran a few laps of a playing field with the junior school, before peeling off to add the rest of the miles needed for my marathon, which I completed around 4 p.m. A quick change of clothes and I was rushed into makeup at the main national TV station. A quick appearance on live TV, then it was back for dinner and bed by 10 p.m.

The marathon itself was a great run, with no rain and one comically slapstick, if not potentially dangerous, incident. Along with the 'Fat Betty Runners' community and long-time Instagram friend Kristy, I was joined on the run by the British ambassador. He and I became engrossed in conversation as we ran, to the point where we weren't really looking where we were going when our chat was abruptly punctuated by a metallic thud. I can laugh about it now, but at the time it was alarming. He could have done some serious damage running into a lamppost. Sorry, buddy.

Having concussed a member of the British diplomatic service, I returned to the home of Jean-Christophe. JC was a new friend about to become a key enabler within my growing network. Luxembourg is his home, and he'd certainly pulled out all the stops. As well as him and his partner Nico kindly hosting me, he'd arranged all the pre- and post-run activities. The publicity he generated for me even resulted in a generous donation from the TV station.

Denmark

Cannonball runners. This is a Danish concept, where runners group together at semi-organized marathon events around the country, and indeed the world. Think Park Run, but more serious. A race had been put on especially for my arrival, a couple of hours outside Copenhagen, and in the company of the 22 other runners I suddenly felt like an amateur. Chatting to them before the race, we totalled up the number of marathons we'd run between us and, incredibly, the total was over 4,000. I met a 16-year-old who, remarkably, had already run 360 marathons, just 100 fewer than me (at that point in Denmark), and he would surpass my total very soon. He effortlessly stormed into the lead and began lapping other runners on the five-kilometre lakeside loop. It was raining and bitterly cold, but with so many experienced runners to chat to, and a short circuit lined with cheering supporters and well-stocked drink and snack stations, the marathon was soon done. With all the puddles, my shoes were pretty ruined and I was developing trench foot, but it had been a bloody brilliant run in the company of some properly mad runners.

Norway, Sweden

Unfortunately, the remainder of Scandinavia was a bit of a blur. Not because of the fast run/fly turnover, but because of a chicken burger.

Of all the places in the world to get food poisoning, I wouldn't have put Norway at the top of the list. I'm no stranger to food poisoning, but this seriously undercooked burger gave me the worst bout I've ever had. (Spoiler alert – my final total of various food-related stomach upsets for the whole trip was 22, but this one wiped me out for days and cost me five kilograms.) Within a few hours of reaching the accommodation by the coast in Oslo, I settled and ate the dreaded burger. I dried my wet clothes and shoes from Denmark and slept early, unaware of the impending unpleasantness, before I woke feeling terrible at 4 a.m. A bloke called Kikkian, a local architect, cycled with me for my entire Norway marathon. He was friendly and very knowledgeable and it was a pleasure to spend time with him. We chatted about his life, career, family and inevitably sport and running. He patiently stayed with me at my increasingly sluggish pace in the rain, sleet and eventually snow, taking me on a magical mystery tour around forest, city, lakeside and over huge motorway bridges. I was feeling progressively worse, but kept my stomach murmurings to myself and tried not to think about it too much. Eventually we clocked the 26.2 miles plus a little extra.

With the run over, I now knew I was about to endure an evening of sickness. It was a small blessing that I didn't know quite how bad it would be. By 1.30 a.m. I was curled up in the once white and clean hotel bathroom, now redecorated in a frightful combination of 1970s shades. My body was evacuating liquids from every available orifice, and I had given up attempting to return to the bedroom between visits, resorting to sitting slumped in the shower with vomit dripping down my chin after every eruption. Not to be outdone, the other end of my now very weak digestive system contributed to the horror, at first alternating with the upper exit, until eventually they joined forces in an attempt to turn me inside out. The cold shower water acted as a dilutant and, after several hours, I fell asleep in a pool of my own effluent. I awoke around 10 a.m. in danger of missing my train to Stockholm. I had a proper shower, packed every available pair of pants in my hand luggage, and ventured out of the hotel to run the gauntlet. My mission: to reach Sweden without shitting myself.

Dizzy, weak, tired, hungry and cold to my bones, my legs, arms and toes cramped occasionally as I shuffled and clenched my way to the station. My body was entirely dehydrated and lacking any form of salts or electrolytes. Not the best preparation for another marathon. In a deeply unfortunate turn of events, it also appeared that my train had been replaced by a bus service.

Toilets on buses are generally either not working or not fit to bear the title, but I was assured by the driver, as he hastily ushered me onto the bus, that this one was in full working order. I took the seat nearest the loo. Very soon into the four-hour journey, I felt the familiar rumbling of an overzealous bottom burp, so in I went. Out of order. Bang out of order. I returned to my seat and spent another hour writhing with painful cramps, before I could stand it no longer. I got off the bus two stops before mine and rushed to a nearby café. Out of order. This was going to be a really long day.

Five hours, two trains and two pairs of pants later, I made it to Stockholm, still feeling terrible. I eventually crawled into bed around midnight and curled up, still unfed. I had at least made it to country 90 and the familiar confines of the Radisson Hotel, with fully functioning toilets. Seven hours later, following another largely sleepless night spent mostly in the bathroom, I had no choice but to try to crack through another marathon. With no time to spare between now and the end of the year, if I was going to stay on track, I'd have to run with the runs.

In sub-zero temperatures around an icy city, double-gloved and with spare pants in my pocket, I got on with it and got the job done. My body crying out for sustenance, I was reminded of the times I'd turned up at aide stations in various ultras in far flung lands desperate for food, but all that was on offer were more bananas or more jelly babies. I was drifting in and out of daytime food dreams, trying to block out the unpleasant likely results. Big lasagnas at family parties, roast Christmas dinners, toad in the hole, my mind was food mad.

With no roast dinners at hand, I tried some small slices of dry bread around the halfway mark, which reappeared shortly afterwards – and were less dry. 'Slow and steady – right foot, left foot, right foot, left foot, try to remain within sight, or at least within a dash to a toilet, at all times.' It's amazing how the body can switch its fuel from carbs to fat so easily. I had, however, by now learnt the differences in performance over such a long time. Fat for fuel was a very different experience to carbs. The body feels like it's using reserves, likes it's scraping the barrel, and it is. My mind was aware that it couldn't do this for ever.

I did my best to spur myself on, and tried to look on the bright side – at least I wasn't injured – for now. With that thought in my mind, I rounded a corner and slid on the ice. My wrist, complete with extra sock layer for warmth, took the brunt of the fall, but my hip also took a bashing, which turned into a large oval bruise that worked its way through the rainbow over the next few days. I was having a shitty time. No apologies for the pun.

I ground out the distance and clung to the positives: I was still on track and not giving up. The fact I that I hadn't let this beat me, I took as a sign that I was in a good place mentally, if not physically. I even had a salad and some carrots that evening, which remained in my body!

Finland

Day 326 – Helsinki, November, and still bitterly cold. As we came in to land, looking out of the window pristine snow blanketed everything. The feeling of cold was enhanced by the look of the suburbs, full of blues and whites, like I was viewing the scene through a cool lens filter. The luggage carts were icy, the handlers wrapped up from head to toe, and defrosting trucks were on standby. We landed with a hard thud on the frozen runway. It was minus 11. I was due to be travelling to Finland by train, via a multi-stop 14-hour journey, but with my stomach still unsettled, the team and I opted for the safer alternative of a short flight. Costly, but it was the right decision and gave me a chance to catch up on some more sleep before running again.

Despite the fact that almost all of the best experiences I'd had on the journey so far were with other people, particularly those that ran with me, I was glad that Helsinki was to be a solo marathon. No host, no runners, just me. It meant I could concentrate on trying to settle my stomach without expending energy talking to the kind souls who'd been giving up their days to spend time with me. Even smiling was knackering at the moment. I needed a rest. Of sorts.

I was weak and certainly still not myself but, to my relief, I ran with no stomach issues, accompanied by the sound of absolutely nothing. By the time I reached eight miles, deep into a forest, it was deathly silent, apart from the sound of the snow crunching under my feet. I carried on, appreciating the peace as I looped around the coast, looking out over countless islands. Despite enjoying the stunning scenery, I was painfully cold, thanks largely to wearing already wet clothing. Drying my kit had been de-prioritized in the last couple of countries in favour of attending to more urgent needs.

Russia, Estonia, Latvia

Scandinavia was done and I was back to eating three square meals a day. Russia treated me well too, despite being even colder: minus 15 in

St Petersburg. After all the hassle and delays obtaining my Russian visa, there were no unexpected problems upon arrival, and the city was glorious. As I ran I took in the stunning architecture, beautiful old Russian cars, huge empty squares, and classic surly-looking police and military personnel, all of course wearing fur hats and thick black coats with the collars turned up. Despite attempting to learn the Cyrillic alphabet, I was none the wiser, but even the look of Russian words was so evocative, and the various signs and street names I passed all added to the mystique of the place.

Tallinn and Riga were similar in look and feel, both bitterly cold, with heavy snow falling. Tallinn was the first marathon I ran in thick snow and, surprisingly, my road trainers, Adidas Ultraboost, which I wore for every single run on the trip, coped just fine. With the squeak of compressing snow under my feet as my metronome, I plodded around Tallinn, alone and content with the fact.

In Riga, as in St Petersburg, the locals shielded themselves from the cold with enormous dark-coloured coats, and as I got further away from the grimy brown slush of the city, the scenery became lighter and was punctuated by fewer and fewer dark-coated figures, blotting the white. Trees started to appear, tiny twigs laden with impossibly balanced heaps of snow. Every body of water, from lake to puddle, was hard with ice, and the sun glinted off the snow as it sunk beyond the horizon. I had this winter wonderland all to myself. The world had gifted me a few days of peace.

The Baltic marathons were just that: Baltic. But having learned my lesson in Helsinki, I had at least been running in dry clothes, even setting my alarm halfway through the night in order to replace dry clothes with wet on the limited space of the heated towel rail. My journeys to and from Riga were, unusually, by bus, which made for a welcome change (the replacement bus in Oslo notwithstanding). The Lux Express not only allowed an overnight sleep on the luxury lounge bus – in a very comfortable reclining seat, with pillows, blankets, mini-TV, buffet and drinks – but was a great money saver. All this luxury for the bargain price of €22, roughly the cost of seat allocation, speedy boarding and one or two other utterly pointless extras on a so-called budget airline flight. To make the whole experience even better, the bus driver drove in a positively soporific fashion and, with that, I was asleep instantly. I missed the buffet and drinks, but it was worth it for the bliss of four hours' uninterrupted sleep.

Lithuania

Lithuania hadn't been a special country when we'd set out the schedule, but arriving in Vilnius on day 337 I received a message from my mum informing me that I was 12 hours away from reaching halfway. Halfway. This meant that, despite being on track, I'd run 94 marathons in the first half of the trip and still had 102 to run in the second half. Not really knowing whether to be pleased, disappointed or worried . . . I knew that at least it would soon be Christmas. I was 29 years old and I'd already visited half the world, and was well on my way to achieving my dream. To top it all, Andy couldn't stay away, and was back for a few more marathons, along with our mutual friend Annabelle, who flew out to run in Lithuania, with her partner Dan.

Despite being in the middle of nowhere, the log cabin I was staying in was well worth the two-hour trip from the city – it was spacious but cosy, with heavy, deep wooden walls and a log fire, situated by a frozen lake and surrounded by immaculate fresh snow. Once I'd checked my calendar, I realized that with just two more nights here it was going to be a busy couple of days, with several interviews and press appointments to fit in around a marathon that had been organized by a local running group, and therefore had to be run at a set time.

In the falling snow, over 100 people came to a sports centre well outside the city to run with me. The organizers had even tapped up one of my sponsors, Red Bull, who had made provision for race timing, bibs, medals, drink stations and even one of those inflatable finish-line arches. I was deeply touched by how much trouble they'd gone to.

Although an experienced runner, Annabelle was anxious about not completing the distance, having not run much in the weeks before, but Andy and I, both hardened runners, weren't going to let her fall short. We ran, chatted and, despite the now slushy and icy conditions, enjoyed ten cold circuits of a loop incorporating woodland trail, main roads and quiet residential areas. I'd run prettier marathons, but in these conditions the known quantity of a repeated lap and easy access to drinks was ideal and, as ever, the company was the highlight. Annabelle made it not only to the finish but onto the podium for her category, and we celebrated with a steaming cup of tea.

The remainder of the day was spent with the log fire roaring and all available chairs acting as drying racks for various items of clothing. T-shirts and socks that hadn't been properly dry for a week were given a much needed handwash in the sink before being baked in front of the fire. Another cup of tea, an extra pair of socks on my feet, and I soon nodded off. The cold was draining, and it wasn't going anywhere before at least Christmas. As Annabelle and Dan flew home, Andy and I flew on to Belarus for more numbing cold.

Belarus

Minsk. Andy and I were joined by Max, Alexei, Yuri and Andrei. Having heard about the journey, this hardy-looking group of runners gathered in our hotel lobby at 6 a.m. eagerly waiting to get out into the cold.

After the ravages of the Second World War Minsk was a city rebuilt for the future, and is very much a product of the Soviet era. We ran past imposingly grand Stalinist buildings and wide empty squares, before turning onto a cycle path which felt out of place amongst the stately architecture. The path followed the partly frozen Svislach River towards the outskirts of the city. As we ran we passed small gatherings of ice fishermen perched on tiny upturned buckets on the frozen water, their hand-lines disappearing down small holes bored through the ice. This wasn't fishing for the faint-hearted. I wondered if they were doing it for sport or subsistence – the latter, I imagined.

Despite the cycle path being of sufficient length to provide all our required miles, we only saw one cyclist, but frequently passed cross-country skiers. Alexei told us about the popularity of the sport in

Belarus and how, in the height of winter, this path would be packed with them. Now, though, with little snow underfoot, there were just a dedicated few staying in training. We completed our out-and-back along the river, and, not wanting to be out for longer than necessary in sub-zero temperatures, made it back to our massive hotel in time to catch the last 20 minutes of breakfast, although the eggs were a bit dry by then. My Strava feed was now also effectively a thermometer: the faster my time, the colder the city. While in Belarus, I'd decided to treat myself to the hotel's express laundry service. Not only were all my clothes now dry, but clean – Christmas had come early, albeit at an eye-watering price, but I smelled much fresher as Andy and I boarded a plane made of Meccano for our flight to Kiev.

Ukraine

At our hotel I came close to revisiting the horrors of Scandinavia. I couldn't put my finger on why, but for some reason I fancied a chicken Kiev. Moments before the first bite reached my lips, I decided to delve into the breadcrumbs to make sure it was properly cooked. Not only was it not properly cooked, but in parts it was raw. I sent it back, re-ordered vegetarian food, and breathed a sigh of relief at having dodged another brown bullet.

Although not as bleakly Soviet as Minsk, under grey skies, with slushy brown ice underfoot, a city run in Kiev wasn't the most appealing prospect. But, thanks to Andy's map skills, we found an alternative and opted for a rare, truly wild run. We scoured maps for a good route in an area outside the city along the 'Kiev Sea', which is actually a wide reservoir on the Dnieper River, and eventually settled on what looked like a small path that followed its eastern edge. It would require a taxi ride to get to and from, and would likely have no water stops, people, buildings or vehicles. Perfect. With each other for company, and both of us carrying phones with downloaded maps, battery packs, water and snacks, it was worth the risk of heading out to the middle of nowhere, providing we could keep our phone batteries relatively warm.

It was a decision that certainly paid off. Our taxi driver dropped us at the south end of the reservoir and, as soon as we found our path, we were running in Narnia. No traffic, no wind and no sound; just our footprints in the otherwise untouched snow, as we crunched our way along the path between snow-laden fir trees while huge white flakes floated vertically down through the still air. We were wrapped up warm, with only our eyes visible in the gaps between our hats and buffs, occasionally exposing our ears to appreciate the totality of the silence whenever we stopped. We only saw two vehicles on the track, one a battered old Lada Niva, the classic Soviet workhorse, and a cement lorry with a wolf and moon graphic on the door, whose driver had ambitiously attempted to use the track to turn around. We helped him dig his wheels out of the snow before carrying on.

Even when the depth of snow on the path eventually forced us up onto the road, the whole place was still deserted, and we now had a view across the frozen water, the point at which the 'sea' and sky met impossible to discern because of the ubiquitous whiteness. At the halfway point, we stopped once again to take in the deafening nothingness of this eerie wilderness, before following our own footprints back the way we came, trying to spot where we'd slipped on patches of ice underneath the snow.

It had been one of the best and most memorable marathons of the trip, but it was tiring: 26.2 miles on the road is 26.2 miles, but 26.2 miles on thick snow and ice is the equivalent of a few more, requiring a lot more muscle energy. We'd certainly earned a visit to what I suspect may have been the world's busiest McDonald's. Most people there seemed to be using the place as a hotel or community centre, with little interest in purchasing food. One chap had brought most of his belongings with him, including all his electrical items, which he was charging using a large cluster of socket splitters, plus a small, dangerously un-insulated heating element, which he plugged into one of them to make his own tea.

The following day we had just enough time before our evening flight to Moldova to visit the site of the world's most famous nuclear disaster, Chernobyl. It's hard to know how to feel when visiting somewhere like this. Any feelings of curiosity or fascination are tempered by respect and sadness for the lives lost there, both at the time of the disaster and in the intervening decades. In the snow, it was undoubtedly an eerily beautiful place. To see Pripyat, a city built for a future that never happened, and once home to 50,000 people, deserted and being reclaimed by nature, is a truly post-apocalyptic vision. As well as the trees and vegetation that are currently eating their way through the buildings, large mammals such as wolves and bison, which have been wiped out from much of Europe due to habitat loss, have now started to re-colonize the area, raising the question of whether normal human activity is worse for the planet than nuclear disasters.

We wandered around the cinema, shopping mall, school, theatre, fairground and hospital, among equipment and personal belongings that still lie where they were dropped, a reminder of the suddenness of the evacuation. Our guide, Sergei, took us to a radiation hotspot out-side the school, which was nothing more than a very shallow depression in the ground near the gatepost of the main building. He explained that it was caused when the children were evacuated from the school and had their shoes rinsed to try and remove as much radioactive material as possible. The water ran down the very slight gradient of the path and pooled by the gate; 32 years later, it was still giving a noisy reading on our Geiger counter. It was these little details that were so haunting. Despite the hotspots of radiation, it's safe as long as you don't stay too long. So no, it wasn't safe, but for a brief visit it wasn't going to harm us enough to be worried. We just took his word for that.

As we neared the checkpoint on the edge of the exclusion zone, we stumbled across eight feral dogs all lying on a large pipe connecting two factory buildings, the only source of heat available. It made for one of the outstanding photos of the entire trip. The whole place is a photographer's paradise, but in the back of my mind was the question of whether photography was appropriate here. Were these tours edu-cational or exploitative? At the time of our visit, the popular TV series about the disaster was yet to air, and Chernobyl tourism was in its infancy.

Moldova

Having passed the halfway point in number of days, this was to be the halfway point in marathons – 98 of 196. Andy, keen to help me make it to the 100 marker, was staying on for another two countries to support me, although he had to get home before the final run in Poland. With the sky threatening snow and/or freezing rain, we layered up, sighed and set out to discover Chişinău.

We soon ran out of a city to jog around and found ourselves running along a busy dual carriageway back towards the airport. A mile or two out of town we happened upon a park, aspirationally referred to as a 'botanical garden', which, technically, it was, on account of having some trees in it. The armed guard on the gate ensured we didn't try to sneak in without paying the 10 Leu (45p) entry fee, and we went for a couple of laps around what was a fairly pleasant green area in this city of grey. Eventually, though, we got bored and headed back out onto the road to eat up some miles, eventually hitting the 13-mile mark at a service station within sight of the entrance to the airport. We were going to need a couple more laps of the park on the way back. Fortunately, our tickets appeared to be valid for multiple entries, and the armed guard waved us in, probably impressed by our enthusiasm for all things botanical.

Romania

Outside our hotel, on the edge of central Bucharest, was a nature reserve. Or so said the map. From our windows it looked quiet, with a vague path around its perimeter, so we breakfasted then went to investigate. We scrambled up a snowy bank and began running, hoping to bag a chunk of our mileage with a few laps. However, with derelict buildings and wasteland backing onto it, this was certainly stray-dog territory and, sure enough, within a mile we heard barking and proceeded on high alert. If we had been walking and chatting, they'd have ignored us, but there's something about runners that seems to wind feral dogs up. Probably the smell. A little further on we could see a group of four in the bushes, all staring at us, and, as they started barking, we armed ourselves with snowballs and slowed to a walking pace to avoid exciting them too much. At a safe distance we started running again, until the next pack of dogs poked their heads out from behind some old corrugated metal, this time right next to the path. We slowed to a walk again, and decided that it would just be easier to run through the city. This stop/start business would make for a long day, and it was far too cold to be out longer than necessary. But to get to the road we still had to pass these dogs. Fortunately, we'd just run past an old couple, walking hand in hand, a few metres back. We decided that the bravest and most honourable course of action would be to let this sweet, elderly Romanian couple walk past us, and then use them as a human shield. They'd probably be far more tender than Andy and I, and they certainly had more meat on them than I did. As they were walking we knew they wouldn't attract any attention from the dogs, and walking close behind them, neither did we. Our plan worked a treat, and as we spotted an exit from the reserve back onto the road, the elderly couple worked out exactly what we'd been doing, and seemed amused. We stopped to chat, mainly via gestures, and thanked them for their unwitting assistance.

We needed miles, and decided to run along what looked like the main road heading south out of the city before heading back into the centre. It was utterly grey and featureless, following a manmade river channel, the only flash of colour being a pair of kingfishers that flew past, looking completely out of place amongst the concrete.

I also had a new problem to contend with, a potentially show-stopping injury. I'd had a niggle in my left ankle, which was starting to become more painful with all the extra movement caused by running on snow and ice. As we trudged along the main road, occasionally hitting sheet ice, the pain had become strong and sharp. This was now a real worry, and I called my doctor back home, mid-run. He said it was most likely to be a trapped nerve around my left ankle, caused by weight loss and my skinny ankle rubbing against the edge of my trainer, made worse by the cold and uneven surfaces of snow and ice. He suggested it was something that would be with me for a long time – or it would just stop. I prayed for the latter. Either way, it was unlikely that there would be lasting damage, so it was either a case of resting to allow it to recover, or taking painkillers and getting on with it. This was marathon 99. Nobody had ever run 100 marathons in 100 countries in less than a year. It was a no-brainer: grin and bear it.

For the remainder of this run I needed an even and predictable surface, ideally a few laps, but as we passed our hotel on the way back into the city centre, we were disheartened to find we'd only clocked 11 miles. We carried on until we reached the almighty Palace of Parliament. Not only is this the heaviest building in the world, weighing in at around four billion kilograms, but also the second-largest administrative building in the world after the Pentagon. Basically, it's massive. But not so massive that we wouldn't need a good dozen laps of it to complete our marathon distance. By now I was in a great deal of pain, and grateful for the small mercy of the ice-free pavements around the building. As we ran, Andy bored me with a lecture on the history of the Soviet Union, in a bid to take my mind off the pain. My other leg was now compensating for my limp, and my right hip flexor started to hurt. I ran the last mile sockless, hoping to reduce the pain by lessening the compression on my left ankle. It didn't work. My ankle was now just cold as well as painful.

As I limped to the end, my relief at having completed this marathon was overshadowed by the prospect of this turning into an expedition-ending injury. I also had the more immediate dilemma of whether to risk jeopardizing the rest of the trip by running in Poland in a couple of days, or play the long game: rest, and miss out on the 100-marathon achievement. I doubled up on painkillers and frantically Googled various ways to try to relieve the problem.

In the end I decided to just go for it and hope for the best. That had pretty much been my mantra for the trip – it had got me this far. To make the end of year one extra special, the cold, wet weather of the Eastern Bloc finally caught up with me, and the sniffle I'd had for the last few days developed into full-blown man flu. I slept for most of the day before saying goodbye to Andy. He was flying home and I was limping on to Poland, doing everything I could to protect my ankle. I even resorted to taking a wheelchair through the airport, reminding myself that my mum's home-cooked Christmas dinner was only five days away.

Poland

As I awoke on day 350, my ankle was still sore but, having fallen asleep with four bags of ice on it, the pain had lessened, and I was confident that I'd done all I could to prevent it from stopping me in my tracks. My man flu, on the other hand, had worsened, and my raw throat and throbbing head made for a tough crawl out of bed.

It was still snowy, but far prettier than other recent cities and, importantly, I had company, in the form of a great bloke called Simon. Simon is a good runner and had arranged to fly out especially to run with me. It was another deciding factor in choosing to run in Warsaw rather than postpone it and, in hindsight, Simon's company was an uplifting distraction as we ran two big laps around a lake, over various bridges then back into the city. We chatted as we ran. But by the end we were both suffering – Simon with sore legs, and me with a painful ankle, sore hip flexor, snotty nose, sore throat and headache. My marathon in Warsaw wasn't pretty, but it was over. That was it. Year one complete: 2018 was the year I ran 100 marathons in 100 countries. Just 96 to go. Once back in my small hotel room I didn't even make it to the shower before I fell asleep, and didn't wake until my alarm woke me for an early flight back to Blighty.

5

Heading East

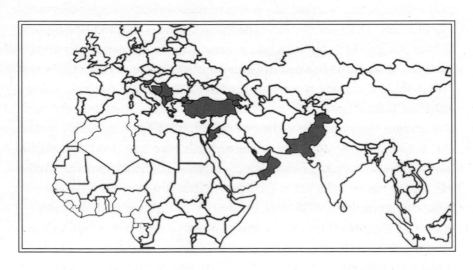

Pakistan
Bahrain
United Arab Emirates
Oman
Jordan
Bulgaria

Turkey
Bosnia and Herzegovina
Serbia
Montenegro
Albania
Slovenia

Kosovo
North Macedonia
Georgia
Armenia

Pakistan

As with any marathon, the first half tends to be easier than the second. The second half of this trip had more unknowns – and the closer I got to the finish, the more I would lose if it had all been for nothing. I wouldn't go as far to say self-doubt was a problem, but if there was doubt, it was about things beyond my control: war breaking out, persistent health issues. The sense of loneliness had just evolved into the resigned solitude of the seasoned traveller.

With my mind on various worst-case scenarios further down the line, my concerns at arriving in Pakistan were real and very immediate. In many areas, this was far from a safe place, and it wasn't much more than a week since my ankle injury had developed. Despite substantial rest over the Christmas break, my trapped nerve was still trapped, and I was still hobbling when walking. Running again would be a bit of an unknown. Would the expected pain continue, would it subside, or, worse still, would the pain increase and put an end to the journey altogether? My mind wandered, and without my permission started drafting a press release explaining how a persistent injury had put an end to my challenge. Not a great mindset with 96 marathons to go. I needed to get on top of my thoughts.

I arrived at Islamabad at 5.30 a.m. After a week among the comforts of a British Christmas, the airport was a striking cultural spectacle, reminding me how quickly and easily you can fall back into the familiar. I was instantly in a different world, and I looked around to reacclimatize. The luggage belts and waiting areas were lined with locals, mostly men, wearing the traditional tunic and trouser combo known as shalwar kameez, almost always cream, white or black. A year earlier I may have found the looks you get as a rare tourist in a Muslim country intimidating, but with half the world under my belt I was soon back into the swing of things, and suddenly felt that paradoxical feeling of being at home in an unfamiliar place. I chatted to people at the luggage carousel, and was immediately made to feel welcome by friendly locals, many of whom invited me for food and a tour of the city.

By 7.30 a.m. I was in bed at my hotel, and managed a couple of hours' napping before the familiar old half-asleep pre-run ritual of getting my clothes on, prepping my watches, downloading offline maps, and putting sun cream on. The latter turned out to be unnecessary; the rain was torrential. With no time for breakfast or drinks, I could only pause for a deep breath before setting out to see what the city had to throw at me – besides quite a lot of water.

With no support and no knowledge of the area, the plan was to just run and hope my nerve damage wasn't going to cause problems but, within ten minutes of stepping out into the rain, I had to turn around. My ankle was causing me so much pain that running or even walking was virtually impossible, and certainly not without loud swearing. I made the decision to return to the hotel to try changing my socks. Rehband compression socks are utterly fab, and I'd recommend them to anyone, but the strong support they were giving my lower legs was also compressing my nerve and causing me agony, so I swapped them for normal non-running socks. This was the first time I'd run without wearing compression for about four years. It felt a questionable move, but there was no way I could carry on as I was.

Sock change complete, I restarted my watches and hobbled out to begin again. The rain was already causing flash flooding and, along the edges of the roads, the filthy puddles were shin deep. Not only was the floodwater too deep to run through, but it would be hiding deeper potholes and obstacles that would, at best, worsen my ankle injury, at worst, cause a broken bone. The only option was to run in the middle of the road, into oncoming traffic. This may sound suicidal, but it was the only way I was going to be able to stay upright, and thankfully, as is often the case in the centre of Islamabad, the cars, buses and motorcycles were moving at a snail's pace.

Twenty-six and a bit miles and four and a half hours later I collapsed, naked, on the floor of my hotel room, with every item of clothing wrung out and draped over things to dry. I had no idea one pair of pants could hold so much water. My ankle injury was still a problem, but the combination of looser socks, painkillers and rainwater had done a reasonable job of numbing the pain, enough to get me through. My feet, however, were ruined. I'd spent a year building up a hardened layer of skin on the soles of my feet, which protected me from blisters, but in one trench-foot inducing run my feet had lost their protective layer entirely. My granite soles had turned to mush, and would have made a banquet for one of those foot-spa places where fish nibble the dead skin off your feet. Not a great start to year two.

Rewinding the clock over two years prior – when I was a year into the planning, and a year before I was due to set off – I trained intensely. I wasn't running marathons – I was just running. Running for as long as I could. Running in boring loops to train my mind, and simply spending time on my feet to build up some mental and physical endurance. One specific training set-up that I took on every other weekend was designed to toughen my mind just as much as my feet and body. From my home in Bristol I'd run from noon on Saturday to noon on Sunday: two miles out up a slight incline, two miles back, have a snack, some water, and then do it again, and again and again until the 24 hours was up and I'd fall into bed. Stumbling through the door after the first 12 hours I'd occasionally change my soggy socks if it had been raining, and often, if I was sweating, I'd change my entire outfit so as to keep fresh-ish. The exercise was rubbish training for a marathon, but that wasn't what I was taking on. I needed to harden up the soles of my feet for the many miles they'd face. I never changed the route. My thinking here was that I could condition a really boring run so my mind wouldn't focus on pain or suffering. And when I'd be running elsewhere the route would, in contrast, always be interesting, even in the most boring situations. I averaged between 80 and 120 miles on those alternate weekends. It was a great mileage booster. My feet were toughening up and my ankles and legs becoming stronger with every mile. Nothing though can prepare me for every eventuality – like breaking my ankle just months before the start.

Given the long flight to get here, we had scheduled in a jetlag recovery day after my Pakistan marathon, and I now had 24 hours to rest and recover before flying to Bahrain the following morning. Like so many large, historic cities, Islamabad has an old town and a new town, and I intended to spend a little time exploring both. In the true essence of the Law of Sod, the monsoon rain had dried up after my marathon and, as I set out sightseeing, there was no sign at all that it had been raining the previous day. Full marks to Pakistan's drainage system. I was expecting the usual noisy bustle and traffic chaos of a large capital city but, despite the inevitable sound of car horns, there was somehow a relaxed orderliness to the place, enhanced by the warm and welcoming nature of everyone I met. On the edge of the Margalla Hills, next to one of the most stunning buildings I've ever seen – the Faisal Mosque – I sat and chatted to locals, including, unusually, a former pro-wrestler. I heard about their city, culture and the languages spoken there. They also talked about Benazir Bhutto, the world's first female prime minister of a Muslim-majority country who, despite being a controversial figure, was fondly remembered.

I spent the remainder of the day with a chap called Kabir. Hailing from Lahore, Kabir went to university in Islamabad with a friend of mine called Razi. Back in my old life, in finance, Razi had been my boss, but he wasn't just any boss. He became a key supporter and enabler of the entire project. Razi believed in me, and not only tolerated my intrusive training programmes and expeditions in the years leading up to the trip, but also backed my pitch to secure sponsorship from our employer. When it came to the good old buzz phrase 'work/life balance' Razi always saw the bigger picture and operated very differently from most bosses. He is a wise, kind and incredibly thoughtful friend who helped me more than most, and had even gone a step further by introducing me to Kabir. Any friend of Razi is a friend of mine, and Kabir treated me to a tour of the city with some expert local knowledge. He drove me to various markets and shops in the main commercial area, Saddar in Rawalpindi, where he treated me to *Gulab Jaman*, an odd-looking but delicious dessert – it tasted intensely sweet and was as if a ball of dough had been drowned in a vat of thick sugary syrup. I also tried *burfi*, another popular dessert, and then a strange hot drink of Kashmiri origin which, despite looking like hot strawberry Nesquik, tasted like tea.

My time with Kabir was the icing on the cake of friendliness and warmth I'd experienced in Islamabad, and his words to me as we drove back were, 'Preconceptions are nearly always wrong.' I couldn't have agreed more. Rarely have I left a country feeling how I'd expected to before I arrived. Thanks to the media, we only ever hear about the worst or most dangerous aspects of some countries, and are fed stereotypical versions of a population and its way of life. I must admit, I think some of that had seeped through to me. I was expecting some hostility, and to feel uneasy and possibly threatened. How I was wrong, and not for the first or last time.

Pakistan had been a real treat, except for the rain of course.

At 4 a.m. the following morning, a hotel driver took me to the airport to fly to Bahrain – originally scheduled to be Afghanistan. However, due to visa issues and some minor safety concerns, this had been postponed. The difficult countries were starting to stack up towards the back end of the trip. It was a niggling worry.

Bahrain

Bahrain was a flying visit, with a jump in temperature. For the first time in nine weeks I was running in what I called heat. Not as hot as I'd become accustomed to in Africa, but still around 30°C, and a big contrast to the minus temperatures of the recent European countries. Rain-soaked clothes would become sweat-soaked once again.

I stayed in a towering skyscraper of a hotel overlooking the city – a freebie, courtesy of the team pulling some strings in response to the budget problem. My bed was luxurious, with pristine, soft white sheets and an excessive pile of plump pillows, and my spotless 40th-floor window looked out onto Manama, a city that was new, clean and more or less empty, a far cry from Islamabad.

The marathon was hassle-free, run on near empty roads, through the conspicuous wealth of Bahrain. In the super-rich capitals of the Middle East, the hot, dry climate and the seemingly limitless supply of infrastructure funding has driven commercial activities indoors into expensive air-conditioned building complexes, leaving the streets virtually deserted. As I ran, I was struck by the irony of the place: even with all the money and resources at our disposal, we'll never be able to control the climate, and yet, through the creation of all this wealth, we are destabilizing it, putting it even further beyond our control.

Before moving on to Dubai I had a chat with some family back home. They asked me about my ankle pain. To which my reply was, 'What ankle pain?' Somehow my mind had squirrelled it away. Moments like this were a lift to my spirits and built an extra layer of trust that my mind would look after my body, and vice versa.

United Arab Emirates

Dubai. Friends had given me mixed reviews ranging from 'vulgar wealth' to 'an amazing feat of architecture'. Either way, I was intrigued to see a city that had sprung up from empty desert in just 50 years to become one of the richest in the world. A few weeks prior to my arrival, I'd read a BBC news article about a British national who had been detained for drinking bottled water on the streets of Dubai. I knew drinking alcohol was illegal here, but water? I never found out the circumstances surrounding the story, but with drinking bottled water outside a necessity for me, I was conscious of not putting a foot wrong.

I landed in Dubai in the early hours of Thursday 10 January 2019, and was collected from the airport by a guy called Rod, whom I recognized but couldn't remember where from. Luckily, he didn't leave me hanging for too long, reminding me that we had shared a few footsteps together during the final stages of the Hyde Park 10k four years earlier. I'd overtaken him just before the finish line (or at least that's how I remembered it), we'd had a brief conversation and gone our separate ways. Skip ahead nearly half a decade and there he was – waiting for me at the airport! He'd heard about my trip, remembered me, and contacted the team.

Rod, his wife Gaëlle, and their three beautiful kids – a French family living in Dubai – are wonderful people, and made my stay very special. Within a couple of hours of landing I was skipping along the beach at sunset with their youngest daughter, Josephine, who, at four years old, liked to chase the waves and name everything she saw, all the time grinning like a Cheshire cat. It was a great reminder how refreshing it is to stop analyzing, judging and overthinking, and just see the world through the eyes of a child every once in a while. Have a giggle, just because you can!

The family and I watched the sunset beyond the famous Burj Khalifa skyscraper and marvelled at the beauty of this absurdly extravagant city. Dubai is a controversial place, and whatever dubious goings on lie behind its skyline, there's no denying it is an astonishing spectacle. Later that night, Rod and Gaëlle hosted a small dinner with their friends. Being French, and having recently returned from a trip to the Alps, it was of course raclette! Perhaps not the most authentic Dubai experience, but I was in heaven. I ate enough cheese to fuel all of my remaining marathons, and slept like a log.

In terms of my ideal marathon, this wasn't far off it. Mountains would certainly be on the list, but in the absence of these, Dubai ticked more or less every other box. It was a glorious morning, and I ran with Rod, Emma, Yvonne, Alaric, Katie, Hannah, Sarah, Alice and Bertie in a buggy. We ran among the gleaming buildings and perfectly manicured parks, past ATMs that dispensed gold bars, and along the canal snaking through the city. I peered up at nearly a kilometre of Burj Khalifa reaching into the sky, completely in awe of its design. Was it, in its own way, even more beautiful than say the Pyramids of Egypt? To cap it all, we even managed a burger, fries and shake – mid-run – this really was my kind of marathon. We placed our order at a burger place called 'Salt' near the beach, and ran on, clutching an electronic buzzer. A few minutes later it buzzed, and we ran back to collect our luxury snacks. I'd had plenty of funny looks whilst running in the past, and today was no exception. In terms of health benefits, eating a burger whilst running, with a milkshake in the other hand, is sending out mixed messages. For a while, I ran barefoot along the beach, completely forgetting that I was on a world marathon mission. I was just enjoying the company, the city and the climate. And that burger.

Thanks to Rod and the gang, I'd had a wonderful couple of days in Dubai, and had unintentionally fallen in love with the place, despite not having really scratched the surface. But maybe in a city this manufactured, you don't scratch the surface; perhaps there's no such thing as an 'authentic experience' in a city this new and international. Either way, once again, my preconceptions were proved to be misconceptions, and in the relaxed atmosphere that the city exudes I felt safer than I do in London. Even with the miles of glass walls shooting into the sky, the 14-lane motorway, the flashy cars, gold bars, glitz and glamour – and extravagances that would put Las Vegas to shame, such as outdoor air-con – Dubai somehow still felt calm and dignified. And it still had one last treat for me.

At 6 a.m. on the day of my flight, I splashed water on my face, tucked my messy, increasingly long hair behind my ears, slipped my shoes on and jumped in the car with Rod. It was still dark. Just around the corner was Bulgari Island, which we reached just before the sun appeared. Within minutes it had painted the sky red, with the jagged skyscraper horizon dominated, of course, by the Burj Khalifa, looking like a huge crack in the sky. It was still and silent. We looked at the stunning view and listened to nothing but the sound of the occasional overhead plane. It was quiet, and calm. I soaked up the rare moment to contemplate the city in relative silence.

We had breakfast and rested, and I even managed a little afternoon nap, something I hadn't done in a long time. Then it was time for one of the hardest goodbyes so far, as Rod and Gaëlle's children went off to various after-school classes and I headed for the airport. Meeting great people and then parting so soon could be brutal when I was spending so much time in my own head.

Oman

I rarely travelled and ran on the same day, simply because it was too exhausting and, more importantly, because I generally wouldn't have enough daylight. I'm not a fan of running in the dark, especially in a new city – it's an unnecessary risk. But with a very short flight and still on a high from Dubai, I decided to go for it. I arrived at the hotel in Muscat, changed and set off, aiming to get as many miles done as possible before the light faded.

Around dusk I passed a beautiful mosque, one of the few highlights of an otherwise unspectacular 20 miles of dull, busy roads, before arriving at a sweeping four-mile stretch of beach. It was flat, calm and beautiful, perfect for my last few miles. As the sun was setting, I noticed a man running in the same direction, just ahead of me, with a water-bladder backpack, usually a sign of a fellow endurance athlete, so I decided to say hello.

Michael was a Danish man, living in Oman with his family, and after I'd explained what I was doing, he decided to join me for the last ten kilometres. I mentioned that I was planning to hitch a lift back to the hotel, as I often did if I wasn't running a loop, but, as he lived nearby, Mike kindly offered me a lift back to avoid me having to hitch at night or part with a hefty taxi fare. After trotting back along the beach to complete the 26.2, now in utter darkness, we arrived at his home around 10 p.m. where, to my surprise, he woke his sleeping wife and son and invited me in for dinner. I felt guilty about intruding at such a late hour, but it felt rude to decline, and in the spirit of travel and meeting new people, I accepted their generous offer, which included a shower and some clean clothes.

Making more of an effort to meet new people meant trusting my judgement, and when you share common ground with someone, such as a love of running, you can tell a lot about them. While accepting an offer of dinner and a shower from a stranger I'd met on a beach would be considered by many people (especially my fellow Brits) to be over-friendly, weird or even dangerous, I could tell that Mike was genuinely kind and selfless. For the second time in less than a day, I said good-bye to a lovely family and, at 2 a.m., Mike dropped me back at the hotel. What a wonderful way to spend 24 hours. I fell asleep feeling like I was really embracing the ethos of making every day count – Kev would be proud of me. The world was gifting me opportunities and I was gratefully accepting them.

Having run on arrival day, I had until 4 p.m. the following day to explore, so took a trip to a local sink hole famous for its crystal clear water. The journey there took me along wide empty roads lined with goats, beautiful homes and, in the distance, mountains, before I made it to nature's bathtub – a warm, glistening circular bowl of swimming heaven. Naturally, I didn't have any swimming trunks with me, so in the tradition of the kid who forgot his PE kit, and to the deep distaste of several old ladies sunning themselves nearby, I went in in my pants, looking every bit the Brit abroad as I did the mincing-over-pebbles walk, getting in and out of the water. Outings on travel days always made me feel a little uneasy, especially in places as idyllic as this. I'd still yet to miss a flight, and with the potential for incidents and distractions that these extra-curricular activities presented, it was always a risk. Sure enough, before I knew it, I'd spent too long there and had to make a dash for the airport, desperate to keep a clean sheet.

Last to board, as usual.

Jordan

Sitting on the plane with my wet pants stuffed into my bag and my straggly, still damp hair restrained in a small bush on top of my head, it had been a fairly close call, but I was now well versed in not giving a shit about my appearance, and was back in the swing of last-minute speed packing and sleeping on the plane. I was enjoying the pace. I was looking forward to more pleasantness in Jordan. Amman, then, came as a bit of a shock.

In my blasé state, I'd foolishly assumed that, as another Middle Eastern country, the weather in Amman would be similar to Muscat. After all, I'd just been swimming in natural spring water in baking sunshine. Turns out Jordan is actually quite a long way from Oman, and I arrived amidst gale force winds and highs of 8°C. It was a wake-up call not to get complacent – a kind of slap in the face from the weather gods for having too much fun in my downtime.

I'm told there are some very beautiful places in Jordan, but Amman didn't appear to be among them, certainly not the city centre. I completed a forgettable 26 miles of bleak weather and busy roads, topped off with a mini-sandstorm. Shortly after I stepped through the door, having finished marathon number 105, it snowed, which would have been unthinkable the previous day, but such was the privilege of hopping from one country to another.

Bulgaria

Marathon 106, day 393, was pretty boring, cold, and generally not very scenic. Sometimes I would get to see all the best bits of a city, but I think Sofia showed me all her worst bits. The footpaths weren't great and, having spent too long trying to find a decent route, I resorted to heading for the biggest park I could see on the map, and running laps to complete my mileage. Although I did actually enjoy the park loops, it was always frustrating when I knew I wasn't making the most of a city. In most places, I would arrive a stranger and aim to leave having seen a few sights, and with at least a little understanding of the culture and history of a country, but with such a short stop here, 24 hours, Bulgaria wasn't to be one of those places. You win some, you lose some. Onwards to Istanbul, the nation of the East–West divide.

Turkey

Thanks to a window seat, I had somewhere to rest my head and arrived in Turkey having slept from takeoff to landing. I was in the home of tea, textiles, and Turkish delight. The stunning Boutique Hotel Amira is situated in the heart of the old town, just around the corner from the Blue Mosque and a short walk from the Grand Bazaar. The Blue Mosque specifically makes it into my all-time top 10 of favourite buildings. The hand-painted blue walls are striking, and at night are illuminated with beams of projected blue light. It's not overly tall but with five hefty principal domes, six pointy, castle-turret-like minarets and eight secondary smaller domes, it is a work of art.

In response to our begging emails, the management of the hotel had generously gifted me three nights of glorious four-star luxury. My thanks never felt like enough.

My marathon route would be straightforward: I'd keep the sea on my right, turn at 13.1 miles then keep the sea on my left. Following the Black Sea coast was effortless, and as I ran, my location evoked thoughts of what lay behind and ahead. It felt appropriate that I was at the gateway to Asia, as I'd soon be moving from Europe onto the next continent. I thought of the other countries just across the water where I'd already run: Bulgaria, Romania, Ukraine and Russia; just Georgia needed to complete the set. The call to prayer echoed around the city, and the sunlight slowly filled the sky, as dog walkers meandered along the corniche and fishing boats set out for an early morning haul.

As the morning wore on, the traffic increased, but to nowhere near the levels I'd experienced elsewhere in the world. On one of several stops to fill my Osprey water-bladder backpack, a local man asked me if I liked Turkey, and if I thought of it as Arabic, Asian or European. His question caught me slightly off guard, as it hadn't really crossed my mind to try to pigeonhole the place in that way. But I think that was his point – it was rhetorical. Cities such as London and Toronto are often referred to as the most 'multicultural' in the world, but this mainly refers to population demographics. In Istanbul, the city itself feels multicultural, shaped by different empires over thousands of years, its historic architecture the product of its position as the bridge between East and West. It has long been a microcosm of what we now think of as global society, and I loved it. I smiled to myself as I ran on.

I ran without music, but still wearing my earphones. This, along with occasionally wearing a buff over my mouth and nose, was a necessary procedure I'd adopted along the way in order to shield my various facial orifices from wind and dirt, especially in drier, dusty countries. With the mileage I was covering, it was amazing how much grime could end up in my ears, and the earphones saved having to carry and subsequently throw away hundreds of earbuds. While running in other more polluted capital cities, I had to think about my lung health, and the more life-shortening particles I could filter out, the better. Simple fixes, but I like to think they made a bit of a difference.

By the time my legs carried me over the invisible finish line, my mind had turned to thoughts of the Grand Bazaar, Hagia Sophia and a photo session, and so I started planning my afternoon outing. The Hagia Sophia is said to have changed the history of architecture. Once the largest building of its time, it started life as the former Greek Orthodox Christian patriarchal cathedral, and then later went on to become an Ottoman imperial mosque. At the time of my visit it was a particularly photogenic museum, though it has since reverted into a place of worship once again. It was on my photography bucket list.

Ever since watching an episode of the *Antiques Roadshow* as a boy, I'd always wanted a proper Turkish rug. Within a few hours, I was the proud owner of a beautiful, traditional handmade silk rug – and feeling very pleased with myself at having haggled my way to 80 per cent off the asking price.

In reality, of course, the process is pretty similar: the customer walks away feeling like a wily traveller, immune to being ripped off, while the shopkeeper hangs an identical rug in its place and thinks, 'There's one born every minute!' But the bargaining, expected by both sides, is all part of the fun, and I was happy to sit and have a chat and a nice cup of Turkish tea with the charmers at the rug stall. This did, of course, leave me with a large heavy brown paper parcel to carry around for the next few weeks. Worth it, though.

With a few exceptions, I found that 40,000 or so steps around a city were enough to get a feel for how safe I was in any given place. I wouldn't walk around London with my laptop on display, but at around 9 p.m. that evening in Istanbul I tucked my laptop under my arm and strolled out to find somewhere to eat and check my emails. This may have been foolhardy, maybe I was even getting complacent with personal safety again, but there was just something about the city that made me feel at home. It felt liberating.

Bosnia and Herzegovina

Squashed into the middle seat of a cramped Turkish Airlines flight, my head lolled around as I attempted to get some last-minute shut-eye before what was to be a busy stop in Sarajevo. It was crisp and cold as I stepped out of the aircraft and I could see my breath as I looked out over a blanket of fresh snow.

It felt strange to be in a city relatively close to home that had been at the centre of world-changing events and conflict, both historically and so recently, although my knowledge of both was minimal. This was one of many countries where I was lucky enough to have British embassy support, and I was collected from the airport by Emir, a local man in his sixties who had lived through the city's recent turbulent history and now worked for the embassy as a driver. I'd made a habit of attempting to elicit from drivers (especially of taxis) something I didn't know about their city. It was always a great opportunity to learn about the history of a place or discover some interesting facts. To me, it felt like collecting stickers, with the knowledge that I would never complete the album. Emir was incredibly knowledgeable about the Bosnian War, and the 20-minute drive to my hotel turned into a fascinating history lesson from a man who'd lived through it. He educated me on the Siege of Sarajevo, as we passed memorials to the thousands who lost their lives in the conflict, as well as painted murals of explosions, a reminder that this all took place within living memory.

Before Bosnia and Herzegovinian independence in 1992 Sarajevo had, over the last 150 years, been part of the Ottoman Empire, the Austro-Hungarian Empire, the Independent State of Croatia, and Yugoslavia; and it was to the city's more historic but no less devastating events that my mind turned as I arrived at my hotel, just a few feet from the infamous spot where Archduke Franz Ferdinand of Austria was assassinated.

As usual, the running day started before I was fully awake. Having unpacked (i.e., emptied the contents of my bag onto the floor) the night before, I located a few warm items (my Do Sport Live running gear, plus a warm jacket and extra buff), covered my knees, ankles and hip in anti-inflammatory gel, took my cocktail of nutritional tablets, downed some water, and attempted to make my hair presentable in the mirror of the lift on the way down to the lobby. In addition to kindly providing me with airport transport, the embassy had made various arrangements for my visit.

As I stepped out of the lift, I was met by a lobby full of people, including a TV crew, and a group of about ten runners who greeted me warmly with hugs. Among them were the British ambassador Matt, and his colleagues Jonny, Jasmin, Almasa, Dzenana and, of course, Nudzemja. 'Nudzy', as she is known, is famous among local running communities for having set up a running group for women wearing headscarves. After introductions, a good chat and a quick press call, we were ready to brave the weather and run. It was wet, cold, slushy, slippery and windy, all the ingredients of an unpleasant marathon, but my fellow runners were a great bunch, and while I covered the full distance, the others dipped in and out, one of them leapfrogging us in a car to get some professional snaps with my camera. I had good conversation, water and snacks on tap for the whole run. On top of this, the mountainous backdrop to the city was beautiful, and I was able to learn more about the country's history from my running buddies.

With all these great distractions, the marathon was done by 11 a.m. A quick shower and change, 20 minutes to scoff down some food, and I was collected from the hotel and taken to local TV and radio stations for interviews. By this point in the trip, my challenge had been fairly well publicized, and while there was more awareness than ever of what I was trying to do, and despite my mission statement of 'a marathon in every country in the world', I would still invariably be asked questions like, 'Which countries aren't you going to?' I don't think people thought I was simply avoiding the difficult bits, I think that there was just an assumption that it wasn't possible, with various current political situations, to visit – let alone run in – every single recognized country on the planet. Only time would tell.

After a late dinner with the runners, I packed my bags and after just four hours' sleep, set off for Serbia at 5 a.m., forgetting various clothing items I had left drying in the bathroom.

Serbia

Arriving in Belgrade minus several key items of clothing, I managed to borrow some from Andy. Yes, Andy was back. The patron saint of world marathons had returned for more punishment. Despite some horrendously cold and fairly brutal runs on his last visit, Andy was here for his fifth support stint and another two marathons which, to his aching-legged surprise, turned into three. As well as emergency clothing provision, it was always a morale boost to have him join me, not just as a friendly face, but as someone who could comfortably run marathon distances in deeply unpleasant conditions.

The first half of the run was, in a word, muddy. As with several other European marathons, we were aiming to follow the good old Danube, as it usually meant miles of nice flat footpath to run along – but with a visit to the British embassy scheduled for mid-morning, we stayed north of the river for the first few miles, where the river path soon led us into a huge construction site centred around an old railway station. Before we knew it, we'd gone too far to turn back and were running through soft, ankle-deep mud that, in places, had mixed with oil from the old engine sheds and scrapped cars that littered the area. To keep our appointment at the embassy we needed to find a way through, and we spent the next mile or so scrambling around old junk piles and over muddy banks before eventually emerging a few streets away.

Having been told off by the guard for taking a dangerous, security-threatening photo of the British embassy plaque, we shuffled through various levels of security, confirmed that we had no weapons to check-in (I find that carrying firearms during a marathon slows you down), and were eventually issued with visitor IDs before stepping into what was a fairly stately interior, where we were greeted by the British ambassador.

It was just a quick stop to meet the team and take some photos, but we soon realized that perhaps they hadn't expected us to arrive mid-marathon. As we were led into a high-ceilinged room adorned with antique tapestries and oil paintings, we offered to remove our filthy shoes, but the staff insisted it wasn't necessary and, exchanging uncertain glances, Andy and I sat down at a very large table set on a rug that looked like it cost more than my car, for a quick chat and some water. Not wanting to spend too long stinking up this grand old room, we told them we were in a hurry, and were hastily ushered over to the fireplace for a group photo, looking down with deep shame at our muddy, oily, black footprints on the ambassador's rug. Looking a bit sheepish, we ended our five-minute stop with a few handshakes before heading back out into the city where, once we were out of earshot, we giggled like naughty schoolboys, despite feeling terrible about soiling the embassy. We crossed to the south side of the river, where we found enough footpath to complete an otherwise uneventful marathon.

That evening, Andy brightened things up by delivering a special package that he'd brought with him from Bristol. A number of schools back home had been following my journey, tracking my progress on globes and world maps, and organizing fundraising activities to support the charity, all of which made me feel incredibly humble. The children of Victoria Park primary school in Bedminster, Bristol, had gone one step further, and Andy handed me a large brown envelope stuffed full of messages and pictures they'd made for me. The untainted optimism and wonder of young children is always heart-warming. I was deeply moved as I read their fantastic messages of encouragement and enjoyed their wonderful drawings of flags, maps, the world and various renderings of me running. Andy and I spent the evening sifting through them before arranging all 60 A4 sheets on my hotel bed to get a photo for my social media update.

The following morning Andy knocked on my door while I was still packing. This was always the case, due to our relative amounts of luggage. Andy prided himself on only ever bringing hand luggage on these trips (having even managed to do so for his five-country visit back in December) and so, for him, packing was a five-minute job. Departure days would generally involve him sitting patiently while I gathered my belongings from their designated positions on the floor and shoved them into my bags. However, the thick sheaf of letters from the school were placed carefully into the inner sanctum of my hand luggage, and day 392 got under way with a short flight to Montenegro.

Montenegro, Albania

Having checked the map before we left Belgrade, we'd noticed that Podgorica, Montenegro's capital, is only a few miles from the Albanian border, and we hatched a plan. Albania was one of several countries that had been postponed due to flight complications and was still to be rescheduled. With an early morning flight, we would have time to run our Montenegro marathon, leaving us with a spare day to try and tick off Albania too – or, at worst, have a day off. Not only would this recover some lost time, but potentially save money too. I called home to let the team know what we were planning. My dad, in particular, was very keen. We hadn't quite worked out the details yet, and Andy had never run back-to-back marathons before, but was keen not to let me down.

Post-flight, we arrived at our strange little hotel, made entirely of pebbles, and had a late 'breakfast' of chicken wraps and chips in the hotel bar before gathering our energy to get into our running kit. The weather was foul. The temperature wasn't quite as low as in recent countries, but we would be running in cold, relentless, driving rain. We set out, and both immediately experienced shortness of breath, thankfully due only to the heavy meal we'd just finished eating – so that soon wore off. In the apparent absence of any footpaths or areas of interest, we ran along a busy main road out of the city, and within a couple of miles were utterly sodden and freezing. We couldn't have been any wetter, although quite a few lorry drivers didn't seem to agree as they roared past, engulfing us with puddle water. It was a miserable, boring marathon, but at least I had good company and, due to the hateful conditions, we were running at a decent pace, desperate to get back in the dry.

Despite heavy legs, due to all the water in our clothes and shoes, we stuck to the pace and finished in under four hours. We were both exhausted, while Andy, strangely, was frothing at the knees. With so much water in his leggings, the pockets of air around his knobbly kneecaps had been squeezed through the fabric with every step, and he'd built up an attractive layer of foam under each knee. It was the most interesting thing we saw in Podgorica.

However, stage one of our plan was complete, and we now needed to find transport to Albania. The car-hire desk in the hotel reception was unmanned and apparently closed, so we got on the laptop and hunted for local car-hire firms, with little success, so we decided to ask the hotel receptionist when the car-hire desk would reopen. In a slightly hushed voice, she told us, in broken English, not to use the large, well-renowned car-hire company. Instead, she would speak to her friend who would fix us up with a hire car.

True to her word, around an hour later, she called my room to inform me that our car had arrived. We met the woman from the hire company in reception and, after completing an alarmingly small amount of paperwork, and handing over a few Euros, we were given the keys to a smart little hatchback which, as luck would have it, had in its glovebox the necessary documents to allow it to be driven out of the country. It all seemed far too easy: we had transport, and a good chance of ticking off a bonus country.

Over a hefty pasta dinner, we studied Google satellite pictures of potential running routes. We'd be running just over the border, we'd be in the middle of nowhere and there were no obvious pointers as to where to run. Then it was ice packs on our legs and an early night ahead of our adventure in the morning.

Anticipating a lack of places to get food and water, we loaded the car up with supplies, checked we had all the necessary documents, and set off. It was only a half-hour drive to the Albanian border, and after a quick scan of our documents, our passports were stamped, and we were in! Now all we had to do was run a marathon. We did a quick recce of the surrounding area in the car, and realized that although we'd have to run along the main road with no footpath or pavement, it was smooth, flat tarmac, and virtually deserted. It wasn't ideal, but if we drove further into the country looking for a better spot, we risked running out of time and daylight.

We parked the car, which was to become our base for the day, at a petrol station close to the border, and changed into our running kit on the forecourt, much to the bemusement of the four men either working or hanging around near the kiosk. Unlike hotels, cars can be stolen, and we made sure to take our passports with us, in case we returned to find we'd be walking back to Montenegro.

We weren't expecting this marathon to be anything special, just a necessary tick in the box, but as we set off it was not only dry but a relatively balmy 14°C. As we ran through the mostly empty landscape we realized that we were actually among some really pretty scenery, with Lake Skadar to our right and forest-covered mountains to our left. Not much happens in this part of Albania and every single person we saw waved and said hello. Even the local police were friendly, and a check of our documents soon turned into a friendly chat and a group photo.

After a sub-four-hour marathon the previous day, it wasn't a fast run, but we got the job done. Two laps of a 13-mile out-and-back with a snack stop at our little car at the halfway point, and we finished, utterly exhausted but very pleasantly surprised with what had been an enjoyable marathon in peaceful, scenic, mild and dry conditions. More importantly, I had completed another country, for a total cost of 50 Euros and zero extra days: great for the schedule, great for the budget. My dad was very pleased indeed. Within 24 hours of hiring the car, we returned to our hotel in Montenegro just in time to catch England vs. Ireland in the Six Nations rugby.

Slovenia

The next day Andy flew home and I flew on to Ljubljana. The embassy staff had really pulled out all the stops: to my delight, I'd been invited to stay in the presidential apartments in the city. On my first morning, I swept back the curtains of my huge, multi-room penthouse suite to see a rare sight: clear blue cloudless sky. After all the grey skies lately, the bright sunlight came as a shock to the system, and I recoiled from the window like a vampire, hissing as my skin sizzled.

My running pals for the day were Urban and Jasmine, a pair of authors who lived an idyllic life, writing and bringing up their four children. Enthusiastic runners, with the courage to leave behind conventional lives and work hard to follow their romantic dream – these were my kind of people. The city looked gorgeous as we stepped out into the crisp morning air. Despite the blue sky, it was still chilly, and my companions put me to shame with their double layers, while I'd wrapped myself in five. We ran along the river, and around numerous nondescript parks, swapping stories of our alternative lifestyles, and chatted about travel and adventure. Assuming I completed this challenge, my next one would be writing this book, and I was keen to get some tips on how to balance writing with a busy life and specifically running.

Marathon done, Urban and Jasmine invited me to dinner that evening, for which I threw on my least dirty clothes. Just as I was stepping out of the resplendent luxury of my room(s), my phone rang. Apparently there was a special guest downstairs to see me. Flanked by security personnel, his assistant and the British ambassador, President Borut Pahor greeted me with a firm handshake and a beaming smile. At the point of shaking his hand, I still had no idea who he was, and it was only after some introductions from his 'people' that I realized I was speaking to the head of state. I suddenly felt very scruffy. It turns out that Mr Pahor is a very keen runner, and a fast one at that, and we shared a few stories over a drink in the lobby. He was sorry not to have made it out for the marathon that morning, but four and a half hours of a president's time is quite a lot. To compensate, we jogged a short distance together, just outside the hotel. I think he did this for my sake more than anything, just so I could say I'd run with him. I wasn't dressed for running, and he certainly wasn't. I could see my face in his shoes. You could only smell things in mine.

He was a very down to earth chap, and had made me feel very welcome in his country, and before we parted ways we exchanged details and arranged to keep in touch. Dinner and chat with Urban and Jasmine rounded off a brilliant day. We spoke of all things adventure, running, and their family life while pursuing such a brilliant laidback author/running career. For a while we plotted the idea of returning to Ljubljana at some point to run from summit to sea. A great bonus for the city is that it's possible to travel from ski resort mountains down to the ocean. Running the distance, just under a hundred kilometres, would take about 24 hours and seemed a great idea. I spent most of the flight out of Slovenia thinking about which mountains to run from, and the logistics involved. My mind ran away with itself.

Kosovo

Arriving in Kosovo, a diary mix-up resulted in me expecting no support, so as I sleepily shuffled through baggage reclaim, immigration and into the shabby arrivals area I was surprised to see my name among the printed and handwritten A4 sheets held by the usual cluster of drivers and hotel staff. The only reason I spotted my name is because it was being held by the only person in the small crowd that didn't have a glum face. The man was smiling and looked eager to greet me. Not only was his face brighter than the others, it was familiar. He said, 'You don't recognize me, do you?' To which I replied, 'I do' – and after a couple of seconds my mind flew back five years to a very wet day at Silverstone.

I had been running for a sponsor and helping to pace someone in the Silverstone half marathon. It rained all day, and before the race everyone had huddled together under any available shelter, shivering. There was no choice but to mingle, and I met a chap named Veton, who was Kosovan but at the time lived in London with his wife. I noted his impeccable English, and how relaxed and at ease he looked, while the other runners looked like they were dreading running in these conditions. We had a brief chat, exchanged details, and he told me if I ever came to Kosovo I should drop him a message. We hadn't said a word to each other since that day, but here he was, a man I'd known for around five minutes, meeting me at the airport years later.

He now lived in Pristina, back where he grew up, and had been in touch with my assistant, Carla. Together, they had arranged the meeting, and Carla had left my diary blank as a surprise. It was to be another very special stop, all arranged by a man whose name I wasn't even sure I was pronouncing correctly. (I wasn't.) Veton (pronounced with a soft v and a long ee) had organized a press conference, a talk at his running club, a route with support cars, and even dinner at the embassy. Despite his laidback manner, he was clearly a master-planner and knew how to get things done.

We instantly bonded over stories of running and travel logistics. Kosovo was one of three countries on my list whose status as a sovereign nation is disputed, and Kosovans generally have problems getting visas to visit other countries. Despite this, Veton had friends not just everywhere but in high places too. I later learned that he had previously worked for the UN and had a network of contacts all over the world. Little did I know at this point just how instrumental this incredible man would become to the remainder of my trip. At the risk of spoilers, it's no exaggeration to say that without his knowledge, help and commitment, completing this challenge would have been impossible.

The three days in Kosovo were very tiring, but I loved every minute. During the first evening, I spoke for a while to the X-Trail runners' community about my running background, and how I'd come to be there. This was followed by some autographs, radio and TV slots, and a very late bedtime, as a result of which I slept through my alarm on the morning of the run and missed breakfast.

Around ten runners were huddled shivering next to the city's 'Newborn' monument, which was to be our start and finish point. I'd had no food and little sleep, and felt terrible for arriving late, particularly as among the group was yet another British ambassador and several people who had taken the day off work to run with me. Our route, mapped out by Veton and his running club, was a big loop that took in the sights of the city and quiet rural areas dotted with villages, farms and lakes, on a mixture of busy main roads and single-track lanes.

We were also accompanied, for some of the run, by camera vehicles with crews hanging out of them filming and taking photos, and I was interviewed mid-run. There were some great people running with me, and I tried to divide my time between each of them, including a young girl who was a superb runner but spoke no English, so we ran together for a while in comfortable silence. Around the middle of the run I chatted to a man called Xhavit, who told me about the war in Kosovo and how the country had changed during his lifetime. His stories of uprising, war and the growing tension will stay with me for ever. Stories of shelling, his friends being killed, and the overall brutality of the war that led to over 100,000 Bosnians being killed. This was the first genocide in Europe since World War Two. There are too many details and snippets of horror to mention, and frankly I tried not to remember them. He was a young man who went to fight for his country, something which I questioned in myself – would I do the same had the war been in England?

Later that evening he presented me with a military pin he had earned before I was even born. I was reluctant to accept it, but he was insistent, and I took it with great thanks, feeling both undeserving and deeply honoured. This is now a highly treasured souvenir in my large collection of mementos from all over the world. As ever, I was touched by the power that running has to bring people together.

Despite it being unpleasantly cold once again, it was a great day, and a fantastic marathon route, if not a little long – I clocked 31 miles as we arrived back at the monument, before being accosted by another media crew for post-run questions. I was so grateful to Veton for making my visit so much more enriching, not to mention educational. I learned of the forces that combined for the creation of the army that fought for their independence. I learned the real extent of how quickly war ignites, and I began to understand how death and destruction in a pocket of the world can cause so many lives to change course for generations. I felt as if I was in the most immersive history lesson ever put on. I vowed to learn more about Britain's history – not just the headline-catching events but the bits in between too. In a place where the horrors of conflict are such a recent memory for so many people, I went to bed that night once again feeling incredibly lucky to have the freedom and privilege to do what I was doing.

North Macedonia

I managed three hours in bed before leaving for Macedonia. In fact, I was leaving for North Macedonia, another country, along with Eswatini/Swaziland, that had changed or was in the process of changing names. The name North Macedonia was being bitterly disputed by Greece, and the day after I left it changed its name to Macedonia.

Veton, in his infinite kindness, offered to drive me across the border, all the way to the city of Skopje, rather than take the train as arranged, which was not only another cost saving, but allowed me to catch up on a little more sleep. I awoke four hours later at the border, where Veton told me we had a small problem. The car documents we needed to cross the border didn't seem to be in the vehicle. We got out and emptied the car of its contents and searched every cubbyhole, but to no avail. Despite the unsociable hour, Veton resorted to calling his wife, who immediately directed us to a small and very well-hidden compartment in the car up and under a small flap of fabric beneath the passenger seat, where the necessary paperwork was stashed. We put everything back in the car and were on our way and, after another hour, reached my hotel in Skopje. With the delay Veton would struggle to get back in time for work and couldn't hang around, so in the small hours of the morning I offered him my heartfelt thanks and we hugged goodbye. An addition to all the support he had provided in Kosovo, Veton was a calming presence, and I made a mental note to try to adopt his unflappable approach.

I didn't get off to a great start in this endeavour, as I realized that my hotel was closed for the night. In my hurry to see Veton back on his way, I hadn't checked to see if the doors were unlocked, and with no contact number or Wi-Fi all I could do was wait out in the cold. I'd hoped to check-in and set out running before dawn but, with my bags, I was stuck. Five o'clock came and went, as did six, and I decided to abandon this hotel and wander the deserted city until I found one that was open. I found a slightly rundown-looking Holiday Inn and sat down in the warm lobby. It was too early to check-in, so I nodded off for a bit. The next thing I knew, I was being woken up by staff at 2 p.m., having slept through the entire morning.

Several broken English conversations later, the original hotel owner had persuaded me to return, and by way of apology offered me an extra night for free, which of course I couldn't use. I slept for the rest of the day, writing it off, which meant a very early start the following day in order to squeeze in my marathon before an evening flight to Georgia. The run was uneventful, but it didn't rain, and I even ran without gloves. Not big positives, but lack of sleep had really caught up with me and I wasn't in the best of moods to appreciate this ancient, historic city, birthplace of Mother Teresa.

Georgia

Day 400 had passed without me noticing, and my 160th flight of the trip took me to Tbilisi. With all these plane journeys, I had developed a fondness for the window seat, as it allowed me to gaze out at planet Earth or sleep.

The city of Tbilisi is small, hilly, bustling and beautiful. As with most cities, a river runs through its centre, the Kura, over which passes what is now one of my favourite bridges in the world. Made of shining steel and glass, the Bridge of Peace is a footbridge which sits in dramatic contrast to its surroundings among the traditional buildings of the city, and looks a bit like a cuttlefish climbing over a fence. I followed the river, running along a path lined by fishermen. Most were untangling line or fiddling with kit and bait, and they all looked grim-faced. I've never really understood fishing.

Post-run, I treated myself to what should have been a short stroll around the open-air market, which is open for 12 hours a day, seven days a week. Looking around at the elderly, weather-beaten faces of some of the stall holders, I realized that a lot of them were lifers. They sold everything, including massive swords, gramophones, tapestries and old cameras, and I ended up spending four hours wandering around and chatting to the market folk. It was great for photos, and the stall holders all agreed to have their pictures taken with obliging smiles.

After a total of eight hours on my feet, I taxied back to the hotel in a lovely old cream-coloured Lada Riva, before showering, packing, napping and going for dinner in a restaurant across the road from the hotel. I was ravenous, and in my indecision ordered two mains: a steak with sauce, potatoes and green beans, and a bread-based dish that looked like a tiger loaf with an egg on top, but its hollowed out interior was filled with melted cheese and eggs. I scoffed the lot and sat back like Mr Creosote, full to bursting – delicious. Before my food coma set in, I waddled back to my hotel room and attempted to bend over to pick up various items in a feeble attempt at packing. It was pointless, and I decided to do it at 2 a.m. the following morning, before my flight.

People often ask me about my diet and weight loss during the journey, and I think it was only the occasional huge meal like this one that prevented me from becoming skeletal. Over the two years, my weight ranged from 54 kilograms to 68 kilograms – that day in Georgia, it definitely felt nearer the top end.

Armenia

Armenia, country number 116, and the final stop for this phase. Apologies to Yerevan and its residents, but I didn't really pay much attention here. My mind was already elsewhere, thinking ahead to obtaining my new passport, getting away from grey cities and rain, and exploring the delights of Asia. My mind was so tired so often that my memory of places has morphed and moulded together with the memories of photos and articles of inflight magazines. Armenia – sorry – I don't remember you at all. Although the running was more than bearable, I needed sunshine and the stimulus of faraway places. I was about as far away from home as you can get in Europe, but it was still Europe and familiar. I was also in danger of becoming complacent again and not enjoying each place I visited.

6

The 'Stans

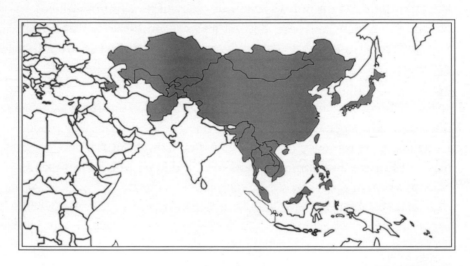

Singapore	Cambodia	Kyrgyzstan
Brunei	Thailand	Kazakhstan
Philippines	Myanmar	Tajikistan
Japan	Laos	Uzbekistan
China	Taiwan	Azerbaijan
Malaysia	South Korea	Afghanistan
Vietnam	Mongolia	

A brief stopover in London. It was a busy few days. Media at this point of the journey was becoming more full on and I was being pulled from one side of London to the other, with cars being laid on to rush me to various studios on time. With a few hundred days left, the trip was far from over, and by this point I'd been on television in 85 countries, and had over 700 media articles circulated about my voyage. I was beginning to get recognized in airports and hotels. The beast that was this trip had gone from pup to teenager and now to an adult. In a similar vein I was maturing in all sorts of ways. Through the wonders of gaining a wider view of the world my perspective had changed. Be it feeling grateful for simple things like getting water from a tap, having food I wanted whenever I wanted it, or some deeper aspects like appreciating religions and the communities they create, or the wonders of air travel, and the privilege of freedom, I was not the same person who set out on this journey in January 2018. The world around me looked and felt so different. My senses had painted a new image of the world. I was far more receptive to things. Be it through the places I saw, the people I met, the streets I ran down, or the smells wafting from drains, food stalls and hotel breakfasts, travelling mostly alone was enriching my understanding of the world I thought I knew.

I tracked all my miles with Garmin, Suunto and Strava, and my routes through a GPS tracker for Guinness World Records, but I used an app called Polarsteps to track each step of the trip with photos and a few diary notes.

In order to add a few pennies to the bank balance I was training a group of runners in London to run the Hackney Half Marathon. The money was only a few thousand pounds, and it was just a drop in the ocean compared to the average of about two thousand pounds each week it was costing to complete the mission. It helped a little though, and it happened to coincide with a passport pick-up and a natural end to one phase and beginning of the next. It wasn't ideal, and everything was rushed, but I did have a day with family as a welcome bonus.

The budget, funding, sponsorship and the overall finances of this mission were frankly underestimated and wildly misunderstood, principally by me. The initial estimates of the trip put the rough cost at around £100,000. This was a figure based on many unknowns, but one that I thought was based on sound approximations and a decent few months of research. The scale of the journey, though, and all it entailed – extra costs like paying bribes, outrageous visa fees, and the cost of drivers to follow me throughout numerous runs to keep me safe – were amongst some of the areas we initially overlooked. In reality, every single aspect of the journey was dramatically under-budgeted and therefore we overspent almost immediately, and things got worse from there.

The funding was the single most draining and stressful part of the journey. In the planning stages so much time was spent approaching sponsors and travelling around the country to speak with brands about potential support. During the journey it got worse, because the money we had accrued was being spent exponentially faster than we could raise it. Even with tens of thousands of emails and many conversations offering support, invariably the support was either tiny or unbalanced in terms of requested responsibilities.

That said, we had around 50 brands involved that were willing to help. This I was and still am enormously grateful for. Ninety-five per cent of these, however, provided product and product alone. While I needed clothing, shoes and a pair of sunglasses, I really needed cash. Even if I sold every single item I was given, it wouldn't pay for more than three averagely priced flights. It's true, very true, that finding funding for this and any adventure is incredibly hard without any proven track record. Even then it's not straightforward. To be clear: my genuine thanks goes to every brand that supported in any way at all. The community that the team and I built with these companies and individuals was invaluable in terms of publicity and spirit. We still, however, needed cash, and lots of it. Nearly all the money we had scraped together from sponsors equated to just over £30,000. This was gone before I even left the UK. Flights, visas and the team costs, small as they were, wiped out every penny. Everything thereafter was down to fundraising on our own. Asking friends, family, the public, using savings, writing emails and, of course, borrowing money wherever I could. I spent every penny I had and was asking for handouts after just six months. My parents and some outrageously kind close family and friends were those who, for the most part, helped me see this through to the end. My dad's elderly cousin, Jean, who I'd only met a few times when I was very young, even organized a tea party at her retirement flats which raised about £100. Consider, then, that just to gain the necessary access to somewhere like Bhutan cost over £2,000; simply to obtain the correct paperwork to grant me access for just 48 hours. We held a launch event, were given stalls at local fêtes and fairs, and I even resorted to selling most of my unused items, like clothes, shoes and old phones.

At first, the notion of travelling around the world after selling everything I had was romantic and enriching – the realities were something else. Consider further that every flight cancellation or amendment lost us money. Every change of plan and every delay meant more money wasted. It got very silly, very quickly. We were massively over budget with less than 30 per cent of the original figure from sponsors. To this day I owe money to many, many brilliant family and friends. Money was a problem and it became a topic that made me feel sick just talking about it.

My mum, dad, brother and I sat snoozily on the sofas around the lounge fire. We were full of Mum's tasty dinner as Barney, our family dog, joined us sitting to attention with his eyes longing for us to feed him, his tail flinging from one side to the other sweeping along the carpet. As the evening went by we collectively slipped further down the sofas. For a brief moment I was back in my old world. My mind, however, was never far from the excitement but also the worry and longing for all that was to come.

That evening around the fire, for the first time, we had some time to share stories of travel, flight frustrations, talk about prostate cancer, cancer in general, and reflected on the many close family and friends in our life that had sadly been taken by the disease. Being home for a short time gave perspective and context on the world.

My dad had a huge map in the kitchen with small black dots stuck to every country I'd been to. I must thank them all for the support. Words don't really cut it. That evening we had a moment. The four of us sat at the kitchen table looking up at the massive world map, and the amount of the world that we'd already covered. Our farmhouse-style kitchen was never very tidy, but the map was pristine and neat always. We stared up at it in wonder, and pondered in silence for a while. An unspoken appreciation of how far we'd come. We had 80 more to go; 80 more countries to complete the world. By November my dream should be realized. I say 'we' because the team effort is real. It's often talked about in any expedition, or sport or accomplishment of any kind but, for this journey the team did more of the work than I did. From booking flights, to adding the expected weather in my calendar so I'd know what I was facing, the team did everything for most of the journey. We shared tantrums, tears and heartache many times over the 674 days. But we all knew it was always worth it.

The next morning it was off to the airport. At 10 a.m. on 22 February I left London for Singapore, my 117th country.

Singapore

Air travel had become a friend and a foe simultaneously. If I was tired I'd be impatient with things like crap Wi-Fi or lack of seating. If I was in a good mood, I'd waltz through practically skipping. My mood was often more volatile in airports than in normal life. I think because they were my safe place so my guard was down. Airports are very strange places. Thousands of people pass through them and yet nobody really wants to be there. Personally, even when I was grumpy airports felt like home, my familiar territory. I knew that I'd have toilets, conversations with other punters, and, more often than not, heavily over-priced food. Airports were one of my only constants. The variety of airports – from sheds in Central America and the

Caribbean, to the metropolis of Atlanta or the new Istanbul terminals – effectively did the same thing but with varying degrees of glitz and health and safety. I placed my laptop, phone, watch, wallet, belt, shoes and passport neatly in the trays to be scanned. The same bag, with the same stuff every time – and yet when asking why the scanner triggered a search, the reason was different every time. In my opinion airport security is abysmal to the point of laughable. Humans are the weak link. More on that later.

Singapore. I would love to have stayed in the Marina Bay Sands Hotel, the infamous hotel known for the biggest roof-top infinity pool in the world. This was obviously out of my price range and so I stayed around the corner, where the price tag had fewer zeros. The one thing I don't miss from air travel is the time-differences, aka jetlag. Arriving in Singapore I felt sluggish and was met by a wave of humidity. Despite arriving at 10 a.m., I slept straight through till 5 p.m. that afternoon. After rousing myself I started to realize where I was, and generally came round from what felt like a general anaesthetic. The team had factored in things like extreme jetlag and so I was happy to rest and didn't feel guilty for it. I even ventured out to the famous Supertree Grove and got lost for a while in the 'nature meets man-made' engineering marvel. Situated in the 'Gardens by the Bay', 12 massive 18-metre high 'trees' resemble the famous baobabs of Madagascar. Despite the trees being made of plastic, concrete and metal, over 160,000 different flowering climbers adorn them. The entire complex is a spectacle of the bridge between imagination, nature and design.

It's safe to say my brain was not functioning at its best but I was content and excited to be in another phase of the mission and edging ever closer to the end. The end was something I longed for, but also tried to avoid in equal measures. A weird oxymoron of the mind.

The day of the marathon involved an early start once again. With the morning light behind the buildings, and the city still fast asleep, the roads were empty as I ran down to the water from the hotel. The smell in each city is distinct, and Singapore was no exception. It's clean, very clean, and there's a stillness to the city. The warm air on my face was a stark reminder that it was to be a hot phase. I was elated it wasn't cold, but instantly wished for it, of course. Before the sun was up and within minutes of stepping outside I was already sweating. With the distant sound of dustbin men and early morning taxi drivers going about their business, I soon made it to the water's edge and was in the heart of the city, not far from the Formula 1 race circuit that I was keen to run.

Despite the tiredness the jetlag worked in my favour. I started at about 6 a.m. and ran to a monument to meet a guy called Chas at 7 a.m. I'd managed four slow miles in the first 45 minutes because I was taking photos and generally enjoying the sights. Chas and I have a friend in common. Adrian had put us in touch so that Chas could show me around. With a 200-kilometre bike ride behind him the day before it was impressive of Chas to drag his body out of bed to help me navigate the city. We ran together for just over a half-marathon before he went off to work.

The route was fantastic: along the water, over the barrage, around the other side of the city and out along a beautiful coastal path. A beach and various sports people were our backdrop: so many cyclists, joggers, skateboarders, rollerbladers, even some Tai Chi, the list goes on. There were so many people being active. They did, though, all disappear after the sun came out, but it was a real treat to be amongst so much sport again after the recent marathons in Europe in the cold winter.

I had dinner at Marina Bay Sands after finding a discount coupon and watched the lightshow over the huge water fountains. As the countries went by, my levels of appreciation for the world and its diversity increased exponentially. Many moons ago I read an article in *The Times* about what the world would be like if everyone was like everyone else. If people and cultures moved around the world so much that everybody spoke the same language, ate the same food and looked the same. On the one hand things like racism and hate towards specific religions would be eradicated, but on the other there would be no awe or amazement, nothing to marvel at. I love diversity. Diversity of people, language, landscapes, faith, food . . . I discovered that the world is meant to be this way. This is what beauty is made of. Brunei was a classic example of that.

Brunei

Being back in the heat hit me hard. It was 40 degrees in the shade –
except I wasn't in the shade, because there wasn't any. Just a hot
sweaty slog along the river, two miles north and two miles back. Not
interesting, but it would have to do.

Early that morning I waited for a while in the lobby of the hotel
reception just after 6 a.m. for a couple who were due to run with me.
Sadly they didn't show up. It was something that happened a dozen or
so times throughout the journey, which was frustrating but I appreciated that people have their lives and I was just a random runner, just
an online personality. Besides, the few times I was let down, it was
usually due to excess heat or rain.

I waited for an hour or so, downloaded the offline map, found some
US currency for emergencies and trotted off quite happy to get my
head down and complete the run. As so often throughout the trip I
had no idea where I was going but knew it was safe, so I could relax
and enjoy myself.

The sun wasn't much trouble for a while, but the humidity was –
then the sun popped its ugly hot head above the horizon too. Up it
came, and my tongue turned white quickly. The dehydration curve
was steep. If you're a runner you'll know just how easy it is to become
super-dehydrated very quickly without realizing it. I am generally
pretty good with balancing fluids, but in this kind of heat it's close to
unavoidable. There was a gentle breeze for a few hours, but other than
that it was me versus the sun. Even the locals were talking about how
hot it was – never a good sign.

In the first few hours of the run I said hello to nearly everyone I
passed. The town was quiet. I was even high-fived by a bunch of
guys I passed over and over again as we ran our out-and-backs of
the waterfront. I befriended a few guys in a local shop; paid for
about five litres of water in small bottles upfront and left them in the
cooler. Every time I passed the shop I'd pop in, grab a bottle and
carry on. They were friendly and kind. I left Brunei feeling I hadn't
seen much but had learnt the people were lovely and the country was

slotted into the 'to visit again' column as I wrote my diary later that night.

Philippines

The car journey from the airport into the centre of Manila was long and full of traffic. I wondered if the roads were too congested to run on. The answer was a big fat 'yes'. No way would it be possible. The noise of horns in the centre of town was an orchestral mess. It took two hours to reach the hotel through a swarm of cars, trucks, buses and thousands of bikes, all bumper to bumper and wing mirror to wing mirror. The journey should have taken about 35 minutes. It was already hot and sticky, even with the taxi's air-con working overtime. Not a promising start.

Every one of the 26 miles through Manila the following day came with a specific smell. Often people would ask me if I could really see a country in the short time I was there, and, honestly, the answer is, 'No, of course not.' Nobody can see an entire country in a day, and you certainly can't experience every aspect in a day. But every city in every country comes with its own unique fingerprint made up of the sights, sounds, monuments, religions, laws, architecture, dangers, attitudes and smells. Us humans are pretty smart at putting them all together in the blink of an eye to create a snap judgement of a place. The way I saw it, it was like every time I stepped through the doors of the airport and began to experience any country for the first time, I had 48 hours to peel back its layers. Running was an incredibly detailed way to get an understanding of a place.

Manila was no exception and was a sensory overload. Smells were so apparent in the heart of the city. From smearing on the sun cream in my hotel room and hearing the sound of dustbin trucks outside, I could have been nearly anywhere. But stepping out into the belly of the city, it treated me to a concoction of smells: lorry fumes, burnt-out clutches, gas from nearby street-sellers' stoves, chicken feet cooking, fishermen's overalls, rain on tarmac, seaweed, floatplane fuel, dog poo, blackcurrant Gatorade, dirty stagnant water and freshly cut grass.

From that day on, I made a point of being more aware of the smells around me. In Manila I smiled as I ran the most wonderful stretch along the coast, past Rizal Park and down to watch a floatplane take off from the small marina. It would take off and land every 40 minutes or so, and in that time I could just about squeeze in three out-and-backs from my hotel door to the marina. It was another solo run, with virtually no room to move around the busy streets, but once I found a workable route that clocked up around three miles out and another three back I was happy to stick to it. People waved or stared at me as I ran. This I was used to by now. It rained, the sun came out, but the clouds stayed overhead for most of the run and it was humid. I clocked up the miles with a reinvigorated sense of adventure.

Once I was safe in the confines of the hotel and preparing for the following day's journey I had my first real sense that time was running out. It was something I hadn't considered before and it took me by surprise. I was recording a short, self-shot video excerpt for an interview back in the UK for Sky TV. I was talking through various bits and bobs and mentioned I only had 77 countries to go. Seventy-seven countries is more than some people visit in their lifetimes, but for me, in the context of the mission, I was certainly closer to the end than the beginning. I suddenly remembered that the trip was a once in a lifetime endeavour and I shouldn't wish it away. As the old saying goes: 'It's the journey not the destination.' The more fun I had and the more I enjoyed each day, the more time sped by like a bullet.

Japan

I landed in Tokyo a little after 7.30 p.m. It was dark, but the neon signs lit my path as I found my way through the maze of underground tunnels covered with Japanese writing. As always when arriving in a new alien land my first step is to find my accommodation, which was just around the corner from the famous Shibuya pedestrian crossing. I accidentally bought a first-class ticket, but it was much cheaper than expected, and the carriage was empty – just me and my huge leather recliner seat that was home for the next 80 minutes or so. With my eyes heavy, the carriage rocked me to sleep to the tune of that whoosh-ing noise as the train hurtled along the tracks and in and out of tunnels.

Once I arrived in the heart of the city, I stopped at the Shibuya crossing with my luggage by my side and couldn't help but stand and stare. I think everyone does this when they see it for the first time. Apparently Shibuya is the busiest intersection in the world; the cross-ing is like a living thing. It's clean, manned with traffic police, and at peak times it can handle 3,000 commuters in a single 11-second cross-ing. It was coldish in comparison to the last few weeks. I wrapped up warm as soon as I could. I stayed for a brief time in the Millennials pod hostel, right in the heart of the student district of Shibuya. The small pods offered only a bed. And I mean only a bed. The key to my 'room' was an iPod – this in itself a world away from Manila. Picture this: a double queen bed in a box with one end a fabric shutter and walls either side. Not only a key, the iPod can turn my pod's lights on and off, tilt my bed into a sofa, and even set an alarm so the bed moves to wake me up. The toilets are also pretty fun – there are more buttons in the bathroom than in my entire house.

Despite the quirkiness of the hostel, I had absolutely no room to move, and my body was achy and sore. I made a snap decision to upgrade and move two miles out of town to an Intercontinental. I had no money and in hindsight this was a stupid decision, but I had room – a lot of it. I sprawled out in my clinically white room and got naked. I was in that mood where I just needed space and a deep clean. I sent off all my gear to be laundered, and I showered for a good hour before falling asleep in my towel. It was a luxury I couldn't afford, but I went for it anyway. (Sorry, Dad.)

The world marathon majors were on my list to complete during the expedition. These are six of the biggest marathon events in the world and despite not actually needing to run them to accomplish my goal of running a marathon in every country in the world, it felt like a good fit, so why not? (And before you ask, no it wasn't as simple to integrate all of them within the 196. For starters, three of the six are in the US. The remaining three, London, Berlin and Tokyo, we did integrate as best we could, although there was always a risk that if flights were cancelled and I missed the actual race I'd have to run in the city regardless.) Everything had gone to plan up until this point, having run four of the six. But between myself, the team and the organizers, we managed to mess this up rather royally. My place for the official race had been lost. I arrived fully expecting to run the race but when I went to get my bib, they didn't have me on the list. In my new-found carefree attitude, which came and went as it pleased, I decided it wasn't a problem and I'd do it another year. Not to worry, it's another reason to come back to Japan.

On reflection I think I enjoyed the day more than I would have had I run the official race. Following advice from a friend Rich, I ran around the city, and then found the Imperial Palace Park. This place was crawling with runners – it was actually holding four different running events on the same day. That encapsulates Japan and Tokyo rather well, I think: 'always more' seemed to be their philosophy, and always done with precision and control.

My 2.5-mile loop had thousands of runners circling over and over again. With a slight incline one side and a gentle fall away for a quarter of a mile on the other side, it made for a perfect loop. I got chatting to some English-speaking locals, expats and other foreigners – the running community once again thrived – 42.195 kilometres flew by. It wasn't hot, which meant my legs opened up and I put in a few fast laps. I sweated less, which meant I drank less, which meant I stopped less to find water. In Manila a day earlier I drank about five litres; for this one in Tokyo I drank less than one litre. What 25 degrees difference can do. With a beautiful blue sky, a gentle breeze, and with runners flying past me, it was another great run.

Tokyo is a wonderful intricate city of history, bright lights, culture, cherry blossom and a whole load of people. It should be on everyone's bucket list. It's orderly and polite; it's calm yet hectic at the same time, and it's above all . . . happy. Even with all the suit-wearing and by-the-book neatness, the city is happy and playful. Even joyful.

A very good friend of mine once lived in Tokyo. That friend (Dani) has another friend, and his name is Rich. Rich still lived in the city and offered to be my guide. He's one of those guys everyone gets on with: placid, friendly and a gent. We spent the day exploring, taking some photos, eating sushi and generally getting lost in a city that nobody can ever know completely. We had time, although only briefly, to take a ride on the infamous bullet train. When we reached the platform in Tokyo station all I could do was stand and stare, waiting for the boom, as one after another trains exited the tunnel and then rocketed past us. It is an engineering marvel, and I was transfixed. The speed and the noise are unique: a deep and rapid roar could be heard in the distance every time a train approached. This was followed by the fast whipping noise of the wind and rain passing over the nose and around the body while the tracks below rattled tightly as it shot by. By now the weather had closed in and the blue sky turned grey. It added something to the spectacle of these breathtaking trains. The cambered rails are an obvious sign of the speed and precision. It was a beautifully clean, crisp white train with large portal windows. We watched many go by before boarding, not because we had to, but because I was more interested to watch as they flew past than to be on one. They came and went in a blink of an eye. There was something so elegant about this train.

Tokyo bid me farewell with the thunder, rain and menacing clouds smothering the city. With Rich caught up with work and a busy life we didn't manage to meet to say a proper goodbye. We did, though, agree that one day we would reunite and spend a little longer together. Perhaps we could surprise Dani with a plane ticket to Japan one day as a thank you to him for putting us in touch.

China

My 61st week on the road started with an orchestral couple of days of extreme thunder and lightning in the mountains of Hong Kong. The day of my 121st marathon I awoke to rain, clouds and heavy grey skies just a few hours after landing from Tokyo. With my eyes still mostly closed I could hear the patter of rain on the window and the wind rushing past. Much like my eyes, the huge heavy curtains of the hotel room let in just enough light to allow a glimpse at the morning over the skyscraper city. My fluffy duvet and crisp white sheets cocooned my tired body. I was curled up like a hibernating cub not wanting to move, let alone venture out and run in a downpour. I was ready to shut my eyes, roll over and drift off to sleep. But with a groan I threw back the covers and slipped on my three-day-old shorts and t-shirt before a long yawn and stretch to start the day.

I was planning to run up to Victoria Peak, which was high and looked out over the city, but my legs weren't having any of it. I was pretty low on energy and so found a path called Burrows Street. It was four kilometres, flat and cut into the city hillside. Half rural, half urban. As I ran west, the path dropped away behind a barrier on my right-hand side. The skyscrapers, cranes and tiny cars were below me, and yet the height of the city still towered above me on the left. The sky was gloomy and I could see the storm coming in. Five hours' running and I had a symphony of noise and flashes to accompany me. I have never heard such loud thunder. The ground shook as the storm came in, and the rain followed. I was soaked within ten strides. I stopped briefly to put my poncho on as the GoPro fixed to my head managed to capture some pretty spectacular shots of extreme rain and flashes of lightning. My feet were wet through and mushy like they'd been in a bath for far too long.

Pre-departure I wandered the streets with camera in hand, my index finger curled and poised ready to pounce on the next shutter opportunity: the classic boxy taxis, the ceiling of lights and concrete, the hustle and bustle of the streets and back alleys. It was an Asian metropolis and a photographer's paradise. Thousands of tiny cuboid air-conditioning units appeared to be stuck to the side of tower blocks, all of which were dirty and rundown and covered with exhaust soot, but, somehow, with the lights and the warm evening air they looked beautiful. A young couple peered out of their window in their oriental dressing gowns, clutching cigarettes and wine glasses.

Malaysia

One of my favourite films as a kid was the 1999 action thriller *Entrapment*, starring Catherine Zeta-Jones and Sean Connery, in which they plan a heist to pinch $8 billion from the International Clearance Bank situated in the North Tower of the famous Petronas Towers in Kuala Lumpur. Naturally things go wrong and there's a chase over the connecting bridge on the 88th floor at night on New Year's Eve. At the time I was ten years old and knew nothing of the world or what an international clearance bank was – but the towers looked *sooooo* cool, and ever since then I'd wanted to visit. I'm pleased to say, 20 years later, the towers lived up to expectations, although even now I still don't fully understand the film.

The whole of Malaysia is a remarkable place, and one of the most economically advanced in South-East Asia, and so I spent my first evening eating gorgeous platters of fresh food while looking out over the infinity pool at sunset to the Petronas Towers.

It turned out that for most of my stay in the city I was either staring up or down at the towers. Running the following day was humid – very humid – but nothing I wasn't already prepared to battle. I had a few gentle miles from the hotel snaking around the high-rise buildings to reach the KLCC Park. The park, my playground for the day, is used by thousands of locals, and even more tourists, every day, no matter what season. There are small ponds, bigger lakes, trees with picnic areas, viewing platforms to the towers above – all with a 1.2-kilometre red Astroturf running track around the circumference. Massive office blocks, complete with floor-to-ceiling blacked-out glass, surrounded the tiny spot of green in an otherwise manmade landscape. Old men walked with purpose around the track as I lapped them feeling smug but realizing they were likely triple my age – and thus feeling immediately less smug. Much like most of South-East Asia, it was way too humid for humans to function, let alone run, and with that came the running rush hour. Pre-dawn, the city was rammed. By breakfast time, slightly less so, and by midday nobody was outside at all. Everyone took refuge in their air-conned office boxes. Everyone except me, that was. In the first ten miles, pre-sunrise, I passed thousands and thousands of runners, walkers, rollerbladers, you name it – they were everywhere. Two hours later, towards the closing stages, I had the track to myself.

Being an economically developed city, water fountains were dotted regularly around the short circuit. I didn't need to carry water bottles, I had no need for a car to drive painstakingly slowly behind me to keep me safe, and the heat, although unbearable, was lessened with occasional shade from trees. 1.2 kilometres wasn't an ideal-sized loop, but I'd run worse, and no matter how many times I looked up the Asian twin towers loomed majestically. I even listened to a podcast about the towers as I ran. One thing besides the materials, the cost, and the sheer engineering feat to accomplish the 1998 building of what is now the seventh-highest tower in the world, is that the design has a lesser-seen eight-pointed star. The Malaysian prime minister back then, Mahathir Mohamad, wanted to not only set the record for the tallest building at the time, but also include a nod to Malaysian identity, hence the five pillars of the Islamic religion was the focus. And when viewing the tower from the sky, looking down as opposed to up, the structure resembles a series of cross sections that reflect the eight-pointed star symbol of Islam. This I thought was rather nifty.

This part of the world isn't like Europe – or anywhere, really. Barring a few exceptions for the odd (indeed very 'odd') African island, the continents that we humans have used to divide the planet pretty much conform to their compartmental states. South America and Asia are worlds apart in terms of the way they feel, but breaking it down to how locals live, they aren't dissimilar, and to this day I struggle to understand why they seem so different. In Asia and South America there are vast similarities between street sellers, the brightly coloured clothing, and the way local trade and communities operate – and yet these two continents are wildly different. As I moved further into South-East Asia it baffled me more and more. Perhaps there's some correlation between economy or governments, or maybe it's down to population or family size. I've learnt above all that labels, names, comparisons don't really matter. The world is marvellously diverse and all the better for it.

Post-marathon I spent three glorious hours watching 50-plus eagles feasting on fish in a nearby lake just 40 minutes from the city centre. As the sun set and the eagles left, rather than calling it a day and getting back to pack and sleep, I stayed for a further three hours and waited for a spectacle that is rarely experienced. On the banks of the Batu Dam lake, as darkness fell, millions upon millions of tiny natural light bulbs emerged. Fireflies. These tiny insects put on the show of their lives every night to a backdrop of still water, no wind and nothing but the sound of an old handmade outboard motor on a long stick. It chugged away, and then was turned off. Silence amongst hoards of tiny glowing lights. I slept well that night, and despite not eating as much as I should, and being overtired, these little critters had given me a slice of peace.

Vietnam

Friday 11 March 2019 I landed into Vietnam's capital, Hanoi. I love this city. Despite my hatred toward constant and redundant horn-beeping I was OK with these ones. Journeying from the airport, the streets screeched with scooters vying for right of way amid the din of constantly blaring horns. The city instantly oozes resilience and ambition, with layers of history, not just in architecture but in the faces of the elders. Be it French, Chinese or Russian, at every turn of every narrow corner, the city offered an insight into the deep underlying pride from every Hanoian.

My hotel and its staff were no different. I was put up right in the heart of the city, in a tiny but well kept five-roomed boutique spa. This was a world away from the backpacker lifestyle but, despite feeling somewhat fraudulent for looking like a tramp and having various hotels offer me luxury accommodation, I wasn't about to turn it down. Where other travellers were met with a pillow case, a key card and a padlock, I was presented with a cold towel, a glass of bubbly and a platter of aperitifs before being invited for a complimentary 15-minute head massage. My first 20 minutes in the city were busy with noise, new smells and now a spoilt greeting from a brilliant hotel. I was not seeing Hanoi as most backpackers do, but I was OK with that. I had slummed it enough in the past – sometimes I even had to make do without the head massage.

Hidden between the narrow hectic streets of the Hanoi Old Quarter lies a world of washing lines, miniature homes, brightly coloured walls and one big train track. Motorbikes are no longer the biggest danger here. Over 20 miles into the marathon I was ushered to the side of the tracks by a squealing elderly shop owner. She shrieked in urgency for me to move. I had read about this train, and seen photos, hence why I was in the right place at the right time. The train wasn't just a little slow train laid on for tourists, this was a working train connecting the capital to Ho Chi Minh City in the south, and it wasn't hanging around. Despite the buildings being less than a foot from the tracks, and railway sleepers that lay disjointed to the point where they appear disused, the high-speed train hurtled through the residential street mere inches from my face. For the locals this is a frequent occurrence but, for me, my sweaty back was pressed up against someone's house window and my feet were squeezed tightly together at right angles to avoid the possibility of any missing toes. My nose was no more than three inches from the speeding train. Too close for comfort. At the time I had no idea how this was still allowed. I know Asia and most of the world isn't as hot on health and safety as the British or the Europeans, but this was crazy. Carefree residents press tight to the walls or duck into nearby doorways at the last minute with a startling nonchalance, and then go right back to walking across or sitting on the tracks as soon as the train has passed. At the time of writing I checked the train hadn't been shut down, and it seems that it has now, finally, been closed due to more and more tourists being injured or killed. The legendary train street is now just that, a legend.

After a very attentive breakfast service earlier that morning, featuring views over the early-to-rise city, I donned my running gear once more for another 26.2 miles of glorious exploring. The clothes, as always, were still damp, this time from Kuala Lumpur a couple of days earlier. I pulled the smelly vest over my head, turned my socks in the right way, then left the beautiful La Siesta Diamond Hotel on Lò Sũ Street and headed west and then eventually north. I passed swarms of smiling local traders, intricate architecture and tangles of electrical cables knotted together draped from building to building. The first stop was a mini-trip around Lake Hoàn Kiềm in the heart of the city; and then on to the much bigger lake of Hồ Tây. Two laps of the lake were enough to clock off the full distance, passing, of course, the memorable train street.

With an accompanying symphony of horns and diesel engine fumes I smelt all there is to smell in Asia on one glorious run: the small road-side fires over which families prepare their food for the day; the street workers jollily smoking large bongs, and the local police joining in. Today was all about the people of Vietnam and their incredible city. As for the lake, it was vast and mostly empty but still with a few fishing boats periodically traversing the pan-flat water, leaving behind a gentle trail of ripples. For the most part, the small roads that cling to the water on all sides are peaceful and quiet in comparison to the rest of the city – no horns or cars, no fumes nor bustle; a great little snap-shot of peace found amongst managed mayhem. To top it off I even passed a brilliant café named 'Marathon Café'. I went in and printed a photo of myself for their community wall made up of thousands of runners from around the globe. It reminded me of the Polaroids I had around my bedroom wall as a kid.

I had persuaded the team to let me have another full day in Vietnam, and then another few days in Cambodia and Thailand, which were coming up. Nineteen days behind schedule wasn't really something I was worrying about – but it should have been. This journey wasn't about racing from one country to the next. Had that been the case I would have fallen short of one of my main goals of the trip: to explore, enjoy and have fun. There was little to no point in living out Kev's advice to grab each day and ram it full of everything I loved if I was doing so with no enjoyment. It's true that if I did this entire journey again, I'd ignore the world record aspect and would saunter mindfully from country to country over two or three decades, as opposed to just 23 months. It's also true that many of the countries were rushed – but with the considerations of cost, time and also setting this world record, I can look back on the journey and say we got the balance between enjoyment, speed and cost more or less right. Everyone knows you can live cheaply in Asia. But I wanted more time here.

My final day in Vietnam and in my slowed down blissful yet naïve mood, I ventured out of the city to the magical islands of Hạ Long Bay, home to the huge clouds of rock formations sprouting from the sea, and barely floating fishing boats bobbing around the islands propelled by shirtless men rowing with their feet, seemingly to nowhere. The sky was grey and hazy but the views were still impressive. It felt as if King Kong could hurl himself from behind a peak in the clouds at any moment. The vastness of the place is hard to describe. Around one corner was another corner, which led to another maze of more corners. More small islands led to offshoots of waterways, these too leading to mazes of crystal clear pools of water squeezed between rocks. The islands are all tall, sheer and teeming with wildlife: monkeys, birds and an array of green plants and foliage. The emerald waters below are still, deep and patchy. Some spots are deep black and others a light, bright greeny blue. The day was long and full. To reach the bay of these 1,600-plus islands I travelled 170 kilometres by bumpy taxi. Once the sun had set it was time to venture back to the little hotel, grab my things, sleep for a short while, and wake for another country.

Cambodia

Moving from Vietnam to Cambodia I couldn't help but spend a few hours pondering the horrors of the Cambodian genocide at the hands of the evil and deadly Pol Pot. The Khmer Rouge, the brutal regime that ruled Cambodia under the leadership of the communist dictator Pol Pot for four years, from 1975 to 1979, was responsible for the torture and death of millions of its own citizens. I watched the film *The Killing Fields* on the plane as I flew into Thailand a few days later. I fell in love with both Vietnam and Cambodia and their people. They have strived in the face of outrageous adversity. They are amongst the few of my favourite nations.

Over the decades since the fall of the Khmer Rouge, Cambodia has now gradually re-established ties with the world community. The country still faces problems though, including widespread poverty and illiteracy. These South-East Asian countries are not just the backpacker-friendly cities of tour books. People are also in chronic need – it reminded me of Sierra Leone and countless other desperate nations I'd seen so far. Once again, I was humbled.

Anyone that visits Cambodia will tell you of the smiles from the locals, the welcoming hospitality and the energy to give and to help. I stayed in the lands of twelfth-century Buddhist temples. My home for four nights was hotel Templation in the heart of Siem Reap, just an ancient stone's throw from the Khmer Empire's temples at Angkor Wat, the world's most visited tourist attraction. I couldn't help but wonder if the National Trust ever got their hands on it, there'd be hundreds of locked gates, security cameras, overpriced cafés and inaccessible toilet blocks on every corner. Not here, not in South-East Asia.

As I ran around the various paths and roads connecting temples, gardens and forests to one another, I ticked off all the major sights: Angkor Wat, Angkor Thom, Ta Prohm, Neak Péan and East Baray. I paid for a three-day pass at a cost of $62, which meant I could also run through and around each area without worry.

Bright orange, green and deep dark brown was the colour palette for the morning's run. Be it the dust hugging either side of the freshly paved roads, or the old ancient rock of the temples, the views were something from a film set. The roads were long, narrow and straight, with gaggles of masked-up Chinese tourists whizzing by on drive-their-own tuk tuks. The stretch that ran north up the Jayatataka lake was the longest straight road I've ever run down and was lined with endless jaw-dropping views. Thank you to the Khmer Empire and for Vishnu, the god it was made for. I lapped the small temple complex about four times to complete the distance. It was hot, but not Africa hot, and so a pleasure to run alone with my thoughts of ancient gods and powerful empires.

Flying to Thailand, I flicked through the photos of the past few days. Thousands of monks, smiling police, adorable children, families living by riverbanks, tuk tuks decorated with lights and snazzy paint jobs, and locals with oversized wicker hats and cracked old faces. Asia never drops the ball when it comes to sensory overload – the very best kind.

Thailand

In Thailand the humidity and hospitality continued. Like with every country, I could have gone to every capital city and ticked off that record too. I was keen, though, to visit those bits of each country I wanted to see rather than box myself into cities that possibly lacked the love or cultural diversity of the countryside.

I have been to Thailand a number of times: from the tropical paradise of Koh Phi Phi, to Bangkok and beyond. For this two-day visit I opted for Phuket simply due to ease, cost and the fact I'd had offers of support from an eclectic trio: Simon from the UK, but living in Bangkok; Chait from Thailand, but living in Boston; and a brilliantly smiley lady named Poom from Phuket, living in Phuket. To this day, I'm not entirely sure how these guys knew each other, if at all. Somehow, though, they all arrived in the lobby of the rundown Benidorm(esque) hotel ready for a marathon at 6 a.m. Embarrassingly, for the entire day I thought Poom's name was, in fact, Poo. This, of course, resulted in a childish inner giggle occasionally spilling out into the real world. I took great pride in shouting 'Poo!' down the road. Poom was adorable and was so excited to run with me. Her classic Thai accent, along with her name and eternal enthusiasm for the day, was one of my favourite memories of how people made my journey so special. Along with failing to grasp Poom's name – despite her repeated attempts to pronounce it for me – I also didn't understand why she was so interested in running. She wasn't running with us, but instead was happy to drive her car as support. Poom, the car, along with a load of bottles of water and snacks, leapfrogged us all the way to the finish line back at the hotel, after a meandering loop around Phuket's coast at dawn.

My heart was in my mouth occasionally as she would swerve around us to get ahead, dump the car in the middle of the road, jump out of the vehicle and attempt to take photos of us. That was, of course, lovely, but I had made the slight misjudgement of giving her my highly expensive top-of-the-range camera, which she treated like an old handbag slung around her neck or wedged under her arm. It swung violently from side to side, hitting her hip and occasionally crashing to the floor as she bent down to get a shot of us running towards her. It regularly banged against the car door as she quickly got back in. I winced and gasped as I heard the camera on the metal work behind us as we ran down the coast road. This was another lovely gesture and I couldn't exactly stop her, take the camera away, and run with it myself. But remember the British attitude prevails regardless. In an attempt not to be rude I asked to change some settings on the camera and sneakily took a battery out and tucked it in my running pouch. I promptly announced that it had run out of battery and wedged it in the back footwell of the car. Phew, it was safe for the time being. Sorry, Poom. I have such fond memories of you, and your exuberant energy – I just needed to keep my baby, my precious little camera, safe.

I later found out that Poom's enthusiasm wasn't short-lived either. She had found out about my journey 13 months before I was due to arrive and was proud to have helped in any way. I was honoured. Simon and Chait were great runners and we trotted around the winding coastal hills at a decent pace until the sun got hotter. We then all started to fade a little. It felt on the most part like we were running through water. We were all soaked through, thanks to the outrageously humid conditions. It may as well have been raining.

Post-run everyone parted company with big sweaty hugs, and I got on the back of a truck to hitch a lift to an elephant sanctuary. Within ten minutes of experiencing this so called 'sanctuary' I abandoned the excursion and walked back to the hotel. It was pretty upsetting seeing how the elephants were enslaved to tourists. It was advertised as a legit sanctuary, but from where I was standing the elephants were not happy. Their tails were stiff, indicating anxiety, their lumbering bodies were constantly swaying from left to right, showing us they were either bored or depressed. Some were even eating their own excrement. Having watched enough conservation documentaries, I knew these signs were not positive. There's plenty of research to show elephants are incredibly emotionally complex, and can often suffer with depression. I left wishing I could have somehow helped. Thailand was done, and although I hadn't sunned myself on beaches and been on wild adventures like many of the visits before, I had made some great Thailand friends. Chait and I even saw each other again briefly in an airport several thousands of miles away in the US – totally by chance.

Myanmar

Despite the abundance of sleep during the flight I was clearly still knackered by the time I reached Yangon, the largest city in Myanmar, because the next morning I made the fatal mistake of missing my alarm. Totting up all 196 countries' worth of running, I later worked out that I ran over 90 per cent of the first half of my marathons before 9 a.m. This, I can assure you, wasn't because I was super-keen or raring to go every morning. It was to make my life easier. The heat wasn't letting up – so by starting almost every run pre-dawn the heat was slightly more bearable. But in Yangon in my sleepy state I had mistakenly pressed snooze one too many times on my alarm. I woke panicked and confused at about 6.30 with the light from the window hitting my face and pillow. Oh shit, it was light. The journey so far had more or less turned me into a vampire fearing the deadly sun.

The city is one of the safest in Asia, and foreigners are seldom bothered. However, the lack of development still remains, which has allowed a certain colonial-style charm to persist, with much of the city's architecture dating back to the days of British rule. This does however also mean that pavements and roads are in a terrible state of repair. For that reason I ran loops around a more evenly paved lakeside to avoid the alarmingly huge potholes of the main roads.

Standing on Singuttara Hill in the north of downtown Yangon, the Shwedagon Pagoda is the largest in Myanmar, standing 99 metres tall – it is also plated with 21,841 solid gold bars and has a tip encrusted with thousands of diamonds, rubies and sapphires. Not a bad view, if from some distance. Reflecting Myanmar as a whole, Yangon is filled with religious monuments – a bizarre but brilliantly vast and diverse selection of historic churches, Hindu temples, mosques and synagogues scattered around the city. From walking past tourists in shorts in Phuket a day earlier I was now walking past monks in golden gowns. I was the short-wearing tourist in this scenario.

Having completed many sweaty laps of Inya Lake, I ventured out to see all I could in my brief four hours before packing and flying. Yangon is a port for many tourists as they enter and exit but rarely stay. For me this was sadly pretty much all I saw, and Myanmar was added to the list of about ten countries I knew I need to revisit to escape into the more rural areas.

Laos

Laos – the land of French colonial architecture, hill-tribe settlements, more Buddhist monasteries and the legendary Mekong River – completed the classic gap-year backpacker section of South-East Asia. A bloke called Carlos was my new marathon companion, but I was cursing him initially. I was ready and waiting to get going at 5 a.m., listening to dogs barking a few streets away while sitting patiently on the doorstep of my hotel. The hotel was opposite the river and, due to the bounce-back of the echo on the building, it was unclear if the barks were coming from the other side of the river or were just around the corner. I hoped for the former.

Carlos, like so many other supporters, was just a name in my calendar, and after a 20-minute anxious wait on the hotel step I gave up waiting and asked the hotel staff to tell him I was running along the riverbank. I had no reception on my phone, so he had no chance of getting hold of me had he tried calling.

I was so often the only guest in the hotels I stayed at, mostly because I was staying in places that needed publicity, so would offer me a free night's accommodation. Such hospitality ranged from lavish offerings of champagne and spa treatments (the former I had to sadly decline), to the opposite end of the spectrum where, rather than champagne in a bucket, cockroaches scuttled over stained bed covers. This hotel, Hotel La Seine, here in the heart of Vientiane, the capital of Laos, was completely new and would soon be a thriving hub for tourists and locals, I was sure. It just hadn't got started properly yet. In fact, I was their first official guest – so they informed me upon arrival, with a ceremonial opening.

Within 20 minutes of jogging down the narrow dirt road next to the Mekong River I was already drenched in humid sweat. Dust covered my lower legs and socks. A scooter pulled up next to me about three miles down the road. A hefty black plume of exhaust smoke belched into the air as the engine chuffed and chugged, and eventually the annoying moped drone ceased. 'Nick,' shouted a man in running gear with an excited yet unsure tone of voice. I had no idea how he recognized me at first, and then I twigged: I was the only person running in the heat and I was clearly a tourist. I stood out like a sore thumb. He jumped off the bike, apologized for being late then called a friend to collect his scooter before running alongside and expressing his thanks for letting him run with me. I was pleased to see him, but wasn't entirely sure if it was the Carlos I had been waiting for or if it was someone who'd responded to a social media post asking locals to join me.

His excitement did eventually fade and he introduced himself, confirming my initial assumption. After several hours of chatting and sharing stories of family, work and travel, we reached the turning point to begin our journey home – a simple 21-kilometre out-and-back route. The turning point Carlos had referred to as 'Buddha Park' for all of two hours, and was quite passionate about, was not what I expected. Imagine a conventional park with footpaths, benches and the occasional plaque and a signpost to the exit or entrance, but all the size of a five-a-side football field. Fine so far, but this wasn't just named Buddha Park, it was literally a park full of Buddhas. OK, so Buddha himself wasn't there, but it was FULL – and I mean crammed full – of concrete, wooden and metal statues of Buddha. Some were tiny, but most were massive, at least ten-feet tall, and frankly rubbish attempts at statues. I smiled and nodded as Carlos explained the concept of the park to me – apparently it was started in 1958 by Luang Pu Thuat, who later fled to Thailand and created an identical park the other side of the Mekong River border, just a few kilometres away. The park is known as Wat Xieng Khuan, Xieng Khuan meaning 'spirit city'. No matter what it was called, it felt to me less spiritual and more like the statue section of a garden centre.

Another couple of hours and we were done, I thought, having completed the distance about ten miles from the hotel. We flagged down a passing truck and jumped on the back for a ride into the city. It was how all locals travelled. Every citizen is a taxi driver. (Genius, really – although I'm sure the class division in the UK and western world wouldn't be able to handle it.) As we ran Carlos had told me of his various projects around the city supporting the local youth. It was an honour and a pleasure to be running with a chap that had contributed so much. A totally selfless guy, Carlos deserves a medal for everything he's doing with the local community and the youth development programmes. We stopped for water and ice creams, most of which he treated me to. Dusty roads, cows crossing, dogs barking, and the heat of the sun steadily cooking us as we plodded slowly – with virtually no focus on running, just sharing stories, being taken to another place with conversation and chatter. Carlos also planted the seed for a run from the north of the country to the south. About a thousand miles. Another adventure for another time.

The next morning I was soaring above the clouds, both in spirit but also quite literally. I had about 30 hours from the moment I stopped my watch hitting the 26.2 miles of the 127th marathon to the time I needed to be at the airport ahead of my next country. Not wanting to miss an opportunity, I organized a cheap taxi driver to pick me up at 3 a.m. for a quick in-and-out visit to Vang Vieng. Three hours later the driver woke me up. We were parked in a huge empty dirt car park in the centre of the city. The light was still dim and the sun hadn't fully woken up. In the distance I saw a couple of hot air balloons just about to take off and so grabbed my camera and dashed over to take some photos. I was still barefoot after taking my sweaty trainers off for the car journey, and had nothing on me except my camera. One of the guys who owned one of the balloons gestured to me as if asking if I wanted to go up with them. Naturally he'd want paying, and I had no money, or even any shoes, so I said, 'No, it's OK. I have nothing on me.' The car was now about half a mile away. And, yes, it wasn't wise to dash over a gravel car park in bare feet, but I wanted a nice shot of them taking off. This was a shot I didn't manage to get because after haggling a little, and agreeing to pay the man the equivalent of £40 once we got back, I was in the balloon and disappearing into the clouds.

I'm not one to miss an adventure, but I am usually a little more conscientious or like to at least make some form of plan before disappearing into the mountains in a hanging basket. I didn't even know where we were going. My driver thought I'd just hopped out for some photos – I'd even left the door open. It did dawn on me that he could steal all my stuff, including my shoes, and I'd have no way of getting back to the city for my flight out of the country. I tried not to think about that as we rose higher and higher. The fiery roar of the two huge burners just above my head was intense, hot and loud. The heat and the noise made me jump every time. There were five of us bundled into the basket, nervously, and before we knew it we were no longer on the ground. The elegance of the balloon as it lifted into the sky was captivating. The people, cars and buildings shrank, and the mountains grew closer as we passed through the thin layer of hazy clouds to reveal the wonders of Laos. The view over this region was beautiful. The small dot of another balloon in the valley floor below put the scale of this place into perspective – gentle, elegant and calm. What a great and completely mad way to travel. Within five minutes of jumping out of the car I was above the mountains in a basket with massive flames above my head, surrounded by strangers. I felt bad for the driver, but he was paid to take me back to the city later that day too, so I hoped he would just hang around.

We got back to what I thought was our starting location after an hour in the air. We weren't anywhere near the original location, but somehow the taxi driver had found me. His English was poor and so all I could understand was that he'd asked someone. I got the impression that the community of ballooners wasn't big in Vang Vieng.

As we came into land we missed the planned landing spot by about a football field and were being pulled into the houses below. The landing aborted, we climbed again and instead settled down in a local dirt park. Their ground team did a great job. I didn't even feel the basket touch the ground. And the best part: the driver didn't steal any of my stuff. He was actually pretty happy not to have to show me around. The price had included some sightseeing, but I'd used most of my available time in the unexpected adventure in the sky.

Soaring about the mountain peaks over Laos was special. The driver and I stopped off at a cash machine to pay for the trip, went to a nearby lagoon and just fell asleep in the sun. The day was marvellous, and I was dropped back in the capital with plenty of time to get to the airport and hop on the flight to Taiwan. This was when I realized I had left my debit card in the cash machine in Vang Vieng. Bugger.

Taiwan

In the excitement of recent high-flying adventures, plus the frustration of losing my only working debit card, I got off the plane a little weary and not really concentrating. I was just going through the usual motions of passport control and baggage collection in a dozy trance. I hadn't looked at the diary correctly, and so was shocked to wander through to arrivals and see both Dani and Andy waiting patiently for me. My friends had both flown out to join me for Taiwan, South Korea and Mongolia. As for my debit card – I can only hope it remained in the cash machine until it was cancelled.

Taiwan's status as a country is disputed by China, which classes it as a rebel state. Simply trying to confirm a definitive number of countries on the planet is tricky: the general consensus of the internet states 193, 194 or 195, for a variety of reasons, but countries that make up the UN-recognized list total 193. It was these plus 3 extra questionable ones that made up the magic total of 196. It was this number that we had to adhere to in order for Guinness World Records to sign off on the record. In nearly every country I'd have someone ask if I'd 'even done North Korea or the North Pole'. North Korea is definitely a country, as per the UN and virtually all other sources, so no debate there. The North Pole simply can't be because there isn't any land to claim – it's just lots of frozen water. It's not always so clear cut, though. There are countries that are on the cusp of becoming a country, or countries that some nations recognize and others don't, and so the team and I decided that we would do these countries too, just for completeness. Andy, Dani and I spoke of this over dinner on the first night in Taipei, huddled around a wonky pool table. There were so many other places in the world that could be a country in the future. The team had decided that we'd settle on 196 marathons – as mentioned, all the official countries identified by the UN, plus those in dispute. Any of the world marathon majors could be worked in if possible, and Beijing was added in addition to Hong Kong due to the ongoing political climate in China during 2019. The London Marathon was run twice as well because I was there and it was good publicity for Prostate Cancer UK. This seemed a sensible and fun approach while thinking of the future political landscape. But with the understanding that for the record, the principal aim was just to run the official 196. Any others, like Beijing and a double London marathon, were a bonus.

Taiwan is, of course, an island that has for all practical purposes been independent since 1950, but China still regards it as a rebel state that must be reunited with the mainland – by force, if necessary. China has claimed sovereignty over Taiwan since the end of the Chinese civil war in 1949, when the defeated Nationalist government fled to the island as the Communists came to power. China insists that nations cannot have official relations with both China and Taiwan, with the result being that Taiwan has formal diplomatic ties with only a few countries. It's not unexpected then that Taiwan feels like a weird mix of influences from China, the US and Europe. It certainly has the historical ties to China, but with all the social efforts to break away from feeling 'Chinese'.

With all this in mind, Andy and I ran through the city with one eye on what was different about Taiwan. I personally found it quite an odd place. Hard to put my finger on it but what we happened upon certainly set off some alarm bells. In the morning we ran past an outdoor cat festival – which to me was classically Chinese, in the sense that it was bonkers. In an extra-strange turn of events I somehow came away with a photo taken of me with a human-size sanitary towel. The festival was small: about a thousand people all gathered together with a main stage, and some music along a riverbank. The perimeter held lots of stalls but no obvious entry or exit to the gathering, just lots of selfie-stick-wielding locals. We inadvertently ran through before stopping to admire the spectacle. Everything was normal(ish) at this point, but as we got deeper into the throng there were cats on leads everywhere, and weird stalls selling everything and anything. The cat element was prominent, and it was clearly a feline-focused happening; an Asian feline version of Crufts. Weirder still were the various adverts and brands in attendance. One minute a boy band was playing, with girls going crazy, the next a sanitary towel with human arms and legs walked by. With no ability to speak more than three words of Chinese, I simply couldn't resist a selfie, and even accepted the free sample. It might come in handy if I was caught short with food poisoning again, I suppose. It now takes pride of place, and a lot of room, in the Taiwan section of my scrapbook.

We moved on past the market, a game of baseball, some marching guards outside a palace in various garish outfits, and even ran a few miles with a broom between each of our legs having stumbled across brooms that resembled those used in Quidditch. I confess, the inner child in me often came out around familiar faces, and we had a laugh plodding around the city.

In my haste to pack for the warm countries on this leg of the journey I had forgotten the likes of Mongolia and beyond, which were about to get colder. Andy, Dani and I spent the remaining time trying to find some warmer garments. In short, we didn't find anything we needed, but it was an opportunity to see the city: we popped into a few odd bars and chatted the night away. The three amigos were on tour once again. We didn't get to sleep until the early hours after wandering around open-mouthed most of the evening. It's fair to say Taiwan is a weird and wonderful place. Taipei has a UFO village, a huge church in the shape of a high-heeled shoe (said to be designed to attract more female church goers), a toilet restaurant, where food is served on and in miniature toilets, and even a house that has been designed upside down. Yes, upside down. Oh, and you can buy pickled snakes in wine bottles. Yum.

South Korea

Due to the long night, we woke up late and were on the back foot from the moment our sleepy eyelids parted. Dani spent all morning in bed feeling sorry for himself in a hungover stupor, while Andy, equally hungover but putting on a brave face, joined me for another 26.2 glorious miles around another new and strange city. In my mind this part of the world is a no man's land in the tourist sense. Not somewhere that springs to mind for Brits to holiday, nor was it tropical enough to attract the gap-year bunch. I came to the conclusion, based on no knowledge, that it would be great for retirees hunting for a country they'd not yet visited. It's culturally rich enough to offer some adventure but not too dangerous or cheap, and so potentially free of youngsters. I'm stereotyping, of course.

Passing various 'Gangnam Style' painted portraits of varying quality on grubby underpasses and walls around the city, we trotted along the riverbank, around some hilly trails, similar to that of the National Trust, well lit and purpose-built for tourists. We got our scale all wrong when looking at the map and for while were lost in a maze of trails with big inclines. We adjusted using the trusty Maps.me offline map and headed for the riverbank again. There was a lot of big construction work going on: bridges and new parks.

In most cities the river is the best place to be, and Seoul was no different – flat, long and with cafés and restaurants at every turn. There were cyclists and runners almost every two minutes for the entire duration. I have never run along a river with so many bridges and yet so few people or cars on them. Virtually every 200 metres a new bridge with a different design was being built. And yet it's known people don't bother passing over them. Maybe the construction work was to encourage people to venture further backwards and forwards across the Han River. Andy and I high-fived and hugged in acknowledgement of another marathon down and one step (well, 42,000 steps) closer to the finish line that was now just 214 days away.

Mongolia

I'd wanted to see Mongolia for some time, ever since my love affair with yurts and nomadic living had blossomed when I was a boy camping with family, and then later building and sleeping in tree houses as a young teenager. The concept of living in a yurt with the freedom to roam, without huge volumes of possessions, seemed peaceful. I guess the harsh temperature and living conditions in Mongolia do make it slightly less romantic, but still, the simpler way of life is hugely appealing.

Mongolia's land area covers an expanse only marginally smaller than all the countries of western and central Europe. Three-quarters of this huge area is pastureland, and with a total population of fewer than three million it has one of the lowest average population densities of any country in the world. The country I had read about is truly amazing, with its vast open landscapes, tens of thousands of herds of horses, snow-capped peaks, mirror lakes and rugged horizon lines containing everything from forests to barren wilderness. Sadly we saw very little of that, as we were mainly confined in and around the national capital, Ulaanbaatar – but Andy and I did manage to venture into the mountains to avoid the smog and pollution.

The temperature in Mongolia can fall to below minus 15° at night, and so we were conscious we didn't need to set off too early in the morning. We decided to flip the day around and leave in the afternoon, which meant a blissful lie-in as the sunlight squeezed through the curtains. I'd not started many runs this late in the day before, simply because I was usually dodging the heat. After four miles Andy and I were away from the city, over the river and heading towards the mountains. It was breezy and chilly – so much so that we both wore socks on our hands as well as gloves. At mile six Andy and I armed ourselves with rocks and sticks to ward off any potential dog attacks due to the increase in what sounded like vicious barking that was far too close for comfort. The sound of the deep, bellowing barks echoed around the valley, and we accelerated in several nervous bursts of speed, with hurried looks over our shoulders.

The next couple of miles were slow and very steep, but we were still on the last of the surfaced roads leading away from the concrete jungle of Ulaanbaatar. Before long we passed a construction area (one of many) and then made it into the mountains. The 'no poaching' signs gave us a hint of the terrain we were about to take on. The bottom of the forest valley was eerie and we were both aware there could be other animals out there, more sinister than dogs. Wolves were on our minds. The going got tougher as we scrambled up the hill on all fours panting, feeling knackered and unfit. Of course, we were forgetting the slight altitude we were already at.

We reached the summit after a long climb with no more chatting. The occasional noise through the trees froze us in our tracks, but the views were worth it and our animal fears were unwarranted. Our plan was to run along the ridge line, staying as high as we could, taking in every peak as we descended, having already made it to the highest point. It was peaceful and to our delight the cold let up a little. Andy and I laughed and spoke of how poorly prepared we were to go running in the Mongolian mountains. No water, no food, and only a phone with low battery that eventually died. For two like us, who like being outdoors, we were certainly doing things the tourist way, and felt foolish for it. That said, the rest of the run was downhill and gentle.

The final unexpected struggle was the last ten miles around the outskirts of the heavily industrial quarter of Ulaanbaatar. The air in the city was bad, really bad. We paced along, running in the road against the traffic, single file, with our heads down and very much in focus mode. The pollution was terrible to the point we could see particles of dust and unclean grains in the air. Our lungs weren't happy. We used the sock gloves and buffs to protect our mouths, running only with our noses exposed. The mountains lived up to my imaginings, but that was just a tiny taster. We meandered back through the city, through smog-filled streets full of the textured black walls of the half-built concrete metropolis, to the hotel and headed straight for the pool and sauna. Dani, as expected, was in his crisp white hotel robe, a beer in his hand, in a blissful state of heat from the sauna and half asleep on a lounger. Andy promptly joined him with a beer and we all chatted for a while as we sweated the Mongolian dirt from our pores in the steam room. This was the night before Andy and Dani said goodbye again. We spent the evening watching a film huddled together as a three, on a double bed, with an average-to-poor pizza and (for them) copious amounts of beer.

Kyrgyzstan

At Chinggis Khaan International Airport I passed glass-fronted boxes displaying confiscated items – things like handcuffs, knives, explosives, nun chucks and rocket launchers. This put the 125ml shampoo you'd find in a bin at Heathrow to shame. Seated and ready to take off I was in the zone, ready to tackle the challenge of the 'stan' countries.

Arriving into Bishkek, Kyrgyzstan's capital, I was in a city I'd never heard of and a country I knew very little about. Experiencing a whole new set of cultures is fascinating and fortunate, but after several months it can become rather exhausting – despite everything being different, the act of experiencing new things becomes the same somehow. I was by now tired of the onslaught of new everything. It was a weird feeling – I liken it to that of an addict giving up a substance by force. I didn't want to stop experiencing the world – that would be madness – just like a drunk often doesn't want to not have another pint of booze. But I was tired. My body needed sleep, and my mind knew it. My eyes were even aching with tiredness, blinking several thousand more times than were necessary. I was in a zombie state. And yet ... although exploring is draining over such a long time-frame I couldn't resist chatting to the people in the immigration queue, or the cabby, or sticking my camera out of the window to take more and more photos.

Bishkek is busy, and the markets reminded me of South America or Central Africa: a frantic attempt to graft hard for your day's wages and put food on the table. It felt poor but workable and people had a purpose. Amongst the unsung magic of travel are the 'eyes wide open' moments – those flashes of unexpected brilliance that bring an uncontrollable smile to your face even when you're half asleep and not entirely with it.

A little pre-trip research for holidays, or otherwise, is fine, but I don't like to know too much. I'm the same with films. I hate watching trailers because they give too much away. I'd rather work it out for myself. This, in the travelling sense, did make my mum a little nervous. I knew nothing of Kyrgyzstan whatsoever but I was quite happy about that.

The morning of the run, the air was cold as I opened the window. With clear blue skies and no wind whatsoever, I opted for just one layer. The right choice. I woke up knowing that the principal National

Park, halfway up the mountain in the distance, was just over 42 kilometres away and so seemed a good fit to give it a go. The plan was
then to taxi back once I'd hit the distance. This idea was short-lived
and sadly abandoned only a few miles in thanks to . . . let's just say
'the needs of my bottom'. Over the four and a half hours I toted up an
impressive 13 toilet stops and drank only 400ml of water. I was the
pinball in a sick game of 'find the toilet' before I shat myself again.
Needless to say I didn't reach the mountains, but I did complete the
marathon, and I'm glad to report that I didn't end up with chocolate
thighs, nor was I locked up for defecating behind someone's car. I'm
not saying that didn't happen, but I was, at least, not caught. I'm not
sure, but I put the blame on plane food at the time, because it so often
was the plane food – the food that I couldn't turn down because I was
so hungry, but which often left me uncomfortable and squirming.
Even before setting out on the run my stomach groaned and gargled
as I left the room, and so I went back in for an entire roll of toilet
paper and simply ran holding it. This wasn't my first rodeo. I knew
what was to come and toilet paper was now more valuable than gold.
By mile three I was squatting down in my first seatless scenario in the
back cubical of a small empty café. When I say 'café', don't think
Parisian elegance, think the kind where mould grows on the plates.
My additional 12 stops were equally unpleasant and I even found
myself rating my experiences, while still able to chuckle to myself.
Not all stops were squat loos, some were seated – one even had a
padded-cushion rim. And, no, I didn't always make it to an actual
toilet. I was at least away from the city centre at the time. All in all, as
I peeled away my clothes in the shower, post-run, I marked the day as
a win. No soiling myself, I'd completed my objective to run another
marathon, and the city was actually rather lovely. Some of the toilets
weren't half bad either. There's something magical about a city that's
engulfed by snow-capped mountains. Looking up at junctions to get
my bearings, the peaks acted as a compass. With the city nestled neatly
in the basin with the mountains around it, it felt like the hills were
keeping the city safe somehow – something I'd experienced in other
cities, such as Santiago or La Paz.

The morning after the poos I ventured into the hills by car to watch the sunrise. Fluffy white clouds sat to attention along the ridges of the snow caps, just like the tips of meringue atop a pie. The whites of the snow and the clouds merged; the sky only separated by a deep yellow band of light as the sun popped over the horizon. The yellow turned to orange and then purple. Within two minutes the sky was transformed from night to dawn and then from dawn to day. The vast beams of light shot across the sky casting long and trailing shadows. The city below was still and sleeping. I heard only birds, a distant tractor engine and the clang of cow bells. I didn't hang around too long. I had a plane to catch, and another bathroom to visit ... I stopped off on the way to the airport to pick up some essentials at the market – more toilet roll and some bread. The bread in Bishkek was some of the most delicious I'd had. The market was small but I could tell it was the place to be on a Saturday morning. Sheep heads, complete with floppy lifeless tongues, were among the many sights that caught the eye. On the long stretch of road through the mountains to the airport I was nodding off and not paying any attention. In a moment of wakefulness I saw a man in a boilersuit and a full black balaclava riding a donkey in the middle of a huge sloping pasture. I decided he was a shepherd, but had I come across him at night I would have shat myself. And not for the first time.

Kazakhstan

All the bad stuff in my gut flushed out, and my little brother was coming out to join me for a few countries. Despite the fact I've run so much in my life all over the world, he'd only ever seen me run that one time in London. We don't get much time to see each other because I'm often away and he's always very busy with work. He was due to land at about 3 p.m., so I had enough time to have breakfast before slipping my shoes on for a mid-morning start. My plan was to run to the airport to pick him up. It seemed the logical thing to do, and the streets and roads in Almaty were safe and easy to navigate.

Miles one to six were about making my way to the First President's

Park. I'd read online that it was a great place to do a few laps. I actually only needed one to get enough distance in. The first six miles were all uphill but got me to the park after running along a nice little cycle lane. It was an easy start, but all in the opposite direction to the airport.

Miles six to ten: a few runners and walkers were around, but it was eerily empty all things considered. I made it to the top of a hill at one end of the park and looked out across the city and the mountains. The views were stunning.

Miles ten to 13.3 were all I needed to get back to roughly my starting point at the hotel. From there I had the last half-marathon to follow the roads to the airport, trying not to run down any lanes or alleys where there would be stray dogs.

Miles 13 to 26.2. I made it. The final half-marathon finished just a few hundred metres short of the airport. Perfect. I gave myself a pat on the back for the map reading and navigation – despite it just being one long road. I looked rather strange, sweaty in running gear, arriving an hour early and organizing a lift back to the hotel with a dodgy-looking bloke who said he was a taxi driver.

Two hours later it was a real pleasure to see Chris be dumped into my world of adventure temporarily. He remarked on things like pollution, traffic, the weather and the overall sense that this wasn't a holiday destination like he was used to. I smiled and said, 'You've seen nothing yet.' The temperature wasn't bad, and nor were the streets. This was tame compared to many other cities I'd trotted around. Chris has travelled, and he's seen far more than me in terms of pain, suffering and death, due to his job as a nurse in A&E. And so although he was in my world, and everything was different, he was still at ease and nothing really fazed him.

As kids we'd fight like boys do, and being bigger and older I invariably went through the phase of bullying him. In our countryside family home, our return walk from school involved a long slow climb up a lane and then our extended driveway. If Chris was too slow, I'd run around behind him and hit him with a stick. This, of course, was bloody horrible, but most of the time he wasn't crying. Since our childhood days we've both been through transformations: me not hitting him any more; him now taller, bigger and stronger than me. This has somewhat changed the dynamic. We also leaned on each other for advice in many areas. Despite my horrible big-brother approach to siblinghood, we have now forged a brilliant relationship and one where we both respect and admire one another. It was a pleasure to have him around.

With a day in hand thanks to my ingenious plan to run to the airport to collect him, this meant we could spend a full 48 hours exploring before heading off to Tajikistan. Despite Chris having a reputation of always wanting to sleep and stay in bed, he was keen to see the countries too. My nature as a child – and indeed now – was one of cramming as much into a day as possible, and never really stopping. This was likely the reason why Chris rebelled and went the other way. For as long as I can remember, when anyone asked 'What's Chris doing?' or 'Where's Chris?', the answer for most of our lives was, 'He's probably asleep in bed.' He was obviously born to sleep for long periods of daylight hours and, be it chicken or egg, Chris for a long time worked on permanent nightshifts, gifting him the perfect excuse to sleep all day and earn money at night. He is 'a man of the night'.

The plan was to immediately find a cab to take us into the mountains to watch the sunset somewhere rural, so we then had the following day to visit one of Kazakhstan's many natural wonders, the Charyn Canyon. We were staying in a large white marble hotel. The place was crap, all things considered, but was supposedly 'outstanding' according to the many stickers and awards stuck to the walls. I'm sure it gained all of its four stars from the grandeur of the building and absolutely nothing else. We had about an hour of discussion with the receptionist, interspersed with lots of patience on our part while he asked us to wait as he answered the phone repeatedly and left us staring at the desk as if we weren't there. Eventually we arranged a car to collect us and drive to the highest point in the city, about 40 minutes away. The driver would then bring us back after sunset. Simple enough.

Six hours later, having missed the sunset and seen nothing but a dirt track on a hillside and an endless line of dusty cars stuck bonnet-to-bonnet in traffic, we were back at the hotel. My attempts to show off the wonders of travel and adventure to my brother were not going to plan. I could see he'd rather be sleeping. Undeterred and keen to actually see some of Kazakhstan, we regrouped and made a new plan. We wanted to see the Charyn Canyon but had already missed some of the best sunrises and sunsets in the world, as boasted of in various blogs. And so we arranged a different taxi, with ideally a more reliable driver, to take us to the canyon early the next morning. The canyon was three hours away but we wanted to be there for sunrise. We would then spend the day exploring and return with enough time to pack and head to the airport. By 1.50 a.m. we were both sleepily in the back of another taxi heading for the canyon. Dawn was over four hours away.

'*Helllllllooooo, Helllllloooo.* Is anybody out there?' My voice boomed around the walls of the canyon, echoing on and on and on. It was still totally pitch black so with an hour before the sun came up I broke out the camera for some night-sky shots. The silence of the valley and mountains beyond was almost frightening. The air was bitterly cold but calm, with practically no wind – nor any trees or bushes to give the wind a voice. The silence was broken only by the occasional bird, or scuffle of some desert-dwelling animals.

Chris held the torch and a solar lantern I'd remembered to pack but not used for over a year. The driver was asleep in the front seat while we pottered around the boot setting up the camera and tripod. For some reason we resorted to whispering. Were we whispering because the driver was asleep? Probably not, it just felt like a moment to whisper. Within 20 minutes I'd captured some of my best night-sky work to date. As the sun shed light on our situation we looked at each other with amazement – it was like we were on the moon. There was nothing but huge craters and cliff edges as far as the eye could see. We spent six hours messing around taking photos of each other in the canyon. What a brilliant, brilliant morning. I had my gear on and ran a few miles of the canyon, not wanting to miss the chance. Before we got back in the car we both took some time to soak it up. We walked down to where a river joined the dry canyon floor, sat and said nothing.

Tajikistan

Chris filled out his mandatory departure card with all the correct information diligently and accurately, while I scribbled a few numbers and letters without any care. I had completed these annoying cards too many times to care, and with the suspicion they never get read anyway. I often made my name up. After some snacks at the airport we eventually flew over fluffy clouds to the city of Dushanbe, the capital of Tajikistan.

With a human development index of 0.6 and a corruption perceptions index of 157 out of 176, you get an idea of our surroundings. It was another poor undeveloped country. Chris got to see what I'd already seen a lot of: street sellers, lonely kids under the age of five wandering around with nothing but a pair of pants and an empty water bottle, and lots of hand-built concrete buildings that had once held hopes of becoming large shopping complexes but were invariably abandoned and left to rot.

The run wasn't a highlight of our brief stay – nothing was, really. We didn't have the time to do much else except mooch around some markets. Tajikistan is a place I'll have to revisit and do properly.

Every now and then I don't even notice how far I'm running. Dushanbe was one of those days. I stopped a few times for water and a biscuit or two in a rundown service station, but other than that I bagged the miles without really being present. I was away in my own thoughts. The route was dull, the city was grey and overcast with no wind. The mountains in the distance were my only distraction. They were calling me, but I had no time to visit. At this time of the year the snowmelt from the surrounding mountains was forcing the river to flow pretty fast downstream. Although it was fierce, it drowned out the traffic noise and so I welcomed it. When passing through the final passport and ticket check at the airport gate, the cabin crew member said, timidly, 'Have a good flight – good luck.' We were on a *very* old plane with very few passengers. Chris and I both exchanged looks. 'You can't say that,' we said out loud in unison.

Uzbekistan

Uzbekistan holds many wonders, not least Tashkent's high-rise blocks complete with rusty Cyrillic lettering stuck to the sides. Tashkent is Uzbekistan's capital. It was completely destroyed by an earthquake in 1966 while the country was under Soviet rule, leaving over 300,000 people homeless. Having now been rebuilt (to an extent) it hosts a charming mishmash of restored twelfth-century mosques and classical Russian architecture alongside blocky brutalist concrete buildings. Statues of workers with bulging biceps seem to be a common theme. Personally, I'd seen enough faded Soviet architecture by this point, but the city did have a rather neat feel to it.

Uzbekistan is, of course, synonymous with the Silk Road, with much of the famous trade route worming its way in and out of what was then known as Mawarannahr. To this day it remains one of the largest exporters of cotton, silk and textiles. The work ethic and the industrial nature shone through here somehow.

We were joined by a chap called Lucas. I'd met Lucas a few months prior when speaking at the National Running show in the UK. Lucas is a character. He travelled with full-size guide books for both cities (Tashkent and Baku) and had planned various outings and sightseeing experiences. All good – but he hadn't run two marathons in the space of three days before . . . Chris wasn't expecting to share his time with anyone else on these few countries either and, truth be told, I'd forgotten Lucas was turning up so soon. By now the planning and organizational element of more or less everything to do with the journey was messy and struggling to stay afloat. Or rather, I had neglected my duty to check-in with the team as often as I should. Opting to sleep instead of searching for a Wi-Fi signal became the norm. Lucas, however, was a pleasant surprise. The three of us shared a room the size of a small double room rearranged to hold three very tiny single beds. I learnt that night that Lucas could snore for England.

We'd had a bit of a débâcle catching our flight earlier that morning, and so by the evening of our first night in Tashkent, Chris and I were knackered. Lucas, meanwhile, had all the energy and excitement of someone just arrived on a new mini-break.

Gathering to begin the marathon, Lucas and I waited around in the sun for a few others who had reached out on social media and who wanted to run with us. Malik and Merchan arrived right on time and we set off. These guys were both locals and were able to explain the earthquake and the country's history, plus knew their way around. Lucas and I learnt about every statue and park in the area. Lucas finished with a burnt red face and was sweaty from head to toe but happy to have made it. He hadn't run a marathon for over 18 months and was pretty pooped and hobbling slightly. He promptly fell asleep. The walrus returned. As a break from the snoring Chris and I went out to find some pre-dinner snacks. I took us straight to what we called the Biscuit Deli. This was an outdoor stall with approximately 100 small cardboard boxes. In each box there were particular types of biscuit: some chocolate-topped and fused together with melted goodness; others were large and cookie-like. We spent a good £10 on bags of the stuff.

A standout photo-memory of Uzbekistan was the underground system. The metro-wall art mosaics, the queuing system and even the ticket system were exactly the same as North Korea. Even the trains were the same colour. It was scarily similar. Another sight I'll never forget was of an elderly woman pushing an old-fashioned pram along a main road parallel to the hotel. She was pushing with some haste and purpose. As we got closer it was clear the pram was full to overflowing with small green fruits about half the size of limes. She didn't appear to be selling them, rather it seemed she was running off with them.

Azerbaijan

If you translate Baku directly into English it means city of wind. This was no Chicago but it was bloody windy. Lucas and I shared all 26 miles with the wind giving us grief as we plodded slowly along the seafront area. Formula 1 was in town the following week and so roads were cordoned off. This tested our navigation a little. For the final ten miles Lucas ran half a mile either ahead or behind me. I got the feeling he needed to focus. Chatting wasn't an option. He shared a few words of appreciation for how many marathons I'd run in such a short time and in far more extreme conditions.

We started in the old town, meandering up and down the steps, passing little stalls selling everything from clothes to fidget spinners, rugs and lanterns. Azerbaijan is a wealthier city than I imagined: high rises smothered in mirrored glass; the oil industry noticeable by advertisements on huge billboards; the streets free from chewing gum, with the ocean seemingly free of plastic or trash. People were well dressed, museums looked grand and majestic – it was obvious money had been gifted to smarten up the city. Give it a few years and the skyline will rival Hong Kong, I'm sure. For miles ten to 26 we spent most of our time jogging along the waterside. The Caspian Sea, although actually a lake, really does look like a massive ocean. This is the largest inland body of water in the world.

Our route was entirely made up on the spot and most of the time I let Lucas lead. It's actually really nice to let another person run in front – for me just to follow mindlessly. I didn't have to think about anything. I even had some time to pop into an old antique shop. A little iron teapot caught my eye, and in no time the shopkeeper had convinced me to buy it. I ran the last ten miles with the teapot under my arm looking like I'd stolen it.

At 11 p.m. Chris and I waved Lucas off. Work commitments called. He was to jump straight on a plane home in the early hours. Chris and I used the following morning for one final little exploration, which ended with a police escort.

We knew that Baku was a major player in the oil market and so hired a guy to drive us to an inland oil field. The photo opportunities were fantastic. Huge oily dinosaur-like machines pulled and pushed pistons into the earth. Thoughts of how the world here and elsewhere has been tirelessly and often mindlessly harvested by us humans lingered on our minds. We stood, listened and pondered. We heard wind, birds and the gargling of oil in the machines as they clunked seemingly endlessly. By the beginning of the twentieth century, half of the oil sold in international markets was being extracted from here. The oil boom contributed to the massive growth of the city to the point that between 1856 and 1910 the population of Baku grew at a faster rate than that of London, Paris or New York. Oil was king. We also learnt that the city takes a crown for a few other impressive stats. As well as being the largest city on the Caspian Sea and of the Caucasus region, Baku is located 28 metres below sea level, which makes it the lowest-lying national capital in the world as well as the largest city in the world located below sea level.

As we were wandering around the oil field with our cameras snapping away at the pre-historical mechanical monsters, we had a feeling we were probably not meant to be there, but with all the signs in the wrong language we carried on. Our driver was anxious to get us back to prevent him from landing in trouble. He called and gestured to tell us to make a move. As he did so, two unmarked police cars came zooming around the corner. They pulled up and gestured to us angrily: 'Out, out, out.' That was clear enough and so we stumbled over the dirty terrain with the backdrop of at least 200 more drills all plunging away behind us and made it back to the taxi. The police then pulled alongside to give us another telling off. This time we understood nothing and just smiled sweetly. It could have been dangerous. Thinking about it, it probably was pretty dangerous, but we knew no better, and being brothers we were feeling rebellious.

Afghanistan

The rest of the evening was free before an early morning flight. Both of us were flying out at the same time but Chris was off home, sadly. It was horrible saying goodbye to my little bro but my parents didn't deserve to have both their sons in jeopardy – especially not their favourite one. I'd spent more time with him in the past week than I had in the past two years.

Afghanistan was my first real war zone and took a huge amount of planning by the team, not only to get me access, but to find a way to safely run 26 miles. My way into Afghanistan was easy enough with a conventional commercial flight from Turkey. I flew to Istanbul from Baku. I landed in Kabul mid-afternoon on 21 April 2019. That was where the easy bit ended.

Visas for all of the war zones around the planet were another matter entirely and proved harder than we initially thought. Lots of documents were passed back and forth, including things like police records and medical examinations. We did everything the embassy asked. Universal Visas did what they do best and sorted everything thanks to copious phone calls to numerous departments and officials in a number of institutions around the planet. On top of this, safety was even more challenging and something that was at the front of all our minds when attempting to organize a 26-mile run in a city known for constant bombings, kidnaps and televised beheadings. Not even the UN are allowed out for a walk in Kabul. How was a scrawny tourist going to successfully run a marathon?

I landed, filled in the forms, waited in the typically slow queues and was met by Visar in the entrance of arrivals. Visar is an old friend of Veton (my Silverstone marathon friend from Kosovo) – both of them are very connected and totally selfless gents. Better still, Veton used to work for the UN, and Visar still does. Lugging my bag over, he met me at the door of arrivals with a smile and an outstretched hand. I was surprised to see more white tourists than usual – at least 15. It was obvious, though, that the rest of the westerners were all military or perhaps foreign aid workers. I stood out. My straggly appearance didn't help. And, besides, I didn't have tattoos or any form of muscle in my arms.

We met, shook hands, Visar took my bags and 20 seconds later a jeep pulled up next to us in the gravel car park. Visar's driver stashed my things in the car quickly. There were no fancy multi-storey car parks here. I went to open the door of the jeep as I normally would. It was locked, or so I thought. Car doors weren't usually as heavy as this. The driver chuckled to himself. It turned out that I was too pathetically weak to open it. The whole car was armoured. There was bulletproof glass in windows that didn't open. In the back there were UN helmets and body armour with a first aid kit and a large fire extinguisher. The letters 'UN' were written in blue along each side. Visar was a short chap with little to no hair, a worn leather jacket and black aviator sunglasses. Imagine the lead character in a classic spy film, minus the gun and serious look but with a slight addiction to cigarettes. I never saw him without one.

The drive to my temporary home was about 30 minutes through the streets of Kabul. Not just any streets either. This was prime car-bomb territory. Visar swivelled around in his seat to talk to me sitting in the back. He explained the basics of Kabul life. My home for my final 72 hours of this phase of the journey was to be the UN compound. More specifically, a 21-by-8-foot container made into an air-conditioned luxury apartment. It was a windowless studio room but was surprisingly homely – there was even potpourri.

Life in the compound itself for all the long-term residents was a microcosm of normal life in many ways – just with huge danger at the other side of your garden fence instead of the road to Tesco. Food shops, restaurants, a gym, a souvenir shop, an art outlet and a football/cricket ground all made the place feel normal and like home. The huge volume of white jeeps with UN written in blue on the side, along with barbed wire on every wall, plus the roaming military dressed head to toe in camouflaged body armour, somewhat brought me back to reality though.

Outside the huge fortified walls that made up the perimeter, life was very different. In fact the dangers had been so high that for many, many months no UN personnel had been allowed out. It was airport to compound, and vice versa. I later learned this was a real frustration for those who had seen it all, over many years. The restrictions were apparent in everyday life. Even things like ordering food from nearby retailers was banned due to safety concerns.

Visar left me with the single key to the door, and instructed that there was little to no point in locking it because everyone inside the compound was not only trusted but vetted thoroughly. Virtually every single person who lived in the compound, of which there were nearly 2,000, had impressive military credentials or was significant in their field. It felt like I had been invited into the inner sanctum of the UN peacekeeping force. Visar instructed me to shower and rest. Before long Paul turned up. Paul was Visar's boss and greeted me with,

'You're the crazy marathon man.' 'Yes, I am,' I replied, laughing like I'd never heard it before. He was senior, well liked and I got the immediate impression he worked very hard and cared hugely about his position and his people in the best possible way. He introduced himself and invited me to attend a one-on-one security briefing with Harris, an Afghan national and the head of security for the compound. He had a strong and authoritative presence with a hint that he was a softy at heart, owing mostly to the array of photos of his family and loved ones that covered the walls. I liked him and respected him almost instantly. This briefing, I wrongly assumed, would be a hello and some basics. Two hours later I'd been walked through every protocol under the sun. Evacuation, bomb threats, breaches, the gunfire I'd hear in the evening, the underground bunkers, and, of course, all the serious stuff too: like where food could be found and when the restaurants were open. Yes, the compound has restaurants. Good ones too.

With help from a large map on the wall and various pins and military symbols Harris explained a little of the context of the UN in Afghanistan, and of Afghanistan's history in general. In short, Afghanistan in all its guises is complicated. War, power, wealth, land, leaders, foreign military, and beyond – Harris talked me through the lot: the provinces in particular and who they are occupied by; Helmand in the south, Kabul in the north-east and Herat on the west. Islamic State, the Taliban, the government, foreign military, and of course allies to all and none, make up a messy mix of politics and beliefs rolled together with violence and ill-educated impatience and anger. I learned that most of the country's conflicts are continuing not for one aim or end, but for many different reasons – none of which everyone fully understands, on either side.

Harris went into further detail about the dangerous areas, the sites which had been bombed recently plus the attack locations and their frequency. His job was to keep the compound safe – no small task in the circumstances – but I felt immediately that there was no one better for the job. He knew everything, and being an Afghan national understood the bigger picture and political landscape first-hand.

We were interrupted a few times over the radio that sat on his desk – the radio would squawk with requests coming in for information – plus various personnel knocking at the door not realizing he was busy. I got the impression he did the job of hundreds, and was too busy to be chatting to me, but he hid it well and was patient and polite.

Visar turned up for the last 30 minutes of the briefing, to ease the burden from Harris and to show me around. He was accompanied by a South African chap called Dirk, who was an environmentalist supporting some projects further out of the city of Kabul. Dirk was a runner too, and was keen to meet me. We joked about Visar running, noting his smoking habit and the fact he could smoke a whole packet in the time it would take him to run a mile.

We left the confines of Harris's security HQ, which was another container made into an office, and headed for a tour of the UN city. It wasn't small, and it was easy to get lost. I remembered only where the restaurant was, where my container was (number 5), and roughly where Visar was, so I could find him if I needed anything. Without fail he could be found on his porch area in a chair with a fag and a phone in his hand. I never did get to the bottom of what he did.

On my first attempt at navigating from the main entrance to my container I got lost and stumbled upon Dirk again. He chaperoned me to Visar's cabin. Visar was in his usual spot on the porch. He invited me in briefly before escorting me back. My container was the equivalent of a spare room, neat and furnished for guests. Visar, having been living in the compound for years, had turned his space into a proper home, full of memorabilia from his various postings, a living area complete with sofa and telly and photos on the walls. It's amazing what can be done with a little time in such a small place – I loved it. One of the larger framed images was hung by the door. It was a black and white film photograph of Visar and Veton back in the day – both looking substantially younger and fresh to the UN world. Originally Veton had been just another kind-hearted selfless friend from Kosovo, but without Veton's introduction to Visar the Afghanistan leg (and others yet to come) would likely not have happened. It was brilliant and bizarre to be in the middle of Kabul looking at an old photo of Veton knowing that he'd put everything in motion. The world seemed instantly smaller. I'd met Veton in Silverstone while at a race on a rainy Sunday, and now I was in hot and humid Kabul in the middle of a war-torn country looking at a photo of the man who had made it possible.

Once back in my cabin I lay down on the bed and listened to the gunfire in the distance. Visar had informed me that there was a big question mark over whether I'd be allowed out to run the marathon. Leaving the compound was, of course, still forbidden in recent months due to attacks, but substantial efforts had been made to organize a five-car armed convoy to allow me to run the distance on the out-skirts of the city in the mountains. As I was landing, just a few hours earlier, completely unbeknownst to me, there had been two attacks in the vicinity and therefore the carefully laid plans to take me to the mountains were looking unlikely – I just hadn't been told yet. Even in my briefing with Harris we spoke of the set-up, the convoy formation and the emergency procedures. Visar's words to me were, 'Don't worry, it's still happening . . . until it's not.' The powers that be were still discussing if it was safe to take me out and risk the lives of over 20 men just so I could run. The answer was obviously, 'No.' It wasn't worth the risk. But they wanted to show support, and many of the military wanted to run with me. It was a chance to escape the walls of the compound. I waited in my room for only 20 minutes before there was a knock at the door. Visar popped his head around the door, dropped off my UN-issue safety helmet and bulletproof vest, which weighed a ton, and simply said, 'It's not looking good for tomorrow, mate. We'll make something work, though.' He came back only an hour later and delivered the bad news. It was off. No running outside the compound. I was gutted but understood, and shut my eyes for a moment, thinking it all through.

I slept for about two hours before being collected from my air-conned box and whisked off to the main communal area. I'd agreed to say a few words about my expedition. We linked up my laptop to a TV and moved a few old sofas and chairs into a semi-circle. I spoke for an hour about the ultimate goal, my inspiration, and the experi-ence so far. About 40 UN personnel turned up to hear my story. I felt a little silly, really. They probably all had better stories than mine.

They were living in the UN compound in Kabul, after all. I explained I'd be running in the morning for several hours to reach the magical 26.2 miles. I was open to anyone and everyone joining me. I asked for any advice about running around the compound, explaining the last-minute change of plans.

To my surprise a lot had already been organized by way of route, support and drinks in just the few hours since receiving the news I wouldn't be allowed out. We settled on a start time of 6 a.m., and by the show of hands we'd have about ten runners. The start/finish line was to be by the main gate. Glen, who was military security, chatted to me about the Marathon des Sables and his hopes to run it the following year. I shared a little advice, and we bonded. He was Welsh, tall and strong, but his soft and gentle voice gave everything away. He was a total softy at heart and a true gentleman. We spoke for a while before he was needed elsewhere. I learnt of various people's stories and how they had come to be in the compound – from military assignments to human rights and humanitarian aid work. The bunch had a collective understanding of the world and it dawned on me that I was surrounded by highly experienced and well-liked people. It was an honour. Every single person without exception was totally lovely and welcoming.

I can't remember who invited me exactly, but I was asked if I wanted to join in the nightly game of Ultimate Frisbee. About 20 people gathered under what looked like stadium lights in a five-a-side Astroturf area in the centre of the compound. Not wanting to miss out, despite feeling like I could sleep for a week, I agreed to join them. In hindsight I shouldn't have been running around on a pitch, barging into people leaping around catching Frisbees, in the middle of a running trip. It was a risk I didn't need to take. Even a sprained ankle would put an end to everything. I took the risk anyway. I avoided injury – mostly, all except a large bruise to my right thigh caused by a head-on collision mid-tackle with a regular pro-player. My team lost entirely because I was crap, but they didn't seem to mind, and I was just pleased I could still walk.

That evening I had dinner with the boss Paul and a few others. We ate and chatted the night away. I turned in early, as they continued smoking and laughing to the sound of bombs and gunfire in the hills. That was the norm to them. I got to sleep by 11 p.m., which was probably a bit late for bed with my mind just as tired as my body. I'd been meeting more and more people of late and the last 24 hours was an onslaught. However pleasant, it's still draining and I could feel the lack of energy ramping up a notch. Not ideal ahead of another 60 marathons.

The run the next morning was heavily supported. So many great friendly folk joined for the first dozen twisty-turny laps around the compound. A lawyer and a fast ultra runner, Stephanie, showed me the route and all its variations with the rest of the team trotting behind us. Only Dirk ran the whole way with me, with the others sloping off to read emails – or so they said! It was hot even at 7 a.m., and only getting hotter. Glen, Dirk and I ran together for most of the last half, Visar puffed away on a cigarette while manning the water station.

The 50 or so loops weren't terrible, although we very rarely did the same exact loop twice. The place was a maze of back alleys and dead ends. I lost count after a while. For the last few miles we ran in full UN armoured security clothing – not because we had to but because I would have been, had I been running in the mountains. I wanted to feel the weight of the gear. I regretted it instantly, and was glad we weren't running out of the compound. It was close to 15 kilograms – weight they could manage but my spindly tired legs could not. It was exhausting. I recorded a little video for social media in my last few miles. It captured my smile of appreciation for all those that had helped. Perhaps my smile was a sign of relief that another potentially difficult country was complete. I was on a high, and watching that video back I get goosebumps every time. An extra 30 or so people gathered on the chalk-drawn finish line. It was a job well done and the atmosphere, although very different from what it would have been in the mountains, was special. It proved one of my most friendly experiences. Lifelong friends were made during those few hours.

My flight wasn't until the afternoon, which meant I had the rest of the morning to myself. With help from a deliberately unnamed group of security and some UN staff, along with two heavily armed jeeps, we found a reason to leave the compound and headed for a nearby lake. I don't want to risk certain individuals getting into trouble and so will keep the story nondescript. Put simply, I had four hours out and about in Kabul eating local food, mixing with children and families in a small alleyway market. At all times I was surrounded by Afghan military with weapons drawn. It was a thrilling time, but we probably shouldn't have been there. I had visions of it all going wrong. The five security guys plus the military were constantly on the scout for trouble and kept me moving. We stopped only to rest under some shade by the water to listen to a local stringed instrument being played. I took a few selfies with locals, and was told of the tribal areas and gangs amongst the suburbs. I was trying to hide the fact everything was quite scary, and instead just tried to enjoy the sights, smells and sounds. It was a relief to be bundled back in the armoured jeep heading back to base. It wasn't until I was safely inside the walls of the compound that I relaxed. I felt bad for putting such a large number of people in harm's way – but they assured me they were all itching to get out too.

Cards, gifts and messages of support for my onward challenge were all bagged up and handed to me as I left. Visar dropped me back at the airport and escorted me through the rather scarily abnormal airport protocols. Being UN, he managed to get airside and sat with me until I left. I really didn't want to leave. I had seen virtually nothing of Afghanistan, but it didn't matter. I'd been immersed in an alternative world where brilliant life-changing work is done. I loved every moment of it. Once Visar had waved me off as I boarded the plane, I did feel a sense of relief at having completed the run. Things could have turned out very differently, but I lived and the mission was still alive.

7

African Revenant

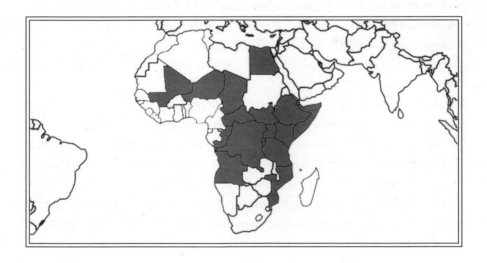

Ethiopia	Democratic People's	Niger
Comoros	Republic of the Congo	Mali
Kenya	Uganda	Chad
Tanzania	Rwanda	Central African
Burundi	Djibouti	Republic
Mozambique	Somalia	
Angola	Egypt	
The Republic of Congo	South Sudan	

When checking the calendar upon landing into Heathrow, I couldn't help but laugh. At the top of my diary it stated 'REST FOR 4 DAYS' – that was immediately followed by a dozen or so appointments on each day. It was laughable how everything was panning out. I couldn't exactly say no to a bunch of nine-year-olds who had all drawn me pictures and written letters from a Devon school, nor could I turn down media – the Chris Evans show, a few radio interviews with the likes of Radio 5 Live, some live TV including Sky, the BBC and World Service – nor the London Marathon.

With the help of a few friends we bundled into a car, whizzed down to Devon and then back in a day. The following day was full of getting on and off trains in London for various media slots, and then my final full day in the country was spent running the London Marathon. I ran, had more interviews mid-race, then to top things off I even had a few moments' chat with Andy Murray and other celebrities in the VIP tent. I stumbled through the door of my parents' house in Dorset later that night. I flew out the next morning. Home had been more manic than being on the road. I hated missing out on opportunities. If we were going to raise anywhere near the money we wanted for prostate cancer then I had to get in front of mics and cameras at every possible opportunity. With a new passport, and a slightly more simplified bag owing to the upcoming extreme heat – vests and shorts only – I took the train back to London from Salisbury and then on to Heathrow.

My dad and I had spent most of my last night in the country chatting through some of the potential security risks and delays ahead. The kitchen table of my parents' farmhouse was the war room. I was nodding off as we went through the last few points of interest, and so took myself to bed. As I left the next morning, to be dropped at the station, my mum came running after me down the drive with a pair of trainers in her hand. I had forgotten my bloody running shoes. This wasn't a good sign. It reminded both of us of the time she'd driven like a crazy person after the school bus to give me some much needed lunch money, which ultimately cost her £4 plus £150 and three points on her licence thanks to a speeding fine.

There was a plan – Addis Ababa, Moroni, Nairobi, Moshi, Bujumbura, Maputo, Luanda, Brazzaville, Kinshasa, Entebbe, Kigali, Djibouti, Mogadishu, Cairo, Juba, Niamey, Bamako, N'Djamena and Bangui were the cities listed in my diary for the next couple of months. I had heard of four of them – but coordinating nearly 40 flights across 19 African countries was not easy. Little did I know it but Addis Ababa international airport was about to become my most visited airport in the world. I went through there a dozen times in 60 days. It is the hub of East Africa.

Before I'd even got going there was another stumbling block. I arrived at Waterloo to change trains to get the Piccadilly line to Heathrow. As I was getting off the train after an uncomfortable sleep, I checked my phone. I had 14 missed calls from home. This wasn't ever a good thing. It turned out that Dad had gone back through the visa validity dates for the upcoming leg. I was about to fly to Africa without the visa I needed for South Sudan. There had been a mix-up because we'd already re-planned South Sudan twice and effectively two identical South Sudan visas had been wasted in old passports. The visa company thought I'd already completed South Sudan and hadn't ordered a reissue of my three-month visa. By a stroke of luck, when Dad called the visa office they still had my old passport which hadn't yet been sent back to me, and importantly it still had a few weeks of validity. Thankfully, everyone else answered their phones on the first attempt. Maz from Universal Visas instantly organized a courier to deliver the passport to me at the station. All I had to do was sit in Waterloo and wait. Time seemed to speed up. My flight was getting closer and closer to departing and I couldn't afford to miss it. I sat on the floor, slumped against the wall of M&S with my bags around me. I'm not sure how long I was there, but I nodded off pretty much immediately. I must have looked homeless. I was woken up by my phone ringing in my hand. Thankfully it was the courier calling. He was wandering around the station looking for me, and happened to be right in front of me when he rang. I jumped up, thanked him profusely, virtually snatched the passport from his hand and ran to the tube.

Ethiopia

In the classic rushed airport style, I was sweating and stumbling as I barged my way through people in the security line desperate not to miss my flight. I skipped getting any pre-flight snacks and got to the gate with only a few minutes to spare. The muffled Tannoy then announced a two-hour delay. Classic mistake, Nicholas. Sure enough, the several hundred passengers I'd barged past eventually sauntered up to the gate. Most of them locked eyes with me and gave a disapproving look. I had to laugh as I sat slumped with my bags thrown down next to me. To make matters worse I looked outrageously unfit. I was a sweaty mess. At least I hadn't missed the flight, and there were positives – I had my visa. Note to self. Don't do that again. For my sins I had drawn a seat between two rather hefty women in the Boeing 727 middle section.

We landed in Addis Ababa at 6.35 a.m. and I found a lift to the hotel. I slept for most of the day, then spent the evening trying to wade through all the jobs I'd neglected. Things like backing-up photos, writing some diary notes and replying to emails from supporters. It was lovely to have so many people all over the world email but it was tough to reply to them all without feeling rushed and like I wasn't giving it my full attention. I gave up after a while and turned out the light. I was in the top floor of another classically average hotel but only paid $40 for two nights so I classed that as a win. The alarm was set: a 6 a.m. start again to try to beat the heat.

There are three seasons in this part of East Africa. From September to February is the long dry season known as the *bega*; which is followed by the *belg*, a short rainy season. May is hot and dry and precedes the long rainy season, *kremt*, in June, July and August. The hottest temperatures are in March, April and May. I'd landed on 1 May.

The following morning started well. As soon as the sun popped over the mountains, the dogs stopped barking and the birds started tweeting. The city felt calm at 6 a.m. There were long tails of deep red and orange light sprawled across the city roads. I'd WhatsApp'd a guy I met at the airport who said he could take me to the mountains to run. Although I know not to trust everyone, I did trust him – based on absolute instinct and nothing else, but it's all I had. Like with many of the poor taxi drivers I hired to support the run, this bloke was patient and, better still, didn't murder me either. The set-up for my deals with the drivers was to agree a price for a number of hours. Most initially believed they were to be my tour guide. They were, in a way, except I would get out of the car and run in front of them for four or five long slow hours. It's safer to have someone nearby. I have water on demand, someone looking out for me and, in Addis, I was able to start high in the mountains for a more classic Ethiopian feel – plus it added a downhill to start the day. The Rift Valley wasn't far away – I was, after all, in the birthplace of running.

After meandering for ten kilometres in the mountains I made my way down into the city. The streets got busier and the traffic fumes bellowed out of every exhaust, most of which I stored in my lungs. The run was much harder than I had expected, but the reward at the end was feeling a greater sense of achievement. That's how running works for me (as I assume it does for most). The altitude battered me. Imagine holding your breath and swimming underwater for as far as you can, surfacing, gasping for every breath – then doing it all again. That was what most of the day was like. I loved it, though. The hills and views over the city were spectacular. I ran past families, groups of schoolchildren and farmers. Cows moo'd, sheep trotted up the hill past me and, as always, everyone stared at me. I even had a group of five kids run with me for a while. They made it look easy running in their school uniform.

The Ethiopian traditional costume is made of woven cotton and is often white or a light pastel colour. Ethiopian men and women wear the same clothes. These are called *gabbi* or *netella*. Sadly Nutella, the chocolate spread, wasn't involved. Women often wear dresses called *kemis*, with embroidered woven crosses as borders. I had my camera in the car and so stopped a few times to ask for photos. I liked

Ethiopia; it was just a shame the developed sprawl of Addis had ruined what was once such a beautiful landscape. When I took my clothes off that evening I washed them straight away in the sink. They were covered with lines of dirt. No matter how lovely the countryside, the city was just as dirty as any other. My sunglasses, which I had worn for nearly every run so far, were covered in tiny flies and needed a wipe too.

Comoros

Up next was one of the few East African islands, a volcanic archipel-ago, and the city of Moroni in the country Comoros. It was certainly an island and a small one at that. I arrived by plane, a twin prop, that shuddered a little more than I would have liked. I collected my bags and went to find whoever was taking me to the hotel. My bags were the last to appear and when I exited no driver was anywhere to be seen. I spoke none of the language, and was now down to only $33, which was useless in Comoros, a country that has its own currency and was financially unstable. In my haste at Heathrow I had forgotten to pick up extra cash as a back up. Not a wise move on potentially such a dodgy leg of the journey. Twenty minutes or so passed with me standing in the sun with my bags, looking glum and increasingly wor-ried. A driver arrived but he wasn't for me. He had arrived a little early to collect two groups of passengers off the next flight. I flagged him down and tried to explain my problem. He agreed to take me but wanted paying – in a currency I didn't have.

I followed this driver around like a lost sheep: I had no Wi-Fi, the driver that I had expected was a total no-show, my battery on my sat phone was dead and I had less than 20 per cent battery on my other phone. It was also getting dark and even more humid. I'm not one to scare easily but I wasn't sure of the taxi driver's intentions. Another ten minutes was spent negotiating a price to be paid in dollars. I wrongly assumed he would take me to the hotel and come back for his other passengers. After all, the plane holding the passengers he was waiting for was nowhere to be seen. Instead of driving to the hotel, he just sat in the car with me and wasn't driving anywhere. A while later, he got out and just wandered around the empty warehouse-like airport. This was when I realized he was waiting for the others and that my hopes of getting to the hotel soon after landing were dramatically fading. With that my frustration and exhaustion ramped up a notch. Another 40 minutes passed and by this point he had gestured for me to stay in the car and wait after several attempts to encourage him to take me and come back for the other passengers had failed. He gestured again in an equally short-tempered vein – he wanted to wait, and for me to do the same – and so, resigned, I did as I was told. I sighed, shut my eyes, and nodded off. Upon waking up in an alarmed confused state, the driver had vanished. It felt like the opposite of a car jacking – I was in his car, and even after trying to find him, I couldn't. When he appeared some time later I couldn't help my outburst of frustration. I must have been more tired than I realized. 'Can we go now, please? Let's go, let's go!' I said, in a slightly deeper, far too annoyed tone. He didn't care and just ignored me. Eventually he was fed up of waiting for the plane and I never found out whether it landed or not. Begrudgingly he at last turned the key in the ignition and off we went. I was angry, overtired and very ready for bed.

From the moment I finished my bartering processes to the point we arrived at what I thought would be my accommodation, over three hours had passed. The hotel, which was a $10 ride, was, annoyingly, only six miles down the road – just too far to walk with heavy bags. But maybe I should have.

My calendar notes from the team stated: 'Owner of hotel, Emilina, will meet you at the airport, and has given you two free nights in her guesthouse.' After stepping through the doors of the guesthouse, which was down a side street but close enough to the sea because I could still hear the waves even though it was now dark, a youngish girl behind the all-in-one reception and kitchen bar area couldn't find my name anywhere in her books. Nor was she willing to call the boss. After much frustrated encouragement she agreed to let me call her. The taxi driver was still waiting for payment, because my thinking was that the hotel could simply charge a card or sort some arrangement that would allow me to keep hold of my precious cash. I got through to

Emilina, who was angry immediately and said I was early. I think she was just embarrassed to have forgotten me. I explained my cash problem but she refused to help, stating, 'That's your problem, you sort it out. I'll come and show you to your room later.' She then hung up. I eventually paid $30, triple the agreed price for the taxi so he would go away, and waited a further two hours for Emilina to show up. Paying triple the price was a classic case of exchange rate distrust. I knew I was overpaying him, but he believed I was drastically underpaying him. I had no battery at all at this point in order to show a currency conversion on my phone to prove my point. Either he was ripping me off on purpose or by accident. Either way, I was beyond caring.

The humidity was horrendous. I had no money left to pay for food and came to realize nowhere on the island accepted cards due to the unstable and limited electricity supply. The guesthouse had no Wi-Fi, in fact neither did anywhere else on Comoros. The intermittent electricity meant there was little point having air-conditioning units too. I was moneyless, hot, sweaty and hungry, and cut off to boot.

Emilina eventually turned up. She was stressed and frantic. She greeted me with a fake smile and apologized for the airport mix-up, but jibed at the point I should have had local cash. I let it go and thanked her for letting me stay. Before I could finish, she interrupted, and while looking at the floor, informed me she had accidentally double-booked my room – aka forgotten about me. She proposed a solution which was to stay in the spare room of a friend of hers. At least I had a bed. The instructions to find her friend's house were, 'Go back down the ocean road and she's a few houses on the right. Big gates and a dog, I think.' You might think she'd know if her friend had a dog or not. I set off but soon realized it was too far to walk. The stars overhead were my only light – billions of them, and beautiful, but still not really bright enough to light my way. I hitched a lift with an elderly bloke who could speak some English and French. He luckily knew where I was talking about. It was a small town, after all. He didn't want paying, but I wish I could have at least given him a gesture of thanks.

The friend's house did have a dog – a big one with a hell of a bark. It was midnight and I was knackered. My final hurdle was to hope they knew I was coming. I walked up the small driveway. Insects and tropical critters, along with the boom of the dog bark, was all I could hear. It was over 30°C and I knew I'd have, at best, five hours' sleep before trying to run a marathon – with no money for water. I was greeted at the door by a couple in their sixties. They were pleased to help, and understood I wanted sleep. They went to bed as I slept on their sofa. It felt like minutes later that my alarm sounded.

It was 5 a.m. and I needed to run before the sun was out in force. I started running just after 6 a.m. It was 44°C by the time I'd completed all 26 long insufferable miles. My route was one mile out then one mile back – 13 times. True to say that day was brutal and unrelenting. The humidity played a huge part, and I was forced to run one mile out-and-backs because I needed water – water that was only available by tap at Emilina's place. She at least allowed me to drink her water. I got through nine litres of it, as well as two Cokes and two Fantas – the sugary drinks paid for on a tab which she had agreed to sort with my team through an online transfer. My sugar was low, my energy was low, and my mood hovered on the fence between tired and over-tired. This journey wasn't supposed to be easy all the time, but all things considered I finished the run and hadn't collapsed due to hunger, so I had to take the wins. Plus the island was beautiful – even if slightly spoiled by pollution and traffic and other signs of human activity, plus several big storms, many landslides, floods and eruptions from the impossible-to-miss volcano over the years. Just a few weeks prior to my arrival the island had been hit by the biggest storm in Comoros's history – so much so, it turned out, that they were still struggling to find power for their fridges. This made my frustrations with food and payment seem rather insignificant. The damage was obvious and sad – the environmental degradation only concealed by cars, a ton of rubbish and concrete everywhere I turned.

The day was a battle to the end. I left Comoros having only eaten bread, some sugary drinks and a pack of bourbon biscuits I kept for emergencies. Life is a rollercoaster, so they say, so what goes down must come back up, right? The small print of 'the real African experience' reads, 'Please bring your passport, luggage, something to deal with the barrage of mosquito bites – and a shedload of patience.' I arrived at the airport at 8 a.m. to find that my flight had been moved from 10 a.m. to 3.30 p.m. And still with no money to buy food or water, I used the last of my patience in dealing with the four-hour queue to get into the terminal building. This was a tin shed that contained, sectioned off in one corner, the 'Kenya Airways VIP lounge'. The VIP lounge had more staff than the entire airport put together, as well as the only air-con in the country, or so it seemed (of which there were four big towers). Plus they had a fridge with food and free Wi-Fi. I was one of about 20 passengers flying out. We were all told the plane was to be further delayed to 5 p.m. There were no VIPs flying and yet they insisted none of us were allowed to use the lounge, or the Wi-Fi or the air-con. We were all livid at the ridiculous situation. We sat in a 40°C tin shed for seven hours while the airport staff sat in the air-conditioning snacking on freebies and streaming football games on their phones. Strangely, it was us who were the paying customers aggrieved by the delay – not that Kenya Airways gave a shit.

Kenya

I was hopeful Kenya would bring new fortunes: maybe less humidity, and perhaps helpful hotel staff. On a journey like this, it was the small bits of faff and wasted energy that I tried to avoid yet invariably followed me. Running in Nairobi was a huge contrast to slogging it out in the crazy humidity of Comoros. The airport delays did leave me feeling exhausted but, once the legs started to turn over, the magic of running kicked in. My legs felt less heavy, my mood lifted and I was pushing through the miles with hardly any effort. The power of the mind is an incredible thing. Everyone knows running is therapy one way or another – the best and healthiest drug for bad moods.

I would have loved to run in Iten, the home of African long-distance running, but sadly time wasn't permitting and I would have had to sacrifice the two-day break which my body was craving. Priority number one was simply to run a marathon in every country, however unglamorous some of the locations. And, of course, to keep myself fit and well enough to make it through to the end. Occasionally my want to explore had to take a back seat, to focus on the mission. I didn't like this at all, but I knew I had to compromise occasionally. Anything more than the marathons themselves – including some spectacular and significant backdrops – was a bonus. That's the mantra I had to start adopting. It was getting more and more serious by the day and therefore I had to become more ruthless with my time, even if I didn't sit right with me.

My only slight hiccup of the day was a run-in around my 19th mile. I was plodding along nicely, coming back into the city after a short time running around some hills. Nairobi was like most cities, polluted, and so I was keen to escape. Returning for the final seven miles I was recording a few pieces to camera for social media. I keep my phone in a small elastic belt made by Arch Max. It's hidden but allows me to check the map occasionally and, of course, take photos and record some content to share the journey as I run. Mid-spiel about the enjoyment of running and remarking on how Kenya had lifted my spirits, I was accosted by a chap who grabbed my arm and asked to see my phone. No introduction. He was in ordinary clothes but actually looked pretty rough. Having previously been mugged far more violently my heart rate shot up and I was immediately conscious to not let the phone out of my hand. He repeated himself, 'Let me see your phone, let me see your phone.' I refused and asked why. He claimed that he was a police officer. All that went through my mind was: 'I'm in Kenya, these folk can run fast, and I'm towards the end of a long hilly marathon. If he grabs my phone I don't stand a chance of catching him.' I refused and asked to see some identification. With that he reached around to his belt towards his lower back. I imagined a gun or a massive knife. Time seemed to slow down and I stepped back. It was just a radio. He called his peers and informed them I wasn't cooperating. Bugger, this was escalating. Maybe he wasn't just a grifter chancing his luck. In fact, he wasn't a mugger at all. He was a fully fledged undercover police officer. But, and it's a big BUT, I was in Kenya and the police, like in many places in the world, could be corrupt.

A few moments later, with his fist still firmly gripping my arm, there were three police cars and an impressive 12 police officers on the scene. I was taken to a nearby building and told to explain why I was filming a specific building. I explained that I was running around the world, I had seven miles left to go in Nairobi, and would very much like to finish. The building they thought I was filming, I wasn't. It was as simple as that. The building in question was an old factory and one I hadn't even noticed.

It turns out there was some confidential activity going on inside the building and some high-level government personnel present. None of whom were in sight, and I'm still not sure if I believed them. They wanted to see my passport, which of course I didn't have on me, plus they asked me to show the photos from the past few hours. Luckily my little piece to camera very clearly didn't include the building or anything other than my face and upper body. They had no grounds to hold me. It was over 20 minutes before they agreed I wasn't a secret runner spy and let me go. I carried on with slightly more adrenaline than usual. Going to sleep that night knowing I didn't have to get up, to get on a plane or put my sweaty wet gear back on, was a little bonus to the day.

The Nairobi national park was only an hour's drive and so I was up early for a full day of exploring. I had no plans, and didn't even know if the park was open to random walk-ins. Luckily it was. My driver left and I found my way to the ticket desk, hired a park guide with a huge open-top jeep and started the day well: zebra, impala, buffalo, black rhinos, crocs, eagles, giraffes and thousands of birds I never knew existed. It was the holding bay of Noah's Ark – except there were far more than two of everything – but sadly no lions. All day I tightly gripped my long-lens camera in the hope of snapping some. Preferably up close. My driver, whose name I tried hard to pronounce but failed, suggested we try in the deepest darkest depths of the park. As the sun got closer to setting over the vast savanna littered with wildlife, I put the camera down and watched as we went further into the bush.

It was my lucky day: 11 lions, three females and eight tiny cubs, were sleeping in the shade. The noise of the jeep's engine woke them up but only momentarily. Most of them nodded off to sleep again. We were less than four feet away. Close enough to smell them. Close enough to hear the deep hum as they slept. One little cub was curious and came right up to the jeep. He was beautiful. I was conscious of time, but didn't want to leave. We stayed for an hour and simply watched in silence. Pure animal heaven. I was mesmerized.

Tanzania

I left Nairobi the next morning with no other thoughts than of those lions. The fact I was flying to the foot of Kilimanjaro, the tallest mountain in the continent, was beside the point. My mind was still in Kenya.

The town of Moshi is the gateway to Kilimanjaro National Park, nestled at the base of the infamous Mount Kilimanjaro. The mountain, despite being covered in clouds most of the time, still has a looming presence over the surrounding villages. Flying into Moshi Airport was spectacular and pretty damn bumpy. Every one of the 40 or so passengers, who mostly resembled hikers, was glued to the window. Thick cloud smothered the hills with the snow-capped peak peeping out of the top.

My Tanzanian marathon was fun but not what I was expecting. Despite it being rainy season it stayed surprisingly dry and warm. I ventured out without sun cream on. At 2,000 metres in 30 degrees, this was a dumb move. My thought was to run as close to the mountain as possible but with the hills and the heat, combined with the need for much water, I decided against it. Running zigzags all over the town of Moshi was the best bet to stay close(ish) to the hotel's drinks and the roaming ice-cream seller with a bath on wheels wandering around the town. Every time I passed him I gave him a few notes and went on my way. I achieved a new record: 0.2 of a mile to down an ice cream while running. A long dip in the hotel pool was followed by an exceptional steak, care of the South African chef who owned the hotel. Bliss.

Burundi

Getting to Burundi via, once again, Addis, was one of the bumpiest flights of my life. We flew over the Congo mountains then swooped in behind them to land in the centre of Bujumbura. The landing made everyone shriek as the plane came in at 30 degrees off centre, hovering in the air like a bird going in for a water landing. I was amazed the pilot even attempted to land. It was beyond windy and a genuine sense of fear filled the cabin.

We landed at 1 p.m. and I was driven ten minutes around the corner to the Hotel Club du Lac. I wasn't expecting a beach resort in the heart of Africa, but it made for a nice surprise. I dumped my bags and smothered my neck and back in the last of the after-sun I'd bought from a fellow guest in Moshi out of desperation, paying $20 for half of his remaining litre bottle, and sat in the shade of a small beach terrace with the waiter serving me food as the sun set. Since leaving Moshi I'd only had a packet of chocolate buttons, a Graze snack box, which I found in the bottom of my bag, some dodgy airplane food and a huge pineapple cut into pieces. The pineapple, of course, was a common sight in Central African airports. Fruit in bags is the equivalent of a box of Maltesers at Heathrow – overpriced but satisfying. I was hungry and so ordered two 12-inch pizzas with double tuna on both. Tuna had become my staple protein, and pizza my trusted carb hit. The pizza was divine and I ate till I could hardly move. Despite it not being particularly nutritious this would at least keep me upright in the heat tomorrow. My diet was just one of the many things that had changed in my life. At home, pre-expedition, I'd never been particularly healthy – but I've always been very aware of what my body needs vs what I want to eat. Sometimes it needs vegetables, when most of the time I want chocolate. The journey had made me appreciate the freedom of choice I'd had before, and now, faced with such limited options, I craved healthy food. Back home, when I'd had a bout of rubbish food for a few weeks I could at least cleanse with fresh fruit, veg and supplements. My diet now was literally anything I could get my hands on that wouldn't upset my stomach. And, as you've seen, I didn't always get it right.

I woke to a collection of messages from friends and family back home. It had been 500 days since I left home to embark on this bonkers mission. I hadn't even realized it was such a significant milestone, but it was. It was day 500. Wow! I had a tear in my eye watching a few of the videos. I didn't exactly miss home, but now, more than ever, I wanted to hit pause and give them all a hug and sit and watch crap telly. But as that thought passed through my head, I also realized time was ticking and my enemy was mounting an attack. My enemy, of course, was the sun.

My day started well. The messages were lovely. My accidental gift to myself for making it to such a momentous milestone was to transition from human to lobster. The bottle of sun cream I had largely forgotten to apply was now empty. I don't know why my brain repeatedly forgot to get more sun cream. So, yet again, I was about to run a marathon in Africa, in 40+°C without any UV protection. The beast in the sky was surely going to get me. And yep, it did. The sun burnt me for a nice long period of five hours as I plodded up and down the five-kilometre stretch of dusty road over and over again. My route was simple: run to as many shops as possible and look for sun cream. Nowhere had water for sale either, due to a shortage in the country, and so the hotel lobby was my safe haven for fluids. I got in five litres just from sticking my head under the tap in the single sink of the reception toilet. I ran the five kilometres along the RN4 highway from Hotel Club du Lac west to the Congo border and back again. I repeated this, in and out of the hotel reception toilet, four times – although it felt like at least 100. Later, I resorted to wearing long sleeves and my buff around my neck to cover my skin. But in the African heat, adding clothes didn't really help.

Water was all around, but there was not a drop to drink. I was running parallel to the huge ocean-like lake called Lake Tanganyika which covers what feels like the entire Burundi 'coastline'. This lake spans four countries and is totally beautiful, pan-flat and massive. It felt weird to be in the centre of Africa, in one of the driest continents on the planet, and still have this body of water. I couldn't help wonder why it wasn't being treated to make it available to drink. Money was probably the answer – and politics. It is however possible, and would likely have a staggeringly positive impact.

The people of Burundi I learnt were unbelievably friendly. In what seemed like a market dedicated to bananas were hundreds of locals of all ages. Every time I ran past they ran out and offered me a banana.

They didn't even want money for them. I accepted and gave them a little money anyway. That's, of course, how it works. As I ran up and back over and over again, the group of banana sales people grew bigger and bigger. From dawn till closing time there must have been something like 100,000 bananas in this one field. To make the spectacle even more elaborate, the bananas were draped over old, tiny, single-geared bikes. I saw my first banana riding a bike about four miles in; 400 or so bananas balanced around a bicycle and rider is a hell of a sight, especially considering some poor banana man inside the banana cocoon had to ride the bike and keep the fruit from falling off while trying to sell it. It also baffled me why they were all gathered in one place. I'm no businessman but I'd have suggested spreading out a little. The friendliness gathered even more momentum when a girl of about ten ran out shoeless and said hello in perfect English. She carried a wicker basket full of yet more bananas and offered it to me. Her mum was looking on and giggling with embarrassment. This time it was a gift, and they wouldn't accept my money. This part of the world and indeed this part of Africa was not rich, but the people were full of generosity. Just down the road from the Congolese countries, health, famine and desperation were ever-present, but so were smiles and a clear sense of happiness. I finished running with another dollop of worldly perspective and felt genuinely humbled by the people of Burundi and their kindness. I explained this to my hosts at the hotel. They simply smiled and said, 'Of course. You are our guest, Mr Butter. Not just of the hotel but of the country.'

Mozambique

It took two days to get to the coastal capital of Maputo owing to several connections and an overnight stop in Johannesburg. South Africa was another regular stopover and one which often involved sweet-talking my way through the labyrinth of connecting security checks.

When I left Bujumbura I was given a handwritten ticket to get to Kigali, Rwanda. These tickets were both ripped in half as I boarded each flight. But when I flew the 'Rwanda Express' from Kigali to

Jo'Burg I wasn't given my onward ticket to reach Maputo. This, I was used to. My flight connection was over 12 hours long and therefore the tickets weren't available 'on their system'. The problem with that meant that I was in limbo. Upon arrival in Jo'Burg I was unable to check-in for my flight to Maputo and, because I arrived into arrivals (as you do), and went through the connecting-passengers bit of the airport ready for my onward flight, but had no ticket, I was stuck in a small area with about a dozen other passengers all in the same predicament. I just wanted food, somewhere to lie down in a quiet corner and, ideally, a bathroom to brush my teeth and splash my face, especially in a tired, mid-transit state. I attempted to get through security to be airside without a ticket. Normally in a British airport there would be no chance, but I wasn't in England so thought I'd have a go. Sure enough, for those in the know, the airport security had devised a way to sort this ridiculous problem. An A4 lined notepad was used to record the names and onward flight numbers of us limbo passengers. I was allowed through but had to pass back through security the opposite way to collect my ticket an hour before my flight was due. It seemed like this was a process they didn't want to advertise, possibly because it was embarrassingly disorganized and could easily go wrong, but I was glad I had found it. I had the rest of the airport throughout the night to myself with a couple of small shops open. The upside of connecting in South Africa is that the airport, despite being shoddy in the organizational sense, was, by African standards, luxurious. It was the most sophisticated airport on the entire continent, with shops, a Starbucks and a few food outlets. From that moment on, whenever I saw Johannesburg listed in my calendar as a connecting flight I knew I was OK. It's the simple things. Over the course of the remaining months, I even got to know the airport staff by name and the Starbucks bloke made me my drinks for free. I did feel a little bad for all the other passengers who hadn't worked out the security notepad protocol. Although mostly I was just pleased I had.

I finally arrived into my freebie hotel south of Maputo. It had a decent internet connection, but didn't have any food, a lock on the door, a fan, air-con, or any sheets on the bed. Plus the Portuguese language barrier hindered me a little. I was in a very rundown shack, really. The lock on the door was the main issue, so I opted to move to a hotel called the Southern Sun, further north and right on the beach. I asked myself if I was becoming too snobby or picky with hotels. Maybe – but, you know, some food to fill me up could be helpful and a lock was essential.

A comfy bed, the window ajar and the warm breeze in my face as the sun rose forced a blissfully long lie-in. The sound of the waves lapping at the shore just a few feet from my first-floor window was preferable to the usual cacophony of motorbikes and horns. 'Do I get up and beat the heat?' I thought. 'Or do I just stay in bed for a few more hours and listen to the waves?' Waves it was.

I didn't linger long, though, and was soon lured out onto the road again. The runner's high hit me. The feel of a spring in my step, that rare rhythm as my strides felt effortless, a smile from ear to ear, breathing not even a thought, shoulders relaxed and then a glance at my watch – I was even running pretty quickly. Sometimes marathons felt utterly awful, and sometimes they felt like Maputo: bliss. I had shops for water and, of course, stopped for my regular ice cream in the last few miles. I even managed to buy some knockoff sunglasses. I was fearful before I began the trip that, like a chocoholic in a chocolate factory, I could go off running. I hadn't.

I ran 4.5 miles up the coast from the hotel, and then turned around and came back again. I did that four times. The sights and smells of local pop-up markets, the fish on barbecues, the seaweed, the crabs and the ocean were all smells that made me smile. I grew up near the sea, and so the beach will always feel better than the city. The coast is king.

I left Maputo with the city close to my heart plus a few souvenirs I didn't need. A wooden box on the floor of a street seller's stall caught my eye. It was handmade, varnished, and had a hefty wooden hinge. It was dark wood with animal carvings embossed into the lid. As I ran past, and without slowing much, I shouted, 'How much for the box?' He quoted me $40. I simply shouted, 'Nope, I'll give you $10.' That was still a decent chunk of money for Mozambique and I knew he would start at least double its worth. Each time I ran past we'd barter a little more, my voice getting fainter as I ran away and then back again. I was certain the chap thought he wouldn't see me again. But, like a bad smell, I literally kept running past him and I eventually ran the last few miles with the box tucked under my arm – $12 plus a selfie was our resting price. This box now takes pride of place amongst my souvenirs. It stores all the various banknotes and coins from around the planet. A reminder of the spirit of bartering and trade on which so many people depend.

Angola

My first morning in Angola, I was lazy. I could have got up and run early, but like so often recently I just didn't. I was in a happy place, and content with the running, but still my body lacked energy, and so I had another lie-in and faced the sun in its full force later in the day.

Luanda is more affluent than I had imagined, but sadly has huge issues with inequality. Like so many developing countries, the rich–poor divide is huge. The homeless live in extreme poverty right next to those with pristine ties, suits and polished shoes. I gave away the last half of most of my drinks. I'd be drinking and then as if by magic a boy would appear at my side looking up in desperation. These kids didn't ask for money. They asked for water and food. That says it all.

After completing the first half-marathon along a stunning bay, and out on a five-kilometre spit with lovely empty beaches, I turned around to complete my last 13 miles running back. On that return leg I spotted a number of people gathering on a manmade groin jutting out into the ocean. I stopped to see what they were all looking at. Perhaps it was a washed-up animal, or something, maybe even a pot of gold? No – a dead body, naked and floating face-down in the shallow waves. People looked on. I stopped, pulled out my earphones and joined the group. I happened to be listening to an audiobook about the realities of poverty, which was now somewhat grimly brought to life.

The principal language in Angola is Portuguese, but a couple of younger blokes spoke to me in French, making the point that this wasn't an uncommon thing in this part of Luanda. One of them said, *'Il y a des centaines de cadavres chaque mois'* – meaning there were hundreds of dead bodies every month in this area. I ran the remaining miles without the audiobook and instead pondered the life I took for granted. I learnt that evening from the hotel staff that it had made the news and that he was a young man who had been caught up with the wrong crowd. Not wanting to sound like a reporter fishing for gossip, I left it at that, and contemplated it for most of the evening. I'd seen dead bodies before, but none bobbing around in the ocean as yet unclaimed.

As I showered and prepared for bed, with my clothes drying on the balcony, I caught a glance of myself in the steamed-up mirror. My body shape had somewhat dwindled, was shrunk and small. I was living on the occasional good meal and snacking on things like Dairy Milk on airplanes and bread in between. I was thinner than ever, likely very unhealthy. Even so, I was far better off than most of the people I ran past in Luanda. The bags under my eyes, my skeletal ribs and cheekbones more prominent . . . in the past I would have been horrified, but now I was just thankful. I could, if I wanted to, change that. Others here had little choice of what they ate, or didn't.

The Republic of Congo

During the 26-hour journey to the Congo the airport lounges became my home again. 29 May 2019, and I had just 135 days to reach the finish line. All that stood in my way was another 52 countries, another 52 marathons, and roughly 110 flights. Athens was getting closer. The official 2019 Athens marathon was on 10 November. My final country and the birthplace of the marathon. I couldn't miss it. Troublingly, there were still visas we hadn't managed to secure. The team were working tirelessly, but it was close, and becoming uncomfortably so.

The Congos are famous for many things, some bad, and some good. Notably they pair up the two closest capital cities in the world. I looked out of the 16th-floor window of my new Congolese hotel room to see just how close they were. Only the 250-metre-wide Congo River separated them. I was in Brazzaville looking out to Kinshasa.

I'd read in a tatty inflight magazine months earlier that Brazzaville was one of the richest cities in Africa. In some parts of the world, if a country claims to be rich, that doesn't necessarily mean the people are rich. In fact, it's highly likely the opposite is true, with just a handful of the corrupt holding most of the money while the rest suffer.

I'd also read about horrendous indiscriminate shootings, extreme corruption within the police, malaria, violence and gang murders. This, however, was thankfully not reflected in the run. I ran with children and dogs, neither of which tried to bite me or hurt me in any way. Most of the kids were barefoot and in small groups. I got the impression they had no other family or even knew anyone else. They certainly had neither education, nor money, and had likely never left the city let alone crossed the river into a different country. I ran relatively quickly so not to draw attention, and to be back in the confines of the hotel as soon as possible. It was eerily quiet. The hotel wasn't far from the Congo River and so I ran out-and-backs along it, never straying too far away from base. The kids roamed the streets with huge nets on sticks and tubs under their arms. From what I could work out, the purpose of the nets was for grabbing fruit from trees and catching it in the fishing-net-style hoop. The tubs were for something different. I watched a few groups of kids cleverly position themselves like human chess pieces ready to trap lizards. They'd identify a lizard and predict where it would run. One little chap had the tub, the others would stand and stamp their feet to force the poor creature into the tub. They did well from what I could see.

The feeling of running in Africa is something I'll have with me for ever. It's utterly brilliant, but I was always on guard, always conscious when taking my phone out for a photo, always gauging the response from my thumbs-up towards passers-by, and always hopeful that it would become less hot, less hilly and more breezy. It seldom did. The phrase being 'situationally aware' is something that my whole being has learnt and is now ingrained like muscle memory. It's exhausting but needed. In Brazzaville, I relaxed after a few miles, but I never turned that alarm system off in my mind. The people of the city, the few that were out, made the run what it was. Kids, adults and even some non-scary-looking military all cheered me on, waving and even running with me at times. Some asked for money and food, but most were either genuinely happy to see a new face, or just wanted to support the crazy white guy running. Once I was finished and made it into the hotel the receptionist informed me it was a national holiday and that was the reason for the quiet roads. It was a shame not to have seen it as normal, but I also wondered why the roads were quiet if it was a holiday. She told me no one had any money to do much else.

Post-run and with my calendar showing nothing for the following day or a path to my next country, I sat on the edge of my bed and reloaded the calendar app a few times. I thought there had been a malfunction and the app hadn't loaded the latest information. I only ever looked a few days ahead, most of the time just scanning the details rather than examining them.

My assistant Carla didn't answer the first few times I tried to call, and so I called Dad instead as back-up. He must know what the plan was. What with the Congo being south of the UK and not particularly too far east, the time zone wasn't dissimilar to home. He answered and said the calendar was correct: 'Remember we talked of you exploring this when you got there. We couldn't find the best way between Brazzaville and Kinshasa. There's a boat but people often drown trying to cross, and the flight goes via Addis and Jo'burg again, so it's either a 24-hour flight to travel 200 metres. Or you risk the river.' The lure of an extra bonus day after a short river crossing, followed by what would then work out to be two days without running or flying, won the toss.

Together with the brilliant hotel staff and Carla we worked out the last-minute plans to cross the river border to the Democratic Republic of the Congo. My initial plan was to find a way to cross immediately the same evening, potentially bagging another day off. It turned out that this was crazy talk. Crossing the Congo River at night was a definite no-go. There were dangers from crocodiles, the official border posts were closed, and the likely occurrence of some dodgy dealing down at the water's edge, be it drugs or weapons, seemed possible. I must have had over 50 phone calls and messages in an attempt to try to work out the best route. There was also another snag. I had the wrong entry date on my visa. This, I'm sure, would have been less of a problem in many other countries, but I was afraid that crossing the river with effectively an out-of-date visa could cause chaos and

Top: Back in Africa, a young lion cub susses us out.

Above: Joined by Andy and a runner friend towards the end of our Niger marathon.

Right: A Nigerien man fetches water.

Above: My Sherpa friend, Ram, outruns me in Nepal with help from James in the background

Left: The bustling streets of Kathmandu.

Left: Some wise-looking men in Bhutan.

Below: Battling food poisoning and a kidney infection in Bangladesh. Lying on the ground just before and after I was sick.

Above: In the Maldives, running along a sandbank in the middle of the ocean.

Below left: Boats and the city of Doha at dusk.

Below right: The empty streets of Turkmenistan's marble capital.

Below: Jeddah Running Club supporting me in Saudi Arabia.

Above: Meeting a junior Aussie rules football team in Nauru, one of the least visited countries on Earth.

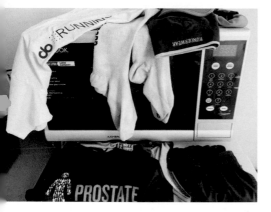

Left: The Marshall Islands – and once again attempting to dry my clothes before packing them.

Below: Kiribati by drone.

Venturing to Tuvalu, the most remote island in the world.

Above: Back to Africa, where in Malawi young kids pose for photo.

Right: Running in the sun on Malawi's empty roads. Heaven.

Below: Running Sudan with UN military support.

Above: Day 673. An emotional reunion with Kev in Athens.

Below: Celebrating one day away from completing the mission.

Left: Kev and I run the final few miles of marathon 196.

Below: Crossing the finish line. Athens, Greece, 10 November 2018.

Bottom: The team and friends assemble moments after completing the final marathon. What an adventure.

potentially result in having me banned from the country, or worse, simply shot. My media-adapted mind had made the Congo seem a very scary place, even more so than others – I'm not exactly sure why. With some advice from various security personnel about various attacks and shootings, I wasn't feeling overly safe. All eventualities really were a possibility.

I resorted to asking the receptionist, people on the street and went to the 'ferry port' myself to get some information. It was all looking complicated whichever way I went. There had been multiple situations of capsized ferries, militia threatening passengers and stealing luggage, and, of course, the very real possibility that nothing would happen at all, and I'd be left with no progress, no river crossing or flight, and end up losing a day in a schedule that was already very tight. With a mountain of help from countless people and further numerous phone calls, emails and even a fax, we managed to arrange and pay for a crossing at 9 the next morning. A driver would meet me at the hotel, take me to the boat. I'd get on, hopefully not die, and get off the other side. Simple.

I closed my eyes to get some rest. I could hear dogs barking in the street and so went to the window to check. There was a bunch of guys with semi-automatic weapons and about 15 dogs – nice comforting stuff before sleep. The saving grace of all the stress of the day had been a totally delicious and belly-enlarging steak with fries and sauce. If I died crossing the Congo tomorrow at least I would have had a nice last supper. From 10.15 a.m. to 12 noon I sat by the water watching as my passport was handed around various people, none of whom looked, nor indeed probably were, official. I should have docked in Kinshasa at 9.30 a.m. Needless to say that hadn't happened, and the lift I'd arranged at the other end would be waiting a while longer. I felt terrible. I had no way to contact them. A hotel was putting me up, and was aware of the plan and pick-up time. Leaving Brazzaville the officials didn't notice my invalid out-of-date visa. This was good. I could at least get there. The boat wasn't as shabby and as rundown as I expected, and it had an engine. I really hadn't been sure if we'd be rowing or not. There were also life jackets. I felt like putting them all on. Nothing was orderly about the boarding process. I just waited and hoped they wouldn't forget about me. I had a dozen or so people come up to me asking if I needed help with my bags. I did, but wasn't about to let a random guy charge me to hold it for me. So I declined again and again.

Eventually a man with a whistle around his neck pointed at me, blew the whistle hard and shouted '*vingt-et-un*' in French at me. I was the 21st passenger. This I assumed would mean we would be boarding in number order. It didn't – I never did work out what the number system was for. The boat was the equivalent of an old small fishing boat that, once full with passengers and luggage, had its stern dipping into the water, with windy waves lapping at the exhaust of the outboards. It held over 25 of us, but in normal circumstances was big enough for a family of four to have a nice day's fishing. It was rammed – no wonder they sink sometimes. I did, though, get on the boat eventually. I just pushed my way to the front and got on. Sod British politeness. Now was not the time. In doing so, after waiting so long, I'd forgotten that some other chap had my passport. Moments before the small boat set off a man shouted, 'Oy, oy,' and with hand outstretched passed me my passport. Thank goodness for that. How stupid I was to forget about the one document I needed.

The boat was cast off and motoring, but there were some crying babies howling next to my feet. It wasn't clear who was with these babies. I just hoped they would be collected. 'I'm not smuggling babies, honest.' I played out the situation in my mind. I helplessly looked around for support and tried to speak to the women next to me. The whole ordeal made me stressed, desperate to get to Kinshasa and not cause more problems to the journey. I was a little delirious in all honestly. As we passed the halfway mark and closer to the other side I was relieved to be nearing land, but anxious about the passport again. This, after all, was a different country, with different laws. The engine noise was too loud and everyone was covering their nose and mouth to avoid the smoke. The engine was old, to say the least, and the smoke black and thick. With a bit of speed the smoke tailed out the back and we made slow progress towards the opposite bank. Everyone was looking at me. I was obviously not a local, and probably oozed a smell of fear. I had my bags, other people's bags, and many other wrapped plastic boxes and badly packed objects all around me. The babies eventually stopped crying, which, I think, was a good thing, and I arrived only five and a half hours later than expected. As I pulled up to the small jetty dock area, I was filming with my phone. I stopped pretty quickly after being told off by a large man with a deep grumpy voice. I was immediately escorted to the immigration booth, which was a container placed at no particular angle to the side of the river. Everyone else grabbed their things and disappeared. Not me, though, of course. I was hoping to be met by a friendly hotel man, but knew it was unlikely, given the fact I was so late.

I was asked some questions, like, 'Where have you come from?' Which I thought was pretty obvious. In fact, they wanted to know other places I'd been, which of course opened up a can of worms. I had my passport taken away and was told to wait. I waited. That is pretty much the only training I should have done more of when preparing for the trip. Waiting. I did a lot of it. The container had a desk, a chair, mountains of dirty untidy paperwork, a fan in the corner next to a mini-fridge on the floor and a hole where a window may once have been. I explained everything – what I was doing, why, the hotel I was staying at – at which point they noticed my visa date. Crap. Here we go.

$200 was demanded for a new, correctly dated visa but I had no money and so was stuck. The conversation continued like this for a while. They threatened to send me back, like an unwanted fish.

I don't fully know why they bothered to hold me in the first place. Being a particularly lawless land, I assumed it was for money. Everything resembled a fish market rather than an immigration area – and they had no real electricity and certainly no Wi-Fi, so therefore couldn't demand the money be paid online. They didn't want that anyway – they wanted cash in their pockets. I got the distinct feeling they pick on foreigners for any reason they can think of in order to extort them. For me, it happened to be a valid reason to stop me, but with no money to pay them they ultimately got bored and just threw me out. If this had been a year earlier I would have been very scared and likely would have found a way to pay. Knowing Africa well enough by now I just kept quiet and waited. It was 5 p.m. when I was let go. I was handed my passport back with a new visa stamp and let through. It felt like a win. Patience and politeness prevailed.

All in all the 200-metre river crossing plus the short drive each end took 11 hours. The driver from the hotel I was now staying at was, remarkably, still waiting for me. He was woken up by an immigration officer and I was handed over. I apologized. The driver seemed fine, though. He had just been asleep.

Democratic People's Republic of the Congo

By the time we reached the hotel I was rather knackered and bedraggled. To my surprise there was a red carpet with uniformed soldiers standing either side of it. The driver pulled up to the edge of the carpet and so I walked down it. I was dead pleased the Congo had literally rolled out the red carpet for me. I waved and smiled at the guards as I walked past them, just like an LA film premier. Later that evening I had a slip through my door explaining that they had important people staying, namely presidents from nine other African nations. The note went on to explain that a previous head of state had recently died and the hotel was hosting the funeral gathering. I wouldn't really call it a wake; it was more a media circus. From my room on the top floor, floor 24, I had a free-standing bath which overlooked the river, and a giant bed. As I looked out over the river, sitting in the bath with the bubbles and the heat making me feel even more sleepy than usual, I realized the only other high-rise building I could see had to be the hotel I was staying in previously. It seemed so close. I must have been able to see this hotel from where I was running yesterday. After the bath I looked back through the photos. Sure enough, there it was, just across the river.

For the marathon, I had support in the form of merry expats and locals. I wasn't expecting it, but I actually had some runners to join me for the entire run: Lionel, Greg, another Greg, Rod (Rodolphe in full), Jack and Georgia. These people rallied at the last minute to get up early and support me after Rod put a post on Facebook less than a day earlier. The run was a looped course around a series of freshly tarmacked roads not far from the river. There must have been close to a thousand runners trotting around the four-mile circuit. I was shocked, but loved it. Early morning was exercise time, and we had hit rush hour. Even in 40 degrees.

We spoke about everything and anything, as is usual on a gentle but lengthy run. I spoke with Greg about a water-aid project to support the fight against Ebola in Africa. He was a true philanthropist with a good heart. Very much like the others – the group was strong-willed, high energy; a well-meaning bunch.

I had dinner that evening with Jack and Georgia – a crocodile special. Post-marathon but pre-dinner the others got in their cars and drove a few miles home while Rodolphe walked me back to the hotel which was just around the corner. Rodolphe is a doctor from France who has been living in the Congo for 11 years on and off. On the way back we passed a boy sitting on the side of the street who yelled, 'Doctor Papa.' Of course, all I heard was 'Dr Pepper'. The term Doctor Papa is not a drink here. It's a term of respect and seniority to elders, and in this case to the guy who'd saved the boy's life. During Rod's first year in the city there were thousands of homeless children on the streets thanks to poor government, as well as decades of civil unrest and war. Back then it was much worse than it is now. The boy had had a motorbike accident and his leg was wounded badly – full of pus, maggots and severely infected. Without treatment he would have lost the leg and potentially his life. The boy had been eight years old at the time, and as a street child he was refused hospital treatment because he had no money to pay for it. Rodolphe couldn't ignore the situation and took it upon himself to use his truck as a portable hospital. Every day he would park up near the boy and his street friends and perform all of the necessary medical work in the back of his van – equipped with a drip, bandages and antibiotics – to avoid the hospital process and the attached fees. The boy was now 19, and looked to Rodolphe as his saviour.

The surprising element to this tale, however, is that another life was potentially saved while speaking with the boy. Initially we walked on past him after a quick hello. It was only a few minutes later, after I'd learnt of his story while chatting and walking with Rodolphe, that I

asked to return and speak to him and take some photos of him and
Rodolphe together.

It then transpired almost exactly the same thing had recently happened to a friend of the boy's: a nasty infected injury from another
motorbike accident. Upon seeing it, Doctor Papa arranged for him to
go to hospital immediately. The leg was oozing and full of maggots.
Rodolphe was now a senior at the hospital and could admit anyone he
wanted. Rodolphe clearly had more important things to do than stay
talking with me, so I waved him off and thanked him for all his work,
energy and kindness.

Lunch at the hotel was interesting. It was a buffet, top-of-the-line
food, fit for presidents. There were a few suited people around, most
of them looking pretty stuffy and smart, and there was me in a blue
sweaty vest I'd worn for about a year. I was dripping with sweat and
tired. I just grabbed a plate and piled the food on as high as I could
and sat down. Knives and forks and manners and etiquette had fallen
by the wayside some months ago. I just tucked in: pasta salads,
potatoes, beef, chicken, some couscous and plenty of unidentifiable
but tasty added extras. The buffet was an all-you-can-eat scenario
and I was going for it.

I sat down next to someone decked out in his finest clobber. He
looked the part. No sooner had I started scoffing, my face within an
inch of my plate, when out of the corner of my eye I noticed some
'Mr Anderson'-like black-suited figures descending on me from all
sides. It was at that moment that my brain connected the dots. Ahh!
It must be someone important. It was the president of Zambia, a chap
called Edgar Lungu. Thankfully he waved them off with a gentle nod
and said 'hello' in a voice deeper than Barry White's. I said 'hello' too,
and continued to shovel food down my throat. Eventually we did chat.
He asked what I was doing. It was lovely of him to pretend to be interested, but I was keen to keep eating, really. I came to my senses and,
to my surprise, he got up and suggested we should run. Having just
been running I was a little fearful, but fortunately he was happy to
have a slow walk around the pool outside. I think he was going that
way anyway, but he said it counted as 'running with the white running
man'. I took it as a compliment.

I came back in and started eating the food I'd abandoned on the table. I called my mum immediately and told her I'd had lunch with the president of Zambia. As if things weren't weird enough I was then joined by four other African presidents. Annoyingly I can't remember who they were or what we spoke about. They were friendly, but I was more focused on the carbs my body so desperately craved. I'd worked in a restaurant for a brief time as a waiter and could carry up to five plates on one arm. So my dessert round was a full arm of sweet treats. I did get some looks, but that no longer bothered me. This food was good, and free.

After a bath and a nap it was dinner time and another chance to take on much-needed calories, this time with Jack and Georgia for company. The night was humid. It was as if the sun had forgotten to turn the thermostat down as it fell behind the horizon. Flies, bad African music, a local guitar player, plastic tables and crocodile with chips. Crocodile is an acquired taste and, if I'm honest, I'd have to spend quite some time acquiring it to vaguely enjoy it. It has the texture of a slightly grisly chop with a spiky skin. I'll stick with the presidential buffet, thank you.

Uganda

I woke early, wandered down to breakfast and was greeted by two hotel staff members. They were beaming with smiles. Hotel Number 5 was a freebie hotel offered by the owner, a chef with strong links to cancer work. It's an immaculate place; a small boutique hotel that is beautiful and calm. I ate breakfast on a large terrace with stillness in the air, set amongst lush green foliage at the edge of mountains filled with gorillas.

There was less traffic around a looped road, which was half tarmac and half orange dust and more or less circled Entebbe. The running was calm too. I ran without music, and with a full stomach paced along nicely.

Later the chef, Mark from South Africa, rustled up a fine steak with all the trimmings. I was in a calm state tucking into dinner, anticipating a peaceful couple of days in perfect surroundings, when a light-bulb moment lit up in my mind. I realized I wasn't far from Rwanda, a country I'd missed due to some shuffling of the itinerary before this leg of the trip began. I remembered a moment in an airport recently. I'd been scrolling through Instagram while waiting for a plane somewhere and noticed a familiar face pop up on my feed. The post was tagged in Kigali. It was from one of my new friends I'd made 15 months ago in the cobbled streets of Antigua, Guatemala, the day when we ran around an erupting volcano. Nick had just moved to Kigali for a three-month stint to organize a race there.

I demolished the steak and mulled the post over in my mind, and then scrolled through my WhatsApp contacts and called Nick. I had three more nights in Entebbe before flying to Djibouti. It might just be possible to fly to Kigali and run in the same day . . . I'd need a route, water and lifts to and from the airport to be reliable, but it could work.

Nick answered within a few rings. Amazingly he was free, able to help, and more than willing. With help from my dad and the team we quickly found a flight, paid for new visas and the plan was set. It cost us about £400 but cut out the country later on and left a gap for anything going wrong. This was good. I went to sleep pleased, but also like I'd shot myself in the foot. I wanted to just relax in this beautiful hotel for another day and eat glorious food. But marathons were what I was here to do. The alarm was set. Joseph, the hotel driver, took me to the airport for 4 the next morning . . .

Rwanda

After breakfast in Kigali, by 8 a.m. the route was set, we knew where we could get water, and it even took in most of the key sights around the city. Despite Rwanda's troubled past, Kigali is one of the continent's safest cities, the roads weren't too chaotic, and the infrastructure was good for this part of Africa, all things considered. However, the heavens did decide to open the moment Nick, his friend Mark and I stepped out the door. With Africa being so hot, it does still rain. And when it rains, it rains. We tucked back under the porch of their Airbnb-style set-up and rolled our eyes. The show must go on, so we had no choice but to grab some rain jackets and brave the torrential weather. Thankfully Nick and the gang had all the gear we needed. I'd just turned up without a bag or any clothes. I was expecting heat.

It rained for virtually every step of the 26.2 miles. Wet through immediately, but with our spirits still high, we chatted as if we were in a café. Gentle running with plenty of hills and some heavy breathing.

Then I saw the memorial as we ran past.

The Rwandan Genocide, also known as the genocide against the Tutsi, was a mass slaughter of Tutsi, Twa and moderate Hutu peoples by extremist members of the ethnic Hutu majority. In just one hundred days, between April and July 1994, 800,000 people were slaughtered. The scale and brutality of the massacre shocked the world, but no nation intervened to forcefully stop the killings. Most of the victims were killed in their own villages or towns, many by their neighbours and fellow villagers. Hutu gangs even searched out victims hiding in churches and school buildings. About 70 per cent of the country's Tutsi population was wiped out. Sexual violence was also rife, with an estimated half a million women raped during the genocide. Rwandans now have two annual public holidays to mourn their families. The memorial was incredibly moving.

I was born in 1989, in England. Had I been born in Rwanda, I may not be alive nor might any of my family. Another brutal reminder of my privilege: to even breathe the air of the planet, let alone roam it freely and joyfully. I got back to Uganda, had dinner and went to bed. My mind kept jumping from the success of the day that Nick had made possible, the pleasure of the here and now, to the horrors that the country endured, the pain and suffering of so many.

Djibouti

The capital of Djibouti, aptly named Djibouti, is more like a Middle Eastern state than an African one. It's on the Horn of Africa, and most people speak either French or Arabic. It's known for its dry shrub lands, volcanic formations and the Gulf of Aden's beaches. It's home to one of the saltiest bodies of water in the world. All in all, it felt dry, very dry. The land was white, bright and dusty. A hostile place for a runner.

Marathon 148 turned out to be one of the most miserable runs of my life. The fact I arrived having run two marathons in two different countries in the previous 38 hours, both of which featured hefty hills, meant I was ill prepared for such a day. A hot day. Scrap that, not a hot day: the hottest day of the entire journey so far. Throw in some humidity, and less available amenities like water, and it was one tough morning.

The people were as lovely as ever in Africa. Everyone waved, cheered, and again I even had some kids run with me for a while. Everyone thought I was mad. I was. Nobody was out in the sunlight. Workers on building sites operated under big manmade canopies of shade, and all the buildings had shutters to keep the heat at bay. I ran an eight-mile loop three times and so I passed the same shops, the same people, the same mounds of rubbish, and the same goats over and over again.

The normal body temperature of a human being is 37 degrees. This rises by just one degree if an infection or illness takes hold. The body's temperature shouldn't rise or fall by more than three degrees either way. Heat exhaustion and heatstroke occur at just 40 degrees. The world of the internet says that heatstroke includes: muscle cramps, heavy sweating, weakness, confusion, dizziness, headaches, nausea, vomiting, a faster heartbeat, dark-colored urine (an indicator of dehydration), and even fainting and seizures. It's safe to say I've had many of these many times during races of all distances. One step further than that, though, and it gets a bit dangerous. Over 41 degrees and you're in serious trouble. Strokes, organ failure and death are listed as the extreme effects once your body temperature rises above 41. I had been running in temperatures of 44 degrees for many months, all over the world, with hills and a lack of water. While that doesn't mean my body temperature was 44, it does mean the body has to work hard to keep the magic window hovering within a degree of 37.

In the dusty, dry empty streets of Djibouti it was horribly hot. It was 49 degrees in the shade – which felt at least 60 in the sun. My body temperature needed to be 20 degrees cooler than it felt. I could tell that my inner mechanics and plumbing weren't keeping on top of this. Dizziness was more severe and blurred eyesight occurred too. My heart was really struggling after lap one, just eight miles in. Humans are so finely balanced that even with nine litres of water, and constant dashes into shade, popping into shops to find cooler air, it was unbearable.

There were four shops open on the eight-mile loop – all very tatty and selling dry fly-covered meat and sugary drinks in broken chillers. One particular shop had air-con, a big unit in the corner as tall as me and wider – a comedy air-con in scale, and set to 38, meaning they were trying to cool the temperature inside to 38 degrees. The heating at home doesn't even go that high. It made me laugh at the sheer absurdity of it all. I stood under it for a couple of minutes and adjusted my chaffing areas. My heart rate was 189 while standing doing nothing. I was born with a heart defect, and while it's never caused me much hassle, this heat was a reminder to be a little careful. In the back of my mind I thought of my mum's similarly dodgy ticker that had resulted in her second open-heart surgery just six weeks before I embarked on this whole journey. It's a hereditary thing; a faulty tricuspid valve. In all honestly I'm not really sure what the matter is, but it does some weird things in my sleep sometimes, and occasionally when I run. It is common that for about five to ten seconds my heart will race and accelerate in speed until it stops, for what seems like for ever, and then carry on again. It takes my breath away sometimes and I go a little dizzy, but other than that I'm fine, so I've just ignored it. The doc seemed OK with me running, so I'll just keep going until I can't. That said, I didn't particularly want the end to be in a grungy corner shop in Djibouti. And so I was careful, and began to take in two minutes of allotted air-con time with each lap, before slogging out again. My feet began to turn to mush too. The wetness in my shoes from the sweat was worse than running in torrential rain. Surprisingly, blisters and black toenails are something I'm not that familiar with. Don't get me wrong, I don't often have all my toenails, but my feet are in relativity good shape considering I've run thousands and thousands of miles. Djibouti, however, was putting an end to undamaged feet.

I eventually made it back. The last mile felt like eternity. The sun was high in the sky and there was no escaping it. I could feel my back burning to a crisp, even with repeated doses of factor 70 sun cream.

I got back and slumped in the shower tray. I couldn't be bothered to move and wee in the toilet and so just did it in the shower. It was bloody. This wasn't the first time I'd been peeing blood, that comes with the job (if you do it badly), but it's never pleasant. About 60 to 70 per cent of a human's body weight is made up of water, and every part of our body needs it to function properly. Dehydration happens when you lose an excess amount of crucial body water. Water helps remove wastes from your blood in the form of urine. Water also helps keep your blood vessels open so that blood, with important nutrients, can travel freely to your kidneys. But if you become dehydrated, like I do regularly, then it's harder for this delivery system to work. Like I said, mild dehydration can make you feel tired, and it can also impair normal body functions. Severe dehydration can lead to kidney damage, so it's important to drink enough when you work or exercise very hard, and especially in warm and humid weather. Some studies have shown that frequent dehydration, even if it's mild, may lead to permanent kidney damage, as well as the formation of kidney stones. Kidney stones I did not want. Blood in my urine wasn't good. I had had some electrolyte tablets in my bag, which were my last two. I moved around the room in a hunched achy fashion and packed my things. I was also sunburnt and so everything hurt. I took myself to bed – not to sleep but to experience being horizontal under the air-con unit. Ahh, cool air at last.

I was dozing off when the team called on a three-way Skype call. My folks, and my new assistant Veton. They gave me some bad news. We had been worried about South Sudan and potential violence blocking us from entering the country. It turns out it was actually the northern part, a country in its own right, Sudan, which was the problem. Violence and protests had broken out and even the UN were evacuating – along with my contact, whom we were relying upon. There was another change of plan. Sudan wasn't possible and would need to be re-jigged. The only saving grace was that we'd gained two days because of Kigali. So it wasn't a disaster, but meant we'd instantly lost any time we'd gained.

I put the phone down and went for a wee again. Still some blood. I caught sight of my naked body hobbling back to the bed in the full-length mirror. I was a skinny sunburnt mess. I noticed red dots all over my body too. 'Oh crap, not bed bugs or shingles,' I thought. Nope, actually these were just small bruises. On top of everything with the tough run, a small boy, about eight years old, had followed me for a few hundred metres every lap, ducking behind battered ruined old cars while repeatedly blasting me with small plastic bullets from a BB gun. I was so knackered and the boy was laughing and so happy, I didn't really care, but it stung – the little shit had left small red dots all over me. I went to sleep knowing that the next day I'd be flying to another war zone. Mogadishu, Somalia.

Somalia

Chelsea Village in London, and Chelsea Village in Mogadishu are very different places. If I had to pick one, I'd choose Mogadishu.

The only commercial route flying in and out of Somalia was being run by Ethiopian Airlines, and hopped between neighbouring countries. The plane was old and hot and buzzing with flies. I'd never been on a plane full of flies before and I wouldn't recommend it. That wasn't the best start to the day, but once my feet touched Somali soil – Mogadishu is the birthplace of the legendary Mo Farah – I had a surprisingly marvellous time.

I was hosted for three nights by a private firm who look after many humanitarian initiatives in the area. Chelsea Village is home to a few hundred medics, lawyers, contractors and security personnel. Basically, a huge collection of well-meaning, dedicated people. The village is made of containers, most situated within a hefty three-metre-thick walled compound complete with barbed wire and lookout posts.

Within a few feet of stepping off the plane, and feeling free from the swarm of flies, I met a British lady called Nooky, a medic who had volunteered to collect me from the airport. She met me with immigration forms already completed, and then, thanks to her becoming friendly with the airport staff over several years, ushered me past various queues and guards, straight out the door to a waiting armoured car. My bags were collected by two other Somali security personnel and brought to the village. The drive was about three minutes in total. It was just outside the airfield secure zone and was ideal for an 'in and out' stay. A guy called Costa and his boss Stuart made my stay possible. I owe them a lot. There was no way I could have completed my run without their help and expertise. Welcoming a British civilian into a hostile war zone is not recommended, and many who we reached out to for support in various countries simply refused to help for reasons regarding insurance and liability. These chaps saw an opportunity to help and did so with humour, personality and patience.

The Chelsea Village is a special place. It's a very laidback setting, complete with bean bags in the courtyard and its own luxury in the sense of top chefs, good food, space for communal living and socializing. After all, I was only around for two days, they'd been there for years – they are still there. It felt a world away from a war zone, but in reality we were literally metres away from where car bombs regularly killed people. If you ignored the gunfire, jets, helicopters, men with weapons, and double-looped barbed wire, we could have been in actual Chelsea.

I had a quick security briefing and was shown to my container (a 21-foot luxury model). It was a similar set-up to Kabul. Costa is a tall bloke from South Africa, who is quietly spoken – rare for South Africans, in my book. He showed me to dinner and I met some of the gang. Posters of me and my journey were dotted all over the place and so I was greeted by name all evening. It was a tremendous feeling to be so warmly welcomed – especially after the trauma of Djibouti. I was told I'd be running an eight-kilometre loop around the coast with vehicle support plus some runners. Anyone was welcome to join, but Costa expected about ten to share the distance.

An early rise at 4.45 a.m. – happily it was only 30 degrees and we even had some breeze. Stepping out of my container door I actually went back in for a jumper before heading to breakfast: a short walk from my accommodation of '5 Regent Street'. 'Anything' I wanted, they said: eggs with plenty of salt, maple syrup on bacon, a cuppa, some porridge and my usual assortment of 11 tablets to keep my salt, electrolytes and probiotics topped up. At 6 a.m. I was greeted by a huge group of friendly faces: Jon, Bill, Alex, Lyle, Stuart, Gordon, Costa, all the medics, and so many more (sorry if I've missed names; I won't forget the faces). We met outside the compound and, still within the confines of the coastal Mogadishu International Green Zone, collectively pressed 'start' on our watches. Sixteen of us lined up on a dirt track to start the clockwise loop past embassies, foreign-aid agencies and military buildings, all with a view over the runway or the ocean depending on which way you looked. Fifty small humanitarian aid flights plus a few dignitaries came and went; I had a constant narration from fellow runners, which helped to pass the miles.

I remember that the waves off the Somali coastline were stunning. The water lapped at the sand on the south-eastern side of the runway as our route took us around the airstrip five times. Road, trail, sand, sea, rocks – perfect. The medics and locals provided brilliant support in the form of three aid stations perfectly spaced. Water, Gatorade, bananas and oranges were neatly lined up using a stretcher as a tray, meaning it could be lifted and moved towards us as we approached. The support was overwhelming: I had reinforcements in shifts, in the form of military personnel – the older guys and their unbreakable stamina, and a collection of those who did a few kilometres then were collected by car. The finish line was an actual finish tape, with extra village staff coming out to clap us over the line. Costa, who hadn't run a marathon ever in his life, did so with ease. It was a blast.

Nooky, the medic, was out supporting all day. Upon finishing she offered me a massage. Everyone in the compound had told me to ask her for one. 'She is the best,' was the phrase that was bandied around the village. She was. I fell asleep too. The team that wasn't running laid on brilliant steak and chips – then arranged for a celebratory get-together on the roof. If all that hadn't already been enough, the folks at Chelsea presented me with a cheque for Prostate Cancer UK. Stuart delivered a kind speech, and we gathered for some farewell photos. I got into bed knowing I'd be flying out and to another new land when the sun rose. I didn't want to leave. I was totally blown away by all the little touches. As I departed, the icing on the freshly made cake quite literally read: 'marathon 149 cake', complete with the Somali and British flags. I was also handed a cap from a local security guy, a Chelsea Village t-shirt and a card with a message of support for the onward journey. I was so elated that everyone had had a good time and they had enjoyed my presence. I blame it on the tiredness, but I cried a little (again).

My last surprise, as I was driven to the airport by Stuart, Costa and Nooky, was an envelope. Inside it was a formal invite to a scholarship. A bloody scholarship to become a Master of Arts in Sports, Ethics and Integrity linked with the Erasmus programme of the European Union, which could be accessed for study anywhere at any time. I was speechless, which is rare. What a fantastic gift. I bonded with them and they with me. It was hard saying goodbye.

Egypt

I landed in Cairo at 2 a.m. two days after leaving Mogadishu. I'd had 22 hours' connecting time in Addis. Addis was fast becoming my least favourite airport in the world. Somalia seemed like such a long time ago. Bedraggled and missing my Somali family I made it to my new, slightly more luxurious accommodation: the Marriott Mena House of Cairo. Despite the five stars it wasn't a container in a war zone, a container that I'd grown particularly fond of with the people I'd grown to admire. No matter how many stars a hotel has, they can't make up for the camaraderie and togetherness of a war zone compound.

Egypt was my 150th country. I had another 'holy moly, I've been to lots of places' moment. Cairo, however, I wasn't that fond of. I ran my marathon. I concluded that I was right to coin the city 'Crap Cairo'. Admittedly, I hadn't seen it all but I had spent several hours running around it. All I could see was the sad state of a city, with rubbish and dead horses on the street corners of the Giza district. I don't think the pharaohs would be very proud. I ran along the Nile and was expecting some form of beauty but there was just more mess and rubble. If I had time to venture further along the river, out of the city, I'm sure I would have been spoilt, but in the city centre and around Giza, nope, I found it dusty, oily, uncared for and ramshackle.

The next day I went in search of the pyramids. I didn't have to go far, because I could see them from my breakfast table. It's no surprise the 4,500-year-old constructions, built at such scale and taking 85 years to complete, trump any modern day building. The ambition of the monuments, built by tens of thousands of skilled workers, using methods that remain a mystery, is just mind boggling, and even though they are so ancient and have been ravaged by time they are still awe-inspiring. The Great Pyramid is one of the Seven Wonders of the Ancient World, and the only one still standing, but the tourist circus that now surrounds the site does somewhat detract from the spectacle. I did think it would have been amazing to see the place before the dawn of tourism, and the hawkers that attend the daily flow of visitors, but of course I was part of that same problem. I hitched a lift from a camel to trek a few miles over sand dunes at sunset to see all nine pyramids in one field of view. Camels are, in a word, uncomfortable. I quite literally got the hump – my thighs were chafing just a little, and I wasn't going to risk soreness that didn't clock up the running miles, so I jumped off and walked the rest of the way, filling my shoes with sand in the process, even if it did look like I was taking a camel for a walk. The camel owner took the most perfect photo for me, with my camera, as if I'm leaping over the pyramid. But that aside, I wasn't sad to move on.

South Sudan

As South Sudan approached, lots of phone calls were being made between various team members, and my message alerts were pinging on my phone far more frequently than I would have liked. I could tell there was panic amongst the ranks but had no energy to understand it all. I mentally put a pin in it, and planned to pay attention later.

Arriving in Juba, the Acacia Hotel put me up, the UN let me into their compound (I was becoming a regular in UN compounds), and the British military hosted me for the day. The Acacia Hotel was a small and friendly place, and they helped me out with phone calls to arrange various logistical bits, and even fed and watered me.

Following a long-running civil war and since achieving independence in 2011, South Sudan was in the grip of a humanitarian crisis, with food shortages and political and economic failings leading to an unstable environment and frequently raging violence. The hotel was deemed safe enough, but the streets were not, so it was agreed that I'd run in the UN compound. The morning after I arrived, I was met by a military unit who drove me to the compound and explained the plan. The two chaps who came to collect me were classic military: tough when they needed to be, they enjoyed a good laugh and shared their usual camaraderie with me. The plan was straightforward. They would take it in turns to jump in and out of supporting the run, with a few members of their regiment joining me for a lap here and there, while I trotted around the nine laps of the perimeter. They'd then drop me back at the Acacia. Simple. In standard military style, timings were worked out, the plan set, and it all worked. Of course.

We ran past tanks, UN vehicles, and a few confused faces who did a double-take on seeing a scrawny civilian running round. The temperature wasn't unbearable, we had plenty of chats mid-run, mostly me repeating the same answers to questions like, 'What's your favourite place?' Or 'What are you going to do next?' I had the answers down. I'd answered these questions for about 18 months now, and so could answer without much effort.

Post-run, my military escort surprised me with a delivery of pizza and allowed me to use their showers. We sat in their section of the compound and discussed fitness, mental health and the general strength to overcome challenges – they had more of it than me. These were good men and women and I was proud to have ran with them, and of the role they were playing in trying to bring peace and stability to the region. With other work to be done, I was dropped back an hour after running – exactly on time. My intention was to have a second dinner and pack my bags. That didn't happen. I fell asleep immediately only waking up at about 2 a.m., some 14 hours later.

Niger

It was a brief stop in Niamey. I'd be flying out in less than 48 hours. Having arrived a little grumpy and tired, I was impatient to get into my room. The only place available was the Radisson Blu. I wasn't in need of an overpriced laundry service just yet, after only recently having one in Cairo, and so was miffed to pay the £200 a night. I just got in, showered and slept again. My body was in another phase of the tiredness cycle. A little extra sleep was all I needed. I woke up with energy. Or as close to energy as I'd felt in a while. My body, despite the pizzas and fancy hotel buffet, was still scrawny and my hair now even longer and knotted.

The Niger River runs through the eastern side of the capital where I was staying. The hotel overlooked it – I had to stop and take it in. I was seeing so much it was easy to become desensitized to it all. The view was broken with some shacks, concrete structures and rundown hotels, but it wasn't an ugly place. I needed to get down to street level and see everything in the way I had become accustomed: on foot, slowly, through a haze of sweat and exhaustion.

To join me on the hazy quest was a tall chap called Andy, a senior British Foreign Office official. He was out on business for a week. By pure chance he a) knew of my adventure, b) was keen to try to cross paths at some point and c) happened to speak about me to a colleague who mentioned I was in Niamey right then. It was very last minute, and we shared some frantic organizational text messaging as I was checking-in to the hotel. Last minute didn't matter, he was keen to join, and I was keen to have some company and someone who knew the area. As with 99 per cent of my plans, I learnt to not expect people to actually turn up, or to be able to run a full marathon, or to even know what a marathon was. My range of enthusiastic supporters was exceptional, eclectic, but not always reliable.

Andy was on time – if anything I was a few minutes late. He could run, and run well, and he had an air of something I couldn't put my finger on. While we ran I realized he was simply a really bloody nice chap. He understood the world, and experienced things with an open mind and an inquisitive train of thought. He was bright, an achiever, adventurous, and not selfish or obnoxious like some so well-situated can be.

Five hours trotting out of the city and along a dirt trail in the form of a dyke meant our run was peaceful and relaxed. We stopped for a

few moments and watched a man wade in his wellies across marsh-
land. He wore nothing but a hat and wellies and carried a watering
can in each hand. We passed donkeys, goats, kids on makeshift
scooters and, for a while, we had a group of three children join us
running, the littlest one being pushed in a wheelbarrow. The day was
hot but cooler than in recent weeks. In the closing stages Andy slowed
more than I did, having not run a marathon in several years. Run
complete, we had some dinner. I spent most of the day in the company of a complete stranger – and yet it felt like we'd known each
other for years. That's the power of sport and mad adventure. Andy,
thank you.

Mali

As mentioned, my assistant Veton is a well connected man and, being
Albanian Kosovan, he has friends everywhere. This particular friend
Shaip knew Veton, just like Visar did – from working with the UN.
Veton blitzed his contact book and without fail came up trumps when
we needed it. Shaip collected me from the airport and welcomed me
into his home. At which point I went to sleep immediately.

I arrived in Bamako, technically, in the morning of a new day, just
after midnight, which was also my only day to run. Despite the heat I
just slept for an extra hour and was up again at 8 a.m. The alarm
sounded but I was already awake. My stomach had yet again been
upset by something and I now knew Shaip's bathroom better than I
did any room in his house, including the spare room I was sleeping in.
The plan, as always, was to take each step at a time. Right foot, left
foot, right foot, left foot – until I've run another marathon.

I dragged my achy body out of bed and slipped into my running
gear later than planned. It was now 9 a.m.

My diary stated that I was to run around another UN compound.
Apparently it was still pretty unsafe in the city – a crime hotspot
where kidnappings were something to look out for. Shaip, however,
was under the impression I had been informed about the last-minute
changes. I hadn't been. The security team in the UN had got cold feet

about supporting my run and I was back to square one. (The red tape in the UN is rather red, long . . . and did I mention very red? The compound was undoubtedly the safest place to be but I suspect they didn't think about the options their decision left me with.) I was grumpy. The lack of sleep didn't help. 'OK, so shall I just run in the street?' I asked – a genuine query.

After a quick discussion around the breakfast table, Shaip asked his member of staff, Dris, to support me by riding his moped behind me as I ran. Shaip felt responsible for me, and to be honest I was glad he offered extra help. I didn't fancy getting kidnapped, plus the need for water still remained so important. I was already dripping with sweat.

Dris is a quietly spoken chap, but has a nice calming slow pace about him. I liked him, and we set off into Bamako. Four hours later we had ventured 45 kilometres out of the city and away into the small suburbs of the capital. He on his bike; me running. He weaved through the traffic supplying me with water and stopping up ahead a few times at junctions while I did my best to keep up.

The Foreign Office advice that appeared in my calendar regarding the threat level was always full of doom and gloom – but there was a rather humorous reverse correlation between their advice and the friendliness of a place. Whenever in a 'dodgy' country, I was always greeted by smiles and high-fives, and general happiness. I am, of course, aware that the advice is based on fact not feeling, but in Bamako I felt welcome, supported and, of course, sweaty. The Foreign Office got that bit right. Hot, it was. Way out in the sticks, and after the watch beeped over the required distance, I jumped on the moped and began the journey back to the city.

On the way back, with the wind in my hair and the dust in my eyes, I allowed myself to smile a little at the prospect of nearly finishing Africa. I was a little delirious, I think, but I gave Dris and Shaip as much cash as I had and thanked them for their 'on the spot' thinking. I was grateful. It would have been a horrible run on my own. Looking over your shoulder when running is not fun. Safety, in the form of water, and another pair of experienced eyes was a blessing. Next stop, Chad.

Chad

On the flight from Mali to Chad some of the passengers adopted the role of air stewards. The trolley that serves food and snacks, or beverages and meals as the Americans call it, was unavailable. Apparently the airline had stopped it some time ago. So, on this flight, some regular and well-liked frequent flyers took it upon themselves to play host. One chap with a leather suitcase walked to the front, propped it on the head-rest of a seat, and opened it. For a moment I thought he was unveiling a semi-automatic. He wasn't. It was snacks and drinks. I opted for some nuts and orange juice. My decision was purely based on the fact the nuts came in an empty wine bottle with a screw cap, and the orange juice came in a sandwich bag with a tie wrap. Crazy! This man had some business sense. He'd sold out before we reached halfway.

With only a day in Chad, and the whole schedule getting a little fraught, I arrived, slept, woke and ran. Marathon 154 was done with relative ease. I yawned for the first ten miles, but was cruising at seven-minute miles(ish) and somehow didn't slow beyond eight-minute miles all the way to the end. Amazingly my stomach problems were gone and I felt fine. Weird, I know.

I had Idy, another saint of a driver, behind me with gallons of water and patience. It cost me a lot of money to pay these drivers, but it was a way to get things done with maximum enjoyment, some safety and minimal faff that sapped the energy I needed. I ran through another dusty Central African concrete-ruined city, past 200-plus camels, 400-plus cows, thousands of goats, a few hundred mango trees and donkeys – that, and a load of pollution, road waste and unfinished Chinese construction sites. Without the time to properly explore N'Djamena I only saw the surface, and my impression was of another African city struggling with internal conflict and its colonial legacy. In 1960 Chad gained independence from France. Since then it has experienced four civil wars, and more recently a rise of terrorism from a number of extremist groups. Fortunately I felt safe enough on the streets, but the destruction caused by so many years of unrest was plain to see. At one point, a young boy wearing only a dirty brown ripped t-shirt was crossing the road in front of me. We were on a long, straight stretch with nothing but trees and dirt on either side. No people, no animals, no noise, just this little boy walking slowly and casually across the road. He was tiny, so tiny. He can't have been more than three years old. He looked desperate, and I couldn't quite tell where he had come from or was going, but as I approached, he smiled, waved, turned and carried on. Some things just stick in your head. I will never forget that three-year-old.

Central African Republic

Landing into Bangui I knew I was going to be met by another Albanian friend of Veton's. He really did make everything possible. My passport was full, I'd even got stamps on pages that shouldn't have stamps, like the page where all my emergency contact information is. I was last off the plane, and stood in the foreigner queue. Airports in the western world are neat, tidy, and most of the time there's some order to it. Africa, nearly without fail, is the opposite.

The 50 or so passengers got off the plane in some humid rain. A storm was coming in. We were chaperoned to a hangar to wait out of the downpour. We waited. The luggage trolley pulled up, the driver got off, and just walked away. Luggage handling wasn't a thing. They just let us get our own bags. It was chaos. Bags were eventually found, all the while trying to stay below the radar and just get through to meet Veton's friend.

I queued again, still airside with my bag. Everyone else was in the same position. Somehow I was still at the back, having had people push past me. It was evening, the sun had just set. The two small cut-out booths housed the immigration officers. They were stamping passports while also screening health checks too. It's common in Africa to have your temperature taken with a radar gun on the side of your head. They did that, took the forms and paperwork, money exchanged hands, and that was that. It was my turn. My temperature was fine, my paperwork was fine, but they wouldn't stamp my passport.

An hour passed and it escalated to the point that they started saying I needed a visa. I didn't, and the sign behind their heads said so. I was asked to move aside while they did some more paperwork. A chap with a round belly and a stern, grumpy face demanded, 'You must pay $400.' He had a smart military uniform on and a big fancy official hat. I had absolutely no cash on me. I wasn't expecting to need any and I was just one stop from home. I suppose this was my mistake, really. No cash, or space in my passport. I was asking for trouble. As I protested he simply said no and shut the shutter of the small office unit. Shit.

I could see Veton's friend, through a corridor. He was looking concerned and helpless. I shouted to him and asked if he had $400. He did, in the car. It was his back-up cash. The problem was, he couldn't be seen to be helping me (and this is the reason he remains unnamed). He had asked the UN, for which he worked, if he could help and allow me to stay with him and his housemate in UN-registered housing. They declined the offer. If they found out, he could have lost his job. With that very quickly relayed to me down the corridor, he dashed to the car to get the cash. It was too late. They locked the airport and he was stuck outside, and I was stuck inside. It was silent. The airport – literally just two hangars – was closed for the night. I banged on the door. Nothing. I banged on the door again. Nothing. I walked around shouting 'hello' louder and louder. Nothing.

Eventually the same stern-looking chap appeared – this time just in a string vest and civilian clothes. He said 'cash' and gestured to give him money. I quickly agreed, 'OK, OK, my friend. Have cash.' He opened the door but kept me behind him. I shouted to Veton's friend, 'Can I have the $400, please? I'll pay you back.' He ran over and virtually chucked the cash at me so as not to be seen. He then vanished into his UN vehicle and waited. Upon giving the immigration guy the cash, he wrote out a receipt and stamped it. He then put the cash in his pocket. I was fuming but, in the same breath, relieved. I kept my mouth shut. He let me go through. There were now only two cars in the car park. It was dark, and a few stray dogs mingled around. I walked up to the UN car but he instructed for me to get into the taxi behind. We were going to the same place but, in case we were pulled over, Veton's friend couldn't be seen with me. I just hoped the taxi would actually follow him.

It did, we got back. I wired him the cash, and he cooked me pasta. I was a little shaken. He was just frustrated with the officials and sorry he couldn't intervene.

The run wasn't straightforward, with busy dusty roads and an air of danger around the city. I just kept my head down and reached the 26.2 with slightly sore hips and joints. My elbow, however, was damaged – substantially, thanks to being knocked over a verge by the hefty wing mirror of a truck. Bones were fractured, for sure. To this day I still can't lean on it with any force without an 'ouch' and an instant memory of the driver's face in the smashed mirror as he drove off. At the time, I just got on with it knowing that a stop off at Heathrow was just around the corner. Perhaps I could see to it then. I was ready for a rest. The stress of the airport, the cash fiasco, and then a slightly on-edge run was enough to wipe me out.

At Heathrow I was met by Mum and Dad, who drove me home. Beyond the smiles and hugs it was straight to business. I needed to look at the plan. This was when I learnt the extent of the damage and how much time we now didn't have to finish the remaining countries. It was bad, and the two-day break was far from what I'd hoped for. We were running out of time and, even worse, we still had countries that were refusing us visas. We were now using borrowed money, and we had 14 countries which we couldn't link up in the timeframe. It looked as if we might need to hire a private plane but the cost of that was out of the question. My little ordeal at the airport in Bangui a day earlier was now actually looking not so bad. My elbow? I never did get that seen to. Painkillers were my stop-gap for any niggles I didn't have time for. I could move it, and use it, so I got on with it.

8

Himalayan Highs

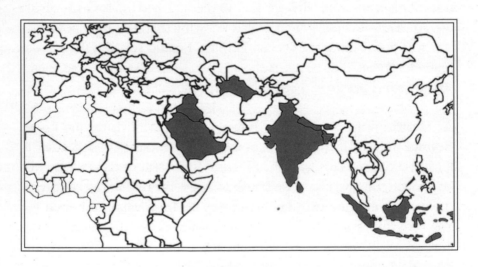

Nepal	Maldives	Cyprus
Bhutan	Indonesia	Iraq
India	Timor-Leste	Saudi Arabia
Bangladesh	Kuwait	Lebanon
Sri Lanka	Qatar	Turkmenistan

The expedition was in bad shape. My dad, who had been stressing for months, if not years now, was anxious to tell me the problems he and the team had been facing. He was keen to get down to the detail and go through the extent of the problems. Having just arrived home and knowing I had limited time between landing and my flight out again, the last thing I wanted to do was worry about everything that wasn't working. It was more exhausting than running.

I now had 40 countries to run marathons in before reaching Greece and the final one in Athens in November. It was July, and at first glance it seemed like the plan was set. The spreadsheet which we used as our bible, and which my dad had created, was neat, orderly and included everything from flight numbers, references, hours in the air, hours in-country to all the connection times. Everything was there. The devil as always was in the detail. There were two principal problems. That's once you cast aside finances, the frequency of marathons and some dodgy connection times, of course.

The first and potentially mission-ending problem was that we still didn't have Yemen, Syria, Libya or Iran 'fixed'– as in entry with an agreed visa. Even if we had visas, we didn't have set flight paths in and out. In truth we couldn't even fly into some of these places. There simply weren't flights, so overland options were on the table too. With those, though, safety concerns were more prominent.

Second was the Pacific problem. I was approaching the phase which was most difficult to string together. Not because of visas or safety but simply due to flight paths. Pacific Islands like Fiji, Nauru and the Solomon Islands are a long way apart from one another. There are 12 Pacific Islands in total, a few quite literally just tiny pieces of land jutting out in the middle of the ocean. The plan had enough time for me to spend 2.5 days in each place. The problem was that most of these tiny, very rarely visited places only have one flight out a fortnight – maybe two if you were lucky. On top of that most flights were returns back to islands the plane had just flown in from, which potentially introduced more stops into every journey. For three months the team investigated funding to find a private plane. The cost range was from £50,000 all the way to £200,000 – without fuel or grounding fees. That was looking out of the question.

The only way round it was to painstakingly try lots of different permutations with flight paths. My dad drew a massive diagram with multicoloured pens highlighting which countries linked and how many days' travel it would take, plus the cost, and our rating of how much we trusted a particular airline. No matter which way we looked at it there was still something like five countries that we couldn't get to in time.

The time pressure wasn't forced by Guinness World Records' rule book. After all, I was the first person to attempt this and so I could technically take as long as I wanted. A real problem with our pre-planned average of two and a bit days per country was our miscalculation of how many indirect flights I'd be taking, and the subsequent time wasted in the air or in airports. Our self-imposed finish line was another problem. My dad and I joked briefly before it got serious again. We recalled all the episodes of *Grand Designs* on the telly where house builders attempt to build their home to budget and on time, and never do. We had royally missed the mark on finances, but were still determined to hit the finish line. The fact of the matter was simple: the official Athens Marathon would start at 8 a.m. on Sunday 10 November 2019. We had picked that finish date because of the significance of the race. According to legend, the Greek soldier Pheidippides ran from a battlefield near the town of Marathon to Athens in 490BC. He ran the approximate 26 miles to announce the defeat of the Persians to some anxiously waiting Athenians. He delivered the victory message, *'Niki!'* – meaning 'Victory' – and then keeled over and died. The rest, as they say, is history. The marathon was born in the town of Marathon, and so it had to be the finish line of this challenge.

Being in Athens to run the official 2019 race was never in question. No matter what happened I'd be there – but we wanted it to be the finish line. If even one country was left, then the finish line would be a huge anticlimax. Friends and family had arranged to be in Athens to mark the occasion, but doing so without it actually being the end would feel like rowing an ocean, celebrating the finish, and then announcing you had to get back in the boat and row some more. I must finish on time. I had to get to Athens having accomplished what we set out to do.

The meeting, which involved many WhatsApp calls to various team members and support staff all over the world, ended with no positive outcome, just more options to look at. That was the best we could hope for.

To make matters worse, I was flying out to Nepal to spend an entire eight days there. This had been arranged, booked and paid for 11 months prior, as were nearly all of the flights in this leg of the journey. Nepal, Peru and South Africa were countries I'd opted to have longer in than the allotted two or two and a half days. I wanted to see more of these countries. Nepal was the last long stint I had but it happened to fall right at the moment when time was running away with us. Pun intended.

Nepal

I flew to Kathmandu via Bangkok. On each flight I managed to scoff down two extra plane meals of questionable chicken dishes. I was now well versed at flagging the airhost and asking for extra food. I now have no shame, not that I had much before. Mid-flight, with my bags repacked and neatly stowed above my head, I got my notebook out and went through some of the stats of the journey. It brought so many memories flooding back.

I'd stayed with over 50 families in varying capacities, I'd sat around 46 camp fires, I'd paid nearly 60 bribes, I'd been in exactly 22 countries I didn't even know existed, I'd run on nearly all of the major mountain ranges and I'd had over 80 flights cancelled or rebooked.

The extent of my journey so far was enough for many lifetimes. As usual my time in the air was reflective. It gave me time to think and regroup. By now I'd also mastered the art of sleeping upright. My neck was now stronger than my legs.

Finally arriving in Kathmandu with a thud, the whole plane woke up. Nepal has mountains, lots of bloody great mountains that ultimately result in a somewhat shorter runway, hence the heavy landing. The Himalayas are what I call the crumple zone of the world. The earth collided with other bits of the earth and, boom, skip a few million years and the human race has a playground of rock. A stunning and massive playground.

Once landed, I waited outside with my bags and a chap called Bashu. Bashu worked with James. James was a friend and contact of Nick Kershaw. This is the same Nick I met in Guatemala, and who had recently helped out with the last-minute marathon in Kigali. Nick, as you can probably tell, is well connected and kindly arranged a mini-trek up the Annapurna Circuit, calling on James to arrange it for me. Bashu was a guide and driver for James. He met me, chatted, and I explained we were waiting for Chris.

Coincidently there were a lot of Nicks, and a lot of Chris's on the journey, which became rather confusing for my parents considering that I was also called Nick, and my brother called Chris. The Chris in question this time wasn't my brother, but we got on like he could have been.

Two years prior to arriving in Nepal I had spotted some beautiful photos of mountains on Instagram. The photographer in question was Chris. I reached out hoping he could help with some photography. It turned out that he was a successful animator and, importantly, videographer too – principally working with some of the best brands in the film business. He was British but living in Sydney. His office was within Fox Studios.

I had no money to pay him, but I was keen to get him out to shoot some film for the documentary. We'd done this with various other camerafolk from time to time, to capture some cinematic shots of me running in beautiful places. Amazingly Chris was keen to support and was happy to get involved for free. We covered the cost of his travel and we split the hotel. Sometimes people aren't what they first seem. Chris was. He's a gent, great at what he does and loves true adventure.

As I couldn't afford to have brilliant filmmakers like Chris out with me every step of the way, we picked and chose the best places carefully. Nepal was the obvious option given his previous experiences and was another reason why we had a little more time planned in the country.

As Bashu and I were waiting for Chris to arrive there were taxis being loaded up with boxes. The boxes were big, and the process seemed a little disorganized, so I wasn't sure what was going on. Bashu explained that Nepalese workers were regularly killed working overseas from poor working environments and healthcare. The boxes were coffins – three or four arriving every day so the bodies could be returned to their families. It was another eye-opening, heart-wrenching moment.

The drizzle started, Chris arrived and we bundled into Bashu's jeep. A hotel called Baber Mahal Vilas, in the heart of bustling Kathmandu, had offered us a complimentary stay thanks to Nick and James using their contacts wisely. We were in Nepal, so I wasn't expecting luxury, but the Baber Mahal Vilas, a fancy white complex of villas tucked away around the back of a side street, were spectacular. It was our little spot of peace and tranquillity. It was booked for seven nights as we needed somewhere secure to leave the majority of our gear, but we'd only be staying for two because we were off to the mountains first thing the next day.

My first afternoon in Kathmandu was immersive – and rainy. We mooched around the Monkey Temple, purchased far too many unnecessary Nepalese souvenirs, trekked up a bloody great hill to see another temple, took thousands of photos with some kids in the market, and fell asleep with dreams of the trek ahead of us.

The schedule for our week in Nepal was in two halves. The first half was to trek the Mardi Himal trail up to 5,000 metres to see Fishtail Mountain. This was also to give us some opportunity for photos and film with Chris. The second half of the week was to get back to Kathmandu and run the marathon which James and his contacts had arranged. The itinerary was exciting in the planning stages, but now with such time constraints and financial worries, it all seemed unnecessary and like we were wasting time. I tried my best to put those concerns aside and enjoy the brief break.

James, Bashu, Chris and various others gathered for a complimentary meal in the hotel. We all got to bed far too late. The next morning our group, of which there were now six, including drivers and Sherpas, ventured into the wonderful world of the monsoon season in a mountain range that plays host to some of the most breathtaking landscapes on the planet.

After the short 25-minute flight from Kathmandu we landed in Pokhara before a two-hour jeep drive to our starting point in Dhampus. Our aim, other than to enjoy the mountains, was to photograph them, do a little running, and hopefully glimpse a sight of the marvellous and still unclimbed Fishtail summit, Machapuchare.

We finished the first day of hiking through leeches and rain in the dark. We huddled around a small smoky wood fire in a damp and largely abandoned tea house. On the trek we'd seen nothing but the canopy of trees above us. It rained for seven of the eight hours' walking. We were all tired and frustrated at the weather. The next day: more leeches, wet feet, caterpillars, dense green forest and lots of climbing up and up into the clouds. From Low Camp to High Camp was due to take around five hours. We did it in two. It was steep, with scary, deadly drops on both sides, and the clouds and rain smothered us all the way. It was the kind of fun you only understand once you've finally reached your destination. Three marathons a week for 80 weeks gives you some fitness, and I was feeling pretty strong. Even so, Ram, our Sherpa, and the rest of the lads that carried the bags always stormed ahead and made it look effortless. I felt pathetic next to them. The grin of an accomplished Sherpa looking at a bedraggled tourist I'll never forget.

Morning at High Camp, the fire on, porridge in hand, I was shown to my room. We were the only people staying, the place utterly still apart from the sound of the rain and the wind battering the tin roof. The flags buffeted in the wind all day as we waited and waited for the cloud to pass. My room was a small brick-built single-storey hut.

The insects, mosquitoes, spiders and general mountain bugs clearly didn't understand that this was my room and not theirs – needless to say, we agreed to share. After drying clothes around the fire and munching down some more rice and vegetables, we all agreed that the best chance of seeing Fishtail Mountain – a rare occurrence because of the weather – would be to stay here all day with the hope of an early sunrise. Due to our speedy accent, we had a day in hand. Despite the miserable weather we all began to settle into our temporary isolated home in the sky. The food was great, and the building classically Nepalese: it was very basic but came with its own mountain charm, and we even had an adorable dog to keep the place feeling like home. The fire crackled away and the rain continued to dance on the noisy tin roof. We were safe in our cosy bubble in the sky.

At 3.10 a.m., while I was still warm and sleeping huddled in my sleeping-bag liner, and with rain dripping through the ceiling onto my feet, I heard the words, 'Nick, let's go,' in a hurried, hushed but purposeful tone. I don't think I've ever jumped out of bed so quickly. Chris had woken up a little before me and managed to prepare our camera gear. It was totally dark. We tested the sky by shuttering a 30-second exposure. To our surprise it didn't just show cloud. We had stars too, and stars meant cloudless skies. We waited quietly so as not to wake the others. We hurriedly snapped away as the sun painted the sky behind the mountains. The blackness of night turned to deep blues, and then the sun shone through. It was glorious.

At 6 a.m. the mountains echoed with our whoops and cheers of joy as we could finally see what was surrounding us. When you climb into the clouds, especially these, even though you know what's there, when you finally see it, it's a brilliant feeling. I'm so fortunate to have had this feeling many times and it never gets old. The mountains were breathtaking. For a magical three hours the clouds parted just enough to reveal all of the six huge peaks around us. Such a rare glimpse of splendour. Although not the tallest, Fishtail was by far the most beautiful. For no more than about eight minutes we had sight of the summit. The clouds just added something magical to our view. We were all smiles as we rushed around changing lenses, adding filters and adjusting time lapses and tripods. Our grumpy, doubtful and cloudy moods were replaced with glee and awe.

By 10 a.m. it was all over. The clouds came up from the valley floor, pushed past us like smoke rising from a chimney and before long the glorious snow-capped peaks were hidden once more. It didn't matter – we'd had our moment – it was almost better and more special that nature took the view away so soon. Mother Nature knew we'd savour it that bit more.

The following day, before descending, we woke early, checked the sky then checked again: clouds, no mountains . . . 3 a.m., 4 a.m., virtually every hour we checked, but sadly no luck. The mountains are somehow innately spiritual and calmed my soul, even with the rain and leeches causing havoc again on the long trudge down the hill. The mist, the dew, the wet ground; the weather was fast becoming our narrative. The leeches hadn't liked it up at 4,000 metres, but once lower we were in their territory again. We covered our shoes in a paste of water and salt in an attempt to keep the blighters from grappling up from the floor to our skin. It seemed to work. It took us nine hours in one intense downward hike. The next day we were to fly back to Kathmandu. That was the plan anyway.

Within ten minutes of arriving at the tiny little airport in Pokhara, our guide Ram informed us there had been a plane crash in Kathmandu due to heavy rain. The plane was the same airline, the same flight that we were due to get on, the shuttle between Kathmandu to Pokhara. Luckily nobody was seriously injured but we were now stuck with a decision: wait for the flights to resume – unlikely for at least a day, which would mean missing the marathon – or we could find a jeep and drive through the mountains in a huge storm for eight hours. Our views all aligned: we didn't want to just sit there and wait – and I couldn't leave Nepal after eight days and not run the marathon they'd organized just because we were stuck on a jolly in another part of the country.

At 1 p.m. we bundled into the jeep in Pokhara, stocked up on some snacks and water, popped back to use the hotel Wi-Fi to inform our families what was going on, and reassure them we were not on the plane that crashed. And then we were on our way. Five hours into the journey, and with potentially hours more still to drive, the rains came hard, the wind increased and we were driving back along the cliffs of the Himalayas in a huge 'unprecedented' monsoon. The words 'unprecedented monsoon' and 'Nepal' are not a good sign, but it did turn our anticipated boring 25-minute flight, into a marvellous adventure within the adventure within the adventure. As we were driving news reports came through on the radio while alerts pinged on Bashu's and Ram's phones. There was severe flooding in Kathmandu, people were being evacuated, roads were closed, landslides were happening all over the place, and a huge traffic jam gridlocked roads in and out of the city. Sadly we heard the tragic news that 15 people had died in neighbouring villages. In the mountains of Nepal that was probably some of the heaviest rain I have ever experienced. We did eventually make it back in one piece, our bodies battered from the squished car journey. The overriding feeling, having learnt that nobody else had been hurt, was one of gratitude. We were grateful for the adventure, for making it back, and for the company we shared. It was gone midnight though and I had a marathon to run in the morning. We all went to bed bracing for rain the following day.

The official marathon that James, Nick and the gang had organized was called 'the Leech Marathon', in honour of our questionable time to visit, during peak leech season. While we were picking our way down the mountainside, the race had been cancelled due to flooding in the city, as well as the fact the weather forecast solid rain for another 24 hours. Enter 'Jimi the Fixer' (James), who rapidly organized a new route along with two cars, water and food to support a potentially very wet run. He knew I couldn't leave empty handed.

One of the many highlights of the, as it turned out, not-so-soggy marathon was the film crew improvising to get all the shots we wanted for the documentary. Chris, who was giving all his time for free, along with support members and loads of gear, hung to the back of jeeps in various positions to film the run, the town and the overall mad experience of running through Nepal. Initially we ran out of the city into the mountains to look down on Kathmandu. Multicoloured roofs and prayer flags littered the valley, the road was wet, but, amazingly, it only rained briefly once or twice. We eventually arrived in a small suburb and completed ten or so loops while avoiding angry dogs, to get the distance up. The sun even came out and somehow I managed to burn my shoulders and neck. To finish we ran through the main square in the heart of the city. A huge Nepalese flag was handed to me as I crossed the finish line. The entire day was unbelievably fun, and ended with a few hard goodbyes.

Bhutan

Coming in to land into Thimphu, the capital, in the confines of a small prop plane, was somewhat bumpy. The runway is beyond tiny, surrounded by mountains on all four sides and looks like a small pond from above. It seems like totally the wrong place to house a runway. At nearly 2,800 metres above sea level, looking down from the sky, the city resembles a lost land in a paradise of tall green trees, with huts dotted in the valley. The heavy bump and braking on landing was the harshest I've experienced of any journey before or since.

To visit Bhutan every foreigner must obtain permission from the Royal government. Tourism is substantially limited in the kingdom, which meant it had taken several thousands of pounds and a carefully managed conversation to grant me permission to enter. Thankfully the team did this well, and I breezed through immigration. The extortionate cost of my brief stay was kindly covered by my aunt and uncle – another pair of the brilliant people who made the financials of this mission slightly less horrendous than they might have been.

The journey from the airport to the city was long and winding. From the air the country was beautiful – now, on solid ground, it was even better. I ran the following day, smiling nearly every step of the way. The kaleidoscope of bright white butterflies, falling leaves and the sun shining through the trees was more or less all I saw. My feet carried me up and around the Himalayan landscape one small step at a time. The world of Bhutan's magical kingdom is calm and precious. I wanted to bottle it somehow. Even the clouds look lighter and more fluffy. They glided around the tops of huge perfectly still pine trees, floating effortlessly up and beyond into nothing. Every mountain face, everywhere I turned, was smothered in a rich blanket of green, with only the sight of colourful prayer flags draped in clusters to break the velvet view. I usually run quite light-footed – leaving Thimphu even more so; my shoes made virtually no noise as I moved to the sound of my gentle breathing. I spent most of the run in a state of total peace. My mind wandered on to new thoughts every mile or so: how this journey had given me such a range of euphoric highs and belly-bunching laughs, as well as agonizing and upsetting lows. That, I concluded, was what I wanted. To be at the extreme end of the scale – to feel every bit as close to living as possible, be it good or bad. Around mile 19, with a few steps before my watch clicked over to 20, I stopped, listened to the nothingness all around me, looked up, opened my arms out wide and twirled with my head thrown back. This place gave such space and serenity; for the first time in a long time it was just me and the trees – a special, rare and blissful moment. I believe nearly everyone who's ever existed doesn't realize how lucky they are to be – just to be. Here I was, 3,000 metres into the mountains of the Himalayas, with not a sound around me.

I stopped a few more times to appreciate the views, took a few photos, then I was done. I didn't really want to stop running, but the hills certainly persuaded me otherwise. I had an evening being shown around various Buddhist sites, monuments and local traditions. The easiest way to describe Thimphu is to liken it to a small ski village without any tourists or snow, and nothing but trees and cabins. I felt like an intruder into a land that deserves to be left alone. It is by far the single most peaceful place I've ever experienced, and probably explained why I'd had such a spiritual time. Even the airport is compact and quiet. Sadly I was back there all too soon.

India

India soon knocked the spiritual calmness out of me. There are plenty of places in India which would have continued the serenity, I suppose, but Kolkata wasn't one of them. We chose Kolkata for a reason, and as usual that reason was logistical. From India I was off to Bangladesh and apparently the flights worked out well from Kolkata.

We circled above Kolkata airport for 40 minutes to avoid a huge lightning storm below. Many passengers got up to be sick. Thankfully my flying legs were used to bumpy rides – this was nothing compared to flying into Bhutan. From gentle, calming ambience to chaotic, full of fumes and hotter than the sun – Bhutan and Kolkata weren't far away geographically but light years apart in every other way.

The day of the run my body didn't want to move from the comfy horizontal bliss of bed. As I rolled over to check the phone's weather app I spoke out loud a little prayer to the sun gods. Cruel reality kicked in: the app had a nice bright orange circle and stated highs of 44, lows of 41. Not what I'd prayed for. I applied sun cream three times mid-run after towelling off the sweat. It was humid too. In order to have water nearby I ran around and around in circles for 35 laps of the Kolkata Stadium. I was running inside the stadium complex grounds as opposed to the actual 400-metre track. So it was a larger circuit and a little less mundane. It was right in the heart of the city, in a district called Bidhannagar, or Salt Lake, presumably named after all the excreted sweat and salt due to the high humidity. The hotel, which I actually paid for this time, was just around the corner.

I could have ran anywhere in the city. I didn't have a gang of supporters and I could have gone on a bit of an exploration. You may think I'm mad for choosing boring nondescript loops, but I had my reasons. Put simply, after discovering my new-found peace in Bhutan I'd had enough of constantly beeping horns and cars and motorbikes whizzing past me like I didn't exist. I was searching for as much peace as I could find.

But after completing just five of the 35 laps I was puffing, tired and a little fed up. I could still hear the bloody beeping motorbikes and hustle and bustle. Usually I'd just get stuck in, but feeling a little internally fragile I was keen to have some peace. I gave up trying to find that peace after another five laps and stuck my earphones in. I listened to Mark Beaumont's *Around the World in 80 Days* audiobook. It was a repeat listen and so I didn't have to concentrate much, if at all. It was nice to hear a familiar friendly voice. Mark is a supreme athlete – especially on two wheels. He holds the record for the fastest time to cycle around the world. Better still, he's a total gent and utterly selfless with his adventure knowledge and contacts. Mark has been an unofficial mentor to me for some years now and I admire him hugely. His books have got me through some dark miles many times. Kolkata was a tough one. The heat and humidity ruined me. I survived on Coca-Cola and water; 12 litres in total. Mostly water, I might add.

The tiny taste of India that I glimpsed in Kolkata left me wanting more. It intrigued me. I will return one day for future adventures. For now though I needed to sleep more than anything. Back at the hotel I glanced through my calendar and realized I wasn't going to find peaceful, tree-lined runs for a while, so slept and came to terms with the fact I'd be running in a few hot, humid and hectic places very soon.

Bangladesh

Dhaka. The day I lost my shit.

Airports combined with rude people really 'grind my gears', as they say in Bristol. It's safe to say the inner peace I'd found in Bhutan was well and truly squashed.

Don't get me wrong, safety is of course paramount, but I'd dealt with the pointless form-filling, endless security scanners and four-hour queues just to reach the airport door – so I refuse to continue to be patient and polite when others aren't showing me the same courtesy. It didn't help that I was overtired, hot, sweaty and in clothes that should have been thrown out several weeks ago.

The minor incident that occurred was a defiant and classically British response to a queue-jumping scenario. India, I hope it isn't an offence to say, is a nation of carefree queue-jumping. The British, of course, do not go in for that – unless you're on an EasyJet flight returning from Magaluf then anything goes. I was waiting patiently in scorching heat with my bags in a queue that snaked around from one entrance to the next. It was a long queue full of lots of people being patient. But like with most riots and incomprehensible idiocy, it only takes one – or a family of six who, carrying enough bags to start a city, trotted by and walked straight through the entrance and into the airport. The airport in Kolkata, like most around this part of the world, required all bags to be scanned on the way in. This, of course, was causing the queue. Being an airport, everyone was also checking their watches, conscious of time. Sure enough, as the family of six waltzed by, another family followed suit and skipped the queue. Within three minutes the queue had dispersed and a large mishmash of various smells, sweat and luggage congregated at the door in a free-for-all. I was at the back and on the back foot.

This on its own wouldn't have riled me so much. It was India. Fine. It then happened again at the check-in desk. I politely gestured to another couple who thought it would be acceptable to just stand in front of me when joining the queue instead of behind me, which is of course the correct way to queue. I said, 'Excuse me,' in a sheepish tone that edged towards aggressive. They simply ignored me. I let it go again, arguing to myself that it was just two people and I'd get to the desk eventually. Then a four-generation family of around ten pushed straight to the front. With that, I snapped as much as a man could snap in this scenario and I grabbed my bags, walked straight past everyone else to the front of the queue and stood immediately in front of them all with my back to them. I was livid, something made instantly worse by the fact that the girl behind the desk then served me without blinking an eye. I, of course, blamed her for my now out-rageously hypocritical behaviour, which left me feeling terrible and I immediately regretted such a heinous act. When queuing for the plane, I was purposely last on in an attempt to right my wrongs. For a split second I had done the unthinkable un-British thing. 'Never again,' I told myself.

Over the course of the previous 18 months I had witnessed some pretty shocking things in airports, and these had been slowly bub-bling away in my soul. Airports, I loved and hated them at the same time. Over the course of 300-plus flights I had seen it all – multiple transgressions that had slowly ratcheted-up my airport rage-meter:

1) Broken scanners in an airport in the Caribbean which resulted in bags being pushed through by hand – even though the machines were switched off. Bonkers.
2) Arriving into Atlanta a security guard asked me to remove the metal rim of my Osprey bag due to safety concerns. This was a bag I had taken on every single flight before and since, and yet nobody else had a problem with the piece of metal that made the bag a bag.
3) A flight where the plane was carrying too many commercial goods in the hold, resulting in everybody's hold luggage being allowed on board. The staff informed us that all our hold bags would to be placed on our laps or in the aisle and door area of the plane – liquids, sharps and everything else included.
4) Top spot goes to a security announcement on a plane broadcast as we were taking off out of Togo. It was a pre-recorded security video instructing passengers to 'avoid use of printers and fax machines while on board'. Oops, next time I'll make sure the printer goes in the hold. Ahh, Africa.

I ranted about these mad happenings to an Australian who was travelling to Dhaka for work. He shared several unbelievable stories with me too and through our rage we bonded. By 7 p.m. my blood had stopped boiling. Embarrassingly, though, he too had witnessed my childlike stomp to the front of the check-in queue, but gladly empathized with me. I reached the hotel by 8.30 p.m. and was asleep in minutes.

My sleep didn't last long. The rest of the night and marathon morning turned into bathroom Armageddon. My sins of airport queue-skipping had come back to haunt me. Men can multitask. Excuse the crude words but I successfully pooed and vomited in unison many times over the course of the day.

Marathon 159 was run in Bangladesh around a smelly city lake. I had great support – but extreme food poisoning, dehydration and likely some kidney troubles all played havoc with the art of putting one foot in front of another. With 20 or so enthusiastic runners waiting in the hotel lobby at 5 a.m. I'd had a tough decision to make in the tortured small hours. I didn't cancel, and explained in the lobby that

I had a terribly sore kidney, my bowels were evacuating involuntarily, and I was throwing up as and when my body needed to. Initially my words fell on deaf ears while high-fives and encouraging thumps to my back ensued, much to my discomfort. After 13 miles of humid, slow and horribly weak running combined with intermittent vomiting and dashing to various squat loos, the gang began to understand I was not OK. We circled a lake, which mostly smelled of effluent and rubbish, for five long sweaty hours. I threw up more times than I could count. It was close to laughable. Every time I drank, it came back up again. The runners fell quieter, and I felt so very bad for letting them down. They were troopers too. Not all natural runners either. The patient and lovely folk of Dhaka had kindly made a big banner for me, organized t-shirts, caps, the full works. They had planned the event and looked forward to it. I had great support but, for once, I really felt like I didn't want it. In reality, they made the whole run bearable. Running alone would have been hell.

For the rest of the day, and most of the following day, I lay in bed, drank what I could and visited the bathroom to poo, vomit or pee blood. I wasn't in a good way. I hoped my kidneys weren't too ruined. It felt like they were. I owe my apologies to the people of Bangladesh. I was not a good guest, and I will return one day and not vomit. I promise. A call home, a call to the team, and to my brother, the experienced nurse, and they all agreed that I probably was damaging my kidneys and I should be careful. Lovely as that was, it didn't really help me. I was concerned my flight to Sri Lanka that next evening was going to be a pooey one. I took the gamble, packed my things, fell asleep, and actually slept.

Sri Lanka

I did make it to Colombo, Sri Lanka, without too much squeaky bum time, but it wasn't comfortable. My stomach wasn't good.

The heritage, history and white sandy beaches of Sri Lanka are, I'm sure, spectacular. Sadly I had no time for any of that. Sri Lanka was what I called 'a sacrificial country', meaning it was one I would have loved to spend months exploring but had to sacrifice that in order to get the mission done. Time was now of the essence. There was no hanging around. The plan had me in the country for exactly 35 hours before moving on. A hokey-cokey visit. In and out, my stomach still not settled, it was another toilet-roll-holding marathon – with tuk tuks, the ocean right next to me and old trains trundling down the coast to keep my mind occupied and distracted from the fact I was still uncomfortable and weak. The sound of waves licking at the rocks on the shore was beautifully calming too.

In the hotel again after 26 miles, my lower back was becoming unbearably sore. I suspected kidney problems thanks to the extreme dehydration. I tried the family doctor, but it was the wrong time of day, so instead slept some more. Having not eaten substantially in days I woke hungry, which I was elated to feel. This, I knew, meant the food poisoning had at least flushed through. I managed to keep down some of the evening meal on the beach, surrounded by paraffin bamboo lamps, the stars in the sky and the waves crashing on the shore. My body may have been pooped (literally), but my mind was enjoying the peace. I lay back on the sand and fell asleep. It was only the bark of several dogs nearby that woke me nearly an hour later. I was dirty, unwashed, still in my sweaty running clothes and asleep on the beach alone. This was as close to a drunken homeless hangover as I was going to get. I felt gross and in need of a long shower.

Maldives

Moving from Sri Lanka's very Asian feel to the much more western-ized part of the tourist-centric Maldives, my stomach was on the mend, and a lovely little hotel put me up for a few nights. The ocean at Malé is bluer than blue, and the waves look like they've been 3D designed and programmed to break perfectly over and over in an identical barrel each time.

I managed to speak to my doctor briefly, who confirmed my worries about my kidneys as best he could without examining me. Due to running a couple of marathons with food poisoning, vomiting and frequent toilet visits, my body, specifically my kidneys, had taken a battering. I hadn't fully realized how little fluid I'd retained during the past four days – in hindsight 99 per cent of anything I was putting in my body was being ejected pretty quickly, which left my kidneys in a bad way. The pain in my back showed no sign of subsiding. I had the remainder of the day to rest before I'd either run in the morning or abandon it and recover. I would take it slow, and if I collapsed I'd stop, but if I was physically able to move forward then that's what I'd do.

A little after 7 a.m. I hobbled around the island of Malé. Malé is the main landmass of the Maldives; it's not that pretty but it's big enough to make the marathon distance possible without too many loops. It was quiet and not too hot. But ten kilometres in I was really struggling with my kidneys. I had got away with so many miraculous recoveries in the past year and a half – everything from slight sprains that fixed themselves to dozens of stomach recoveries, to potentially life-threatening situations. I just wanted one more lucky escape.

I stopped and walked for a bit. My body was hurting, and my vision blurred. For 20 minutes or so I was convinced I was losing my sight. I was delirious, hot, and hurting. The problem with the vision turned out to be sweat dripping into my eyes, a common reality of heat running – but for some reason my body wasn't functioning on all cylinders and took my mind into a panic.

Over the course of five laps around the mainland I repeatedly passed a fancy private hospital. I used it for shade, water and, on lap three, even asked to see a medic. The costs were too high, and I didn't have any paperwork or ID. I just limped out of the building, got my head down, gave myself a pep talk, and put one foot in front of the other. Each step was like being violently kicked in the back. It was unpleasant, to say the least. Excruciatingly slow, painful and really not the marathon I was hoping for. I clung to the fact that I was now at least retaining fluid and topping up my electrolytes with hydration sachets and salt tablets. By mile 22 I knew I was going to make it. I just plodded on and on, stopping occasionally under trees and porches of people's homes to find some shade. It was 20 degrees cooler than Dhaka, but I was ruined.

Stopping the watch outside my beach-front hotel, I walked straight into the sea holding my phone above my head. The water wasn't even vaguely cool, and so I abandoned that and had a long cold shower, once again slumped in the corner. I was asleep by 12.45 p.m. and didn't wake till the next morning.

I dragged myself out of bed at 11 a.m. My back was still sore, but I felt I was more with it. Better still, I had an entire day of nothing before a late flight to Bali, via Singapore. Not wanting to waste a moment of my time in a world of paradise islands I found a guy with a boat to show me as much as I could cram in – golden sand, crystal waters and, importantly, wildlife. I found the paradise that everyone dreams of: turtles, sharks, stingrays, manta rays, clown fish and the most diverse range of small fish I've ever seen. I spent the best part of the day on a beautiful sandbank in the middle of the ocean. When I wasn't in awe of the white sands and vast seascape, I was snorkelling around various tiny islands, floating and with no focus on my back pain whatsoever.

I've always wanted to swim with sharks. Three pretty big sharks circled underneath me as I gazed through my mask down into the blackness below. From the bright colourful coral of the reef to the cliff edge that led to the ocean floor, I hardly lifted my head, bobbing around in the middle of the sea. For the first time in a long time I appreciated the alternative world us humans so rarely see. I spent a while just sitting on the sand of a tiny patch of land contemplating the planet, my trip, and what a peaceful place this was. I could have stayed there all day, had I not needed some shade, the toilet and to catch a plane.

Indonesia and Timor-Leste

If you have to leave the Maldives, Bali isn't such a bad place to end up. Finally touching down in Bali after a long 30 hours of travel feeling rough, I was rewarded with the most beautiful sky, and better still I felt better. I wasn't perfect but the rest and long sky sleep had helped a lot. Bali was the light at the end of the tunnel: a happy, warm, chilled place. I was on the mend. I dumped my bags and went straight to the beach. I had four full days (due to onward travel arrangements) and so could rest before running again – the fortuitous gap my body needed (or so I thought).

In the south of the island I sat on the sand of Kuta beach. The sun painted the ocean waves, clouds and beach with stunning bright pinks and reds. When I was little I used to wear a t-shirt to bed; an old one which my dad had bought years ago on the beaches of Bali. I've sadly since misplaced the t-shirt but I distinctly remember the big circle of the sun and three people in silhouette on the beach. For a long time I'd wanted to see the beach and the sky here.

Western shops selling familiar brands as well as various bars and outlets lined the road parallel to the beach. I ate fish and chips just sitting in the sand soaking up the spectacle of hundreds of surfers, families and travellers enjoying the sunset. Things were on the up. I had, however, made a little mistake. I'd forgotten about East Timor, now called Timor-Leste. When checking my schedule at around 10 p.m. I noticed I was actually flying out the next day at 8 a.m. Shit! I'd not run my Bali marathon. Had plans changed and I didn't realize? In my delirious knackered state had I ballsed up?

I called the team and home too. Yes, they had squished Timor-Leste in during my four days in Bali, hoping to save some much needed time later on. A whole new plan had been drawn up and, despite being informed of this only a week ago, I'd totally forgotten. I was angry at myself and immediately hung up and turned out the light.

Timor-Leste was a 'there and back', so at least I could leave all my stuff in Bali. I hadn't missed a single flight, but this was close. The sun was still rising as I left the tarmac of Bali's small airport. Landing at noon, I darted to the hotel, chucked my bag down, quickly threw on my running gear and a shedload of sun cream and headed out to begin 26 glorious miles, crossing my fingers that my stomach and kidney issues wouldn't cause me too much pain. I took this one slow too.

On my way out the door a lovely lady called Tracey greeted me. She had put a great deal of effort into organizing some runners for the following day, which I hadn't been fully briefed on. In reality it was low energy causing a lack of attention to the new schedule that caused the mix-up. I explained my sickness, the new plans, and apologized for the confusion. As with all the brilliant people who supported the journey, Tracey understood and offered her services for the rest of the day. She later tracked me down mid-run to give me a SIM card, water and even offered coconuts. Tracey was a true gem, someone who knew more or less everyone on the island and was rather a big deal in her own right.

By mile 16 my stomach and kidneys were settled, but I was tired. In a bit of a mid-run booster, out of the blue I was joined by three people who pulled alongside and hopped out of their car to run with me. Apparently they had planned to run the next day but had heard the news and moved their lives around. The island being small they managed to guess where I'd be and came to run the last ten miles. They were a great group, and it was nice to be a part of Zida's first-ever ten miles. We chatted about running, adventures and everything in between as the four of us continued until it got dark. The sunset was an extra prize towards the end of a great day, with glorious views over the ocean and a lush green landscape of trees as a backdrop.

Back in Bali, after four hours of bobbing around in the water and generally exhausting myself even more by crashing around in the waves, I called it a day, reminding myself I still had a marathon to run. I spent the evening watching another brilliant purple masterpiece be painted across the sky. Bali – what a stunning place; the atmosphere, the people and the waves; and a barefoot marathon run entirely on the beach – 42 kilometres of white sands, splashing in the shallows and even singing along to a few old classics, 'singing' out loud. Sorry, Bali beach-goers.

Running barefoot on the beach was a risky move, really – having run in shoes for nearly all of my running life I was careful not to tweak tendons and muscles that weren't used to the uneven sand and camber of the beach. I finished with a little pain in my lower legs due to the change of running style and soft sand, but overall it was a great run. I could have run inland and still been next to the coast, but the beach was just too good to miss.

I avoided several washed-up puffer fish and other various sea folk along the water line, but I didn't manage to miss a few sharp shells. My feet were now pretty battered with a few cuts and scrapes and several blisters on and around the toes where the sand wasn't too kind – but it was soothing to go back in the sea and heal my feet with the salt water.

After a nap, some tasty lunch and a failed attempt to de-sand my body in the shower, I drove north-east towards the island's volcano to explore waterfalls deep in the mountains. I waded through shallow stoney water to reach a quirky waterfall under a canopy of trees. It was completely surrounded by green mossy rocks with plants climbing the walls of the canyon either side. Further on were some rice terraces with the volcano as the backdrop beneath a sky slowly turning red as the sun dipped. Then it was back to a cute little bamboo-frame Airbnb in the mountains, some tasty food, a shower and, before I knew it, it was dark and time for bed. Nodding off to the tune of birds and insects chiming all around, I slept like a baby.

Kuwait

Leaving the tropical colours of Bali to arrive in the dusty concrete metropolis of Kuwait City was slightly disheartening. The Middle East has a uniquely dry quality about it which makes running somehow more two-dimensional. The real problem in countries that are so hot is that outdoor sports are limited to hours of darkness, so when you run you miss the culture and vibrancy. Not to mention the fact that by day there's not a soul outside. Maybe that's it – there was no soul.

Having arrived, I was whisked off to my temporary 48-hour home. This time it was the residence of the British embassy, who hosted me far too well. Rather embarrassingly they gave me my own building and a butler. Just a week earlier I'd been shitting myself by a Bangladeshi lake – now I was eating from the embassy's best bone china dinner set. Dinner cooked by their chef. The British ambassador and his family were incredibly accommodating and, again, I felt like a simple thank you wasn't enough. That's sadly all I could give. Annoyingly, it just so happened that a particularly hot spell had hit a few days before and the temperatures were causing significant concern for locals, let alone a runner under the care of the British embassy. I was in for a harsh battle with the elements and it was a little scary.

Obviously, I was no stranger to heat – I'd run through Africa, and the Sahara Desert for a week racing the infamous Marathon des Sables. Kuwait City, however, is actually hotter and, unlike the Sahara where the temperatures lowered to just five degrees at night, there is no relenting. So, waking from my slumber at 2 a.m I reached for the snooze button on the day of the marathon. Pramosh, the embassy butler, was not only awake so early but had been for a while. He was incredibly kind. He had made me some last-minute provisions for the early start, commenting, 'You need your energy.' He even brought me a cup of tea. A quick glance at my phone's weather app told me it was already going to be a hot day. It was expected to reach 44°C with outrageous humidity by 8 a.m. That big ball of gas in the sky always kept me on my toes but, in Kuwait, it came out all solar flares blazing.

I literally laughed out loud when I saw the extent of my middle-of-the-night escort. Three chaps – Nick, Dave and Matt from the British embassy – were ready to give me the most luxurious personal escort of my trip so far. They stood in front of a brand new flashy Jag, and had an impressive crew of Harley-Davidsons with riders alongside. All eight of them.

The Harleys were loud and, as great as the gesture was, it was going to be one hot and very loud marathon with a Harley gang surrounding me. I think they had overestimated my running speed, for within the first three miles all the bikes had packed up. They had all overheated. With no air going through the bikes, due to my low velocity, they didn't stand a chance. The riders too were fried. They were wearing leathers. And they called me mad!

With the bikes abandoned I was left with the new sparkling Jag and the boys dishing out water and motivation from the window. Even the car was not enjoying the slow pace and heat combination. The roads were empty, it being early and so desperately hot. I trudged on, and with every step the sun turned up the thermometer a notch. Matt and Dave occasionally stuck their heads out of the car window to give me temperature updates. They couldn't believe I was even moving, let alone running – neither could I, really.

Our highest recorded temperature for the day was 59 degrees in the shade, according to the car's display. My phone said 56 but it felt like 200 – 59 in the shade is about 70 in the sun. It was horrendous. With the recent kidney issues I was keen to avoid repeating any severe dehydration and lost count of how much I drank (but I know it was at least 11 litres). And I was still peeing bright orange fluid at the end. At least it wasn't blood. To try to paint a picture of what 59 degrees feels like, combined with the sun, turn your oven on, open the door and stick your face up close. I wouldn't recommend this because you'll likely burn, but the oven doesn't even have UV, which still got me, even with my special factor 70 on. The plus side of all this heat was that I now very rarely complain about being hot anywhere. The end did come, and I'd actually had more brutal runs. It was only thanks to the boys in the car, the supplies, the flat coastal route and my mind firmly on whatever the chef was going to make for dinner that I got through it. A little tinkle on the ivories of a beautiful old piano at the residency that evening, plus some tasty food and a long cold shower and it was time for bed.

I had my luxurious breakfast served by Pramosh in the confines of the British embassy residence while trying to sort out the mountain of digital correspondence I'd failed to respond to. I'd often ignored messages from friends, intending to get back and chat. With the hectic nature of the journey, I had either forgotten, or time had passed and I'd missed the opportunity to reply. But I was incredibly lucky to have a fantastic group of mates who all understood the nature of the task I was engaged in – at no point did anyone remark on my extreme lack of contact or delayed replies. For that, I'm astounded and grateful.

Messages of encouragement from friends all over the planet were the unsung saviours of the trip, and my sanity.

But at the same time, as well as missing life updates from friends, I also missed weddings, funerals, significant birthdays and new babies. The world was spinning and I was gone for a long period. I knew life wouldn't be waiting for me to return – this was now my new world. Reality, it seemed likely, would never feel the same again. I comforted myself with the thought of what was being achieved. Doing something for the first time in history, as long as it is positive, is a good thing to do. I just hoped all my friends saw it like that, and truly believed that too. I think they did.

Qatar

The following morning I ran early along the coast in Doha only six hours after leaving Kuwait. I started at 3 a.m. to avoid most of the heat again. All I saw were the lights of the high-rise fancy buildings on the skyline and a small cluster of old wooden fishing boats bobbing around along the wall of the corniche. As night gave way to day the city magically transformed into an entirely new and earthly place. For the first 13 miles I ran in darkness, in a humid 37 degrees. The eight-mile stretch of waterfront was a constant stream of runners, walkers, roller-skaters and cyclists. Once the sun reared its ugly head, however, the people vanished like vampires. I thought I would be alone in the dark, but not so. I was alone in the day. I should have known. By 6 a.m. there were far fewer cars, nobody on the streets, and even the ocean seemed more still and calm. It was like I had a 'two cities for the price of one' bargain. I set my camera up along the edge of the fake-grass frontage to the corniche and pointed it towards my running route, with the cityscape in the background. As I often did, I ran away out of shot from the camera and then back in front of it – a little video to remember the space and emptiness of the city.

Qatar has money, and it shows. Everywhere is clean, with spotless pavements and the glitz of the financial sector so close. I used a Costa

Coffee shop which was midway along the water's edge. By night it was bustling, by day empty. I stocked up on water and ran alone in silence with only the gentle splish-splash of water lapping at boats moored alongside.

The Middle East is hot, everyone knows that, but I never realized how much it controls the communities that live there. Everything operates at a different time and a different pace – especially in the height of summer. As I ran I wondered how many air-con units there were close by. I think there could be more air-con units in the Middle East than there are rats in London.

Cyprus

Given the ease of flight times, it made sense to fly into Ayia Napa. The party town of Cyprus is of course notorious for drinking, drugs and horrible hangovers. None of which I'm a big fan of, so it was a short stay.

That said, I had a pretty decent run. It was just me and the open road. I landed, dumped my gear in the cheapest hotel I could find, and ventured out. It wasn't even 30 degrees at 2 p.m. – a whole 20 degrees colder than I was used to. Setting out so late was a rarity for me. The heat might no longer be a problem, but eventually it would get dark and so I picked up the pace for the first half. I had no idea where to run, other than knowing that the coastline from Ayia Napa all the way up to the airport was over 50 kilometres, so I had plenty of space next to the water to run. It felt weird to not have the onslaught of new surroundings to adjust to; it felt like being on a hot holiday somewhere, with ATMs and readily available shops for water stops – relatively speaking, it was a breeze, a totally mindless run. I was jogging along, topless, singing away to some music. I very rarely listen to music when running, but occasionally it feels right. I put on a 'party bangers' playlist and ran. Bloody brilliant. The beach was never more than five metres away. I even played a game with the stray dogs. I let them catch me occasionally and then would sprint off again, keeping them following me for as long as I could. I recalled cyclist and adventure legend Sean Conway's anecdotes of his tales 'chasing dogs' while cycling around the world.

Fourteen miles out, and 14 miles back. I'd somehow forgotten to turn around halfway and so completed the run having totted up 28-plus miles. I was in a world of my own and happy for it. The coastal paths with nothing but small fishing boats, some big luxury houses and the occasional classically Cypriot restaurant were my only sights after I'd left the confines of the city. It was a blissful run. I immediately called friends mid-run and suggested a training trip to the Cyprus coast. It was stunning.

The roller-coaster of life only gets more extreme when you're out of your comfort zone – and, sure enough, you learn more, you feel more extremely and, above all, life is lived rather than just survived. As I left Cyprus and flew to Iraq I had a positive head on, and was grateful for all that had been.

Iraq

Via the city of Amman in Jordan I eventually arrived in Erbil rather than Baghdad. Baghdad is somewhat more hostile and I would have had to rely on military personnel again, whereas in Erbil, by some miracle, the team had found a few people to help out and even run with me. I landed in Iraq at 4 a.m.

As always I had no idea what to expect. Far from being a war zone I was shocked at how lovely, neat and tidy Erbil was – and how very friendly everyone was in the peaceful capital of Kurdistan in northern Iraq. After trying hard to sleep in the middle of the day, fighting my body clock, I was met in reception at 4 p.m. by a brilliant chap called Star, who drove me to the Sami Abdul Rahman Park to discover five news channels were waiting to interview me. Somehow I'd forgotten to eat. Hungry, and with my body clock still struggling, I was desperate to get the job done, find some food and sleep again. I was in Iraq though and so did my best to soak it up. I wasn't planning to come back any time soon.

While the news channels were somewhat less equipped and totally disorganized, the run seemed like it would be a good one, once – several hours later; it was now dark – we got going. I had ten runners, some of whom would run the whole way, a water-stand with bananas and oranges, plus the TV station filming me running past them every lap. Star, as his name suggested, acted as my beacon of support. Running at night in Iraq in the middle of a city I had never seen, I was well aware of absolutely needing him to stick around. Mostly for comfort than anything else.

Star, Mustafa and the rest of the support crew plus all the runners made the evening really enjoyable, with an abundance of genuine enthusiasm and excitement. Sami Abdul Rahman Park was just a simple park but it felt like an oasis. It was about 1.4 kilometres in total around the red spongy track that encircled it. I saw more runners in this park than I did in Cyprus and Qatar put together. It was obviously the place to be. The other runners spoke little English and so the running was pretty mute, but I was fine with that. My eyes were closing towards the end, my body screaming at me to sleep. I blame the walrus of a snorer on the plane over. By 11 p.m. we crossed the finish line. Three of the ten runners managed the whole distance and were chuffed. We hugged and exchanged details with what little language we had.

Ramadan had recently ended and there were 50 or so families having midnight picnics in the park, looking over at the curious runner as he jogged past. Once the post-run interviews were complete I was mobbed for signatures. I was sure nobody knew who I was but I was being filmed by every news channel in the country and so they assumed I was someone important. Sorry, folks, just a scrawny runner. In film-star fashion I was ushered into a car and driven all the way to my hotel. And in a very diva(ish) way I asked if we could stop for a pizza on the way back. The gang joined me and we gorged on pizzas in the lobby of the hotel, before I took myself to bed.

Saudi Arabia

I reached the city of Jeddah at 2 p.m. with a plan to run the same evening. With the Iraqi marathon finishing just before midnight, it was still the day of Eid.

For those of you that are unfamiliar with Eid, there are two key

Islamic holidays 'Eid Al Fitr' and 'Eid Al-Adha'. The former is celebrated at the end of Ramadan (a month of fasting during daylight hours), which begins after the new moon sighting for the beginning of Shawal which I experienced in Africa earlier in the trip. The latter, which was taking place today, is always on the tenth day of Dhu al-Hijjah when Hajj (Arabic for pilgrimage) takes place. This lasts for four days.

Despite it being Eid, I was shocked to have so many people want to get involved. I had no idea Jeddah was such a running hub in the Middle East. I was being hosted by the British embassy again. While I didn't meet anyone from the embassy itself, I was shown to my little room by the security guard. It was all a bit weird and abandoned. I later found out it was a lodgings reserved for nationals working on government projects. They hosted me out of the kindness of their hearts rather than obligation, and for that I was thankful.

A lovely girl called Asmaa arrived at the embassy lodgings to discuss the run and the accompanying support vehicles, route and plan. About 5.30 p.m. we met with all the keen runners, seemingly in a random part of town between two buildings, ready to run out to the coast and along the corniche. By this point it was dark and I couldn't see any support at all. It turns out they were all waiting around the corner to surprise me. It worked. About 20 of them introduced themselves, with an excited energy, to run for as long as they could. The seemingly random place we had met was their usual meeting point. Asmaa was a member of the Jeddah Running Club, a community of runners that had been set up by a guy called Mohammed. This new running club and their eclectic group of newbies and trail runners greeted me with open arms; they even presented me with a special medal and trophy as they spoke about how inspiring I was. We hadn't even run yet. For the life of me I can't remember what we spoke about but it was an honour to chat and spend some time with them.

We started a little late after waiting for more and more people to arrive. Most of the runners enjoyed a fast ten kilometres, some a slow five kilometres, but it didn't matter: we grouped along the seafront every so often. By 10 p.m. we were still hugging the coastline. I

stopped for a moment, unplugged my earphones, and just took everything in. By this point I was now on my own – the rest of the runners
had tailed off to go home for various Eid celebrations with family
members. Asmaa and Mohammed were to meet me back at the start
line once I'd finished. I threw my arms up in the air, lifted my head
towards the sky, and twirled around in a state of happiness and
pride – just like I did in Bhutan. This was a different kind of brilliance. It was a treat to be in and amongst the culture of the city – Hajj
being Islam's annual pilgrimage to Mecca, just down the road (relatively speaking) – at such a momentous time in the religious calendar.
Running along the corniche, the atmosphere was special and enchant-
ing. With the sun down and the night alive with stars, the entire
waterfront promenade was full of families nestled alongside other
families, all eating, praying, laughing and fishing. Hundreds of kids
were out playing. Due to the nature of the holy period Hajj, most folk
were on holiday. The vibe was amazing. The sight of so many families and friendships led me to think about my parents, who had
effectively come out of retirement to help make this trip possible. I
owed them much thanks.

Lebanon

Beirut greeted me with hordes of semi-naked oily men. Gladly, these
weren't for me as such. Looking right out of the taxi window as we
drove from the airport to the hotel, there was nothing but buildings
and small food shops. On my left was the ocean. Between us and the
ocean however was what looked like a rocky beach full of basking sea
lions. The huge smatterings of blubber – oiled up to the eyeballs in
tiny white pants, and lying over rocks and concrete water features –
were quite a sight. Large, perfectly round bellies would occasionally
rise from their draped position and puff their chests out in an attempt
to catch the eyes of women walking by. I must admit, I couldn't stop
staring. It was almost art, or like a zoo, I suppose.
    Out running the next day, away from the posturing men further
along the coast, the corniche was lovely: wide, open and bustling. I

ran listening to a few podcasts, the last of an audiobook and some rare music – none of which was noteworthy but were pleasant and got me through. I was in a world of my own, enjoying my love of running, still enjoying the high I'd found in Cyprus. It's easy sometimes to forget about the actual act of running – if that makes sense. So many times I ventured out of the hotel after pulling on my damp and dirty running gear without really acknowledging what I was doing. It became so normal for me to step out into a city I'd never seen, or sometimes never heard of, just on autopilot. I wanted to get amongst the locals a little more and see something of Beirut. The morning after the run, I skipped breakfast and opted to find a gym. Not because I had excess energy – rather, I was losing a lot of muscle mass and beginning to feel some aches and pains in my core and hips. It's amazing how easy it is to lose so much weight without keeping on top of muscle mass. It's also not wise to travel with kilos of protein powder, so I had to make do with some canned tuna, milk and nuts. Occasionally, if I was lucky I'd get to spend a few hours in a basement hotel gym on my own. Maintaining my wiry frame was the least I could do to keep my body from disintegrating. But, as so often before, I rarely had energy to try: I found a gym, spent ten minutes feeling tired then gave up.

Turkmenistan

Arriving in Turkmenistan's capital city, Ashgabat, I knew to expect a bizarre place. I had read and been told of many hilarious stories about the leadership of the country, along with the laws and the weird goings on. Nothing could have prepared me for what I found. Ashgabat is plain and simply bat-shit crazy. I had to keep reminding myself that I wasn't in a film or a fantasy book. I was in a real life capital city where over a million people live. The abundance of hideous horse statues, grand boulevards, fountains and glistening white buildings heralded just the start of a bonkers 48 hours. All madness aside I felt incredibly grateful for the chance to visit somewhere so few people have an opportunity to see. Turkmenistan is one of the least-visited countries in the world; owing mostly to how difficult it is to satisfy the visa requirements.

Stepping off the plane, I was immediately greeted by a large golden-headed statue of the former leader. Despite the fact he died in 2006, most of his laws and personality still ring out throughout the land. After the country gained independence from the Soviet Union in 1991 the local Communist Party leader Saparmurat Niyazov, aka Türkmenbaşy, took power. Immediately he started his rampage of incomprehensible madness. He renamed the days of the week and the months of the year after himself and his mother. He banned opera, ballet and the circus. All this, while opening a giant theme park based on a book of Turkmen fairy tales which he wrote himself.

To make things more complicated, the country is now run by Türkmenbaşy's former dentist, Gurbanguly Berdimuhamedow, who cultivates and presides over his own creepy look and laws. Images of him can be seen all over the city. He has jet-black hair, atop a fat squishy face, in the same manner of the great Türkmenbaşy and, indeed, Kim Jong-un of North Korea. Berdimuhamedow and Türkmenbaşy can be seen in massive gold-framed paintings in every building in every corner of the city. While many of Türkmenbaşy's laws were changed once Berdimuhamedow came to power, some still remain and new ones emerged. For example, black cars are now forbidden in the city in favour of white cars – because white is the colour of good luck. Of course.

Running through the central part of the city was fascinating. In a very North Korean style, the new part of the city is also full of massive white marble buildings – meaning, as well as all the cars, all buildings were white. In fact, there is so much marble that the *Guinness Book of World Records* has awarded Ashgabat with having the highest density of marble buildings in the world. It's surreal and yet marvellous. The buildings are not just tall, they are wide, fat, long – everything about them is huge. Like the streets, they are mostly empty. Nobody can afford to live in them. The real people of the city live on the edge, in shabby rundown shacks.

Throughout my time in the airport, at dinner, in the hotel and, of course, on the run, I believe I saw no more than 100 people, most of

whom were police in ridiculous hats, road sweepers and other workers cleaning statues and buildings. Huge eight-lane motorways were
left so empty I ran down the middle of them. Ashgabat is a pristine
apocalyptic space station on Earth.

I was lucky enough to have Kumush and Kerim as my guides and
chaperones. These two treated me so well and were honest and open
about living in the city. We had lunch and dinner together on both
days. We ate in one of the many marble buildings and despite its gran-
diose façade, on the roof of the building was a small Shoreditch(esque)
café-cum-restaurant. Kumush and Kerim kindly treated me to steak.

On the run Kumush, Kerim and three other runners trotted
through the city with me, together with a car for water and support.
We passed all the mad sights in this kind of deserted Lego town –
built with all the white Lego in the world, but with only a few little
Lego people standing amongst it. I also struggled for those two days
to make contact with the team – I couldn't; it became clear the country has no internet. I sat in my small hotel room – shabby and built to
rip off tourists – and pondered the recent weeks. Turkmenistan had
been astonishing – I thought I'd seen it all, but I hadn't. Crazy childlike empires of marble, fairy tales and deserted cities existed in real
life. I flew out of Ashgabat thankful for the opportunity, along with
all the support I'd had, to give me an authentically Ashgabat experience. The fact I had fewer than 26 countries to go had sort of passed
me by. I was that close now.

9

An Ocean of Islands

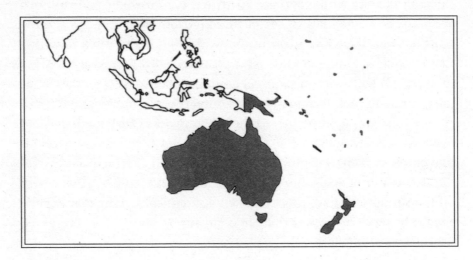

The Marshall Islands	Vanuatu	Kiribati
Micronesia	Australia	Samoa
Palau	Papua New Guinea	New Zealand
China	Solomon Islands	Tonga
Fiji	Nauru	Tuvalu

17 August 2019. I arrived back in London to recharge for the last push. Twenty-six countries, relative to the 170 in the last 19 months, felt like a small number. But I knew it wasn't going to be easy. What lay ahead of me were two significantly difficult stages: 14 Oceania countries, including the Pacific Island nations. And then, there's nothing like leaving all the outrageously tough bits till last, like, say, war zones: Libya, Iran, Sudan, Yemen, Syria and a few more countries that were either hostile or beyond difficult to access legally and safely. I felt like a little boy again and as if I'd left all my homework until the last day of term.

Back in the war room in Cranborne we reeled out the now scroll-like manuscript from one end of the table to the next. This document had been my itinerary for the past 21 months. Thousands of lines on an excel spreadsheet, all carefully managed by Dad, which, when printed out and Sellotaped together, ran to over 12 feet in length – great for the kitchen table in Cranborne, but my copy, once neatly rolled and secured with an elastic band, became more or less pointless, crusted and crunched up at the bottom of my bag, ruined by rain or spilled drinks. Plus it was almost instantly out of date as soon as I put it in there. We changed the plan more than I changed my underwear.

We still needed visas for at least six countries – and we didn't have fixers on the ground in Libya, Syria or Iran, meaning even if I got in I wouldn't have any support to get the run done safely then get out again. And we still had four Pacific islands to link up – all a long way away from each other, in the middle of the ocean. Plane journeys to and from these islands were few and far between, airlines unreliable, and most flights heavily dependent on weather and how many passengers wanted to fly. To meet the Athens date we needed to link all of them up in no more than 26 days. Dad's fancy spider diagram of the various different permutations, from plan A all the way through to plan D, set out our options.

My patience, my dad's patience and my poor mum's patience were all thin. Dad was thinking with his head all the time, Mum with her heart. I just wanted to go to sleep and forget all the problems. Without Mum, my dad wouldn't have coped. She is the glue that holds the entire unit together. I leaned on Dad, Dad leaned on Mum. If I lost my patience with how things were turning out, I'd have a go at Dad, then Dad would be supported by Mum. Whichever way you looked at it, the chain of frustration was always propped up by Mum. She was – is – the selfless saint of our success.

We were still waiting on many questions to be answered by airlines, the visa guys and various embassies when, two days later, I left the UK after 48 hours of intensive panicking – I mean planning. This was it. To Heathrow once again. This time to finish what we started.

The Marshall Islands

I spent the day after my 30th birthday flying, via LA and Honolulu, to Majuro, the capital of the Marshall Islands. I had started this voyage when I was 28. That's no small chunk of time. I was also, potentially dangerously, allowing myself to get excited. For the first time ever my mind wandered off to a place where I had crossed the line. I allowed myself to think of the finish line, the relief, the joy. Was that the wrong thing to do mentally? Maybe. But I did. I had fun, I put my feet up and braced for the remaining 26 intense countries. It couldn't be too bad, I was about to visit islands that people dreamed about.

Day 599 was the shortest day of my life. The International Date Line played havoc with my body clock and sleep time. I left Hawaii at 7.45 a.m., travelled for four hours and 40 minutes then landed at 10.40 a.m. the next day, 19 hours ahead of the UK and so confused I was ready to sleep at 3 p.m. in the afternoon, basically feeling like I was a day ahead, in the future.

Waking up to run wasn't easy. I stretched out to hit snooze and noticed it was already light. I was staying in a small rundown but very popular shack called the Robert Reimers Hotel – low ceilings, lots of wood; the outdoors was almost inside. The whole place gave off a hostel atmosphere. The cheery American receptionist was a lady in her fifties, bubbly – I could tell she'd worked and probably lived behind her little receptionist window for some years. The first thing I was handed, almost before any pleasantries, was a stick a metre long. I could see from the large pile of other sticks that this wasn't a special piece of equipment just for me. She passed it through her reception portal as I hunched over the counter.

'Thank you?' I said, questioningly.

'It's for the dogs – don't go outside without it, the dogs tend to like ankles.' She went into some more detail about how vicious the wild dogs on the island were. Apparently nobody on the island opts to either walk or run on the streets because of the dogs. I'd been given many words of advice like this in other countries, most of which proved to be a little over the top. But never a stick.

At 6.30 a.m., with the sun already beaming down, I set out for the furthest point on the island, just 15 miles to the north. The chain of islands that makes up the Marshall Islands is a sprawling set of volcanic lands and coral atolls in the central region of the Pacific. They lie between Hawaii and the Philippines. In the northwest of the cluster is the Bikini Atoll where the largely undisturbed waters play host to a Second World War ship graveyard. It's now a popular wreck dive site. Majuro Atoll is the largest settlement. The island is shaped like a long boomerang and so water is always just a few steps away. A coral reef called Kalalin Pass teems with marine life just a few miles from the mainland. Despite so much life around, my view for the day was to be rather different. I set out expecting tropical beaches and blissful waters. Within 250 metres of leaving the hotel I had over 20 dogs barking, fighting with each other and chasing me. A few aggressively ran straight up to me growling and snapping their jaws just like in Tunisia. When one stealthy black beast came up behind me within a few centimetres of my legs, and I heard only his jaw snap shut, I realized this was going to be a problem. Fortunately I had the stick with me – if I hadn't turned and swiped my stick at him, he would have bitten me. I continued for another 1.5 miles hoping that there'd be fewer dogs. There were more, and more, then some more. I was on high alert and making myself dizzy looking over my shoulder, crossing the road to avoid packs of them glaring at me and snarling. It was horrible; I was shaking with fear. It seemed only a matter of time until I was bitten again over the 23.5 miles I had remaining. I couldn't afford to miss countries again for re-exposure rabies jabs, and I especially couldn't afford to have my Achilles snipped. I needed my legs. I came to a stop. I had 40 if not 50 dogs in my field of view. At least 20 of them had formed an attacking kill zone with me in the middle. The snippet of detail from the receptionist about the locals not walking on the streets was true. There was nobody around and there was just the one main road that ran to the other end of the island and back. Either side of me were some shacks and the usual semi-completed global deposits of Chinese abandoned investments. Half-built homes were scattered amongst some tropical trees, with the ocean behind them. A whole lot of it. There was no escape.

Scratching my head, and swirling around to keep the dogs at bay with my stick, my only other option was to find a spot where there were fewer dogs and just run. I didn't even know if that was possible. I walked back fast, swiping my stick in a 180-degree motion in front of me like a metal detector but quicker, then did the same behind me. My heartbeat had increased. Every time I tried to run they'd get closer and bark. It was as if they hated runners. I later found out that the island has a significant diabetic crisis because of the lack of outdoor exercise.

I made it back to base and spoke with a different member of staff. I'd had an idea. Maybe I could run on a different bit of land that was still within the country of the 'Marshall Islands'. Even if it was tiny, maybe there was an island with no dogs. I paced around the car park outside to try to find an option using the Wi-Fi from the hotel. The guy from the hotel was making some calls and understood the situation. Failing on the Wi-Fi front, I was told that a boat could collect me in three hours and take me to an island where there were no dogs. Brilliant. I'd have to start the marathon again, but I'd get it done at least.

As I was being told about this alternative a couple of cabin crew who were tucking into some basic canteen-style food overheard. They flew to this part of the world a lot and had been to the island I was intending to visit. They asked why I was going, then looked confused. It turned out that the island had no space to run. It was about a mile wide but was full of big rocks and sinking sand. Their words were, 'Not a chance to even run a mile.' They also advised that I could get stuck out there if the weather deteriorated further – it was now raining hard, the winds picking up.

Feeling frustrated and aware that the next morning I was flying out, and so only had the rest of the day to get it done I started to panic a little. I couldn't balls this up now. I was the guy with two jobs. Don't miss a flight and don't miss a run. I had to find a way. I sat on the step for a while and realized that there were no dogs in the fenced car park of the hotel. The car park was just a bit of gravel, a boatyard more than a car park, really, but still – no dogs.

I went for it. I measured the car park's perimeter. It took me about 40 to 50 seconds to do a lap. It was about 125 metres in circumference. This was possible. Horrible, but possible. And so with that I set off again. Around and around and around I ran. Occasionally stopping at the hotel porch to take in some water – 335 laps later, after battling a huge thunderstorm, I reached 26.2 miles, on an island with hundreds of dogs. I had completed a marathon. I hadn't seen the beach. I was wet through. As I stuffed my face with some tuna fillet and rice, I sat on my bed feeling like a drowned rat. This wasn't the start of a tropical paradise I'd hoped for. I hoped the island of Chuuk in Micronesia would host me without so many problems. I left the next morning and handed the key back along with the stick. It had many more bite marks.

Micronesia

I left for Micronesia having not checked my diary properly and was shocked to have four separate journeys through the skies, hopping from one miniature patch of earth to the next via lots of tiny prop planes all landing in what felt like the middle of the ocean. The view from the air was utterly stunning. It was like this leg of the journey was on a different planet. The world of high rises, traffic, cities and people was long gone. I landed on the tiny atoll of Chuuk, at two in the afternoon, checked in, immediately scoffed down some more fresh tuna and chips at the beach bar, and then got chatting to locals, who were a merry bunch of hardened wreck divers. These weren't islanders but 'seasonairs'. Mostly men over 40, they all assumed I was a diver too. That was the reason why most people came here, apparently. They were all amazed when I rattled off my story. I soon had a few groups of divers sitting around, very intrigued as to where I was going to run. A few of them mentioned the dogs and that I shouldn't run far from the hotel complex. Brilliant, another island full of dogs. One lovely chap, who heard I was due in New Zealand in about five weeks, jumped on the case to try to support me and further my mission. He emailed some buddies of his in Auckland, to hook me up with a triathlon club. Once again within minutes of explaining my task the kindness of strangers resulted in more connections. No matter where I was, if there was a kind human being, I felt welcome and at ease.

My temporary home was the Blue Lagoon Hotel, where 99 per cent of all guests on any given day were staying to dive the Second World War shipwrecks. There are hundreds of them in the waters around the islands. One chap showed me a map on the canteen wall. There appeared to be more boats than islands. The canteen was one of a dozen or so wood-clad outbuildings, all slightly down at heel and damp but fully functioning and appealing; a cool gated complex next to the ocean. While not all the light switches worked, and there was a bucket instead of a tap in my room, the toilet paper had, however, been folded over in a nice pointy arrow shape. Somehow that arrow made up for all the insects in the walls.

As my first evening on the island was drawing to a close, I spent the last 20 minutes or so chatting with Frank, a local who'd been living in Hawaii for ten years. It was obvious he was an out-and-out islander, though – covered in tattoos, a few missing teeth, some of which were replaced with misshaped gold fragments. It's people like Frank who could earn a fortune standing in front of school kids, telling their tales. He just drank and told me stories of island life that were a world away from a childhood in Dorset. Had I not been halfway around the world by now, I would have probably been scared to talk to him. Slightly drunk and with more ink on his skin than not, he had an intimidating look. Somehow we connected and chatted the night away. It was just me, a barman and him. We sat by another wooden outbuilding, a square with a very basic-looking beach bar. We stopped chatting for a while to admire the view. I was pleased to hear that even Frank doesn't get bored of nature. The sun dropped below the horizon and the red and orange hues gave way to the blackness of night. Endless twinkling white dots littered the sky. It was deafeningly still, silent and calm. With the bats flying feet above the water, I was sitting right next to the pan-flat ocean, not a ripple in sight. The vastness of the ocean was scary – the horizon had never looked so far away, just a blanket of velvet blue, with the water merging with the sky. I really was in the middle of the Pacific Ocean.

The next morning's run was spent mostly avoiding rabbit-size holes made by crabs in the grass. Under the fine layer of grass was sand, much like a sand dune that had been flattened and some turf laid. This was the perfect home for crabs, but played havoc with my eyesight. I was focusing so much on not spraining an ankle. It was a problem I'd never experienced before. Many trail marathons are spent looking at the small space of ground just in front of your feet. I always tried to remind myself to look up and enjoy where I was. Otherwise, what's the point? On Chuuk, though, no such luck, I had to avoid the ankle-turning holes.

I'd made a decision to run around the hotel's perimeter, or at least as close as I could. The thought of getting myself into another dog-biting scenario, I wasn't keen on. A few of the others, plus Frank, had also made comments about dogs. This time I had no stick. The hotel perimeter it was, and I set off after a 9 a.m. breakfast. The heat wasn't terrible, it was just humid. I always found that the humidity sort of burnt away as the sun got hotter, acting as if it was drying the damp humidity out. The route was simple. It had five sections. I started in the lobby. Section one was a 120-metre run on a paved wobbly path to the front gate. Section two, a 90-metre section, went from the gate to the beach – this was mostly the uneven crab-hole territory. I then had a flat but tide-dependent 80-metre stretch along the beach. Section four reached the bar, just a 40-metre heavily uneven grass and sand mix. Finally, section five took in the short stint back from the bar to the lobby to begin the route again. This was paved but wound around the buildings near the canteen, and was also 40 metres. There you have it, my route complete. If I did that 113 times, I'd have the job done by lunchtime.

It was dull and slow. Wary of the dogs, but fighting the tedium, each time I got to the front gate I was tempted to venture out a little further, but resisted, at least for a while. Like a cat I did eventually give in to my curiosity and each lap I pushed the boundaries and went out 20 metres, then 100, then 500. It seemed fine. Finally, I made my mind up to run out of the complex on my next lap and so grabbed some bottled water.

I reached the gate and, as if they knew, I immediately had four dogs in a nice neat line about 50 metres away. They were just standing there. I'd obviously set off a trip wire somehow and alerted the captain of the dogs. I turned around and finished my measly route again.

I set my camera up against a rock in the beach section and ran the small 80-metre laps of the beach over and over again. The time-lapse looked fantastic, but after an hour of that I got bored and finished the rest of the run with another several laps of the grounds. It wasn't pretty, and I could have been missing some lovely trail route in the mountains, but it was a marathon. By the time I finished I had most of the complex residents standing outside their buildings clapping me around the last lap. It was a merry occasion to end five sluggish hours.

Palau

The main island of Palau is called Koror. Thanks to having to wait for the next available flight out, I was to spend three sweaty days battling with Koror's tropical rainforest climate. At least dogs were scarce.

It's amazing how tiredness, nutrition and muscle soreness could

affect my attitude. Running something like 41,000 miles had taught
me that sport and its enjoyment is mostly in the mind – a few crappy
runs and I just want to stop and have a burger. The last few marathons were dull at best, not really what I was hoping for from the great
islands of the Pacific. At least on Koror I was able to run freely and
did a few out-and-backs along all the island's three single-lane roads –
but then the wind increased and I was fighting a fierce headwind for a
good five miles. Still, I was mentally happy, my legs were doing as my
mind dictated, and I hadn't seen any dogs either. In training for big
ultra-endurance events I would run four-mile hills: four miles up, four
miles down, then repeat. At the height of training, as mentioned, I'd
do this for 24 hours straight to build up mental as well as physical
endurance. The roads in Koror reminded me of those slogs of training. But I just got on with it, in a full-throttle mindset of success. The
island wasn't much to look at, really – more half-finished Chinese
construction. I got the run done and even made friends with a crab, as
much as you can make friends with a crab. 'Clawford', as I named him,
just sat and patrolled along a wall near a crossroads. This intersection
led me to various other areas of the island and I'd come back to it occasionally to get my bearings. Clawford was my mascot for the day and
never left his post. He was an old boy, bigger than a football. He was a
stunner. I'm sure he waved to me at one point. Maybe this was island-
life madness setting in. I even spoke to him, out loud in front of people
on my final pass. 'Bye, Clawford.' Yep, I'd gone mad.

A slight change of plan meant I'd have to be up early if I was to see
the famous lagoon full of jellyfish – a marine lake located on Eil Malk
Island, a boat ride away. Every day, millions of golden jellyfish migrate
across the lake. While they do this, you can go swimming with them –
and the best part is, they don't sting. Swimming with the jellyfish had
only reopened weeks before I arrived. In recent years horrendously
declining numbers of jellyfish had led to it being banned. Jellyfish
Lake is around 12,000 years old – a remnant of the last ice age, when
the sea level rose to the point where sea water began to fill the basin.
But when the glaciers receded there was no place for jellyfish or any
other fish to go. This isolation allowed the species in the lake to evolve
in a unique way. These lovely little jellyfish, some not exactly on the

small side, have evolved without their stingers because they don't need them – they live on algae that are attached to them. Twice a day, the jellyfish in the lake swim from one side to the other so the algae can grow. There are about 70 other marine lakes located throughout the Rock Islands, all with millions of golden jellyfish migrating horizontally across them daily. I spent about three hours with these beauties, called papua etpisoni. The lagoon on Eil Malk Island is truly magical. If I'm honest, beforehand, I wasn't a big fan of slipping into a lake of jellyfish, but to my surprise it was much clearer than I was expecting. I just dipped my head under the surface and watched. I was extra fortunate that there was hardly anyone in the area when I arrived.

I wasn't back and showered for long before some of the Filipino ladies brought me some dinner to the room. I ate the lot – a sort of sticky rice with mixed root veg. I then promptly fell asleep. I'd touched little more than the surface in Palau but could see the attraction of living on, or at least near, one of the lagoon islands. The locals live simply, have nothing, but told me they coveted the lives of city-dwellers and the 'west'. All I wanted to do was sit and watch the waves.

China

Day 609 I flew from Koror, Palau to Beijing, China. The world feels very small when you're in a tiny lagoon with some rare species of jellyfish and a country of just 18,000 people. To then fly to a city of 25 million people . . . Technically, China was a country I had already 'completed', having run a marathon in Hong Kong. But, as mentioned, the team and I had discussed the possibilities of trying to fit in as many of the disputed countries as possible. China and Hong Kong are not separate countries, of course, but with the rising tension and the real potential that Hong Kong may gain independence one day, we were keen to try to do both. The team realized that one route from Palau to Fiji took me via Beijing and that there was time to run another marathon there, and so I did as I was told.

Within hours of landing in Beijing I was really not a happy bunny. I travel with a lot of camera gear: tripods, huge lenses, about 15 batteries, a drone, three GoPros and two very expensive cameras which are rather precious to me. Or at least they were.

Once in my hotel in the centre of the city I unzipped my bag to get my clothes ready for the following morning's run. The camera gear, complete with batteries and lenses, was gone. Somewhere between getting on the plane and arriving at the hotel, someone had taken my things and zipped my bags up. A while later, once I'd angrily tipped my bag upside down, I came across a folded note typed in Chinese. The authorities at the airport had removed every item without informing me in advance, and had let me leave the airport believing I had all my possessions.

I was fuming. I tried to get online to contact the airport, the airline, and my insurance company. Nothing. The internet restrictions in China are infuriating, and just one of the ways in which the state censors daily life. That evening, having calmed down a little, but not entirely, I had the news on in the background while I ate dinner. The TV turned itself off when news of the current Hong Kong protests came on. These two incidents combined with no access to WhatsApp, no access to news, and a sense of being cut off from the outside world, or at least only permitted access to it under government control. Everyone had been pushing past me at the airport, people were spitting on the floor right in front of me, all my camera gear had been stolen, and now there was no internet either . . . I was struggling to warm to the place.

My diary had details of a 9 a.m. meeting point in a park in the heart of the city, at a location called West Gate 4 where I was to meet a group of about five, all of whom were from a local running club that had heard about my trip. Using the ever handy Maps.me offline app, I found it, and ran roughly in the right direction for 20 minutes. I arrived on time, and there was nobody around. Because there was no access to Wi-Fi, I had no way to message any of the numbers in my phone. I also had no calling credit. I was only staying for 48 hours, after all. I was even more frustrated at this point. I decided to give up, and just run.

The park has numerous entrances and exits. Annoyingly, all of them required a payment to enter. With everything being written in

Chinese I didn't stand a chance, not to mention the fact I had no money either. I'd left my usual stash of cash at the hotel. My diary informed me that the park had water fountains and I wouldn't need anything because I was to be met and supported.

Just as I was asking the member of staff in a booth by a side entrance if I could pay on a card – forgetting again that my digital cards attached to my Chinese-ready WeChat app wouldn't work because I had no Wi-Fi – I turned round to run back to the hotel to find some cash when a kind Chinese gentleman clearly saw my predicament. He handed me the exact money and nodded gently, not saying a word. With that I nodded back and attempted the Chinese for 'thank you' ('*xièxie*'), which sounds a little like you're trying to say something beginning with 's' and 'sh' at the same time. I think I nailed it. (I didn't.) But I was in, thanks to the lovely elderly gent. Things were looking up.

I started my watch again, and ran through the park. After a few miles a person shouted my name. It was a member of the group that was supposed to be waiting for me. Bingo. ('Who needs Wi-Fi?' I thought, immediately taking it back. 'I do.') It wasn't long before we'd all met up in the park and were running together. The group just kept growing and growing as we ran. I relaxed into the run, they bought me some electrolyte drinks and plodded on with me around the park for a good few square miles. There were plenty of water fountains and ornate bridges over lakes. I particularly loved the old men singing opera as they walked, belting out a track with not a care in the world. This apparently is traditional. What a brilliant way to enjoy the park.

We all shared some steps together and had a pretty good time doing so. It was by now the afternoon. The faff of getting back to the hotel with my phone battery dead was another challenge.

On the route back, with little to no idea if I was heading in the right direction, by pure coincidence we ran past the office of Koryo Tours, the company that had helped me get into North Korea to complete the official Pyongyang marathon.

It was a friend called Adrian who worked at Koryo who not only organized that trip, but had organized this marathon too, or at least put me in touch with the right people. He's a top bloke and went out of his way to make sure I had a hotel to stay in too, knowing I was coming from the Pacific Islands and might need some comfort. Adrian is one of those friends to be especially thankful for.

I eventually got to the bottom of the stolen camera gear. Everything had been illegally taken by the staff working at Beijing airport under the pretences of an official search. Apparently it isn't uncommon and there is little chance of ever getting it back. Unfortunately I had to replace all my gear. In a new slightly less angry mindset, I was just thanking my lucky stars that I kept one camera in my hand luggage and so could still take decent-quality photos. I also kept all the memory cards safely about my person when I travelled, to ensure I didn't lose my photos in case my bag didn't follow me. China, I haven't forgiven you.

Fiji

With islands being, well, surrounded by water, I'd lost count of how many times I'd needed a boat to take me from the airport to the hotel, rather than a taxi. This leg of the trip was very 'oceany'. Over some dinner I did a little research about the country, and got chatting to locals. I learnt that Fiji has 300 islands, a large Indian population, the traditional drink is Kava, they have three official languages and rugby is everything! The rugby bit I knew, the number of islands, I didn't. My hotel bed being full of insects, with unwashed bed sheets, came as something of a surprise too. I Googled if there was an alternative nearby. To my surprise there was, and it wasn't extortionate. Another boat took me to another island. The hotel was substantially better and I also had enough land that I could run four-mile loops with no worry about dogs, water or getting lost – all for £54 per night.

Palm trees gently lapping water at the shoreline, and the occasional coconut throwing itself to the floor, sums up my marathon day pretty well. I love running and I especially love running when it feels easy and enjoyable. Running on a tiny island in Fiji helps. Towards the end – after the hotel guests saw me running at breakfast and then again past their morning dip in the pool, before running by them once again at lunch – I started to get some strange looks. The place was so peaceful and yet there I was in the heat plodding the same steps over and over again. It was nice to have some kind words of encouragement as I walked back from my last lap. I think everyone thought I was crazy till they knew what I was doing. And then they still thought I was crazy.

Some coconut water downed, I ordered room service, and me and the mosquitoes had a date on the balcony until the sun went down.

Vanuatu

Erakor is an island of Vanuatu. Both of these places I'd never heard of prior to planning the journey, and so had no idea what to expect. Erakor Island Resort Hotel offered a room for free, and Erakor, being its own tiny island, was totally peaceful. There were no shops, no cars, no roads – nothing, really, just some rooms, a kitchen and restaurant and a few boats next to palm trees on white sandy beaches. It has everything the front of the tropical holiday brochure depicts, plus thousands of starfish that line the shore. This was more like the Pacific Islands I imagined.

But as the ocean waves increased and the dark skies rolled in I battened down the hatches of my waterfront accommodation. The hotel room was a beautiful, simple, single-floor hut by the beach – with the rain pelting against the glass double doors it felt like I was at sea. With a stormy sky I fell asleep to the sound of the ocean, but I dreamt in great detail about all that could go wrong with the countries that were around the corner.

Before I knew it I was up and out running another marathon. The single-track path under the green jungle canopy led from one end of the island to the other. It rained, and rained, and rained. It probably hadn't stopped since the previous evening. Despite the rain, and the fact I was running in a storm in the middle of what felt like the ocean, I got more odd looks from hotel guests. The Erakor Island Resort Hotel felt more like a family home than a hotel – small, connected and together. After two dozen one-mile loops, or thereabouts, and a few stops for some fizzy drinks and water, I was done. Totally soaked, my ears slightly sore from the wind, I nevertheless rather enjoyed the rainy challenge. Being an 'all weathers' runner is a must. I just love running; I'm a simple human being. I looked out to sea and just laughed.

Australia

I had to run, of course, but thanks to the lack of flights to Papua New Guinea I had a couple of days to spare after flying into Brisbane. It's rarely a bad thing to hang around in a beautiful country, so I used the time to my advantage. I hired a car for £38 for 24 hours and set my compass south and drove as close to the water as I could. A 7 a.m. start meant that even with loads of stops – to hold a koala, feed some kangaroos and photograph some wildlife – I made it to my resting place in Byron Bay at around 9 p.m.

Byron has a reputation as a small, chilled-out village with some glorious beaches where surfers and travellers congregate from all over the place. It was just that, and just my style. Byron was a place I fell in love with instantly.

I parked the little hire car and walked to the beach just as dusk was turning to night. Feeling peckish I set off to find something to eat and spotted a busker in an alleyway. The atmosphere was great, and much better than a paid-for concert: two little speakers on stands in the narrow graffiti-filled alley; nothing special at all and yet totally captivating. Armed with a sandwich and a drink I joined the other 20 or so onlookers taking in the music all sitting on the floor with beers. The evening was warm and the atmosphere calm. All we were missing was a campfire. Bradley Stone sang the night away, and now I listen to him often.

It was a super-early start the next morning to chuck my stuff back in the car, watch the sunrise over the beach, and then head back north to Brisbane just in time to drop the car off and dash to meet Jacinta and her girlfriend Alyse at their apartment in the city. This pair are super-inspirational themselves but also host many other far more brilliant and experienced people than me on their podcast *Fearless*. After a great chat I realized that I'm really not a very 'good' runner. I mean, I can run, but when it comes to all the other bits you're supposed to do . . . I just don't. We spoke about pre- and post-race rituals, and what protein I use, or what stretches I do, or my warm-down routine. I know what I should do, and I know enough to help others to train and improve – and, of course, all these bits do help – but in my opinion a warm-down is not an absolute must. I vowed to one day focus on such marginal gains. But for now I had a routine and was going to stick to it. Over 175 marathons I'd had a grand total of four massages, stretched about twice (probably by accident or after waking up), and I'd certainly not done some fancy yoga routine or downed raw eggs. I just wake up and run. No fancy stretching, no fancy massages, no proper ice baths, no foam-rolling, no overnight compression, and no deep-tissue pain mats to stand on . . . I just put my trainers on, and run, and then stop, shower and eat. It's true I have occasionally iced my legs if they've been stiff but, for the most part, I just try to chill out. So what's the secret? In my opinion, there isn't one. It's all in your head, plus running very slowly and not straining muscles too much keeps many of the niggles at bay. I guess I had become rather practised, but I still to this day don't class myself as a good runner, or even a marathon runner. I like to run long distances and enjoy the journey. A similar ethos to my life, I suppose. That's all. I'm just a runner.

Over the years, I've learnt that my body can handle much more than it is reasonable to expect if my mind is in the right place. I know how much I can train, what food I can eat. But I also understand that you, me, and nearly all of us, don't absolutely need to learn any of it. It helps, but it's not necessary. Just run and enjoy it. That's what I try to do.

The next morning I lay in, and instead ran in the evening. I had no heat to avoid in the day so started late after catching up on some sleep from the long drive. I started running at 4 p.m. and the sun set pretty soon afterwards. All things considered, especially the jetlag, I felt pretty awake, and so I meandered along the water's edge. The river in Brisbane is amazing, and the network of paths and cycleways is better than in most cities. With hundreds of runners and bikers commuting along such a long stretch of river, Brisbane is a city I feel I could live in. I just ran and ran until the distance was done. I listened to my audiobook, got my head down and cruised to the finish. Jacinta and Alyse even came to run the last few miles with me. It was a totally chilled run. The city is so pretty at night. The big purple bridge and all the restaurants along the river supply the perfect excuse to stop for a few moments to take some photos.

Papua New Guinea

I stocked up on painkillers and some Soothers and cough medicine in Brisbane. I could feel I was getting a cold. The huge amount of flying, extreme heat and then extreme cold, plus the running, probably had something to do with it. I landed in Port Moresby, Papua New Guinea's capital. 'PNG', as it's known, has a reputation for a few things: notably tribes, cannibalism and an extraordinary diversity of language. It occupies the eastern half of the second-largest island in the world (Greenland, the largest, is an autonomous territory within the Kingdom of Denmark, which is why I didn't run there). The other half, Papua and West Papua, is part of Indonesia. It's a place that has an outstandingly complicated and fascinating history.

In a country of over 700 languages there are always going to be differences. During my run along the coast I was taught the history, the struggles and the sad realities of tribal living, including the fact that the biggest cause of death in the country is snake bites. With so many tribes living remotely and not having any access to anti-venom, a snake bite is the most feared thing among families.

Port Moresby is well maintained, but has expat communities in safer areas with gated housing, while 80 per cent of the nation lives in highly rural areas far from any conventional civilization. The country has seen huge change, and the British were not without impact, first arriving in 1885. It was the 44th anniversary of Papua New Guinea's independence the day before I arrived. I'd missed many of the celebrations but the lingering confetti, extra graffiti and litter along the seafront indicated it had been a party. It was also very clear I wasn't in the safe zone of modern society like Australia any more. I was back to island life – developing and neglected.

I was hosted for my 48-hour stay by a rice-producing company called Skel Rice. My team had put the feelers out to ask for support, knowing that it was likely unwise for me to run solo around the city. Reports of muggings, attacks and generally violent behaviour were common along the built-up seafront. Skel Rice organized everything, from the hotel, to the runners and the support vehicle. Jacob and Henry were my escorts for the day. I had brilliant runners for support too, but strong and silent types Jacob and Henry kept us safe with an armoured car, some big smiles from behind metal mesh windows, and some even bigger shotguns.

The most significant thing I underestimated about this whole journey (other than the cost) was the people. Yes, the world has idiots, violent people and some that simply frustrate me – but most, and I mean virtually all folk in the grand scheme of things, are lovely, smiley human beings. I was joined and supported by another five of these fantastic people running the five miles out along the coast and back again. We stayed relatively close to the gated compounds in case trouble kicked off.

The run done, having battled rain and wind along the coast, I woke the next morning full of cold, a snotty nose and a stinking sore throat. My immune system often took a battering and I had tried to stay on top of it. It's not always possible, though, and running every two or three days is, of course, not an ideal process for recuperation. The rain and storms had probably not helped my cause either. I curled up and slept for the morning before a later evening flight.

Solomon Islands

Groggy and feeling under the weather, I flew into the mainland of the Solomon Islands, Honiara. I immediately had an argument with the receptionist of an over-priced casino hotel. The islands elsewhere were, I'm sure, stunning, but the mainland was awash with construction and, in the centre, it was frankly hideous. My brief spat with the hotel management was down to their price increasing from the original booking. I had booked and reserved my room some months earlier – well, the team had – and now they were asking for more money per night. This equated to a not insignificant sum of $45. I accepted reluctantly, knowing that my options were limited (four other very expensive but not fantastic hotels), but when I was passed the keys I was informed of a hefty fee for breakfast on top, and then various other charges. I wasn't in the best of moods: the heavy cold, it was raining again, and I'd been ripped off for what felt like the gazillionth time.

I put some music on and trotted out. Not having any support runners was sometimes a blessing because it meant I could dictate my own route, the time and day I ran – and I could run at my own pace. My preference was always to have people with me, and to meet new people and experience local living, but now and again I welcomed a peaceful run where I could just be in my own head. I decided to run along the coast in an out-and-back fashion, not straying too far from the hotel, where I'd collect water every time I ran past. This, as I'd done in the past, was my lazy approach to the marathon, and meant I would hopefully be less prone to picking up problems such as dehydration, lessen the likelihood that I'd sprain an ankle on unfamiliar terrain, and, of course, meant I didn't have to think about where I was.

I'd been running the out-and-backs several times at a good pace considering I wasn't feeling well. Every few miles I'd pass a group of young skaters. Initially I'd run past and they'd stare with an evil look and stop what they were doing. Once I'd decided to wave and smile, they waved and smiled back. This, by the way, is the universal equivalent of wearing a sign around my neck that said, 'I don't mean any harm, I'm friendly. How are you?' It worked. If I waved at someone friendly they waved back. Occasionally I'd get some verbal abuse. Towards the end of the run I popped over to say 'hi' and explain my constant and slow running. They were friendly, but clearly desperately poor; a few kids had no teeth and handmade skateboards, and all had a good inch of mud under their nails. One boy had a badly infected leg and seemed unaware of his urgent need for medical attention. I tried to offer advice but, with no money, what could he do? They waved me off as I went on to finish the run while they continued their skateboard antics on the corner of the street.

Once the run was done, I still had the kids on my mind. Some of them looked nearly 16 – so not really kids – but they just oozed utter hopelessness and seemed like they had no ideas or ambitions to dream of. In an attempt to brighten their day like they did mine, I ran back and handed them $40 for soft drinks and treats. I gave a little extra cash to the boy with the gammy leg in the hope it might help in some way. Before I was out of sight along the road, I looked back and could see they had bought a crate of Lucozade and a handful of chocolate bars each. Giving like this is never selfless, more an act of guilty recompense for the world's inequalities. It brought me some happiness, though, and I hope it did for them.

Seeing deprived boys on a concrete building-site corner I became increasingly unimpressed with the Pacific Islands, many of which are a mess, with poor infrastructure and totally overrun by Chinese investment, which might sound like a good thing but seemed to be serving foreign interests rather than local ones. I'm sure such interventions had benefits to public life and the economy, but it felt messy, imposed, and out of the hands of the local people. I felt uncomfortable as a tourist. I left the island in a mixed bag of a snotty cold, feeling tired, humbled, and with an overall concern for the islanders.

Nauru

Nauru must invite you to the island prior to travelling. It's such a small place, with a tiny community, and so access is rightly monitored and tightly controlled – it's the least-visited country in the world. Arriving onto the island I was greeted with big smiles and a friendly welcome from a chap called Neil. He consults for the only TV channel on the island. A quick interview and he was on his way as I waited for my taxi. Word of what I was doing had, remarkably, reached even this tiny, tiny place. I was beyond amazed.

A while later, after no taxi had arrived, some incredibly friendly locals called my hotel, who sent someone to come and get me. The hotel Menen was old, a little shabby, but gave off a nice community feel. I was informed by Veton (my legend of an assistant, and the guy who now manages my life) that these guys were 'excited to meet me, and would do anything to make my stay special'. There had, however, been some communication breakdown. In the few months since the booking, the hotel manager had left and hadn't told anyone I was coming. It turned out nobody was expecting me, nobody knew who I was, and so I was left standing in the lobby rather confused. A kind lady called Pina came to my rescue. The interim manager listened to what I had to say, apologized and then went on to wait on me hand and foot. It was a bizarre turn of events but I'd already got a feel of how the island operated and I loved it. The island was much smaller than I thought and had so few people that it is a family in itself. Brilliant.

With the day turning to night I was given a lift by the ever helpful Ima, who I wasn't sure was a staff member or just a local. She drove me to the shop to get a SIM card and some data, as the island had no Wi-Fi whatsoever. The network shop, or building, was by far the most visited place on the island – it was the hub of the community.

On the way back we stopped to chat with some boys playing Aussie rules football. I watched for a while before the game was abandoned due to dogs stealing the ball (uh oh!!). I was in the process of being blown away by another unique and entirely wonderful island.

That was until I discovered the dogs of Nauru are worse than those of the Marshall Islands. Ima had mentioned them but was a little sheepish to talk about them too much, so I used my new data package to do some digging. Online there were a number of articles about people being mauled to death by big dogs on Nauru.

Still, the next morning, having spent several hours orchestrating a top-notch protection racket in the form of two locals – Clay and Nash; one on a moped with a whiny engine, one on a push bike – we set off to run around the entire country 12 times. It was the slowest circum-navigation of their lives, but I couldn't have done it without them. Positioning the bikes between me and any dogs was the plan, which worked for the most part – a few sneaky dogs managed to creep up behind me undetected. It wasn't just the occasional dog, there were literally hundreds. Walking passers-by don't have a problem, but smelly runners, they seem to hate. Packs of five or more were the most scary, often surrounding us and bringing me to a standstill. The stick was used many times. Needless to say, the answer to my Google question – 'are dogs a problem in Nauru?' was: yes, dogs are a problem.

Clay and Nash seemed rather impressed with my feat of running in the rain and wind. I was more impressed with their constant smiles even when the rains came heavily as they continued sitting on their bikes patiently driving close to me on high alert. The ring road was right next to the beach, so all the way around we were accompanied with a stunning view of endless ocean. I tried to put myself in the shoes of a local, someone who hadn't ever left this island and may not know of the outside world. They probably wouldn't have a clue how beautiful their home is. I loved the island: it was simple and untouched by nearly all the external social norms. Nothing that existed on Nauru was from an outside source – aside from a few food and health products they make do with what they have and live off the land. Shame about the dogs.

Kiribati

Tarawa Atoll is one of the 32 islands of the nation of Kiribati (which I later learned is pronounced 'Kiribass'). Day 630 – Kiribati, Tarawa, the day of marathon 180. Just 16 to go. Having arrived at night the evening before, and to then wake up with a tired body in a small shack, feeling rather confused, today was one of those days. I simply wanted to stay in bed and roll over. Only when I half-opened one eye with the breeze from the sea wafting over my toes at the end of the bed did I realize where I was. I'd been collected by the guesthouse owner's son, and shown to my room in silence in the dead of night. The hut I was staying in was right on the water's edge. The bottom wall of the building was several feet from the ocean. The windows of my room were in fact just cross-hatched netting to keep the bugs out, and with a big porch over all four sides I was effectively sleeping in a car port with some fly nets and a bathroom. As I opened one eye all I could see was the morning sun and bright blue water on both sides. It was like waking up on a boat.

The Dreamers Guest House was one of a dozen small B&Bs on the island. Being an atoll there looked to be much more land at low tide, but once the waters came in the mainland was reduced to a small u-shape that was wide enough for a road down the middle and occasional buildings either side. The rest was beach or ocean.

Stepping out of bed on my first morning, pushing the creaky wooden door open, I was met with the most beautiful sight: for as far as the eye could see there was blue calm water with fish and white sand underneath. The horizon line was broken up by another couple of small islands with palm trees and green foliage. This was the place I'd been dreaming of.

The owner, a woman in her sixties, and her son, were both charming and had big smiles as they brought me tea and toast. I sat with my feet dangling in the water, looking out to the morning sun. Neither of the hosts spoke a lot of English but it was plenty to get by. It turned out there were just two other guests: Fraser and his daughter Francesca introduced themselves a while later as they appeared for breakfast. Fraser was originally from Sheffield; he and his daughter were here on a mini-holiday from the Solomon Islands where they now lived. Fraser, having left the UK 21 years earlier, had subsequently lived and worked in ten far-flung countries, latterly with Francesca, who was 12, by his side. She was by far the most knowledgeable and mature 12-year-old I'd ever met. I was over the moon to learn that Fraser was a runner too, and a strong one at that. I mentioned I'd be heading out in the early afternoon so I could finish at sunset. He remarked on the heat, which was hovering around 35°C. I'd been in far worse and so felt I could run at that time of the day. A couple of hours later we had our running gear on. Fraser hadn't run a marathon in close to a year and so was a little apprehensive, but although we slowed a little, he was a pro and I was impressed.

Fraser, with his tight curly locks of long grey and brown hair, was about 50 and had stories to match. He had lived all over the place, and his daughter had seen more of the world than most adults ever do. Moving from place to place, Francesca had received both a formal and an informal education, and spoke four languages. They loved the world, and clearly had a special dynamic. I loved and envied their way of life.

We ran down the one narrow dusty road the country had – from the guesthouse as far west until the island ran out, and then back past the guesthouse again, only turning around finally at the other eastern end of the u-shape, about 15 miles in total. Backwards and forwards, we finished running about 40 minutes after it got dark, and were struggling to see thanks to being in the middle of the ocean with no streetlights to guide us.

I'd found the gem of the Pacific. The homes and simple appearance of every building personified this place. Some were brick, some tin, some wood – some seemed to comprise just hammocks hung between trees. It was simple living without the extremes of rich and poor; the smell of freshly caught fish in the air, the sound of the sea lapping at the beach, and the occasional thud of coconuts dropping from palm trees leaning towards the ocean. The people smile, the cars and motorbikes drive so slowly you may as well walk, and there's absolutely no sense of urgency in anyone's life. Catch fish, cook them, sell a few, repair some lines, wash in the ocean, feed the pigs, then do it all again the next day. There are four places to eat on the island – a couple just people's homes. Needless to say the menus are limited – fish and chips was my meal every night, with breakfast consisting of oddly sugary toast and tea. I'm sure some people would hate to live like this. I loved it.

On my final afternoon we borrowed the guesthouse car and drove as far as we could until the road disappeared, to see a sunset at the end of the island. Fraser and Francesca came along too for an ice cream, some time to chat with locals, then the sun finally dropped below the 12 or so cargo ships on the horizon and the island shut down for the night. Tarawa is darker than dark after sunset: generators are turned off, the very few streetlights powered by solar are also shut down, and the whole island hunkers down as if there were an unspoken curfew.

The last sunrise of the island was its farewell gift. I luckily woke up two hours before my alarm at 4.30 a.m. I guess that's what a whole extra rest day means for my body now. The light was just starting to appear. Still in my boxers, sleepily rubbing my eyes, I pushed the faded pastel guestroom door open. I was met with a gentle warm breeze and the sound of the waves. Barefoot, I stepped out into the new day. It was totally still. The birds slowly woke up as the kettle whistled to the boil. The sun appeared. I sat in an oversized chair on the porch. The chair was handmade: a few nails held together dried bark from palm trees. I sat and smiled. What a morning. What a lovely way to live on our planet.

Samoa

I had just 24 hours in Samoa. I arrived late, ate, and fell asleep. It was time to run again. Little did I know what was about to happen.

Having woken early and checked my phone for a local weather forecast I knew it was due to rain in the afternoon, with temperatures predicted to not pass 35°C. I made the mistake of believing a Pacific Island forecast again. It was wrong. The temperature reached 44°C and it didn't rain at all. In fact, the heat just kept coming. Despite a lovely flowing route between lush green trees, no rubbish, no noise, just an island going about its business, the hills and the heat caught me out. It turned into a rather brutal run.

I started at 11.20 a.m., running through the heat of the day, expecting rain. I wasn't alone. I had the company and support of Sani, a very patient and totally underprepared support rider. Without wishing to be unkind, Sani was not in the shape of a god, or even someone about to cycle 42 kilometres. With eight miles still to run I was waiting for him at the top of a hill, and not for the first time. Sani's knees, back and neck were hurting him. I learnt he hadn't been on a bike for 20 years and had never cycled more than five kilometres. Despite this he never complained – until he was broken.

I had asked the hotel to provide me with some support, and was happy to pay for it. I'd said it would be nice if I could have a cyclist with some water in a backpack. That way the peace of the island wouldn't be ruined by a running engine and I'd still have someone to guide me and provide water. Samoa is bigger than other islands and the small villages are spread out, which meant it could be ten miles between any form of shop. Sani was the friend of one of the hotel workers, and needed some cash. I was pleased to have him join me. That was until I learnt how unfit he was – and that Sani was chosen only because nobody else was available.

At mile 24 – after helping Sani push his bike up a hill owing to his knee pain, and having run out of water – I was struggling. We had left late due to the faff of waiting to sort out the bike, and so I ran a little faster at the beginning in order to get it done so I could pack and be ready to leave. Suddenly a strong compression-like pain filled my chest almost as if I were being squashed. It was enough for me to gasp and let out an audible sound of pain. It got stronger and my head felt light and things went hazy. I sat down, struggling to catch my breath. My arm hurt briefly and the compression didn't fade as I expected it to. I sat holding my chest and panting like I was running at full speed up a hill. Was I having a heart attack? I had no idea, but it sure felt like it. This was worse than Juba. Thoughts of my heart problem reared up again – I could be in a rather bad way. I sat in the shade with Sami's bike on the floor. Eventually he appeared after a long trudge up the hill. I sat for a while, and the pain subsided, but I was still short of breath – and more than anything alarmed at what had happened.

Thankfully, Sani took the bike and told me he'd catch me up. I hobbled through the last few miles dodging the sun, hopping into shade wherever possible. Maybe I had just overheated.

Having spoken with a doctor and some family members it was confirmed that I had likely had a minor but not insignificant heart attack. Crap. This can't be happening. Should I stop running? I was adamant that I would carry on even if it killed me. Obviously this was madness. I grabbed my bags, paid Sani when he made it back, and left for the airport. I was in shock, I think. I felt fine again, more or less, but was worried that it may happen again and worse. At least the continent's second-biggest island, New Zealand, would have far more medical support.

New Zealand

I fell asleep as soon as I arrived in Auckland and rested, trying to monitor my heart closely. It seemed fine and by the afternoon of the following day I'd almost forgotten it had happened. I felt totally fine. I concluded that I was probably just overheated and over-exerting myself. Looking back that was an absurd rationale, because I'd been running much harder, in much harsher climates, hundreds of times. Either way, I put it behind me and moved on south to Raglan.

I slept the following day, as instructed by the medics back home, then hired a camper car – basically a big car with a bed in the back. I had two more days before moving on, once again thanks to limited onward flight options, to Tonga. Having stopped off at a few beauty spots to take photos of sheep and mountains, I drove south-west to Raglan then further south-east to Lake Taupo. By midnight I'd climbed over the front seat, having pulled up by a roadside inlet, and fell asleep in my ready-made bed in the back. I woke up and peered through the curtain of the car-camper combo. I had picked a pretty decent spot, but my body wasn't happy with the weather. It was cold, very cold considering recent climates. This had been the first time I felt cold for months. But the best feeling came when I realized I could run without the thought of being attacked by the sun. With that, I hurried to sort my things ready to run.

I had nothing with me except a few dirty vests and shorts. In fact, I had nothing clean at all, or warm. I got out my phone, found the nearest outdoors store and bought a jumper, a hat and gloves, plus leggings. A waste of money, entirely, knowing I had hundreds of all of these items at home, but needs must. I hated being cold, but now, problem solved, I was ready to run – after bacon and eggs prepared on the small rusty pop-up stove in the camper. I wrapped layer upon layer around my shoulders and boiled some water for tea. I sat, ate and stared out onto the lake, smiling at the cold feeling on my face. I had warm clothes and was in a cold country. This was a novel feeling.

I ran feeling a little chilly, but with no heart issues, along the side of Lake Taupo below a blue sky with a gentle breeze. It was what I needed as I got closer to the end, before what I knew was going to be a tough time with some difficult countries.

With a day in hand I made a beeline for the city of Hamilton, back north, to see an old friend. I hadn't seen Zoe in 11 years. I went to school with her and we're both from the same sleepy village in Dorset. She and her boyfriend Fletch cooked me a super-tasty veggie curry and we drank non-alcoholic wine while catching up. It was a lovely few hours to cram in 11 years of news. It was a pleasure.

I left Hamilton at about 10 p.m. and drove through the night, 200 kilometres north to a cozy spot famous for star photography. I reached Omaha Beach in the dead of night and stepped out of the car to stretch after a long time behind the wheel. The sound of nothingness proved again to be so peaceful. You couldn't even hear the sound of the sea because the tide was so far out. I looked up to the sky. It treated me to the most amazing show of glistening crystals of stardust. I could have faffed around with photos and got the tripod out, but instead I just stared and admired the cosmos.

With a deadline of 4 p.m. to drop the car off and a long journey until I'd reach the airport, I left very early in the morning and took my time. The colours of New Zealand are nothing but a palette of green. Even with some rain and cloud it's beautiful. A few more beaches, a few more sudden roadside stops to snap a few shots of animals and amazing views, then it was then time to hand back the keys of my trusty camper car.

Tonga and Tuvalu

Tonga was sadly a flying visit. I had breakfast at 6 a.m., was changed and out by 7, started running at 8 and was finished by midday. An interview, shower and then it was time to head off to the airport again. I hadn't seen much of Tonga except the few miles out and back along a rainy seafront wall. The town of Nuku'alofa was pleasant but by now I had seen enough Chinese half-finished construction. It was my fastest in-out of the trip so far.

I flew back to Auckland again, fortuitously, as the watch I needed for tracking mileage, which it had done for every mile up till now, was broken. The watch-charger and the watch itself didn't seem to like each other any more. I wasn't sure why, but the watch just wouldn't charge – and I needed at least 40 per cent battery to complete a marathon. Hours later, after much help from friendly stores and research by my dad, the watch shop Ponsonby Time helped clean the connections under a microscope. I later discovered, with the help of Bivouac Outdoors, a classic New Zealand outdoor shop, that I only needed a new charger. They had one charger in stock. Close one. New Zealand came to my rescue – I probably wouldn't have found one in my next country, Tuvalu being the second-least-visited country in the world.

The island of Tuvalu is so small that there's virtually no space for people, let alone an airport. We hit the ground with a hard thud, like all the other small runway landings. As we were taxiing in I peered out the window and noticed that the plane was ushered into its parking space by a chap hanging off the edge of a roof. On both sides, the airport parking spot was wedged between two buildings. One was the two-storey national bank, constructed seemingly by someone who liked wooden sheds but wasn't quite sure how to build one. The other side was a concrete structure painted in yellow, with a roof supported by some pillars but no walls. I later found out that this was in fact the building of the only school on the island, where lessons were taught with natural air-con. The other building, the bank, was the only place anyone in the entire country could get cash, buy Wi-Fi tokens or collect parcels. It was the hub of the island. Before I'd even got off the plane I'd seen most of the substantial buildings in the entire country.

Unlike the usual airport etiquette, I collected my bags from the rear of the plane and went through to have my passport stamped. No ground crew existed here. The building was no larger than a big kitchen and went directly out onto a dirty track the other side. What with so few passengers arriving there was hardly anyone waiting to be collected. I did, however, have a lady there to greet me holding a sign which said 'hotel' written on a piece of paper. I was expecting the usual hello, walk to the car, drive to the hotel and check-in. I knew the protocol well. Instead, she smiled at me and, without opening her mouth, simply pointed at the building about five metres to her right. The hotel was the building the other side of the yellow wall-less school. The bank, the airport, the school and now my hotel were the sum total of public buildings on the island, all of which were directly next to the runway. There was no fence, no security, and there were goats, pigs and dogs wandering around all over the place.

The lady who ran the hotel explained that the runway wasn't just a runway, it was the country's community centre, open to the public. The tarmac had trees, a couple of buildings and the ocean either side. I was shown to the room that I'd been given at a bargain rate, which worked out to be not much of a bargain at all. It was a small box room with a single bed made of pallets on one side, with a mattress and a pillow plus an old rusty fan in the corner. I had windows without glass, but no door. I actually quite liked it until I discovered the bed-bug bites the next morning.

Excited to run a marathon on a live runway, I was out and running fairly soon after landing at 11.35 a.m. It was one mile up then one mile back, but the novelty of running along a runway was enough to keep me smiling. The bank had a siren and some cones to signify when a plane was landing. There were three scheduled flights in and out per week, all of which went to and from Fiji. All the locals knew the times of the planes, and turned up to buy a ticket like you would for a bus, on a first-come first-served basis. The place was magical and bucked all trends of modern living.

As I ran, and it got a little cooler, the runway started to get busy – not with planes, but with people playing sport: a dozen different groups of footballers, five volleyball matches, cricket, and even kids riding bikes. As the sun set over the airstrip I stopped a few times to say hello and take pictures. I finished running in the darkness as it began to drizzle. It was a marvellous way to finish the Pacific Islands.

I had a quick shower and a meal of the hotel's finest chicken and rice. A classic, and indeed the only dish available for hundreds of miles. Unfortunately, shortly after placing my knife and fork together on the plastic outdoor table by the bar, I spotted a huge rat in the kitchen tucking into the rice. This was when the owner caught me looking horrified. She wasn't unfriendly exactly, but I wouldn't say friendly either. She simply looked at me and said, 'They are all God's creatures.' I had to smile – before wondering about what I'd just eaten. Either way, it was tasty and too late now. I'd probably eaten worse.

The other two hotel guests maxing out the room capacity were a lovely chap in his fifties called Michael, from the UK, and a woman in her sixties called Lea, from Australia. They were unrelated. Lea was working, and Michael was on a mission to visit every country in the world. He had been at it for 30-plus years and had just 21 to go, ticking off a few places each year. His stories were fascinating. Lea's were too. She proudly introduced herself as a sex worker. I was a little taken aback by this, but could see a twinkle in her eye, and realized she meant in a different way. She had spent her life educating individuals, institutes and, in this case, entire nations on the mysteries of contraception and the rights and wrongs regarding personal sexual health.

Sharing stories about sex education and tribes around the world, the conversations that evening were the essence of travel and adventure. A brilliant evening. I was also invited to join Michael for an exploration to one of the furthest-out and hardest-to-reach islands in the world. Tuvalu is a series of land masses, sprawled out, that look very much like droplets of land spilled on the ocean. Michael had already paid for the excursion but kindly invited me along to share the journey. Early the next morning we met in reception, filled our bags with bottled water and, cameras in hand, went to meet a guy about an island.

Ripples of turquoise water capped with white crests swelled around us as our little blue boat motored through the waves further and further into the endless ocean. We visited four islands that day, each more beautiful than the last. We feasted our eyes on bright white sands, huge flocks of island birds – and the skeletons of crab, fish and lobster that lined the beaches. The slow tug, tug, tug of the tired engine took us far out into the blue to reach the very last of these distant untouched islands, rarely frequented by anyone.

The furthest out was breathtaking: an island of white sand and perfectly picturesque green palms, with washed-up branches, bits of boats and eggs from various birds. Through fallen trees and massive pristine shells, we meandered around the perimeter of the island. We sat for a while without speaking and just took in the truly magical and rare moment.

We reluctantly left the island after a few hours, noticing that we'd both become rather red-faced – in fact, burnt to a crisp thanks to the wind fooling us for most of the morning. Our journey from the island and back to the 'big' island complete, we stopped for a dinner in the only half-decent 'restaurant' on the island – burgers, milkshakes and fries through the hatch of a converted trailer. It was literally the only food that wasn't rice, chicken, fish or rat on the island – in fact, thinking about – I guess it could have been rat.

We both needed to get on the only remaining flight out of the country this week, so we packed and just sat on the runway, waiting to be told the plane was coming. The plane left a few hours later than planned, but before long my return connection in Fiji was complete. I'd transited again through Sydney and then Doha and I eventually landed in London for a 48-hour pit stop. My final passport, with all the documentation I needed for the last 12 countries was ready and waiting for me. The mammoth multi-hop flight took two and a half days, but I was home one last brief time. Up next was everything I was worried about from a safety perspective. The flights didn't quite work out, we had gaps in at least three war zones where I still didn't have ground support, and still no approved visas. The team were working around the clock, but the time had come to face what lay ahead and work out the bits we'd ballsed up. There was a lot that could go wrong.

10

The World or Bust

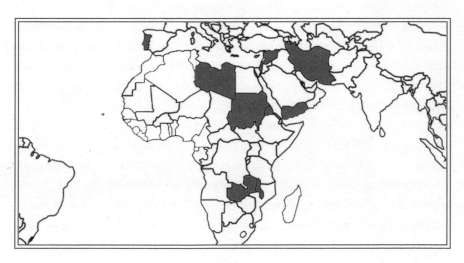

Libya	Eritrea	Portugal
Iran	Sudan	Cape Verde
Zambia	Yemen	Israel
Malawi	Syria	

The last supper. Day 649 – 17 October 2019 – one year, nine months and ten days since I said goodbye to everything in search of the dream to run a marathon in every country on the planet. I knew I would return penniless, without a home, car or belongings. It was 'the world or bust'.

I also knew that when I set off we didn't have enough money to finish – I just didn't know quite how short we'd be. The overspend turned out to be horrendous. The finance was just one of many stumbling blocks. We had countless obstacles to overcome, some of which we weren't even aware of entirely, and above all I knew that it would be the most difficult yet most enriching thing I'd ever do. And despite understanding all of that, it was still a battle of logistical, financial, mental and physical endurance to get anywhere close to finishing.

This journey was a dream to see the world, to live by my dear friend Kev's advice. To not wait for a diagnosis. To not wait for something terrible to happen before realizing the tremendous unfathomable privilege we have as western, educated, wealthy and healthy humans. I also wanted to know what was out there. I want to one day – hopefully not for a long time yet – be on my death bed knowing I followed my dreams and had the courage to do what nobody had tried before.

The only slight problem was: 12 countries to run – in just 24 days. The catching up and cramming in was the result of earlier re-jigging. Zambia and Malawi had been missed due to the dog bite back in Tunisia. I sacrificed these two countries to return to the UK to have the much needed rabies jabs, plus sort a tooth infection. Sudan had been moved because of violence and the UN pulling out of the country, and therefore our support contact going with it. An account of the difficulties in obtaining visas for Libya, Iran, Yemen and Syria, all dangerous and volatile countries, would run to a book in itself. If we'd put these close to the beginning and things went wrong, the onward travel could have been severely affected. Israel had been kept to close to last simply because having an Israeli stamp in your passport can cause havoc with onward travel to many countries, for obvious reasons. Then last there was Athens, of course, with that famous finishing line.

Before that there was Portugal. Guinness World Record guidelines stated that I must progress from one country to the next at least every 14 days. This, of course, I'd been doing somewhat more quickly – but on the off chance I was injured and needed rest, Portugal was kept as our emergency close-to-home. If I were in the UK recovering for ten days, say, I could still hopefully limp around a marathon in Portugal, which was only a couple of hours' flight from the UK, and required no visa or on-the-ground support. Cape Verde was linked to Portugal in the itinerary because, as an ex-colony and popular holiday destination, it was easier and cheaper to get to this Atlantic island, off the coast of Africa, than almost anywhere else.

Leaving 'home', or Dorset, for the last time felt odd. By this point I felt far more at ease on a plane, or in a strange hotel I'd never set foot in before, or chatting with a stranger. I felt out of place in my parents' house. It was weird, but I knew it meant I'd embraced the journey and had lived it well and truly. I was exhausted and ready to finish. We'd need a miracle for everything to link up but I just kept thinking, 'Twelve marathons.' It was off to Libya.

Libya

I slept most of the journey to Turkey, and then again from Turkey to Libya. By dusk everyone was sleeping as the sun set and people pulled blankets over their heads as they snoozed. The occasional cough or stir of movement is a common soundtrack to life in the sky. Mostly, there's nothing but the gentle hum of the aircraft cutting through the sky. I love the feeling of being totally still above the clouds in our tubular communal dwelling. It feels as if we're floating rather than hurtling at hundreds of miles an hour. I peered through the portal windows to see the light was warm but fading, as my eyes got heavier.

We landed in Misrata at 9 a.m. and I realized, 'Holy shit! I'm in Libya.' This was to be a quick 'in and out' in a day, via the previously unheard of and hard to locate Libyan Wings Airways. Leaving Istanbul at 6.10 a.m. and returning on the 21.55 from Misrata meant I had less than 13 hours in the country. The airport was tiny. Unsurprisingly, the luggage-belt situation was chaos, situated in a rundown hangar about the size of a double garage. My bag took far too long to arrive and I was getting a little nervous. Having flown in from Turkey with a planeload of Libyan nationals who had flown back various food or luxuries like TVs and fridges, these all began to arrive on the same belt amongst the luggage. I've seen many weird and wonderful items rattle past me on luggage belts all over the world. But it was me who was getting the funny looks, along the lines of, 'Who is this slightly sunburnt western man, and why is he here?' Again this was not for the first time, but somehow it felt more threatening in Libya. I had a handful of people offer to help with bags, which was also not uncommon, but these folk were of course after some cash in return from the rich westerner. Eventually my little Osprey bag arrived and I was reunited with my trusty pack. Yaseen was also waiting outside, crouching down on the floor happily having a smoke. Yaseen was Universal Visas' doing – this was one of many contacts that they'd found as support at the last minute. The problem with arranging things so far in advance was that things changed over the course of two years. Therefore, we had to rely on some luck to find the right people, ones who were trustworthy, not too expensive, could not only speak English but be available and understand what we were trying to achieve and appreciate the importance of not letting us down. This was rare, but we'd accept anything close. Yaseen, thankfully, was all those things and more. He helped because he wanted to. This was the best kind of help, and he was funny too. With a grey beard and traditional dress, he spoke with humour in his eyes. What I didn't find out until later was that my flight had been originally bound for Tripoli before being re-routed to Misrata, 200 kilometres to the east. There had been frantic goings-on between my parents and Yaseen to determine where the flight was going to land due to the runway in Tripoli being rendered unusable through constant shelling. Yaseen had assured Mum and Dad that despite the airline showing Tripoli as a destination – and it was shown as such on the departure board in Istanbul – it was going to fly to Misrata, where he would collect me.

As we drove for no more than 20 minutes to our temporary accommodation (laid on to store our bags), Yaseen said, 'I think your dad was a bit worried about you being in Libya – but this city is fine. We have everything organized. What can possibly go wrong?' He knew of the reality of living in this part of the world, but his words were genuinely reassuring.

We arrived at a little hotel in the middle of the city, where five of Yaseen's friends that he'd recruited to help were in the lobby waiting. I introduced myself and we sat for a while to make plans. Yaseen was fantastically diplomatic and just wanted what I wanted. I said, 'All I'm after is to run a marathon safely and then leave.' I also went on to explain that I would love to see some of the country too, and maybe the route of the run could take us to some sights? They already had a plan A and a plan B. I opted for plan A, which was to run 13 miles out in the safest part of the city, and then run back. The alternative was to weave through the city to make the distance. I thought this unwise. The rest of the lads, who were all 20 years younger than Yaseen, agreed that an out-and-back route would be easier. I was just happy to have such understanding support. I'd had countless times when support runners simply didn't understand that I didn't want to race them, and I wasn't interested in making the route longer.

The run turned into a very well supported one. Some local media turned up too, plus another friend of Yaseen's in another car. Before we knew it we had a convoy. We started the run beneath an underpass with a blown-up tank off to one side. The roads were dusty and I could see the heat shimmer above the odd patch of exposed black tarmac. I was anxious to get running and to not be standing in a place where we could easily be attacked. Being under an underpass felt dodgy, but then I realized we were there to shelter from the sun. Maybe I'd been watching too many action films on the plane. In reality I had no idea if being attacked was likely or not, but I figured I'd rather we just started running. As it happened, the roads were safe, and by mile three I had support from a vehicle a few hundred metres ahead of me with a camera crew hanging out of the boot at the back. Apparently the local TV wanted to air the entire run. Yaseen was also on hand in his jeep behind me, and another truck was off to my left in the middle of the road. As I ran, all the crew in all the vehicles offered me water, snacks and took photos. They did this for five hours all the way to the finish. I ran the full distance with an impressive 22 people – some of them from the local running club; some old, some young. Each one of them was totally polite, patient and pleased to be involved. I was taken aback at how the entire crew of nearly 30, including the drivers, were so lovely and cheerful. They just wanted me to succeed. I was even handed a flag from one of the younger kids with one mile to go. We all linked hands, held the flag and ran to a monument in the centre of the city for the big finish. A sweaty group hug signified the end.

I was buzzing, very hot, but buzzing. Everyone chipped in. We hugged some more, bumped fists, and swapped details. I still have many of these guys on WhatsApp and we keep in touch from time to time. Libya was not the Libya on TV. That, right there, is the power of people.

With my flight still a few hours away I suggested we find a pizza place, if that was a thing in Misrata, so I could buy everyone some dinner. We'd been running past tanks, bunkers, blown-up buildings, shops littered with bullets, and cars on fire in the distance. I assumed they'd have a pizza place, but, thinking about it, we'd run past exactly zero buildings that looked like any form of store or restaurant. To my surprise, just around the corner from our finish marker was a pizza joint big enough for us all to sit in and eat.

The country isn't all war and fighting. Like so many places, the news headlines don't tell the full story. I wanted to buy everyone food to say thanks, and to acknowledge that I was totally honoured to share my miles with such generous and welcoming people. It would have been easy for them to see me as obnoxious, travelling so far and seeing so much when they in all probability would be denied such luxury. But instead they just welcomed me with open arms. I was moved.

Pizza vanished into our bellies much more quickly than we could
order it, then I shot back to the hotel, got showered, packed and we
made a beeline for the airport. We made it, but only just. Ahead of me
was a two-day journey to reach Iran. The Iranian government had
specifically refused my visas twice, and everything had only been
finalised literally hours before I flew out of Misrata. Arriving into any
country where they have effectively told you not to visit isn't wise, but
doing that in Iran is madness.

Iran

En route to Tehran I had an 18-hour-layover in Dubai. Remember the
family that I fell in love with, Rod and Gaëlle and their kids? Well,
they very kindly opened up their home to me once more for my brief
stopover. It seemed like decades had passed since I'd last seen them.
In reality they hadn't changed much at all. I had been doing so much
that time had been warped in my mind. In the few hours I had with
them I played with the kids in the sea, splashing around and collecting shells. Rod had lent me his swim shorts – of course, I hadn't
packed any for this leg. Swimming wasn't exactly on the list of things
to do in Syria or Iran. Gaëlle, the kids and I had a great few hours
catching up on the beach, but I was getting fidgety, anxious to not
miss my flight. Gaëlle very kindly dropped me at the airport three
hours early.

    Despite my flight being at 5 p.m., it wasn't straightforward. Due to
the rare amount of flights and the non-commercial or non-mainstream
nature of the airline 'Kish Air', I hadn't been able to buy a ticket online
anywhere. All flights were agreed on a first-come, first-served basis and
would need to be paid for in cash. Crazy, I know, but when dealing
with Iran you just have to toe the line. I had specific instructions to
find a door in the airport that said 'Kish Air Office'. My diary said
'brown door, back office, must ask for Kish Air ticket'. After faffing
and panicking a little I came across the mysterious door. Better still,
the lady behind the desk knew me by name and greeted me saying,
'Ahh, you must be Nick. We reserved you a ticket, your dad was very

insistent it was important you have one.' 'Yes, yes, thank you so much.'
I was so relieved and thankful. I paid the $700, she stamped some
piece of paper and gave me a handwritten scrap of paper with the
number 13 on it. Unlucky for some, but this was apparently all I
needed. And, yes, $700 for a flight to Iran is extortion in itself. I
boarded the plane bound for Kish Island, Iran.

The problems we'd found with Iran was that they didn't like the fact
I'd been to so many places and so had simply refused my visa twice
after months of back and forth. The mainland of Iran was therefore
out of the question. We had investigated that from a number of angles,
to try to bypass the system or even attempt to access the country illegally. But this was obviously stupid – we were clutching at anything
we could. My mum, being the saviour as always, found a contact that
knew another contact who suggested going to Kish, an island just off
the mainland that didn't have the same sort of access requirements.
While I'd still need an official guide and wouldn't be allowed to be on
my own, it was possible to visit the island for less than 24 hours without a visa. Why the visa conditions were different, I have no idea – but
I felt it was a lifeline and we took it. This was our chance. Mum had
found the answer. It then of course took several months to find the
right company with the correct understanding of what we were
doing – to facilitate running a marathon safely, without being
deported, and without any trouble from the notoriously strict and
crazy government – and to sort the flights in and out. Finding flights
was a whole other conundrum. Kish Air we came across through a
string of contacts because no mainstream aggregator like Sky Scanner or Jet Cost listed it. Even then, the website was in Arabic. Mum,
the team and even more contacts eventually found an English-
speaking office in Dubai after much frustration.

I boarded the plane and was getting comfortable across the two
seats I had to myself when I noticed the young man on the other side
of the aisle looked incredibly scared. He was literally dripping with
sweat and even physically shaking. My mind was on high alert. I
asked him if he was OK. He just ignored me and turned away. This
was even more alarming. All I could think was, 'Please don't be a
bomber.' It's frustrating how my mind immediately went to that, but

then I realized he was just very scared, and I decided it wasn't because he was about to become a martyr. Rather, a group of ugly, obnoxious and loud men in their fifties were sitting behind us and had started yelling abuse at this guy and taunting him. They were speaking Iranian, or a similar dialect. I only found out what was going on by asking the all-male cabin crew. One of them informed me that the guy was being deported back to Iran – he was being sent to prison for breaking laws in Dubai. The men behind me knew this and were verbally abusing him and getting him very worked up. He was pale. Very pale. I felt sick to my stomach for this guy and without thinking I turned around and shouted at the guys behind me, 'Just stop it. Stop it now.'

To my surprise they did, and the plane fell silent. Oh shit, I'm flying to Iran and I've just hurled abuse at some Iranian nationals. On top of everything I'm not really supposed to be in Iran at all. Shit.

We landed about 40 minutes later. Pulling into the landing space the airport was scarily hostile-looking: lots of barbed wire everywhere, then the plane was surrounded by military and police vehicles as we disembarked. Most of the arriving passengers, of which I was the only 'tourist', were taking it in their stride. No one seemed to have a single worry, except for the poor guy who was manhandled down the stairs by the police as we were boarding an old bus to go to the terminal building. Then everyone gasped suddenly as the deportee made a break for it, running away across the tarmac. A policeman took out his gun, yelled something and fired two shots into the sky. The man, who was really just a boy of about 20, froze and put his hands up. He was immediately taken to the floor with a hard thud by a group of military men with stupid big hats. They held him at the back of the arrivals queue, as if they were waiting for everyone to leave the airport before they dealt with him. As I got closer and closer to the front of the queue, every now and then I would glance around to see what was going on. The young man was standing in handcuffs, shaking and terrified. I had no idea what he had done, but this was the behaviour of a man in fear of his life. I was two people away from the front of the queue when the youth had a fit and collapsed, smacking his head on the floor in the process. The Iranian officials didn't help, they simply stood on his shins with full force to hold him down, while another held a foot on his head. This, I knew, was not the right way to help a man who was fitting. He didn't stop convulsing, and to my horror the guards just started kicking him.

At this point I was called forward, my passport was taken off me and I was asked to stand aside while the other passengers were dealt with. I was now standing with no sight of the boy on the floor. I was shaking, myself. Every ounce of my being wanted to help, but I didn't. I protected myself. I didn't want to be locked up, or worse. I felt the strongest surge of powerlessness I'd ever felt. I was close to being sick.

An hour passed while I patiently stood exactly where they'd asked me to stand, virtually without moving my feet at all. A different guy eventually came back, shoved my passport and some papers at me and, without making eye contact, ushered me away with a grunt and a hand signal towards the exit. I collected my bag, which was now the only one left in the little luggage hall, and walked out of the building for my brief 11 hours on the island. I never saw the deported man again.

I wandered around the car park looking for my chaperone guy, feeling increasingly worried that I was on my own. After what felt like an hour, a man pulled alongside me in his car and shouted, 'Niklas?' He apologized over and over again. He had fallen asleep waiting for me. I told him it was OK, as long as he looked after me now. Relieved to be in the car, we were finally on our way to the hotel that had been arranged as part of the package of support – included within the several thousands of pounds we'd spent on getting the help we needed to ensure Iran was trouble-free. I was relieved he had found me but slightly unnerved by the obvious fact that he didn't seem to know how to drive an automatic car.

It was dark by the time we reached the hotel. This, of course, meant I had to run in the dark. I checked in, changed and met the driver outside. I still had adrenaline racing through my body. I just wanted to run and get out of the country as soon as possible. I double-checked with him that I had water and plenty of it. It was close to 40°C still and very humid, plus I was hungry, having had the long delays. The driver assured me that we would be picking up supplies en route. His words were, 'Just two minutes and there's a garage with a shop and water.' He pointed straight ahead. With that I reconfirmed the plan and started my watch. The plan was to loop around the city, and that we'd need to run it twice to reach the 42 kilometres. All I asked of him was that he stayed behind me and kept an eye on me, and that we could get water asap. He agreed and nodded his head over and over: 'Yes, yes. We go now.'

And so we went. The roads were very similar to that of Turkmenistan: large, empty and sprawling. It was late and there were virtually no streetlights. The driver's headlights were my guide. Two minutes passed, then ten minutes. I asked the driver where the water stop would be. 'Oh no, I forgot. Sorry. We go to next one.' OK, I said, believing it was going to appear soon. It didn't. Four hours and 22 miles passed before I had any water. I was angry, horrendously dehydrated, light-headed and so fed up with this total lack of understanding that water was so important. I must have asked him at least 30 times during those 22 miles. To make matters worse, at every large roundabout, of which there were many, he decided it was best to drive ahead of me about half a mile after the roundabout. I couldn't understand why he did this. Not only could I not see where I was going – it was pitch black – but I was now left to cross a big roundabout on my own. He did this a few times before I put my hand in the air to signal I wanted to talk to him. He pulled alongside and I asked him not to keep doing this, and patiently explained why. He apologized – and then did it again, and twice more. I got very angry and shouted at him through the window. I was hot, sweaty, achy and scared. I couldn't see where I was going, and I still didn't have any water. I felt bad for shouting but it was the only way to get him to finally listen. He held back for two more roundabouts then he forgot and went back to his own ways. I gave up and just picked my way across the uneven roads myself. I was cursing this guy out loud. My head was not in a good place.

Eventually water turned up, but it wasn't quite what I had in mind. My watch read 22.8 miles as I took my first sip of water, which was from a water-cooler machine using my hands as a cup. Having failed to find any shops open, we were basically cruising the Kish Island ring

road, and the only water around was in the back of a car mechanics'
workshop. It was dusty and the place had been abandoned for the
night but left open. I squeezed through a gap behind a petrol station
building and got in. I drank as much as I could while also taking in
quite a considerable amount of air from sucking the water up from my
hands. The driver saw me return to the car and as I walked towards
him he put his thumbs up. A double thumbs-up. I wanted to scream.

I carried on, knowing I had just a few miles to go. Eventually a taxi
pulled alongside me with another guy in the passenger seat waving a
big two-litre bottle of water. My driver had finally got the message
and called his friend to turn up with water. I was grateful – but two
litres. I felt like I could have drunk a lake. I kept smiling as I needed
the driver to get me back to the airport. He confirmed that he'd collect me in three hours, at 5 a.m., and that he wouldn't be late.

I probably don't need to state this but, of course, he was late – by
20 minutes. In fact he was so late that I never saw him again. I gave up
on him and just asked the hotel to order me a taxi instead. At the airport I checked in without trouble, and thankfully made it off Kish
Island with a massive sigh of relief.

Zambia

It was shocking how quickly I was re-immersed into the African ways.
I'd not missed the nightmare that is African air travel. Uganda and
Rwanda are countries of which I have fond memories, but the chaos
of the airports is rather silly. Iran had been brutal. My body took a
battering and annoyingly I was still peeing blood. I'd tried to rehydrate as much as possible during the connecting flights but my body
was still craving water. The Iran run had hurt me. Every time I went
for a wee I'd cross my fingers and hope that it was orange and not red.
I didn't want to do my kidneys any lasting damage, although I probably already had.

I woke up to face another marathon. This was number 187 and a
little cooler than Iran, so things were looking up. I went for my morning wee in the hope that my body had waved its magic wand and

sorted the blood problem in my urine. It had a little, but I was still nowhere near health. As I got my clothes on I remembered I'd already been to Zambia earlier in the trip. I'd jumped off a bridge over the Zambezi. In hindsight I should have run in Zambia and got it out of the way then but, at the time, it was in the plan for later.

The Hilton Garden Inn in Lusaka had put me up – pretty grand, all things considered, but I was just happy for some breakfast and some water. My body was crying out for sustenance. Having had a chat with the general manager and some staff, I found out that they wanted to support the run. I hadn't had any notes in my diary for this one, and assumed I would be running alone. I wasn't. They suggested I run at night because of the heat in the day. I'd told them I'd had worse and would rather get it done so I could sleep, but somehow they twisted my arm and a compromise was reached: a 3 p.m. start. This was a little frustrating but I'd agreed simply because everyone who was due to help me was working until then, and they were looking forward to it. It was one of the decisions that I could have done without. If I ran early it meant it was done and I could relax, but I'd miss the support and they'd be let down. If I ran late, I could sleep, but would have the worry that something would go wrong. Everything mattered so much more now, this close to finish line, and it was draining. I ate a triple breakfast of bagels, beans, rice, chicken, juice and tea. An eclectic mix but the calorific one I needed. After two hours of gorging myself I went straight back to sleep and tried not to worry.

The lift doors opened and I stepped out onto the ground-floor level. To my surprise there were 20 or so staff and a handful of media to greet me. I answered some questions for the local news, had some photos taken, and off we went. I ended up running most of the afternoon on my own, but for the first two kilometres I was joined by a few enthusiastic if totally unfit and not suitably dressed staff. They were all smiles, though, and I was grateful for the company and glad I'd waited. Despite their lack of any form or fitness they tried, and were enjoying it. For that I was pleased.

For the remainder of the run in Lusaka, up until about 19 miles, I ran the two kilometres up and two kilometres back outside the hotel.

The road immediately in front of the hotel was first conceived as an uninterrupted link to Cairo and was named appropriately. Running on this road however was apparently a bit silly because of the traffic, but it was tree-lined and the hotel had put on a water station for me with some oranges in the ground-floor lobby. Thus I decided to run short boring out-and-backs, and tried to rehydrate to the point where I was peeing clear water again, or at least close to it.

At mile 20 John, a local runner and president of one of the city's running clubs, joined me until the finish. As did the general manager and his wife. It got dark pretty quickly and so they laid on the hotel bus to drive behind us as we chatted and the loops continued. It wasn't long before my legs had clocked another 26.2 miles. Every marathon now actually felt like a marathon. They felt like an accomplishment, I assume, because I was so close to the end. They all mattered so much more.

As I saved the run data on my watch and turned into the hotel, I was met by some of the staff, who had ordered everyone pizzas and fizzy drinks for the finish. They cheered, we fist-bumped and tucked into the pizza. I was beyond tired still, but my body had taken in fluid and I was now eating. I wasn't just eating, I was feasting. Feasting like an animal possessed. It was glorious. The cheese dripped down my chin, and my mucky fingernails gripped the pizza, scoffing it without even raising my head. I couldn't care less if I looked like a pig. I was, and I enjoyed it. The longest sleep I'd had in days followed: a whole ten hours.

Malawi

A short flight from Zambia, with no hiccups, I landed into Lilongwe at just gone 4 p.m. I was met by a chap called Goliath. The only way I can describe Goliath is to suggest thinking of all the things that the word Goliath conjures up and then think of the opposite. He was not much taller than five feet, had small features, and was incredibly calm and gentle in nature. He worked for Mel and Tom, who were hosting me at their guesthouse. Goliath only spoke when spoken to, I think probably because he was scared of getting his English phrases wrong and because I was a client. Little did he know that I was just a runner in tramp's clothes. I was a long way from the well-dressed business-man or contractor that the guesthouse often hosts. I tried to tell him this but he kept a business-like politeness.

For two nights, I stayed in the fab Wendels Guest House on the outskirts of the city. Built by the owners, Mel and Tom, they wel-comed me and didn't expect a penny in return. They cooked a scrummy supper complete with strawberries and cream for dessert. We shared travel stories and before long it was time for bed. The insects made their bedtime noises, and the humidity of night increased.

Tom was to be my support for the following day, and being the guesthouse chef he rustled up a hearty breakfast and drinks, along with a jeep-load of water in preparation for the run. At 5 a.m. we crept around the kitchen quietly so as not to wake anyone else, and eventually headed out through the back door to begin the run.

Tom is a tri-athlete himself, and could have run or cycled with me, but instead opted to sacrifice that option in order to stay close by with the car and provide me with anything I wanted. He had bananas, oranges, fizzy drinks and snack bars on hand, plus he even drove far enough behind me to keep an eye out, but not so close that I could hear the engine. This way I could enjoy the peace of the countryside and had water on tap.

The velvet orange trails of Lilongwe's countryside treated me to a gorgeous run as the sun gifted me with one of the most spectacular sunrises I'd ever seen. The dry, single-track paths resemble a carpet of fine dust linking one village to the next, acting as the veins of the nation. As the sun came up, the reds and oranges were projected onto the trees, the trails and the hills. It was marvellous.

Occasionally we'd pass through a town with a couple of mud huts or a stone-built church. Other than that it was just gentle rolling hills of countryside with goats, cattle – and every so often a car or truck would curiously drive past. This was the Africa of my imagination: open plains, a textured pastel pallet with wide boundless skies. Maybe it was because I wasn't expecting such a peaceful run, but I was so happy and light-footed the run seemed to fly by. I even picked up the

pace towards the end. It was all thanks to Tom and Mel, and little
Goliath, for making my stay so easy and by totally understanding my
mindset. I vowed to go back and see the rest of the country, and to
thank Mel and Tom properly. Before I knew it, I was inside Addis airport again, for the 22nd time, connecting to my next flight to Eritrea – my
final mainland African country before the end, and the last where I
had support from the British embassy.

Eritrea

From Addis to Eritrea's capital Asmara is just an hour's flight. As
soon as the wheels touched down it was straight to the embassy to
meet my contact Simon. Simon was the deputy ambassador and a
keen runner. As with all British embassy folk – how can I put this? –
they all have their certain charm. It takes a particular type of person
to be pinballed around the world to work where you're needed. Most
embassy staff I've come across, including ambassadors and their
families, have such fascinating lives of travel and stories of misadven-
ture. Simon and the gang were the same. In fact, as I walked up the
steps of the embassy residence and was greeted by Simon, I could see
the ambassador's wife and an assortment of five others gathered
around a small projector and screen. This group included a British
contractor, some younger kids, and a nun. Everyone looked so wildly
different, with accents from all over the world; it could have been a
real-life game of who's who? With such a short time in the country I
was expecting to be rushed out the door immediately to get running,
but no, this being the British embassy, I was handed a china plate and
a scone with all the trimmings, along with a cup and saucer for a
cuppa. I especially love the rather well-to-do pockets of extreme Britishness in British embassies, but the best bit is that everyone who lives
and works in the residences or at the actual embassies doesn't realize
how odd it is. Be it Nigeria, Italy, Barbados or Eritrea, the outside
world is nothing like the inside of the embassy. It's a little piece of
Britishness on steroids. I'm not knocking it – I love it – but it's just so
very odd.

Everyone was watching the rugby, and so with my cuppa and two or three scones I sat around on British furniture with British people, watching rugby – England versus Wales, no less. England won and shortly after the whistle blew the ambassador returned from a meeting and the other guests dispersed. It was time to run. I was leaving the next day and it was late afternoon already so we got a move on to get running as soon as our British responsibilities of watching the rugby were complete.

With only a few hours before it would get dark I changed into my running gear and headed out with Simon, who led the way in a perfect loop of 42.2 kilometres around the city. He had very kindly measured it all out in advance and was excited to see what I thought of it. Thanks to the drivers and the support team of four, we had water and snacks whenever we needed it. Again it was another day of feeling guilty for people waiting on me, but being grateful and overjoyed that it was an easy run without any worries.

Something shocked me mid-run. Something that I simply wasn't expecting. I'd run all over Africa and had various different languages spoken to me, many I didn't understand. I'd got to grips with some dialects of African languages but was still pretty useless, all in all. Despite that, I'd always make an effort to say hello to everyone and anyone I ran past. Around our fourth mile running through the streets of Asmara, I passed an elderly gentleman with a stick. He was weathered, to say the least. I said hello and waved as I always did. His response was prompt and friendly, but in Italian. He said, '*Ciao.*' *Ciao*?, I questioned and looked confused. I knew that Eritrea had had much influence from Italy but I had no idea that this little part of Africa spoke mostly Italian. I spoke with Simon and the others about the strong Italian influence in East Africa, the lingering colonial legacy. The more we ran, the more I noticed the odd mix of the old Ethiopian and Italian world. The buildings were all classically Italian and beautiful. The town was quaint and more like a village, complete with farmers walking their cattle down the street, church bells and little, very Italian coffee shops with street-front seating. I really started to love the place.

At the halfway point Simon had arranged for some British friends to join us. Tom and Kate were teachers, a young couple who ran with their little baby, Nia, in a pushchair. Another cheery chap called Justin, from the US, also tagged along. We chatted as we continued the loop as they taught me more and more about the country and the city. There was a gentle breeze, sun on my face, and the air was crisp owing to the altitude. We took it in turns to run with Nia in the buggy. I hogged her a little, but they welcomed it. Pushing a little baby in a buggy along a dusty street with pigs and cattle wandering about, to the sound of church bells in an African country, I formulated plans to run future distances pushing a buggy. I even took photos of the make and model so I could buy one and run with my food and supplies in it on long running missions.

Once the light began to fade the temperature dropped. For the last ten kilometres the ambassador joined me and kindly lent me his long-sleeve top to keep warm. At a height of nearly 2,500 metres above sea level, the city gets cold quickly and I wasn't used to anything like this in this part of the world. My teeth chattered as I finished the last few miles. We all finished in good spirits, though. I had a shower, pizza, and some further chats with the ambassador and his wife. I left Asmara wondering about its future. Obviously, the nation has had its fair share of political issues and war in recent history, but despite that the country does seem calm and on the brink of something great. Eritrea could be a real gem. There are however a few blockers. The totalitarian dictatorship, ruled by president Isaias Afwerki, still enslaves all its citizens to a lifetime of national service against their will. This doesn't necessarily involve joining the military but could be described as a service to the state in general. There have been huge numbers of people fleeing or attempting to flee the country because of it. I just hoped that soon all the turmoil would be in the past for them. From an outsider's perspective Eritrea feels like one of the most peaceful places in Africa and Asmara could be such a beautiful and happy city. I got the feeling many people were waiting for the president to die in order to redesign their nation. He's in his eighties and so with new leadership maybe things will improve. There certainly appeared to be plenty of hope for the future.

Sudan

A day after leaving Asmara I arrived in Khartoum, the capital of Sudan. The Corinthia Hotel is supposedly the best hotel in the entire country, and amazingly they were happy to host me for free. I settled in to get some kip before the morning's run. Having missed Sudan earlier in the journey due to the substantial conflict, I was now going to bed apprehensive of what lay ahead. My principal contact in the city was nestled within the confines of the UN, but several months earlier even the UN had pulled out – and with it, my support. This time we had a new contact, who would act as my driver.

The 4 a.m. alarm sounded. I went through the usual rituals of sun cream, covering my knees in some pain-relief gel, downing some water and grabbing an apple before meeting the driver in the lobby. Due to Khartoum's recent and not-so-recent volatility my driver was my blanket of protection. He was my navigator, water provider and safety for the morning and did well to stick by me in horrendously busy traffic. Having ventured out into the early morning light and begun running various loops around the city to make the distance, I concluded just in time for the hotel breakfast. Khartoum was yet another dusty, noisy and busy city to run around – I'd had enough of these drab, grey, largely concrete soulless cities. For a while I thought maybe I was seeing the city in its post-conflict state, but in reality I feel this concrete was just the general fabric of the streets. I think I was at the brink of overkill. I'd seen so much, and I knew what I enjoyed and where I enjoyed running and also what I'd had enough of. I'm sure the people of Sudan and Khartoum are lovely; for now though I was just in the mood to get this mammoth mission completed. I was terrified of spraining an ankle, or something happening that would end the journey.

Plus Yemen was on my mind when I had a phone call. It was Dad. This was never good. Mum and the rest of the team would call with updates; if Dad called, something was wrong. 'Nick, we need to discuss something. Actually, two things.'

'Yep, go for it.' Said with a deep sigh and intake of breath. (Here we go.)

'Your journey into Yemen tomorrow. You might be refused entry. We are still waiting on word that your visa has finally been approved.'

'Right,' I said, wondering what the worse news might be.

'Also, your route into Syria the day after. You know we had planned for you to be driven from Beirut with the driver we'd found through a British-based travel office.'

'Yep.'

'Well, a driver was shot and killed yesterday morning taking another client on exactly the same route you are due to be taking.'

'How? Where? Why?' I needed to know all the details.

Dad explained everything to me. The simple facts were that protests in Beirut had caused extra friction with rebel fighters. The driver had been ambushed and shot through the windscreen mid-journey.

Dad ended the call by saying, 'Think about it, tell us what you want to do. We are thinking of options our end, but it's your decision. We recommend you don't go, and instead run the Syrian marathon another time, after you finish in Athens. We'll work on the Yemen visa for tomorrow. I've got to go, the other phone is ringing.' Naturally my mind conjured various horrible scenarios of death, kidnap and being in that ambushed car.

I thought about our options before leaving a five-minute voice note on the team group WhatsApp, which essentially said: 'We must carry on regardless – make Syria happen – whatever it takes.' I was stupidly just thinking about the mission and not my safety, but I was focused on the finish line and hoping the team could pull off a miracle.

Before I knew it, the time had come to leave the confines of the hotel and head to the airport to begin my journey to Yemen, a country I'd had a visa refused for twice already and as yet was likely to be turned away at the border. Wednesday 29 October 2019. I had just 12 days to reach the finish line, and all I had to do was run another six marathons.

Yemen

Having attempted to push the negative thoughts to the back of my mind, but overall failing to do so, I landed in Muscat, Oman, some-what anxious for the connecting flight to Salalah, the closest city to the Yemen border – where I'd be met by a man called Sadam-Ali, who would drive me the rest of the way. It was a four-hour trip. We still didn't know if my paperwork had been approved. With no embassy and no mandatory responsibility from the British government to come and rescue me if I was to get myself into a spot of bother, Yemen was a country where I'd be totally on my own.

A fixer called Abdulhameed Ghanima worked with a tour com-pany for clients travelling to conduct business in the area. Sadam-Ali was one of his drivers. My trusty bag and I exited the luggage collec-tion area of the pretty snazzy airport in Salalah expecting to see taxi drivers, family and friends waiting for other passengers. There was nobody. It was a ghost town. I frantically called all the numbers I had to try to fix the problem. I even thought I might be in the wrong place. Sadam-Ali finally appeared as I was mid-phone call about 20 minutes later. He wasn't rushed at all, and just pointed at me and said, 'Butter.' He was a quiet chap but I sensed he was a bit of a lad in the right cir-cumstances. Either way, he didn't speak any English, and so our relationship from then on was close to mute despite my best efforts. Heading to a war zone with little to no Wi-Fi and knowing I couldn't rely on my British 4G allowance or coverage, I purchased an over-priced SIM card with a data plan from the small airport kiosk. $40 got me 30 days of up to 8GB of data. Little did I know that the moun-tains between the airport and the Yemeni border were utterly barren and without cell signal, and therefore no access to data.

Sadam-Ali ushered me into his car and off we went. I assumed, wrongly, that we were going straight to the border as planned. We weren't. He muttered the word 'passport' and I understood that we had to do something to resolve some access problems before we could leave. After only ten minutes in the car, Sadam-Ali parked up on a dusty verge and jumped out with the engine still running. He went into what looked like a garage and brought out a car windscreen with help from another bloke. I jumped out to help then moved my bag so they could fit it in the back. This was not how I imagined the day going.

It turned out that he was doing a favour for a friend. He picked up the new windscreen, presumably his friend needed one, and drove off. Within an hour we were on another dusty roadside with some small white concrete buildings. Sadam-Ali instructed me to get out and gestured something which I understood to mean that we were swapping vehicles. We left his car behind, along with the extra windscreen, and climbed into a jeep – bigger, but with no air-con.

In the glove box of the jeep was documentation in an envelope. It had a photo of my face and some writing in Arabic with a few official-looking stamps along with a photocopy. OK, so this was good. Maybe this was the paperwork we needed. Now, Sadam-Ali announced, assertively, 'Yemen' – and pointed toward the mountains ahead. Right, we were finally off. The sun was close to setting already.

The road from Salalah to the border was empty, barring a few trucks that hurtled past in the opposite direction. The mountains were glorious. Despite my nerves about where we were going, and being outrageously tired and hot, I had enough energy to admire the view. Camels occasionally strolled the roads, and driving through the winding hills was a bit like ascending and descending the Alps – albeit with fine dust, some rocks and the occasional small hut or garage and nothing else for hours. I nodded off for about an hour but woke up when Sadam-Ali turned the engine off. We were apparently at the 'hotel' that had been arranged by his boss, Abdulhameed Ghanima. For a while, Sadam-Ali wandered around some 'Biffa' bins on foot, while camels grazed them like a trough. It was pitch black and eerie. He wandered around an abandoned building on what seemed to be a building site while I sat in the jeep looking on, confused. After a long anxious hour of being abandoned in the vehicle, he returned with a worried look on his face.

There was nobody around, just the camels and a dirt road. I later worked out that Sadam had been trying to get in touch with Abdul-hameed to tell him the hotel that his boss thought existed, and that I'd paid for, was in fact just a building site with no doors, windows or roof. Nothing.

Our plan had been to stay here overnight and then travel about ten minutes down the road to the border and cross in daylight. I was keen to sleep in the jeep and wait till morning, but Sadam wanted to go over immediately and find another place to stay in Yemen. It took us about another hour to work all this out, thanks to a friend of his that he called to translate. He spoke some English, but not much, and it was a battle to get my point across. My point being, 'Isn't it safer to cross by day?'

Through various hand signals, gestures and attempts by him to speak English, and my attempts to speak Arabic, we hadn't got much further, but he'd persuaded me to travel over the border at night, and not wait for the morning. I said a number of times that I'd rather wait for the day, but I got a sense that I should just go with his instincts. He knew this region far better than I did – maybe there was a reason we shouldn't stay and travel in the morning.

This all made me far more nervous, mostly because this was a deviation from the plan. We could have slept in the jeep, surely? But no – off we went – I blindly accepted his suggestions, on the most part because I didn't have much choice. I also didn't want to protest too much and cause him to be so pissed off that he'd abandon me.

It was close to 1 a.m. as we reached the border crossing. A dirty track led to a gate with double-looped barbed wire on top, and five men standing around or sitting outside. As we approached they opened the heavy metal gate and beckoned us forwards. We entered and were held in a holding pen for about five minutes while they chatted about something I couldn't understand. Then Sadam gave them my passport, and within a few minutes the next barrier opened and our passports were handed back. We were through.

We weren't through at all. That was just wishful thinking. This was just the security check before the border itself, which was a short drive ahead.

A similar gate with more barbed wire and a vehicle blocking the entrance appeared. We needed to pass through not just Oman immigration but then through to Yemeni immigration. We were now in no man's land between the two countries. The Oman border was fairly quick and I smiled nicely at the guards and their dogs. They let us through. I glanced over to Sadam as we approached the final checkpoint, the Yemeni bit. Alarmingly, Sadam smirked a little and put his finger to his lips and said, '*Shhhh*.' Shit, what did '*shhhh*' mean?

We presented our papers out of the window and Sadam pulled over, jumped out of the vehicle and went inside a building. We were now parked up in a classic border-like car port with walls both sides and barriers ahead and behind us. It was totally dark and silent, except for the occasional dog bark and gunfire in the distance. I could feel my heart beating harder and harder. 'Come on, please let my paperwork be OK, please.'

All of a sudden a chap with a torch came to the window and shone a light in my face. I was pretending to be asleep at that point so as not to cause trouble or start a conversation. I opened my eyes and smiled and said, '*Salam*,' timidly. He ignored me and used his torch to peer in through the windows. Sadam had come back by now, and was speaking in a slightly louder, more commanding voice. More and more military men with AK47s and big stupid military hats came out of the building, their dogs with them. Sadam was asked to open the boot, along with the side rear doors, so they could search the vehicle. Instantly voices were louder and some form of verbal conflict broke out. A few of the guards were now pointing their guns at Sadam. 'Shit.' I just sat still and did as I was told.

An hour later, every single item that was once inside the jeep was now lying on the floor outside the vehicle. Sadam had used me to smuggle counterfeit goods along with some marijuana-like local drugs. I was his excuse to enter the country. I was now standing with two guards either side of me looking at everything on the floor. How had I been so stupid and not noticed what was in the boot? I'd just got in and trusted him. 'Shit.' This isn't good. All I could think was how long I'd be in prison for before they killed me. My mind was racing. They took Sadam away while I was told to sit back in the passenger seat.

Another hour went by with my heart rate going through the roof. I wished I could speak the language and cursed myself for not being able to talk us out of the situation. I should have learnt more Arabic. It was all made worse by the fact I had no way of messaging or calling or telling anyone of the situation. I hadn't had a signal since the airport some five hours ago.

It must have been 4 a.m. by the time Sadam reappeared, looking sheepish. He had somehow bartered with them to let us through. He had sacrificed all of his gear to the guards. For once I was thankful for corruption and said nothing. It seemed they could see I was an innocent mule and they waved us through, allowing me to keep my bag. Sadam said, 'Sorry, we get to hotel now.' He was frightened too, which made me more so.

About five minutes later we had driven slowly over bumpy rocky roads down a hill and arrived at the only visible building for miles around – a small concrete rundown shack serving rice and some stringy meat from a can. The 'hotel' we were staying in looked almost identical to the building site the other side of the border. It had no roof, no windows and there was rubble everywhere, with just a mattress on the floor and a stove with some leftover food in the corner. It was just a concrete shell. But, above all, we were still alive – and I had made it into Yemen. I needed to run a marathon and was livid with Sadam but didn't let it show. He was my only ally for hundreds of miles. I decided to change into my running gear before I slept so that when I woke up I could run immediately. I needed to charge my running watch, which I'd forgotten to do in Sudan. I lay down listening to gunfire in the mountains with my portable charger, phone and watch laying on my chest. I was too nervous to sleep.

Sure enough, Sadam was still sleeping like a baby as I watched the sun appear just after 7 a.m. He had taken something (some drugs?) before he slept. I had to shake him to wake him up.

As I was waiting for him to get ready, I went to use the loo. There wasn't one, of course. I was on a building site and found an alternative hole in the floor. Fortunately I'd remembered to steal a toilet roll from the hotel in Khartoum in preparation for just such a moment. Runners know a morning poo is all part of the prep. Running with a full bowel isn't fun. I used a hole in the floor in a corner of one of the other half-built rooms to do my morning business. Annoyingly it was still half light and I couldn't see how big the drop was. I guessed it was a few inches deep. It wasn't. The splashback covered my compression socks and shoes in shit. My own shit, along with probably other people's shit too. I tried my hardest to compose myself and not scream in frustration – it had been a hell of a night and now a hell of a morning. To make matters worse the temperature outside was on the rise and I was still not running. I had to laugh – otherwise I'd have sobbed for weeks. I cleaned up as best I could using a bucket in the corner with some foul-smelling water in it. By 9 a.m. I'd finally cajoled Sadam awake and had four miles up and down a small but steep hill. Sadam had finally got hold of Adbulhameed, who wanted to talk to me. He apologized for not answering the phone to Sadam the night before, giving the excuse of driving to the border with the wrong paperwork and having to go back. Whether I believed him or not didn't matter, he was at least calling and speaking to me. He informed me that I should run all the way down the mountain to the ocean, where he'd meet me and support Sadam with another car. I agreed tentatively, knowing I'd have to come back up the hill later. We had to be back to Salalah for the 8 p.m. flight out of Oman.

Adbulhameed, with his full face and shiny head, did thankfully meet me at the bottom of the hill and, in an extra turn of luck, I had some signal to message home and tell them I was OK.

Sadam buggered off somewhere else and I didn't see him again, nor all of my bags that were in his jeep, until the run was finished. I ran five miles out and back along the coast near an unnamed town. Unlike most of my preconceptions around the world that were totally wrong, my image of Yemen was spot on. There were many tanks and vehicles full of kids holding AKs dotted along the roadside. Surreally, at one point I passed a family sat on the beach with a kite. All the buildings were littered with bullet holes, there were no obvious shops, and there were frequent bursts of gunfire slightly closer, over the other hills ahead of me. As much as I was frustrated with Abdulhameed, he kept with me in the car with water close by and watched me slog it out in the heat and hills. I was in the last four miles, and the plan was to run back up the hill to the 'hotel', meet Sadam, jump in his jeep and go straight back to Oman. But I was keen not to run up a massive and very steep hill to finish my already horrendously hot and stressful marathon. I asked if we could do another out-and-back instead and then drive up the hill. Adbulhameed informed me that this wasn't possible, explaining that I had pissed off some farmers: apparently my running had scared off some camels in the area and the local famers were livid that they had to walk a distance to find them again. I was totally unaware that the camels were actually owned. In hindsight, of course they were: I'd followed a gaggle of camels down the hill for a while and they were obviously spooked by my running. Abdulhameed explained we should probably just get on with it, concluding, 'Besides, some of the local gangs will know you're here now. So the sooner we leave the better.' I finished my run at the top of the brutally steep four-mile hill.

Still knackered and sweating, and with time running out to reach the airport to get out of Oman and onto my next country – Syria – I bundled into the jeep with Sadam and Abdulhameed and headed to the border. It took two hours to get back through, with some security wanting written reasons from me as to why I was in Yemen. I wrote everything I could in an old leather book, and eventually, after much nervousness, they let us through. The relief at being back in Oman was phenomenal. I was so grateful, despite everything, that Sadam and Abdulhameed had actually made it possible.

My target for this journey was every country in the world. Yemen was number 191 of the official 196. I had one very big hurdle to jump before that target would transition from looking unlikely to likely. That hurdle was Syria – the epicentre of some of the most deadly conflict in the world. With food in my belly, the plane on time, and having actually pulled off the Yemeni marathon against all odds, I was ready.

Syria

Doha was another common connecting hub in this part of the world, and so I knew it fairly well. I went to my usual lounge and buried my head in the 'all you can eat' buffet while I waited for a call from the team. I still wasn't sure what the plan was. I was flying to Beirut, I knew that much. The only option from there was to travel overland into Syria. I was waiting to know if the team had found any miracles to make the overland crossing possible and safe.

The phone call came. There was still no safe option – the original plan to drive across the border from Beirut, along the road where a previous guide had been shot dead, looked to be all we had. The good news, though, if I could call it that, was that the British company, with helpful connections, had found another driver who was willing to drive – but with a slightly different plan. The team had been told that the likely reason the original guy had been shot was to do with him driving a Syrian-plated vehicle within Lebanon. The new plan, if I accepted it, was to meet the new driver at the Beirut airport and use a car with Lebanese number plates. That was the easy bit. We'd then drive to a particular spot between Beirut and the Syrian border before I'd swap into a Syrian-plated car, with a different driver, who would have my visa and then take me across the border and all the way into Damascus, ideally safely. So there it was – a simple but terrifying plan.

I had about four hours to decide if it was all worth the risk. It was a horrible decision to make. I was putting people in danger, along with myself, in order to finish the mission. After reasoning with myself that the drivers would know more than me, and wouldn't want to drive if it really was still dangerous, I called the team and told them it was on. I have no idea how my poor parents coped. Having the relief of me getting out of Yemen, they now had to hold their breath while I transited from Beirut, in the throes of civil unrest, to Damascus in war-torn Syria, and back again.

I had specifically asked for a driver who spoke English so I didn't have the same problem as Yemen. I wanted to at least be able to com-municate. With our options limited, that was supposed to happen but didn't. I was met by an elderly chap in a clapped-out Ford with the boot of the car missing. He held a sign with my name on it, we exchanged some basic hellos, and off we went. The only problem was we were driving the wrong way. We were driving into the centre of Beirut and not out along the road to Syria. I had studied the route on various maps just in case any trouble was coming my way and needed to navigate. My heart sank as I tried to express the problem. He spoke a little French, but it was a Lebanese mix and we couldn't understand each other. I gave up and waited to see what happened.

A while later and literally on the edge of my seat not knowing what was going on, he pulled up outside a small internet cafe and pointed. I'd forgotten that we had requested the driver provide me with a SIM card as part of the package. A lovely bloke called James, the guy who owned the British-based travel company that the team had tracked down to help with the logistics, had suggested this – in the hope that I could at least make contact with the team if things went wrong. The sat phone was useless, as always, and the SIM card would likely be useless too, but we had to at least prepare. I parted with some cash, picked up the SIM card, and then I got back in the car. The only alarming difference was that my driver wasn't the same guy. I had no idea what was going on or where the other guy had gone to, but the new driver pointed forwards, just like Sadam had in Oman, at the road ahead and said, assertively, 'Syria, we go.'

About three or four miles out of the city centre we passed a road-block with a few burning tyres at the side of the road and some banners in a ditch. A couple of rebel-looking blokes wore bandanas over their faces and gloves and hats to shield their identity. This was in protest at the planned hikes in taxes, gas, tobacco and even the pla-cing of charges on WhatsApp calls. The economy was drowning, the government was acting, but in the worst possible way, and the people of Beirut were taking to the streets.

The first protests had taken place on 17 October, but by the time I was there, a few weeks later, things had got worse, and various polit-ical establishments had broken ranks to cause chaos, some say with ulterior motives. The roadblock we faced was nothing more than a simple blockade and checkpoint designed to intimidate, but as we progressed the blockades turned into towering, flaming roadblocks that were impassable. Every car was being turned around, but my driver just looked at me and smiled. This time the blockade was run by his people, or so it seemed. He took a card from his wallet and flashed it at the masked man at the side of the road. We were the only car allowed through. This happened again and again as we passed several big flaming roadblocks surrounded by rebels wielding various weapons, from handguns to semi-automatics and baseball bats. It dawned on me that the driver switch was no accident. My new driver, I soon realized, had to be a member of Hezbollah, the Shia Islamist political party, aka Beirut's militant opposition. By British or American standards the Hezbollah military arm of the party are classed as terrorists and persons of interest. I had no proof this was the case, but with the symbol on the card he flashed looking remarkably like the Hezbollah icon it wasn't hard to put two and two together.

After we'd passed the blockades, and with the driver looking smug, I settled a little – but I also really needed the toilet and so asked him if we could stop. It took a while to get my point across, but he eventually understood and then declined. His words were, 'Caution, caution.' Then he signalled to me to put my head down as we drove the last section, before we switched vehicles. He pulled up in a lay-by with a few other vehicles nearby and told me to grab my things. I was out of the car for less than a minute before my bags and I were loaded into the next car, and I was being driven by a guy who spoke a little English to the Syrian border. We had done the easy bit.

Now to see if the officials on the border were (a) expecting me and (b) would let me in. I knew the drill. I had to queue, hand in my documents, explain why I was travelling, along with why I had so many stamps, including a Yemeni one, and then wait. The driver and I just stood at the desk for about 20 minutes. My passport was handed from person to person behind the desk. I was in an old concrete windowless building. Various immigration officers were watching TV on their phones. The room was about the size of a five-a-side football pitch, with no chairs, no tables, no queuing system, just a long bar-like desk along one wall. I had come at a quiet time and, before long, my papers were stamped and we were accepted. I was in Syria. The only extra weird happening which took me by surprise was an immigration officer asking me to hold my forearm out. He grabbed my arm, moved my bracelets down to my wrist and wrote in permanent marker the numbers 1660089. He said, 'Use this, come back, use this' – and pointed. I think he was doing me a favour somehow. The number was my foreigner ID also written on my paperwork. I think he wrote it on my arm so that I wouldn't have any problem leaving again.

It was a long 40-minute drive to Damascus, but we made it, and I was dropped at the door of Hotel Beit Al Wali into the hands of a guy called Mohammad. The streets of the old town are like the streets of Rome: tiny, beautiful and built of stone. Plenty of houses had shutters and small flower boxes on the window ledges – I had no idea how quaint the centre of Damascus old town was. As for the hotel, it was gorgeous. I was met with a cold flannel, a goody-bag, and two receptionists to show me around the building, a collection of three ordinary Damascene houses from the eighteenth century. In 2009 they were bought, converted and restored to form a charming and modern take on Syrian architecture. There were wooden ceilings, big high-backed chairs and small fountains in most communal rooms. It was truly one of the most beautiful boutique hotels I'd ever seen. One minute I was scared for my life, the next I was chilling out in five-star luxury. Mohammad was my principal contact while I was in the country, and we had dinner together the first evening. He shared stories of his childhood, the violence, the occasional calm, and the external and internal views of Syria. His stories opened my eyes more than I could have expected. His life was not straightforward but, like many other Syrians, he was making the most of it, and largely making do. For me, he spoke English and was knowledgeable; he was the perfect tour guide. I just didn't have any time for touring. I was up early the following morning to run again. This was my last significant marathon to overcome. Run in Damascus, get out and the path ahead looked relatively easy. Sadly Mohammad had to see to some Russian clients who were visiting at the same time and needed to be shown around the city. Instead, he informed me, I would be in the capable hands of Hussein.

Running in the centre of Damascus, although some 200 miles south of Aleppo and the majority of the fighting, would still open me up to a number of potential troubles. Mostly I wasn't worried about being shot or killed, but instead being arrested and detained. It felt like I'd been so lucky for so long that I desperately didn't want the wheels to come off. Was I pushing it too far? I just had a sense that something might happen.

So, with a feeling of nervous excited tension I left the hotel at about
8 a.m. after a breakfast of porridge, bagels and heaps of Nutella. It
was totally peaceful – something of a contrast with what was going on
outside and inside my head.

I was expecting to run around the city with Hussein in the car to
offer me water and a route, but as I stepped outside he met me and, in
his quiet and calm way, described two options for the day. We could
either run around the streets of Damascus with him in the car, just as
I expected, or try to get an agreement from the minister of sport to let
me run around the big football stadium. I know nothing about football, and didn't really expect Damascus to have a stadium or a football
team. I quickly jumped for option (b), any option which would mean
I was safe and could get in the miles. With that he said, 'Good choice.
Now let us go to find the right permissions and we can get you running.' He was enthusiastic and totally accommodating. He'd been a
guide in various cities around Syria for years, and he was good. He
put me at ease and we drove to the stadium, about a 40-minute journey along busy roads from the old town, various passers-by staring at
me through the car window. We made our way to the 'chief of sport',
as Hussein called him. This guy had a triple-barrelled name and an
office that overlooked the stadium, with some fancy-looking painting
on the walls. His office was somewhat cluttered and I could tell he
practically lived in it, but we were in the right place, speaking to the
right person. Hussein informed me later that we were very lucky he
was available. We spoke for about ten minutes about my journey, and
how he could help make my life a little easier and indeed safer. He
eventually agreed and was happy to help, but suggested we don't stay
'too long', because there was a football team coming to train. He
signed some documents, gave them to me, shook my hand sternly and
said, 'You're most welcome in my stadium any time, Mr Nick. Thank
you for visiting Damascus.'

Hussein and I left with our literal stamp of approval and wandered
around to the stadium entrance. It wasn't much to look at, and there
certainly hadn't been any spectators for some years, but the pitch was
immaculate and the faded red running track was flat(ish) with just a
few weeds poking through here and there. As soon as I entered the

stadium I relaxed – halfway there; I just needed a successful exit from the city back into Beirut. I tried not to think about that too much.

Skip ahead four hours and 13 minutes and I'd not only run the marathon without trouble, but I'd actually made friends and played some football. In the most brilliant and bizarre turn of events the under-19s female national football team had turned up to train halfway through my run. I'd initially panicked, thinking we'd be kicked off the track, but instead they stopped me and asked what I was doing. A barrage of requests for selfies and signatures followed, along with a few laps of them running with me.

Then another football team from a neighbouring district turned up to train too. They were older, all men in their twenties who had a match against the Damascus team in a week and so were getting some last-minute pitch time in. We all got on well and they spoke good English. We chatted for a while, and they even let me take a penalty, which I missed. I was just pleased I actually kicked the ball and didn't break my toe. I am crap when it comes to football and so connecting my foot with the ball was something. We laughed.

As I ran on, they watched and waved, and all the while the ever patient Hussein was waiting in the wings. The football team were so well known in the country that they had their own security and their own camera crew to document their training. The whole day was a million miles from what I expected and I even had some pro photos taken of me while running with the team. It turned into one of my favourite days, full of emotion and the unexpected topped off with another lesson in how I should never assume I know a country or a group of people by what I see on the news.

I finished the 26.2 miles, stopped my watch, saved it, and hugged Hussein. I don't think he was expecting that, but hugged back anyway. I was so happy to have completed the Syrian run. When we'd planned it years ago, who would have thought a day in the world's major conflict zone would end up being full of laughter, smiles and togetherness – and culminate in being befriended by two football teams?

Amazingly, after an early dinner, I caught a lift with a party of Russians back to Beirut. The group of middle-aged rich Russian historians were visiting the country for a week. They were heading back to Beirut a matter of hours before I was and had overhead conversations I was having with Hussein and Mohammad at dinner. One of the group, who could speak English, suggested I ride with them for safety in numbers. I was initially conscious not to stray from the plan, but I was thankful and later agreed, having had a phone call with HQ. By dusk I was back in Beirut, after having no trouble at all on the roads going back. It was quiet and some of the blockades had been removed. I shared a couple of hours of exhausting, mostly unrecognizable, conversation with the Russians on the way back, with my eyes heavy. But I was on a high. My brilliant mate Andy had managed to wangle some last-minute time off to pop to two of the three remaining countries before Athens.

Portugal

From a war zone it was weird to step off the plane as if I were suddenly on holiday. I have no idea how soldiers, brave men and women, deal with returning from the horrors of war. I'd not experienced anything like the stress our servicemen and women do – there's not a chance I could hack it in that world – but I spared a few thoughts for the heroes in the world as I waited for my luggage to appear on the carousel in Lisbon airport.

Once I'd reached the hotel and looked myself in the mirror, I had such a sense of relief and elation I cried a little. Maybe it was something to do with my overtired emotional state, I don't know. I was just a mixed bag of happiness and relief. Syria was my line in the sand. The line that signified the last barrier to a successful 674 days on the road to become the first person to run a marathon in every country in the world. It wasn't over yet, and I couldn't hear any fat lady singing, as they say, but I heard a whisper. We now had flipped from unlikely to likely. After Portugal, it was on to Cape Verde, then Israel and then to the finish in Greece. I'd now completed 98.4 per cent of the world.

Marathon 193 was a rather different affair to the last few runs. Andy arrived and we spent a few hours in the lobby bar together talking about what had just happened in the last couple of weeks, not least my being used as a mule for getting drugs into Yemen. As he sipped a beer, and I went for my usual litre of water, he could now own up and tell me how he really thought things would pan out; how he'd bought tickets for this trip half-thinking I wouldn't make it.

I woke up at 6 the following morning to the sound of Andy knocking on my door. This was Andy's 17th marathon with me in total, and his fifth trip out to support me. A trooper. We'd developed a little routine that we didn't even need to discuss any more. He'd wake at the time we agreed, and then come to my room to find me either still asleep or still getting ready. He is a patient man. I was never ready on time. This morning was no different. The British embassy in Portugal had organized a car to pick us up, and a spritely and classically Portuguese duo by the names of Flavia and Ricardo greeted us in reception with the car waiting outside. We were to run a ten-kilometre race that was already going on in the city, cross the line, continue up the coast till halfway then run back. We did just that and they followed in their little Mini with water and supplies. I was very grateful for their support, but in all honestly we really didn't need it. I felt the most comfortable I'd ever felt. Despite the constant drizzle and coastal winds off Lisbon the run was over quickly and without drama. Andy was fresh and I was on a high from having made it through recent weeks.

We made it back in time to catch some late breakfast and then mooched around the markets and the small stone-built back alleys of the old town. It wasn't dissimilar to the old town in Damascus, except cleaner and the shops were somewhat more upmarket. That evening we gorged on steak and chatted the night away.

Cape Verde

Andy, for reasons we still don't understand, had booked a different flight from Lisbon to Praia, Cape Verde, to me. Once I'd landed, to be met by another kind hotel owner, this time a guy called Jorge, I connected to Wi-Fi to find that Andy was having some troubles. His flight had been delayed and was likely not going to arrive in time to run the following day. He was as calm as ever and simply said he'd see what he could do and soldier on. We spoke for a while about the fortune of the delay being to his flight and not mine.

The Picador Hotel is owned and run by Jorge. He had contacted the team after seeing my journey on social media. He's a keen runner, and what he lacked in height, he made up for in hospitality and charm. He was a lovely man who wanted to assist in any way he could. We ate dinner together and spoke about his life as a hotelier and as a chef, sharing tales of travel and adventure. The hotel looked like a series of container-ship boxes from the outside; it was the hospitality on the inside that made it very special.

I drifted off to sleep knowing I couldn't really afford to wait for Andy the next morning. I had to run regardless. But, just before 2 a.m., I woke up to Andy slowly opening the hotel-room door. Jorge had hosted us but we'd agreed to share a twin instead of using two double rooms that he could sell to someone else. Andy was trying to arrive without waking me up. Not a chance. Somehow Andy had travelled through various different connecting islands to make it on time. We turned the light on and chatted for a while. I couldn't believe he'd made it. The flights looked to be close to impossible. Where there's a will there's a way, as they say, and don't I know it. Unfortunately for him, he was not only knackered from the travel faff but if he wanted to run the next morning he'd be getting up in four hours. Andy being Andy, he did just that and didn't complain once.

The next morning saw a media-heavy, out-and-back run along the coast repeated four times. Jorge, along with his friend Orlando, who was chair of the local youth running club, had laid on not only a route with water stations, and a car with music, but also a truck with various TV cameramen clinging to the side. I was expecting a slow plod around the coast with Andy and maybe a couple of others. Instead we had a group of ten, plus Jorge and the gaggle of camera crew. In a slightly weird but lovely way, the TV stations thought it would be good to film the entire run. I'm not sure how long their news segments lasted, but I wondered how on earth five hours of sweaty, mostly grey-skied running footage was going to feature. We all formed a line at mile 26, and ran the last 0.2 hand in hand as we crossed the invisible finish line just outside the hotel where we'd started. I stood for a while beaming into the cameras outside the hotel, explaining to the Cape Verde people live on TV that I had finished Africa, and I was going on to run my last two of the 196 countries in the world. I felt virtually no tiredness from the run at all. I suppose this was adrenaline taking over. Andy and I hugged and I thanked him again for his endless support. We'd seen some pretty great places together, ever since he flew out to Rio to join me the first time, which seemed like a lifetime ago.

Israel

Country number 195, Day 670. Despite being tantalizingly close to the end, I still had to successfully get into Israel and out again. Israel has one of the most stringent security and immigration checks of anywhere in the world, and with my passport and my recent travel history leaving a trail through Syria, Yemen, Libya and beyond it wasn't a guarantee they'd let me in. This was another massive unknown and all I could do was hope, cross my fingers, and arrive with shedloads of paperwork explaining why I wasn't a dodgy character and that I was just a dodgy runner trying to set a world record. I was nervous, very nervous. Landing into the airport in Tel Aviv I didn't know what was going to happen. Having been allowed to board the plane to fly to the country in the first place I hoped was a sign they would allow me in. Once I was there in the immigration queue, though, I realized that wasn't necessarily the case.

The airport was neat, tidy, clean and orderly, with lots and lots of cameras and even more officials standing around looking official. It dawned on me as I stood in the queue awaiting my turn that I had in fact already been to Athens and run a marathon there about six years previously, so although it didn't count for the record, for me in my lifetime, I had now been to every country in the world, and only really needed one marathon to have run in every country.

Standing in the queue I had sweaty palms. I'd been carrying around several reams of paper, on and off, for the last month, outlining my

journey, who I was, and why I was coming to Israel. It was all a bit battered and tatty, but I had everything I should need to be admitted.

I could see that every so often someone would be turned away as
they reached the glass immigration booths at the sharp end of the
queue. For those that were sent away, they were given a piece of paper
and chaperoned to an office in the back corner. With ten or 15 lines of
30 or so people in each one it was a busy room, full of mostly tourists
queuing for entry, but still quiet. I think everyone was just as anxious as me. I moved slowly in the line. I'd been in so many airport
queues my calculation of two hours to reach the front was only nine
minutes out. I felt smug that my maths had somehow worked that out,
even without a big enough data set. I walked up, handed the chap in
the glass booth my passport and said, 'Hello.' He looked at it, flicked
through the pages, and twisted his head and the passport at all angles
to examine various stamps. All went quiet for a moment before softly
and politely he looked over his glasses and said, 'Syria?' 'Yes, a few
days ago,' I replied. 'Yemen?' 'Yep, the day before Syria.' I promptly
handed him my paperwork along with the pre-typed letter explaining
why I wanted to be in Israel and what for. I then went into full polite
mode, spieling off the explanation I'd said so many times before: 'I'm
running a marathon in every country in the world.' There was a brief
pause. He smiled and said, 'OK', closed my passport, and then gave
me a deli-counter-style ticket and summoned a chap to take me away
to the naughty corner. I thought for a moment I was straight through.
No such luck. He was toying with me, or at least it felt like it.

It took another two hours of sitting nervously in the corner tapping
my foot while watching plane-loads of people filter past before I was
seen. It was an agonizing wait. A very smartly dressed young woman
with a gun-holster and Tomb Raider-like appearance beckoned me
over as she shouted my number, 61. I shot up out of my seat and braced
myself. She was distracted a little, and wasn't really paying full attention, while I was transfixed on everything she was saying. I did
everything I could to appear the best possible citizen. She asked, 'So
why come to Israel? And why have you been to so many places?'
I spoke quickly, explaining everything, and finished by saying, 'I
can show you my website, if you like. I've been on the telly.' I was

desperate. She said, 'Yes please,' and also asked to see my Instagram. I flicked through the web pages and my Instagram, reeling off the stories from the past few weeks, and my motives for why I was raising money for charity too. She interrupted me and said, 'Wait here' – but looked at me and smiled. I wasn't sure what was going to happen, but a few minutes later she came back with two other officers. She explained to them what I was doing, and then surprisingly asked for a selfie. We posed, and she laughed a little, and told me to follow them. I was escorted to the entrance of the luggage hall. They simply said, 'Have a nice day, nice to meet you. Good luck.' That was that. I was in.

Daniel was waiting for me with a sign written by hand. He was British but had moved to Israel some years ago with his family. He was pleased to see me, even if he had been waiting for over five hours for me to appear. He, like the rest of the saintly people on the journey, was a patient man and understood the importance of getting through. I explained that most of the problem was just waiting to be seen.

My penultimate marathon was organized by Daniel. He had heard me on the radio some 15 months prior and was keen to help, but had been expecting me to arrive months earlier. The expedition website had the wrong information on it. Only thanks to the work of Veton and the team had it all been rearranged. The website was one of many things that had not been properly administered because we had no money, time, energy or resources to do anything about it. It was mostly right – but by this point I was beyond caring.

We jumped in Daniel's car and drove the 30 minutes to his house on the outskirts of Jerusalem. By now it was dark and a little chilly, plus his family were all asleep, so we made a quiet entrance as he showed me to the guestroom in the attic. Daniel is a strong runner and therefore knew many other decent runners in the city. He had put a call out on Facebook to ask if anyone wanted to support, and a group of about ten turned up the next morning.

I think anyone who visits Jerusalem, religious beliefs asides, is struck by the uniqueness of the city. The history, the faith and the political and turbulent past of both sides of the fence can't be ignored. Putting all the classical Israel/Palestine-focused discussion to one side, the city, surrounding suburbs and countryside are all beautiful and thought provoking. Even just driving to our starting point from Daniel's home was mesmerizing. Everyone needs to see Israel at some point in their lives. Its place in religious history is something very powerful. (It's worth noting that Palestine is not technically an internationally recognized country in its own right and therefore we made the decision early on that it was unnecessary to run there. Unlike other questionable territories, this was a place that wasn't on any of the 'official country lists'. Coupled with the fact it would pose a substantial risk to my life, it was an easy decision. Palestine is not a recognised country. Simple. It also didn't make it into the Guinness World Record Guidelines based on the official United Nations list.)

We gathered a little after 8 a.m. on a side road by Daniel's car. We waited for a few stragglers and off we went. My penultimate country of the expedition was completed in style. The run was such an escape into a different world. I learnt loads about the city, the people, religion, history, you name it. I had a crash course in everything Israeli and more. From Tel Aviv's Bauhaus architecture, the fact it's one of the rare countries to have more trees than it did 50 years ago, and that it takes the crown for creating voicemail technology. Much of the discussion was centred around religion – which was fascinating – even if I can remember very little.

The group of runners I shared the 26.2 miles with had carefully picked a route around Jerusalem that took in all of the most famous sights, plus a market halfway round. For most of the four hours spent jogging around the city I didn't leave the side of an American guy called Jonathan. He had lived in Jerusalem for some time and worked as a tour guide. He knew everything and anything.

In the market I purchased a couple of bowls and some spoons, which I then realized I had to carry for the remainder of the run. I'd done this kind of mid-run shop many times before and so just tucked them under my arm and ran the last half marathon with them neatly stowed. A little uncomfortable but my uncomfortable bar had been lifted somewhat and so it didn't bother me at all.

The official Athens marathon started at 8 a.m. on Sunday 10 November. I left Israel on the morning of Friday 8 November a little after 10.20. I was just two days away from success as I left Tel Aviv. I boarded my flight, smiling internally as I looked out of the window of the plane. We touched down in Athens just after midnight. As my feet touched Greek soil my body fizzed with overwhelming joy and I was blanketed with goose bumps from head to toe. I was smiling from ear to ear. I stepped off the plane onto my final piece of untrodden tarmac. I was in my final country, to finish what I'd started 672 days ago. But it wasn't over yet.

11

195 Down, One to Go

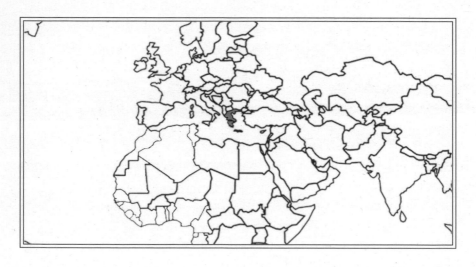

Greece

Greece

Standing in line at Athens airport I looked around at the 500 or so tourists all eager to get through the boring bit and enjoy a break in the city. Most of the others here were likely to be running the Athens marathon too, an event that attracts 20,000-plus runners each year to the birthplace of the marathon. All of a sudden I was surrounded by runners for the first time in a long time.

Before I reached the baggage claim area I called my dad. No answer. I called my mum. No answer. I wanted to share my joy and relief to have made it to Greece on time. I wanted to express my thanks and excited impatience to hug them. Nobody I called answered. Everyone was in the air flying to see me. I had arrived before anyone else. Typical.

Then Chris, my brother, arrived, and we hugged. He said, 'Well done, bro – never do that again.' He was smiling but was referring to the fact that Mum and Dad had sacrificed the last few years of their retirement to propel me around the world from the confines of a laptop back at home, and I really shouldn't put them through that again. He was right. Chris and I taxied to a hotel in the centre of the city called Coco-Mat. It was new and fancy and had agreed to host us and the gang at an impressive discount. The team had arranged for me and various guests to occupy most of the hotel for the final few days of the journey and to use it as a base pre- and post-marathon. At first, it was just me and Chris. Then suddenly everything started happening too fast. I couldn't keep up with the flow of friends and team members arriving. The videographer and photographer from sponsors Pro Direct arrived first, and then some fans who had been following the journey, and then Scott, who was filming for the

documentary, and more and more and more. Every time I saw someone I was so pleased to see them, but had no time to say a proper
hello. It was hectic and intense. The group that assembled later that
evening was 40-strong with close friends from school, friends from my
old life in finance, and many, many friends from around the world
that I'd met during the challenge.

It was especially moving to see Rowena again. Ro had hosted Dani
and I when we travelled through Barcelona for our 30 days of interrailing two summers earlier. She went above and beyond by also
driving us to Andorra and then on to Nice to save us the hassle. I had
briefly disappeared upstairs to my room to grab my laptop when I
pushed the button for the lift to come back down, the doors opened
and Rowena was standing there with her friend Lynn. It was so great
to see her. She is one of the most kind-hearted people in the world.
She had supported more or less from the beginning and was now here
at the end. She was a stranger, a total stranger before I started, and
now I'd move mountains for her. She, and everyone else converging
on the hotel, had made the journey not just possible but enjoyable,
enriching, happy and full of brilliant life-changing memories. At
dinner that evening there were too many people to speak to and
thank without cutting every conversation short and feeling rude.
Besides, I was running around like a madman trying to orchestrate
everything from moving tables to speaking with kitchen staff. I was
now doing more than I had in years. I was in turbo mode. I knew
I had no need to preserve any energy for future countries because I
had none left. I was on autopilot trying to play host as best I could.
I hadn't even considered that this would be what it was like, but I
wasn't complaining.

We were nearly all assembled to have the final meal before the big
day – but Mum and Dad still hadn't arrived. They were late. Classically late. They had a reputation for being late to any party, but I'd
expected them to at least be on time for this one. They weren't, but
eventually they arrived with big grins on their faces and outstretched
arms, having negotiated the see-though glass steps leading down from
the hotel entrance without mishap. Most of us had nearly finished eating, but I didn't mind, it was just so lovely to see them again. I hugged

them both and we shared a few tears as we held each other for a while standing in the lobby. It was the hug that meant the world. Quite literally. They had endured as much as I had, and in less than 24 hours it was to come to an end. Mum and Dad had with them Brenda and Yvonne. These two lovely ladies are like family to me. Both of them and their brilliant, but sadly late, husbands had been so, so pivotal in my life that it was wonderful to have them with me for this special of very special occasions.

I was also waiting for Veton to arrive. Veton was one of the most valuable people in terms of making the journey happen. He'd pulled strings that I didn't even know could be pulled. He did eventually arrive after a long nine-hour drive from Kosovo. Then the other missing couple I'd not caught site of yet, Laura and Leo, godparents to me and my brother, emerged through the crowd. This was getting overwhelming.

As if things weren't emotional enough, the face I'd been waiting to see walked through the door. Kevin. The man who started this thing. The man who had changed my outlook on the world. The man who had inspired the journey walked through the door with arms open wide and his smile even wider. Kevin Webber, who was diagnosed with terminal prostate cancer and given two years to live, walked through the door five years after his diagnosis. Sadly there is no way out of the grips of cancer for Kev, but he lives like he has beaten it; with a smile and love in his eyes. He was the reason I'd dreamt up the challenge, but at the time I discussed the idea with him we weren't expecting him to be around to see the start, let alone the end. Amazingly, he was not only alive but he was there to run the final marathon with me.

Seb and Seren, two community fundraising managers from Prostate Cancer UK, had also come out to see the mission to a close. We now had the whole 196 family under one roof. When I met Kev out in the desert running the Marathon des Sables I'd also met other brilliant athletes, brilliant minds and friends who I'd trust with my life. Jeff Smith and Chris Patterson were two of those brilliant people and were also in the Coco-Mat hotel, about to celebrate the end with me. It was to be the finish line of my dreams. I had all the people I admired the most in the same place. They had all selflessly followed, supported and chipped in to make the journey complete.

I was a mess by all accounts but held it together till gone midnight when we all eventually withdrew to bed ahead of the big day.

The meetings with the camera crew had been had. The runners who planned to run with me were organized, and Veton took the reins to conduct the final 24 hours of the mission. The runners, supporters, sponsors, media and camera crew met outside at 7 a.m. on day 674. My final marathon was upon me. Athens – I'd run the race before many years earlier and so knew what the deal was. Hordes of runners from all over the world jostle for places on the coaches lined up at various points throughout the city centre, ready to ferry everyone to the start line. It was chaos but, magically, with umbrella held aloft to show the way, Veton took control and mustered us all onto a coach amid the convoy. We drove the hour or so through suburbs then eventually reached the small but historic town of Marathon. Everyone was still pretty sleepy and the atmosphere subdued. I was excited, but content and just taking it all in. Then, in the mayhem of the start line I got snarled up in a lovely but protracted interview with Vassos from the *Chris Evans Breakfast Show* and I lost nearly all of my group. I turned around and they were gone. Crap, this wasn't ideal.

About an hour later, with only minutes before the official start of the race, 95 per cent of the group had miraculously found one another. Then came the rain. We huddled together under our ponchos and makeshift umbrellas that we'd fashioned from plastic sheets, waiting for the race to begin. It was chaos, but we were all happy, laughing and ready for a run. Veton, in all his wisdom, had a brilliant idea of holding one of the oversized massive orange balloons used to denote each starting pen of the race as a marker for our group. That way we could look ahead or behind and see where the body of the group was throughout the race. He would be our pacemaker. It worked, despite the fact the balloon wasn't easy to hold.

We ran and ran, occasionally waited for others, ran some more, rejoined the group, had some photos, ran as a solid unit for a while, separated again, made it back together and eventually, just a few miles from the end, managed to somehow re-form as one solid group to run to the finish line hand in hand. The last ten kilometres of the Athens marathon are more or less all downhill, and so we progressed gently, with little effort, making sure the whole team was more or less a unit as we approached the Panathenaic Stadium. Also known as Kallimarmaro – literally 'made of beautiful marble' – the stadium, an extended horseshoe-shaped, white-tiered marble monument to running, was a fitting finish line to such a journey.

We crossed the line, hand in hand, with our smiles bigger than ever and tears in our eyes. Everyone was feeling the emotion of the day; even the sun had come out. The crowd of team, family and friends in the grandstand were louder and more visible than any – with a huge '196' banner brought out especially by my folks, flags and balloons, it was impossible to miss them. After crossing the line I hugged Kev. And then Mum and Dad. 'We did it, we did it, we did it,' that's all I kept saying to them. We had indeed done it. I had run a marathon in every country in the world. We jumped for joy and embraced with one big family hug. Kev and I crossing the line hand in hand was the best finish of any race I'd ever had. I was elated, relieved and emotionally spent.

The finish line was captured perfectly in a single photo. It shows Chris, who I met in the desert when I met Kev; Gary, who I'd trained with for years and who I used to work with; me; Andy, who had now completed 19 marathons with me around the world; Kev, who inspired the whole mission; and Veton, who had helped to make the whole thing possible.

We'd always said 'the world or bust', and although I'm now penniless, we didn't go bust. We had done it. I may now be poor in money, but I'm rich in life beyond my wildest dreams. And, better still, we had raised over £200,000 for Prostate Cancer UK – and are still receiving donations. Even better than that, the awareness of this cancer has spread far and wide, and through conversations lives have been saved. If you're a man and over 40 years old, you need to have your prostate checked now. Don't wait, don't be embarrassed – it could save your life. If you're not a man or over 40, the chances are you know somebody who is.

Unlike that sundial I'd stumbled upon in Croatia, it had most def-initely not been brief and it had not been tedious. A marathon in every country in the world in 674 days, 12 hours, and 2 minutes. A world record and a world first.

Would I do it again?

Oh, go on then.

Dad . . . shall we?

Kit List

My kit varied from continent to continent. Bigger bulky jackets in places like the Arctic Circle and sweaty vests in the likes of humid Asian summers. My nutrition, clothes, gadgets and passports all changed frequently in an often failed attempt to travel light with what I needed most. The list below is everything I took with me at some point during my 674 days on the road.

Osprey backpack – Farpoint 40
Osprey running backpack
Passports (multiple)
Flight documents
Visa documents
Plane tickets
Wallet
Backup wallet
$1,000
£250
Diary
Notepad
American Express Platinum
Priority Pass lounge access
4 digital banking cards for
    Europe and the world
Pen and pencil
16GB SD cards x 60

128GB SD cards x 40
SD card case
iPhone XS
iPhone 7
iPhone charging cables x 4
Portable battery pack x 2
iPad Pro
iPad Pro charger
MacBook Pro
MacBook Pro charger
Canon 5D Mark IV
24-105mm lens
400mm lens
50mm f/1.4 prime lens
10-18mm lens
GoPro HERO5
GoPro HERO6
GoPro HERO7

GoPro batteries x 22
Canon batteries x 11
Canon battery dock charger
Garmin watch
Garmin watch charger
Suunto watch
Suunto watch charger
US extension cable
Universal travel adapter
Do Sport Live shorts
Do Sport Live leggings
Do Sport Live vests x 4
Rehband compression socks
Prostate Cancer UK banner
Prostate Cancer UK vests x 2
Mavic Pro Drone
Mavic Pro charger
Mavic Pro batteries x 4
Adidas Ultraboost trainers
    (running)
New Balance trainers
    (non-running)
Juice Plus tablets x 500+ (fruit,
    veg and nutrients)
Every injection under the sun
Kinetic Six satellite phone
SPOT Gen tracking device
Tile tracking devices x 4
Underwear x 4
Normal socks x 4
Travel trousers x 1
Hairbands x never enough
Soothers

Imodium
Lifesystems water bottle
Hand cream
Painkillers
Very strong painkillers
Malaria tablets (*c.*220)
Toothpaste
Toothbrush
Mouthwash
Electric shaver
Soap x 2 bars
Life Venture sun cream
Compeed blister plasters
Life Systems first-aid kit
Spare plastic bags for wet
    clothes
Dry bag
Flipflops
Souvenirs – far, far too many
Special items that went to every
    single country in the world:
Set of Do Sport Live clothing
Arch Max running belt (worn
    for every marathon)
New Balance shorts (worn for
    every marathon)
Buff (worn for every marathon)
Kev's water stamp card from
    MDS – gifted to me to take
    around the world
A photo of my family
A photo of Jeff, Kev, Rory and
    me on the first day of planning

Running the World in Numbers

196 countries visited

211 marathons run

755,000 miles flown

8,271 kilometres run

10,000,000 running steps

6,303 daytime kilometres

1,968 dark kilometres

-25°C coldest marathon

+59°C hottest marathon

22 pairs of trainers (3 pairs lost, 2 pairs eaten by pigs, 17 pairs worn out)

690,000 calories burnt while running

1,200 litres of water drunk while running

101 marathons run with no food

34 marathons with food poisoning

9 presidents ran with me

41 British ambassadors ran with me

5,000+ running buddies ran with me

400,000+ photos taken

9 passports

60 bribes

499 airports

344 flights on big planes

111 flights on tiny planes

5,900 kilometres driven

18 trains travelled

50 buses

290 taxis

29 metros

11 hitch hikes

100 per cent carbon footprint offset

400 Mission teas drunk

500 nutrition supplements taken

1 hit by a car

3 marathons with kidney infection

2 muggings and attacks

35 no-meal days

1 horrendous tooth infection

1 dog bite

489 different beds

159 hotels stayed in

59 host families

88 school visits

29 camp fires

92 different animals seen

40 languages in contact with

29 volcanoes

5 mountain ranges

700 interviews and articles worldwide

3 billion people reached

Acknowledgements

I was the lucky one who travelled the world to run a marathon in every country, but I wouldn't have even started, let alone finished, without such a vast network of unfathomably selfless and brilliant people.

To my mum, thanks for being my shining light in times of darkness and the voice on my shoulder that gave me the confidence to continue.

To my dad for booking every flight, for the endless spreadsheets, the patience, and the unwavering attention to detail.

To my brother for the phone calls of stability that kept me sane.

To my family, loved ones and those who lived it with me, thank you. A million times, thank you. The list below is my attempt at recognizing all those who deserve their name in lights.

My Enduring Team

Ali White, Carla Kerr, Veton Kasapolli – My right hands
Chrissie Barnett and Rina Domi – Accommodation Management
Rebecca Edmond – Insurance Management
Laura Penhaul – Performance Coach
Mark Beaumont and Jeff Smith – Mentors
Evie Seventi – Psychologist
Dawn Rushden – Travel Editor
Craig Sykes – Security, Kinetic Six Ltd

Nick Haddock – Security Support
Colin Davidson – Doctor
Maz, Faisal and team at Universal Visas – Visas
Emily Blackman, Patrick Warner – Social Media
Scott Barnett, Spark Media – Production
Bonny and team at Spark Media – Photography, Filming and Editing
Chris Debney, Stage 23 Productions – Production, Photography and Filming
Andy Swain – Running Support
Dani Baugi – On the Road Support

Extended Support

At Prostate Cancer UK my thanks to Angela Culhane, Seb Pearce, Seren Evans, Gary Haines, Mike Banks, Ellie Ulrich and team.

For specialist travel consultancy thank you to Koryo Tours, Lupine Travel, Stan Tours.

From Tent 105, my running companions from the Marathon des Sables, Kev, Jeff, Selina, Rich, Chris, Rory and Phil.

An extra-special thank you to everyone who donated online, offline and everything in between. I've tried to name everyone who donated in the list at the back of this book. Inevitably there are thousands of names that were either not given in full or were left anonymously. You have all helped to save lives. From myself, Kev and Prostate Cancer UK – thank you.

I also owe special thanks to staff, personnel and individuals from: the United Nations; the British embassies and the ambassadors; Presidents from around the world who met, ran and hosted me; the prostate cancer clinics I visited; families who hosted me; every running club and runner who joined me on the road; all my friends who sent messages of encouragement and didn't forget about me while I was away; the drivers and security staff who kept me safe; the hundreds of schools I visited, along with their staff and pupils; the camera crew; the production company; the private benefactors; social media supporters; the TV stations; reporters, podcasters and newspapers who all helped to spread word of the journey so crucially; the various celebrities and athletes who reached out, plus the ones who will continue to inspire me; the hospitals I visited both as a patient and as an interviewer; and of course everyone who made access to the dangerous and volatile countries possible and safe.

The true extent of those who deserve thanks is literally worldwide, and despite these long lists, I fear I've missed many names. To anyone who played a role in this journey or joined me on the road, your actions and kindness have not been forgotten. Thank you.

Special thanks to

Abdulhameed
Adrian Sandiford
Al Rawashdeh
Amy O'Rourke
Ana Maria Ruano
Andre Hewitt and family
Andrei Safronenko
Andy and Claire Ryall
Andy Swain
Angel Cortizo
Anna Davies
Annabelle Richards
Antonov Artiom
Ardian Haxhiu
Atkina Alina
Avamada Lodge
Berhan Araya
Bernhard Garside
Bertrand Dijoux
Bob Bracken

Brenda Atkins
Céline Coyac Atindehou
Christian Rebehn
Colin and Pip Davidson
Craig Sykes
Dani Baugi
Daniel Pearlman
Danijela Čičarević
Dario Pitta
Dennis Whitelaw
Diamond House Guesthouse
Dinah Newton
Dominik Baxa
Douglas Lee
Dragana Kilibarda
Duncan McBaine
Eleonor Tress
Ene Vithla
Evelyn Talavera
Farah Mjalli

Fiona and Giles Vigar
Flávia Lima
Francesca Filipet
Frederik Hulsmans
Genevieve Haddock
George Culmer
George Fahim
George Redman and Dilcia
  Aguilar
Guranda Tordia
Hajar Bennouna
Heinz Prelle
Henry Vines
Howard Wang
Ivo van Haren
Janet Brixey
Janet Stokes
Jannatul Abedin Rumpa
Jar Cher
Jardin de la Paix
Jacques Hamou
Jay McBain
Jean Christophe Dauphin
Jean Hartland
Jenny and Martin Baxendale
Jess and Vannesa Calderon
Jocelyne Charpentier
John Ragatz
Jon and Julia
Jorge Silva
Julie Vandassen
Kate Lush
Katharina Bohnmag
Kikkan Landstad
Kim Freestone

Klassik team
Kudzayi Nheweyembwa
Laura and Leo Lions
Laura Penhaul
Lennart Rasmussen-Lagnehag
Leonida Manochi
Lidiane Andreatta
Liliana Yanez
Lord Cranborne – Ned
Lord Shaftesbury – Nick
Lorelle Misikam
Lucia Nunez
Lufi Huakau
Maja Katarina
Marco Pino
Maria Huete
Mark Beaumont
Mark Duffy
Martin Lake
Mary and Gerrard Leroy
Matt Field
Matt Knights
Matt Nottingham
Mayhew Grace
Maz and Faisal
Mehdi Elmejdoub
Mel and Tom
Michael Woodward
Michelle Yonkeu
Mike and Sue Reynolds
Mike Ellis
Mirjam Heldmann
Natalie Doherty
Natasha Reid
Nelson Annandale

Nicholas Albert
Nick Haddock
Nicoleta Voinea
Nikki Tombs
Norman Swan
Oli Wareham
Orna O'Beirne
Patrick Warner
Quartier Sabangali
Radka Königsmarková
Rafayel Khachikyan
Rangga Permana
Razi Ahmed
Rifa Naser
Riley Maule
Rodolphe Cazavant and family
Rodrigo Quezada Ramirezon
Roesil Black
Rosemary, Tony and Kate
  Duckett
Ruairi O'Connell
Sarm Strong
Sheena Worrell
Sheldon Silvera
Simon Winter

Simone Jorge
Stuart and Lisa Grant
Sue Batten
Sue Shewell
Tai Smith
Tasa Sirinarachatr
Tawhidul Bari
Terry and Jean Gauntlett
Thinley Dorji
Tracey Morgan
Tryphos Nghitewa
Tumeliso Mokhethi
Val and Julian Forder
Venta Santigua
Veronica Enciso
Veton Kasapolli
Visar Vrenezi
Xavier Miamb
Xenyia Buyukcelik
Yaseen
Yasmin Li
Yosra Makky
Yvonne Pharoah
Ziad Matta

Hotels

My thanks to everyone who provided me with accommodation of any kind – be it a plush hotel, a spare room, a bench, a tent, a car or an airport bench. Many people who helped to put a roof over my head will go unsung, but the following hotels all kindly hosted me for free and their support was invaluable.

One King West Hotel &
Residence

Hostel Miami

Orange Hill Beach Inn, West
Bay Street

Bel Fle Missions Hotel

Renaissance Jaragua Santo &
Casino

Chateau Miramar

Jasmine Inn

Monique's Guest House

Maca Bana Luxury Boutique
Resort

Blue Lagoon Hotel & Marina

Fox Grove Inn, Mon Repos, St
Lucia

St Kitts Marriott Resort & The
Royal Beach Casino

Ocean Point Resort & Spa

Blue Bay Antigua

Mango Island Lodges

Cobblers Cove

Dreams Sands Cancun Resort
and Spa

Ramada Princess Hotel and
Casino

Courtyard Marriott San
Salvador

Porta Hotel Antigua

George Redman & wife Dilcia
Aguilar

Crowne Plaza Managua

Costa Rica Marriott Hotel San
Jose

Panama Marriott Hotel

Bogota Marriott Hotel

Venezuela Marriott Hotel Playa
Grande

Guyana Marriott Hotel
Georgetown

Torarica Resort and Casino

JW Marriott Hotel Rio de
Janeiro

Sileo Hotel

Sheraton Montevideo Hotel

Aloft Asuncion Hotel

Matildas Hotel Boutique

Casa Fusion Hotel Boutique

JW Marriott Hotel Lima

Tierra Viva Arequipa Plaza Hotel

Inkaterra Machu Picchu Pueblo
Hotel

JW Marriott El Convento Cusco

Yanggakdo International Hotel

Casa Gangotena
Boutique Hotel

Renaissance Boston Waterfront
Hotel

Days Inn by Wyndham London
Hyde Park

Marriott London West India
Quay

Moroccan House Hotel

Ibis Casablanca Hotel

Semiramis Hotel

Lamaraz Arts Hôtel

The Palms Luxury Boutique
Hotel

Kololi Beach Club

Dunia Hotel Bissau / Azalaï
Hotel 24 de Setembro

Villa Oasis

Grand Hotel Central
  Conakry
The Farmington Hotel
Accra City Hotel
Royal Beach Hotel
Ahomé Maison d'Hôtes
Maison Rouge
Hôtel Résidence La Falaise
Cesare Balbo Inn
Hotel L'Adagio
SH Boutique Hotel
Protea Hotel Windhoek
  Fürstenhof
Thaba Bosiu Cultural Village
Diamond House Guesthouse
The Gift Hotel
Tequila Moon Hotel
Cuningham's Island Guest
  House
Tube N Axe Boutique Lodge
  Backpackers and Camping
Addo Dung Beetle Guest Farm
Crocodile Bridge Safari Lodge
Berry Bliss Guest House
Pennywise Cottages
Simunye Country Club and
  lodge
La Mariposa Mauritius
Avamada Lodge
Coral Strand Smart
  Choice Hotel
Centric Atiram Hotel
B&B Hotel
Hearth Hotel
Holiday Inn Express
  Berlin – Alexanderplatz

Boutique Hotel Seven Days
  Prague
Living Hotel Kaiser Franz
  Joseph
Hotel Parlament
Brim Hotel aka Reykjavík Hotel
  Center
Dream Hotel
DoubleTree by Hilton Zagreb
Generator Copenhagen
Radisson Blu Waterfront Hotel
Hostel & Apartment
  Diana Park
Alexander House & Utopia Spa
Tallink Spa & Conference Hotel
Clarion Collection Hotel
  Valdemars
Comfort Hotel LT Rock´n´Roll
  Vilnius
Victoria Olimp Hotel
Ibis Kiev City Center
Klassik Hotel
Rin Grand Hotel
Dream Hostel Warsaw
Envoy Continental Hotel
The Domain Bahrain Hotel
  and Spa
Centara Muscat Hotel Oman
Kempinski Hotel Amman
Hostel Mostel
Hotel Amira Istanbul
Hotel President Sarajevo
Hotel Šumadija
Hotel Podgorica
Antiq Palace Hotel Ljubljana
B&B Hotel Park

Astera Apart Hotel
Ibis Styles Tbilisi Center
Yotel Singapore
The Brunei Hotel
Ramada by Wyndham Manila
    Central
The Millennials Shibuya
Ibis Hong Kong Central And
    Sheung Wan
Platinum Suites Bukit Bintang
Hanoi La Siesta Diamond
    Hotel & Spa
Templation Angkor
Arinara Bangtao Beach Resort
Central Yangon Hotel
La Seine Hotel by Burasari
Grand Hotel Taipei
Pacific Hotel Seoul
Novotel Ulaanbaatar Hotel
Smart Hotel Bishkek
Hotel Novotel Almaty
Hilton Dushanbe Hotel
Hostel Art Palace
Auroom Hotel Baku
Getfam Hotel
Jardin de la Paix, Ambassador
    Quarter Place
Wildebeest Eco Camp
Mount Kilimanjaro View Lodge
Hotel Club Du Lac Tanganyika
The Atlantis Hotel
RK Suite Hotel
Mikhael's Hotel
No. 5 Boutique Hotel
Atlantis Hotel, The Palm
Peace Hotels

Marriott Mena House, Cairo
Acacia Village, Juba
Radisson Blu Hotel &
    Conference Center, Niamey
Baber Mahal Vilas
Hotel Bhutan Suites
Hyatt Regency Kolkata
Ascott Palace Dhaka
OZO Colombo Hotel
Paralian Hotel
Hotel Timor
Villa Hideout Falcon, Bali
Concorde Hotel Doha
Tasia Maris Oasis
Cristal Erbil Hotel
El Sheikh Suites Hotel Beirut
Hotel Robert Reimers
Blue Resort
Palau Hotel
The Opposite House
Erakor Island Reservations
Swiss Belhotel International
The Stanley Hotel and Suites
Coral Sea Resort
Menen Hotel
Sinalei Reef Resort & Spa
Emerald Hotel
Filamona Hotel
Hilton Garden Inn, Lusaka
    Society Business Park
Wendels Guest House, Lilongwe
Corinthia Hotel Khartoum
Hotel Vila Galé Ópera
Boutique Hotel Pescador
Hotel Beit Shmuel
Coco-Mat Hotel Athens

Sponsors

Lloyds Banking Group
Nomad Travel Clinic
Osprey
Universal Visas
Natural Capital Partners
Rehband
Mission Tea
Energizer
Hiscox
LalaLAB
LifeSystems
LifeVenture
Runderwear
Curtis Sports
Do Sport Live
Elephant Gin
Firefitness Clothing

Great Dorset Steam Fair
Hammer Nutrition
Hydraquip
Juice Plus
Kinetic 6
Mereo Performance
New Balance
Pro Direct
Pulsin
Red Bull
Scarpa
Sundog
Suunto
TouchNote
TouchPaper Productions
Tile

Prostate Cancer UK Donors

I am extremely grateful to the following people for their generous donations to Prostate Cancer UK:

Abbe Mayston
Abbey Pollock
Abdul H. Baluch
Adam Hilton
Adam Miller
Adam Underhill
Adam Willis
Adam Withers
Adele Nicholson
Adrian Beisty
Adrian Brain
Adrian Robertson
Aga Plombon
Aimée Humphreys
Aimee Shaw
Aine Lincoln
Aisling O'Neill
Aislinn Mulreany
Alan and Chris
Alan and Elsa Smith
Alan Anderson
Alan Bailes
Alan Daring
Alan Harding
Alan Mcknight
Alan Robertson
Alana Parker
Alaw Flur Hughes
Alec Tinsley
Aled Davies
Alex Atkinson
Alex Beaman
Alex Bousfield
Alex Michaels
Alex Spekes
Alex Walker
Alexander Learmonth
Alexander Martin
Alexander McAfee
Alexander Troeller
Alexandra Bright
Alexandra Damazer
Alexandra Grimes
Alexandra Morgan
Alexia Threlfall
Alexis Faulkner
Ali Dolphin
Ali Green
Ali Pryor
Ali Smith
Alice Bennett
Alice Lamb
Alicia Barber
Alison Aderyn
Alison Aikman
Alison Blyth
Alison Butter
Alison Coller
Alison Corfield

Alison Evans
Alison Jamieson
Alison Rawcliffe
Alison Smith
Alison Thomson
Alison Woodroffe
Alistair Phillips
Alix Bingham
Alix Fauvel & family
Allan Downs
Allan Kelsey
Allan Steele
Allana Isaacs
Allie Ford
Allison Hughes
Allyson Pringle
Allyson White
Aly Rook
Alysha Hayes
Amanda Gerlam
Amanda Jordan
Amanda King
Ambrose Duffy
Ami Nash
Amie Green
Amy Houston
Amy Idun
Amy Jackson
Amy Kalinowski
Amy Linnington
Amy May
Amy Molloy
Amy Mugford
Amy Packham
Amy Pickup
Amy Powell
Ana Chaplin
Andie Humphreys
Andre Hewitt
Andrea Boggon
Andrea Butler
Andrea Lawrence
Andrea Mills
Andrea Pearson
Andrew and
    Samantha
Andrew Bell-Smith
Andrew Blair
Andrew Burke Walsh
Andrew Callaghan
Andrew Campbell
Andrew Cowles
Andrew Creak
Andrew Davidson
Andrew Forster
Andrew Fraser
Andrew Frawley
Andrew Gower
Andrew Johnson

Andrew Lazer
Andrew Nagle
Andrew Peach
Andrew Poole
Andrew Primett
Andrew Richer
Andrew Roberts
Andrew Ryall
Andrew Smith
Andrew Tripp
Andrew Walmsley
Andrew Watkinson
Andrew Webber
Andy and Lorna Price
Andy Harris
Andy Orrom
Andy Robertson
Andy Rudall
Andy Scott
Andy Thompson
Angel Cortizo
Angela and Mark
    Turvey
Angela Brown
Angela Challis
Angela Culhane
Angela Harvey
Angela Lamb
Angela Males
Angela Nicholson
Angela Pannett
Angela Wishart
Angie Bell
Angie Natingor
Anil Raghoonath
Anita Carr
Anita North
Anja Ekelof
Ann Forrest
Ann Gleave
Ann Howard
Ann Perrin
Ann Smith
Ann Staveley
Ann-Marie Ryan
Anna Arnold
Anna Brown
Anna Caines
Anna Davenport
Anna Morley
Anna Overy
Anna Savage
Annabelle Richards
Anne Bracher
Anne Goldstone
Anne Grace
Anne Grove
Anne McClelland
Anne Oliver

Anne Slater
Anne White-Douglas
Anne-Marie Castro
Anne-Marie Eames
Annemarie McLean
Annette Foulds
Annette Hewlett
Annette Jensen
Annette Leddington
Annette Newton
Annie Bush
Annie Pickard
Annie Watson
Annie Williams
Anthony Blake
Anthony Collier
Anthony Devlin
Anthony Drake
Anthony Hilton
Anthony Powell
Antonella Bertucci
Antony Sapsted
April Clough
Ar Hobson
Arabella Chalmers
Arvind Ahluwalia
Ash Wilcock
Ashley Vandyk
Ashling Lillis
Asim Rashid
Audrey Hughes
Audrey Smith
Avril Briers
Avril Griffiths
Azevedo José
Babs Jolly
Bacchus and Green
Barbara
Barbara Barnet
Barbara Hall
Barbara Wyatt
Barnaby Johnston
Barry and Sarah
    Gibbs
Barry Matthew
Barry Snelgrove
Becca Leonard
Becca Morris
Becca Sands
Beckie Armson
Becky Brennan
Becky Startup
Bekky Williams
Bel Thompson
Belinda Harrison
Ben Avery
Ben Geleit
Ben Graney
Ben Hayward

Ben Humphrey
Ben McGlashan
Ben Murphy
Ben Webster
Ben White
Benjamin Foster
Benjamin Stanton
Beryl and Simon
Beth Edwards
Beth Shannon
Beth Wilson
Bethan Hubbard
Bethan Lewis
Bethany Browne
Bev Johnston
Bharat Bhatia
Bill Begley
Bill Geddes
Billy Wylie
Birju Buhecha
Breda O'Connor
Brett Peacock
Brian and Barbara
    Hodges
Brian Golden
Brian Hardy
Brian Hill
Brian Hurst
Brian McDougall
Brian Ronald
Brian Solts
Brooke Lynch
Bruno Gisquet
Bryan Glass
Bryan Leaker
Bryn Jones
Bryony Grimes
Bryony Parker
Bullyment family
Burt Johnson
Callum Swatman
Calvinum Hille
Camilla Barden
Camilla Down
Camille Bonomelli
Cara Edwards
Carey Wilcox
Carina Disney
Carl Hughes
Carl Gaywood
Carla Hudson
Carla Louise
    Thompson
Carlie Pease
Carlisle Bay
Carlotta Olivero
Carly Pleydell
Carmel O'Donovan
Carmen Oliver

Carol Brightwell
Carol Flint
Carol Groombridge
Carol Hedges
Carol O'Boyle
Carol Ross
Carol Sills
Carol Stovin
Carol Wood
Carole Vincer
Carole Webster
Caroline Allen
Caroline Barlow
Caroline Eaton
Caroline Lukic
Caroline Moulding
Caroline Park
Caroline Peters
Caroline Shaw
Caroline Stagnell
Caroline Waite
Caroline Wellingham
Caroline Williams
Caroline Wright
Carolyn Gardner
Carolyn Merson
Carolyn Smith
Carrie Hatfield
Carrie O'Brien
Caryn Farms
Cassandra Keable
Cat Markwell
Catharine Leith
Catherine Barrett
Catherine Beeches
Catherine de Rusett
Catherine Pavitt
Catherine Read
Catherine Woodman
Catherine Wright
Cathy Mosely
Ceri Herbert
Ceri Linder
Ceri Pritchard
Ceri Renwick
Chad Heinemann
Charles Ellis
Charles Wollaston
Charlie Jones
Charlie Maguire
Charlie Melvin
Charlie Watson
Charlotte Powell
Charlotte Baldwin
Charlotte Bennett
Charlotte Evans
Charlotte Foot
Charlotte King
Charlotte Pebody
Charlotte Smith
Charlotte Springett
Charlotte Wenban
Chas Pope
Cher Kilroy
Cheryl Smith
Cheryl Wild
Chris and Jan Wujiw
Chris and Jill
  Lazenby

Chris Beale
Chris Berry
Chris Blair
Chris Bull
Chris Chamberlain
Chris Corrigan
Chris Galvin
Chris Goss
Chris Graves
Chris Hartshorn
Chris Inger
Chris James
Chris Jones
Chris Lowe
Chris Maples
Chris McMahon
Chris Moore
Chris Murphy
Chris Patterson
Chris Sowerby
Chris Tilney
Chris Westbrook
Christine Barr
Christine Bell
Christine Collins
Christine Donaldson
Christine Walker
Christopher and
  Lesley Everard-
  Evans
Christopher Brett
Christopher Buswell
Christopher Deakin
Christopher Harris
Christopher Smith
Clair Phillips
Claire and Andy
  Ryall
Claire Bolitho
Claire Cooper
Claire Fletcher
Claire Grundy
Claire Hazleton
Claire Head
Claire Husband
Claire Huson
Claire Marshall
Claire Parker
Claire Pavey
Claire Riley
Claire Smith
Claire Stanley
Claire Stewart
Claire Wootton
Claire Wright
Clare Boret
Clare Clifford
Clare Foley
Clare Kitchen
Clare Megginson
Clare Rideout
Claudia Balneaves
Claudia Roberts
Claudia Sanker
Colin Argent
Colin Bowen
Colin Day
Colin Murray
Colin Richards

Colton Yesney
Constantin
  Stromback
Craig Brown
Craig Fletcher
Craig McLean
Craig Phillips
Dai Roberts-Harry
Daisy Knibb
Dale Kirsop
Dame Kelly Holmes
Damian Minchin
Damon Miller
Dan Harlow
Dani Chapman
Daniel Frieder
Daniel Pridige
Daniel Bloom
Daniel Bye
Daniel James
Daniel Magrath
Daniel Newman
Daniel Skelton
Daniel Wright
Danielle Beckford
Danielle Hardy
Danielle Parsons
Darrell Jones
Darrell Read
Darren Cunningham
Darren Gizon
Darren Holland
Darren McLeod
Darren Wright
Darryl Cornelius
Daryl Foster
Dave and Carol
  Longmate
Dave Birchall
Dave Fyfe
Dave Limpenny
Dave Pittuck
Dave Ross
Dave Sinclair
David Alford
David Anderson
David Attree
David Bailey
David Bridgen
David Carden
David Cox
David Evans
David Fisher
David Furness
David Fyfe
David Gray
David Harvey
David Hibbert
David Horspool
David Jeffery
David Jones
David Lee
David McMasters
David Mills
David Moore
David Neale
David Oliphant
David Parry
David Pay

David Pearson
David Renshaw
David Scott
David Shepherd
David Sherman
David Smith
David Snape
David Sutton
David Thomas
David Treacy
David Wagstaff
David Warrington
David Wood
Davinia Smith
Dawn Beck
Dawn Jones
Dawn Middleditch
Dean Norris
Dean Plant
Debbie Ellery
Debbie Howie
Debbie Leeland
Debbie Roberts
Deborah Chaundy
Deborah McWilliams
Deborah Wilson
Deborah Wright
Debra Michael
Deep Patel
Della Pearce
Delyth Jones
Delyth Morris
Denise Bradley
Dennis Hall
Dennis Vance
Derek Bradnum
Dermot Toberty
Diana Braid
Diana Montgomery
Diane Hickey
Diane Ouzman
Diane Robinson
Diane Self
Dominic Hall
Dominic St George
Dominik Baxa
Dominique Pichon
Donald Oates
Donna and Peter
Donna Deans
Donna Mole
Donna Pratt
Dora Moon
Dotty Reid
Doug and Karen
  Helmer
Douglas Mills
Duncan Anstess
Duncan Greenland
Duncan Hurley
Duncan Leaning
Duncan MacBain
Duncan Malcolm
Duncan McLean
Duncan Oreilly
Duncan Tyler
Ed Wallace
Eddie Dovey
Edward De Stefano

Edward Forshaw
Edward Simpson
Eileen Gillon
Eira and Ron
  Aspinall
Elaine Hubbard
Elaine Lang
Elaine Martin
Elaine Robinson
Elaine Wilders
Eleanor Gill
Eleanor Harvey
Eleanor Miller
Eleni Dioufa
Eleni Syrimi
Elinor Chamberlain
Elisabeth Bond
Elisabeth Meiklejohn
Elise French
Elitsa Stoycheva
Elizabeth Cannon
Elizabeth Crabb
Elizabeth
  Hebblewhite
Elizabeth Mounser
Elizabeth Nuttall
Ella Higgs
Ellen White
Elley Rushmere
Ellie Abbott
Ellie Jamieson
Ellie Wahba
Elliot Wonfor
Elly Smith
Elspeth Freeman
Elwyn Jordan
Emily Andrews
Emily Burrill
Emily Cunningham
Emily Delgado
Emily Guppy
Emily Halley
Emily Harrendence
Emily Korosec
Emily Latham
Emily Lovell
Emily Pountney
Emily Scott
Emily Titcombe
Emma and John Burt
Emma Ashley
Emma Blackburn
Emma Busby
Emma Cantillion
Emma Coulter
Emma Crawford
Emma Jenkins
Emma Johnston
Emma Konstantinou
Emma Lumley
Emma McNally
Emma McPeake
Emma Palmer
Emma Sellers
Emma Smith
Emma Sprules
Emma Thomason
Emma White
Emma Woodley

Emma Wright
Emmie Radford
Empire Runner
Eric Williams
Erica Bewsey
Erica Simmonds
Erika Couling
Estelle Jackson
Esther Swaffield
Eurig Thomas
Evelyn Dyer
Ewan Macaulay
Fabian Yeo
Fairweather
  Tandemers
Family Mingay
Felicia Ponacz
Felicity Burrows
Felicity Hares
Finley Becks-Phelps
Fiona Bryce
Fiona Byrne
Fiona Conlen
Fiona Cornell
Fiona Greenwood
Fiona Lamb
Fiona McLean
Fiona Morris
Fiona Randall
Fiona Vigar
Fiona Weekes
Fionna Tait
Ford Beveridge
Fran Randle
Francesca Caleb
Francesco Maria
  Saviotti
Francesco Rodondi
Frank Alexandre
Frank Atherton
Freya Demmery
Freya Mehta
Freya Morris
Gail Campbell
Gardiner family
Gareth Bristow
Gareth Fletcher
Gareth Jones
Gareth Kennedy
Gareth Morris
Gareth Rees
Gareth Thomas
Gareth Tidmarsh
Gary Hampson
Gary Hobbs
Gary Jones
Gary Simmons
Gary Toward
Gary Vale
Gavin Clarke
Gavin Copus
Gayle Kerr
Gaz Sproson
Ged Mills
Gemma Batterby
Gemma Bramston
Gemma Briant
Gemma Dracup
Gemma Parker

Gemma Smedley
Gemma Tutty
Geoff Hill
Geoff Lawes
Geoff Loader
George Lewis
  Warwick
George Hamilton
George Hughes
George Johnstone
George Rossiter
Georgi Mann
Georgie P.
Georgie Smith
Georgina Castle
Georgina Cove
Georgina Dixon
Georgina Huxley
Gill Caunt
Gill Haw
Gill Wright
Gillian Acham
Gillian Atherton
Gillian Bunting
Gillian Hodge
Gillian Lynch
Gillian Moore
Gillian Spaxman
Gillian Wickers
Gin King
Glaysher Family
Glenys Bailey
Glyn Wright
Glynis Buchan
Gordon Glancy
Grace Butler
Grace Jeffery
Graeme Allison
Graeme Stringer
Graham Holroyd
Graham Brown
Graham Brownett
Graham
  Bushnell-Wyc
Graham Everson
Graham Lees
Graham Lund
Graham Rickard
Grahame Burnip
Grainne and Charlie
Greg Hunter
Greg Penberthy
Greg Rose
Griffiths Family
Gully Foyle
Gurchathen Sanghera
Gustavo Cirmi
Gwynneth Purnell
Haley Morgan
Hamish Robertson
Hannah Billington
Hannah Black
Hannah Davies
Hannah Emerson
Hannah Gilbert
Hannah Harbron
Hannah Keech
Hannah Ledwold
Hannah McAdam

Hannah Mcgrath
Hannah Murray
Hannah Newton
Hannah Pike
Hannah Price
Hannah Smith
Hannah Watts
Hannes Hauenschild
Hanya Gordon
Harriet Lees
Harriet Milligan
Harry Robins
Hayden Story
Haydn Squibb
Hayley Cooper
Hayley Lauder
Hayley Rampton
Hazel Breen
Hazel Smith
Hazel Thompson
Heather Foxton
Heather Gordon
Heather James
Heather Rogers
Heather Wheeler
Heidi Bartholomew
Helen Atkinson
Helen Barlow
Helen Hamblett
Helen Harris
Helen Longstaff
Helen Marriott
Helen McCay
Helen Smith
Helen Urquhart
Helen Whysall
Helen Wood
Helena Little
Helena Taylor
Helene Blick
Hilary Cockshaw
H.J. Lewsey-Gillmore
Hollie Shirley
Holly Henderson
Holly Isted
Honor Wearden
Horia Astalos
Hugh Tollyfield
Huw Knee
Iain Ross
Iain Smith
Iain Stirling
Ian Brumby
Ian Godfrey
Ian Hornett
Ian Hughes
Ian Jones
Ian Martin
Ian Moore
Ian Vaughan-
  Arbuckle
Ian Wield
Ilona Clifton
Imogen Binnian
Imogen Gold
Imogen Johns
Imogen Taylor
Imy Briscoe
India Young

Irene Pitcher
Isabelle Huggan
Issy Pettit
Ivan Bentley
Izzy Rust
Jack Gerry
Jack Haug
Jack Noble
Jackie Cushen
Jackie and Steve
  Sheehan
Jackie Baugi
Jackie Cresdee
Jackie McCready
Jackie Noel
Jackie Parker
Jacqueline Hunt
Jacqui Winn
Jacqui Parker
Jacqui Phillips
Jade Clarke
Jade Crombie
James Arnold
James Biggs
James Charteris
James Clark
James Clough
James Coates
James Dickson
James Finnie
James Fraser
James Hemmaway
James Hughes
James
  LaBouchardiere
James Leith
James Ljustina
James Moran
James Mortimer
James Murray
James Pattinson
James Perkin
James Piper
James Plunket
James Quinn
James Randall
James Roberts
James Searle
James Treloar
James White
Jamie Casey
Jamie Derbyshire
Jamie Peacock
Jamie Skinner
Jamie Thomas
Jan Clarke
Jan Oldaker
Jan Ollis
Jan Wood
Jane and Ian W.
Jane Brazil
Jane Collier
Jane Davison
Jane Everest
Jane Fazal
Jane Godfrey
Jane Henderson
Jane Hollstein
Jane Humby

Jane Johnson
Jane Lockhart
Jane McCallum
Jane McHale
Jane Mckeown
Jane Powell
Jane Stephens-Ford
Jane Tanswell-Davis
Jane Walkington-Ellis
Jane Wareing
Jane Wingrove
Janet Bell
Janet Howe
Janet Ryan
Janet Tetlow
Janey Reading
Janice Mancktelow
Janine and Nick
  Whitty
Janine Hartland
Janis Young
Jason Mainwaring
Jason McKnespiey
Jason O'Leary
Jason Vivian
Jayne Broughton
Jayne Faulkner
Jayne Owen
Jean Armstrong
Jean Barron
Jean Christophe
Jean Coopet
Jean Sanoy
Jean-Christophe
  Dauphin
Jeanne Stephens
Jeff and Uta Tombs
Jeff Best
Jeffrey Boekstein
Jemima Price
Jemma Love
Jen Burden
Jen Richardson
Jenna Gabriel
Jenna Wells
Jenni Bull
Jenni Wilkes
Jennie Crosby
Jennie Harrison
Jennifer Brown
Jennifer Aubry
Jennifer Green
Jennifer Hammond
Jennifer Hopkins
Jennifer McDonald
Jennifer Needham
Jennifer Smethurst
Jennifer Tonge
Jenny McPherson
Jenny Randle
Jenny Smith
Jess and Dan Jeffries
Jess Morgan
Jessica Barrett
Jessica Buchanan
Jessica Clarke
Jessica Higley
Jessica Lester
Jessie Stanbrook

Jill Bourton
Jill Burslem
Jill Harris
Jill Lodge
Jill Moran
Jill Quick
Jill Saville
Jill Waite
Jill Whitford
Jillian Grant
Jillian Phillips
Jim Morrison
Jim Rimmer
Jim Spratt
Jimbo Manson
Jo Davies
Jo Dewar
Jo Gooch
Jo Jenkins
Jo Lofthouse
Jo Lutas
Jo Meek
Jo Natt
Jo Newey
Jo Strong
Joan Abrams
Joanna Cooper
Joanna Keshishian
Joanne Davidson
Joanne Churcher
Joanne Cook
Joanne Cowie
Joanne Glenn
Joanne Grant
Joanne Haynes
Joanne Heslop
Joanne Hudson
Joanne McNestry
Joanne Nicholson
Jodee Mayer
Jodi Conner
Jodi Maple
Jodie Phillips
Jodie Simpson
Jodie Wilson
Joe Dewar
Joe Meegan
Joe Ryall
Joey Morris
John Eastwood
John Armitage
John Arnold
John Ballantyne
John Beston
John Blackburn
John Burrill
John Cleminson
John Clubb
John Dawson
John Deffenbaugh
John Eary
John Gilpin
John Helliwell
John Innes
John Ireland
John Isham
John Kuczer
John Lee
John Lowden

John McAthey
John McErlain
John Milton-Polley
John Montgomery
John Myers
John Palmer
John Perrins
John Raglan
John Rolfe
John Rook
John Stevens
John Tibbott
John Wilberforce
Johnathon Figg
Jon Higgins
Jon Marland
Jon Wright
Jonas Aagaard
    Madsen
Jonathan Abrahams
Jonathan Capes
Jonathan Eggett
Jonathan Horn
Jonathan Mace
Jonathan Orellana
Jonathan Wright
Jonny Harding
Jordan Hinks
Josephine Adams
Josephine Berrill
Josephine Rickards
Josh Cooper
Josh Darby
    MacLellan
Joshua Flood
Joshua Welsford
Joy Cockle
Juan Munoz
Judson Stone
Judy Beighton
Judy Powell
Julia Argent
Julia Cobham
Julia Kellam
Julia Loecherbach
Julia Terry
Julian Pearce
Julie Drew
Julie Eaton
Julie Edenborough
Julie Foakes
Julie Gibbs
Julie Goble
Julie Lawson
Julie Lewis
Julie Mitchell
Julie Rose
Julie Scollon
Julie Sidaway
Julie Twist
Juliet Heffernan
Juliette Hooper
Juliette Smith
June Bayles
Justin Wignall
Karen Ellis
Karen Bristow
Karen Coke
Karen Dawes

Karen Frankis
Karen Galvin
Karen Gillan
Karen Heard
Karen Macey
Karen Malins
Karen Perry
Karen Pett
Karen Turner
Karen West
Karen Wilson
Kat Owens
Kate Hall
Kate Spink
Kate Stewart
Kate Webber
Katerina Roze
Kath Thorpe
Katharine Clark
Katharine Davis
Katherine
    Armstrong
Katherine
    Melton-Scott
Kathleen McNulty
Kathryn Ball
Kathryn Kinney
Kathryn Payne
Kathryn Phillips
Kathy Swindles
Kathy Pritchard
Katie Arnold
Katie Black
Katie Dempsey
Katie Ford
Katie Masters
Katie Maughan
Katie McLean
Katie Paine
Katie Pryor
Katie Sadler
Katie Spyrka
Katie Starkey
Katreena Bellman
Katrina Day
Katy Davidson
Katy Green
Katy Palacio
Keir Simons
Keisha Cousins
Keith Sutton
Keith Willmott
Kel Marcus
Kelly Burke
Kelly Devine
Kelly Haines
Kelly Jones
Ken Back
Ken Bing
Ken Ferguson
Ken Shrimpton
Ken van Someren
Kendra Cardy
Kenneth Tunstall
Kenneth Turnbull
Kenny Horsham
Kerr Reid
Kerrie and Simon
    Driver

Kerry and Ian
    Howlett
Kerry Fitzpatrick
Kerry Lister
Kerry Randall
Kevin Blair
Kevin Bower
Kevin Doyle
Kevin Pyke
Kevin Reed
Kim and Steve Foy
Kim Barough
Kim Brooks
Kim Markwick-Day
Kim Mundy
Kirah Bradley
Kirsteen Steel
Kirsty Dimitrov
Kirsty Hall
Kirsty Keegan
Kirsty Parry
Kirsty Steven
Kirsty Young
Kristy Burch
Kristy Thibodeau
Kyla Adams
Lara Tapp
Laura Perks
Laura and Leo Lyons
Laura and Paul Holt
Laura Akhtar
Laura Ayre
Laura Beth
Laura Clark
Laura Clews
Laura Disley
Laura Harding
Laura Hodgkiss
Laura Hunter
Laura Knowles
Laura Linney
Laura Marie
Laura McGlashan
Laura Morley
Laura Murray
Laura Newcombe
Laura O'Malley
Laura Piccirillo
Laura Smith
Laura Stirling
Laura Taylor
Laura Townsend
Laura Wilcock
Laura Wright
Lauren Ashby
Lauren Baybutt
Lauren Booth
Lauren Fitzgerald
Lauren Foulds
Lauren Gregory
Lauren Holley
Lauren Mackay
Lauren Nopondo
Lauren Rowley
Lauren Tait
Laurence Good
Lawrence Jackson
Leah O'Connor
Lealand Pearce

Leanne Cahill
Lee Fallaize
Lee Jones
Lee Snowball
Lee Winters
Leigh Brownsword
Leonie and Andy
Les Tonkinson
Lesley and Paul Smith
Lesley Jones
Lesley Lane
Lesley Titchmarsh
Lester Hugill
Lettice Hunter Bell
Lewis Mitchell
Liam McGuirk
Liam Taylor
Liam Williams
Lian Wilson
Libby Colet
Lilian Tse
Lillian Pearson
Linda and George
    Missen
Linda Beard
Linda Havard
Linda Lewis
Linda Packman
Linda Probert
Linda Staunton
Lindsey Mansfield
Lindsey Ramskill
Linsay Pritchard
Linsey Paterson
Linzi Langdon
Lionel Uren
Lisa Ashdown
Lisa Bailey
Lisa Bichard
Lisa Bowman
Lisa Gane
Lisa Inman
Lisa Lind
Lisa Nolan
Lisa Reed
Lisa Southern
Lisa Thomas
Lisa Walker
Lissa Carnelley
Liz Warbrick
Lizzie Baptiste
Loren Mcbay
Loretta Kellman
Lottie Gregory
Lou Best
Lou Phillips
Lou Toogood
Louisa Corbett
Louisa Houghton
Louisa Moreton
Louise Jenkins
Louise Acher
Louise Aylwin
Louise Bailey
Louise Binnie
Louise Brookes
Louise Cusack
Louise Fox
Louise Gough

Louise Hewetson
Louise Jones
Louise Judge
Louise Melbourne
Louise Moodie
Louise Morgan
Louise Rawlings
Louise Roberts
Louise Saville
Louise Steel
Lowri Evans
Lucie Gower
Lucie McLean
Lucie Usher
Lucie Wilson
Lucinda Cobb
Lucinda Newbound
Lucy Barraud
Lucy Bennett
Lucy Berriman
Lucy Brodie
Lucy Davies
Lucy Finn
Lucy Jackson
Lucy Jennings
Lucy Kinahan
Lucy McManus
Lucy Putt
Lucy Ransley
Lucy Richardson
Lucy Roberts
Lucy Skerritt
Lucy Sugiarto-
  Hedges
Lucy Vickers
Luke Green
Lydia Bolwell
Lydia Roberts
Lydia Sollitt
Lyn Dillon
Lyn Freeman
Lyn Thomson
Lynda and Tom
  Ralph
Lynda Charters
Lynda Stark
Lynette Mitchell
Lynn Fleck
Lynn Grover
Lynn Harman
Lynn Macfarlane
Lynn Sharp
Lynne Haddow
Lynne Phillips
Lynne W.
Lynsey Davis
Lynsey Fojut
Lynsey Goodman
Lysette Taylor
Maddie and Bob
  Parker
Maddie Kearney
Madeleine Bailey
Maggie Bull
Maggie Taylor
Malcolm Magnet
Malcolm McFarlane
Malcolm Wood
Mandy Orford

Mandy Smith
Marc and Mary
  Mason
Marcia Douglas
Margaret Harris
Margaret Hewitt
Margaret McMechan
Margareta Malanca
Maria Clancy
Marian Bradley
Marianne Emler
Marie Chappell
Marieke Chatelain
Marikyn Lock
Marina Penny
Marion Baud
Marion Rowlinson
Mark Giles
Mark Beaumont
Mark Burgum
Mark Howarth
Mark Hyde
Mark Irving
Mark Kingsley
Mark O'Donnell
Mark Proctor
Mark Quinn
Mark Sayers
Mark Smith
Mark Spandler
Mark Thompson
Mark Tipping
Mark Wright
Martin Crozier
Martin Curno
Martin Day
Martin Disney
Martin Ferries
Martin Greening
Martin Hughes
Martin Jackaman
Martin Levoir
Martin Lloyd
Martin Morse
Martin Pettett
Martin Thomas
Martin Workman
Mary Ellis
Mary Hamblin
Mary Johnstom
Mary Jones
Mary Ridler
Mary Wang
Mathew Beaumont
Matt Bergum
Matt Brown
Matt Murray
Matt Newman
Matt Pocock
Matt Reed
Matt Robertson
Matt Williams
Matthew Beswick
Matthew Clark
Matthew Hole
Matthew Jones
Matthew Tushingham
Matthew Waterer
Matthew Wilson

Matthew Wright
Maureen Lockyer
Maureen McMillan
Maureen Plumstead
Mavis Black
Max Mulley
Max Remezov
Maxine Carpenter
Maxine Harding
Maxine Thomas
Maz Iannone
Meg Burgess
Megan Claytor
Megan Howlett
Megan Pearson
Megan Sutton
Mel Dawes
Mel Kite
Melanie Briere
Melanie Denning
Melanie Elston
Melanie Furnell
Melanie Kielczewski
Melanie Russ
Melanie Saunderson
Melanie St. Clair
Melissa Jewer
Melissa Randall
Melissa Solly
Melody Bridges
Menno de Vreeze
Michael Aston
Michael Bailey
Michael Briggs
Michael Cook
Michael Curran
Michael Darke
Michael Docker
Michael Godfrey
Michael Hall
Michael Hanley
Michael Harley
Michael Hibbs
Michael Reynolds
Michael Simpson
Michael Tipple
Michelle Chafe
Michelle Johnson
Michelle Jones
Michelle Key
Michelle Meehan
Michelle Sturdy
Michelle Wozencroft
Michelle Yeabsley
Mick McCormack
Mick Morton
Mike Barrett
Mike Byrne
Mike Cain
Mike Fox
Mike Lally
Mike Quinn
Mike Smith
Mike Stevenson
Mikhail Zverev
Minogue family
Miranda Quigley
Mireille Mailey
Mohamed Amin

Mollie Lewton
Molly Ropner
Molly Threlfall
Monica
  Krzyzanowski
Morag McGilvray
Morey Andrews
Morgan Brazington
Morwenna Davenport
Moshe Moses
Nadia Tuckwell
Nadine Helling
Nan Richards
Nancy Ambrose
Nancy Anderson
Naomi Holloway
Natalie Brown
Natalie Crawford
Natalie Doherty
Natalie Edwards
Natalie Green
Natalie Luck
Natalie Pearce
Natasha Walker
Nathan Randall
Neal Mathias
Neal Weekes
Neha Vasta
Neil Bant
Neil Cameron
Neil Hughes
Neil Paton
Neil Pickering
Neil Smith
Neil Watson
Neill Whiteside
Nelson Martins
Nia Cannon
Nia Stewart
Niamh O'Donovan
Nichola Massey
Nichola Robinson
Nicholas Molloy
Nicholas Petrie
Nicholas
  Wnekowski
Nick Albert
Nick Archer
Nick Elliott
Nick Hales
Nick Hopkins
Nick Lindfield
Nick Rose
Nick Simpson
Nick Vero
Nick Wilmore
Nicky
  McMenamin
Nicola Aslam
Nicola
  Chamberlain
Nicola Coyne
Nicola French
Nicola Gale
Nicola Hill
Nicola Jenkinson
Nicola Jennings
Nicola Kelly
Nicola Lewton

Nicola Reith
Nicola Ross
Nicola Simmons
Nicola Toomey
Nicola Watson
Nicolas Younes
Nicole Duke
Nicole Hartley
Nicole Kennedy
Nicole Pegg
Nigel Goulding
Nigel Whitbread
Nik Timms
Niki Gott
Nikki McBride
Nikki Tombs
Nitanj Patel
Norma Morgan
Norman and
  Rosemary
  Grossman
Norman Davies
Nubia Robleto
Oliver Drew
Oliver Hiller
Oliver Jackman
Oliver Koch
Oliver Leggett
Olivia Pike
Olivia Sadler
Olivier Emond
Oly Coddington
Owen Bartlett
Paddy Phipps
Pam Barry
Pam Janke
Pam Taylor
Pamela Taylor
Pamela Wilson
Pat Roberts
Pat Webb
Patricia Jones
Patricia Joyce
Patricia Lambert
Patricia Marquis
Patricia Mattinson
Patrick Wood
Patrik Koppanen
Patsy Lamb
Patsy Morrisey
Paul Bayliss
Paul Billin
Paul Booker
Paul Bunning
Paul Carter
Paul Colvin
Paul Cruickshank
Paul Day
Paul Donnelly
Paul Farenden
Paul Gallimore
Paul Gower
Paul Griffiths
Paul Gurling
Paul Hibbitt
Paul Hodder
Paul Humphrey
Paul McInerney
Paul Meads

Paul Norris
Paul Price
Paul Ryder
Paul Watson
Paul Whitbread
Paul Williams
Paul Wilson
Paula Duffy
Paula Evans
Paula Hassett
Paula Heath
Paula Turner
Pauline Bale
Pauline Chung
Pauline Lewin
Pauline Morris
Pauline Pavely
Pavel Grushin
Pavlo Poluektov
Pennie Aspinwall
Pennie Whitty
Perina Bishop
Pete Ashplant
Pete Hobden
Peter Beckett
Peter Brown
Peter Campbell
Peter Cox
Peter Downes
Peter Hansen
Peter Howarth
Peter Jones
Peter Leigh
Peter Leverkus
Peter Maskell
Peter Seynaeve
Peter Staveley
Peter Vaughan-
  Fowler
Peter Willmott
Peter Wright
Petra Gowans
Petra McEntegart
Phil Andrews
Phil Humphries
Phil Kavanagh
Phil McCusker
Phil Sandford
Phil Savage
Phil Scott
Phil Shaw
Phil Smith
Phil Walker
Philip Brownbill
Philip Grace
Philip Haney
Philip Holt
Philip Jacobson
Philip Rowson
Philip Turner
Philip Uren
Philip Wright
Philippa Daniel
Philippa Johnson
Philippa Tyrwhitt-
  Drake
Philippe Suzor-Morin
Philippe Varrin
Philomena Bull

Pia Ault
Pindor Samra
Pippa Graeme
Pippa Wall
Polly Phillips
Polly Sargent
Popplewell family
Poppy Marello
Qamer Yasin
R. Jane Murrant
Rachael Levermore
Rachael Ord
Rachel Booth
Rachel Cornthwaite
Rachel Deacon
Rachel Flanders
Rachel Goodwin
Rachel Hale
Rachel Hills
Rachel Jeffrey
Rachel Johnstone
Rachel Kilner
Rachel Legg
Rachel Lillie
Rachel Massey
Rachel McGovern
Rachel Ng
Rachel Pollard
Rachel Roberts
Rachel Smeysters
Rachel Southwick
Rachel Wintie
Rachel Wise
Raphaela Bührer
Ray Veck
Raych Di Mauro
Razi Ahmed
Rebecca Porritt
Rebecca and Barry
  Impson Greenleaf
Rebecca Bannocks
Rebecca Bright
Rebecca Croft
Rebecca Day
Rebecca Dicello
Rebecca Ellis
Rebecca Goodwin
Rebecca Hitt
Rebecca Jones
Rebecca Lawrence
Rebecca Loake
Rebecca Moore
Rebecca Naylor
Rebecca Reddington
Rebecca Scholes
Rebecca Shepherdson
Rebecca Shonfeld
Rhian Cogle
Rhian Davies
Rhian Grounds
Rhianna Wilding
Rhiannan Scott
Richard Attwood
Richard Barrett
Richard Bennett
Richard Boxhall
Richard Broad
Richard Caughey
Richard Cox

Richard Deaman
Richard Gibson
Richard Green
Richard Hansen
Richard Jones
Richard Pickin
Richard Sanders
Richard Styles
Richard Swift
Richard Thomas
Richard W. Kennedy
Richard Wheeler
Richard Whitehead
Richard Youle-
  Grayling
Rick Askey
Rick Betts
Rishi Kakati
Rita Rake
Rob Baker
Rob Billance
Rob Broad
Rob Cutts
Rob Evans
Rob Johnson
Rob Murray
Rob Regester
Rob Sibley
Rob Stead
Rob Tipper
Rob Yeadon
Robbie Smart
Robert Bradshaw
Robert Coker
Robert Cranborne
Robert Gillespie
Robert Goodall
Robert Gormley
Robert Haughton
Robert Hunt
Robert Johnson
Robert Leeson
Robert Ogden
Robert Pelham
Robert Poole
Robert Underhill
Robert Walker
Robin Fox
Robin Llewelyn-
  Leach
Robin Stevens
Rodney Fraser
Roger Fenwick
Romola DeVile
Ron McAndrew
Ronald Jannaway
Rory and Sue
  Banham
Rory Allbutt
Rory Dyer
Rory Penny
Roselle Fisher
Rosemary Nunn
Rosie Dooley
Ross Bain
Ross Crombie
Ross Darch
Roxanne Cox
Roy Banham

Roy French
Ruaridh Welsh
Ruby Wilson
Russell Hardman
Ruth Benfield
Ruth Freckleton
Ruth Herlihy
Ruth Williamson
Ryan Dennis
Ryan Houghton
Ryan Weaver
Sabiqa Younus
Sabrina Niewiarowski
Sadie Guymer
Saide Banoo
Sally Palmer
Sally Warner
Sam Ashton
Sam Batchelor
Sam Beake
Sam Johnson
Sam Lewis
Sam Patrick Lewis
Sam Sturges
Sam Warman
Samantha Perry
Samantha Summers
Samantha Torgersen
Samantha
  Willoughby
Samual Cocking
Samuel Bowden
Samuel Robson
Samuel Yeates
Sandie Gill
Sandie Smith
Sandra Fagan
Sandra McMorrow
Sandra Mullins
Sandra Parkinson
Sandra Peake
Sandra Walker
Sara Alliss
Sara Das
Sara Miles
Sara Similien
Sarah Bennett
Sarah Biggs
Sarah Blanshard
Sarah Browne
Sarah Cooper
Sarah Cornwell
Sarah Goodall
Sarah Gooding
Sarah Hill
Sarah Lambert
Sarah Laycock
Sarah Lund
Sarah Matthews
Sarah Mayne
Sarah McLeod
Sarah Merchant
Sarah Merriman
Sarah Nangle
Sarah Palfreyman
Sarah Price
Sarah Read
Sarah Shaw
Sarah Shergold

Sarah Smith
Sarah Stringfellow
Sarah Taylor
Sarah Thi
Sarah Todd
Sarah Tomlin
Sarah Trickey
Sarah Turner
Sarah Wilson
Sarah Wood
Sarah Woods
Sarah Young
Scott Carmichael
Scott Horan
Scott Smith
Scott Speirs
Seamus Whitehead
Sean McKenna
Sean Smith
Sean Thomas
Sebastian Key
Sebastiano Ingallo
Sebastien Hugues
Selina McCole
Shannon Murphy
Sharon Allen
Sharon Brown
Sharon Griffin
Sharon Roe
Shaun Mckinlay
Shazia Saleemi
Sheena Wade
Sheila Rendall
Shelley Oregan
Shelly Holloway
Shelly Johnson
Sheryl Joy
Shirley English
Shirley Noble
Shirley Ottley
Shirley Waddell
Shirley Woodall
Shirlie Mitchell
Shona King
Shona Patterson
Si Walton
Sian King
Sian Parker
Silvia Stravolemis
Simon Aird
Simon Allfrey
Simon Baron
Simon Bellamy
Simon Bodman
Simon Christian
Simon Entwistle
Simon Grundy
Simon Hancox
Simon Ibbotson
Simon Lucas
Simon Malster
Simon Stapleton
Simon Templer
Siobhan McKenna
Sandra Wilson
Snooky Grubb
Solar Sare
Sonia Peters
Sophia Tanner